A CITY ON THE EDGE

A CITY ON THE EDGE

PANDEMIC, PROTEST, AND POLARIZATION

DENNIS R. MCBRIDE

INDIANA UNIVERSITY PRESS

This book is a publication of

Indiana University Press
Office of Scholarly Publishing
Herman B Wells Library 350
1320 East 10th Street
Bloomington, Indiana 47405 USA

iupress.org

First Printing 2025

Cataloging information is available from the Library of Congress.

ISBN 978-0-253-07406-5 (hdbk.)
ISBN 978-0-253-07407-2 (pbk.)
ISBN 978-0-253-07409-6 (ebook)
ISBN 978-0-253-07408-9 (web PDF)

To my mother, Marian Dunne McBride, who brought John F. Kennedy to the Wauwatosa Civic Center for a rally in 1960, served as vice chair of the Wisconsin Democratic Party, and worked as an award-winning political reporter for the Milwaukee Sentinel. But for her example, I would not have become a public servant and this book never would have been written.

CONTENTS

PREFACE

THROUGHOUT THE HISTORICALLY TURBULENT YEAR of 2020, America's cities faced challenges that mostly could not have been foreseen. While most of the tumult occurred in big cities, smaller cities were not exempted.

In April 2020, I was elected mayor of Wauwatosa, Wisconsin. Bordered on three sides by Wisconsin's largest city, Milwaukee, Wauwatosa (pronounced "wow-wah-TOE-sah") has been called an urban-suburban "edge city."[1] The term was coined by *Washington Post* reporter Joel Garreau in his 1991 book *Edge City: Life on the New Frontier,* in which he observed that the edge city had become the standard form of urban growth worldwide, representing a twentieth-century urban form unlike that of nineteenth-century downtown business districts.[2] Wauwatosa's older East Side, developed during the nineteenth and early twentieth centuries and seamlessly connected to Milwaukee, is largely urban and residential, while its more suburban West Side, developed during the second half of the twentieth century and bordered by even more suburban (and more politically conservative) Waukesha County, is home to a regional medical complex, colleges and universities, office parks, sprawling factories, a busy shopping mall, and hotels that supply hundreds of rooms for conventions and tourism.

In all these ways, Wauwatosa functions as Milwaukee's second downtown—and as an edge city.

But it is also true that Wauwatosa and America teeter on an emotional edge. That became distressingly obvious in 2020, when I became mayor and faced all the challenges confronted by mayors of bigger cities. My hometown, racked by turmoil, was constantly in the national and international news. In part, we were just unlucky, but like most of America, we were also paying the price of our troubled history.

Though that tumult has largely subsided, America will continue to suffer periodic upheavals if it does not solve its lingering challenges of political polarization and racial inequity and exclusion. City officials cannot solve these problems alone, but it is to us that people turn first, at the level of government closest to home. We must not ignore the lessons we learned in 2020. "But [there is] one large caveat to making the decisions that lie ahead," Dr. Kent Sepkowitz, an infectious disease expert at Memorial Sloan Kettering Cancer Center in New York, wrote in 2023. "Historians . . . understand they stand at a safe remove from the events they are recounting," he said. "They acknowledge that being in the middle of total chaos is very different than writing about those who were in the middle of total chaos. The eminent historian Bernard Bailyn warned against the distortion this can impose: 'The fact—the inescapable fact—is that we [historians] know how it all came out . . . and they [those involved in the events] did not.'"[3]

There is value in the perspective of historians. But as other mayors and I navigated through the events described in this book, we did not enjoy the advantage of hindsight. Instead, we found ourselves amid chaos and could not be sure how it would all come out. Now it is time for reflection.

A CITY ON THE EDGE

MICROCOSM

SOME YEARS ARE MORE MEMORABLE than others.

In 1775, American farmers fired a shot heard round the world and turned the world upside down. Napoleon's defeat at Waterloo in 1815 ended 23 years of European conflict. In 1848, famine and revolutions gripped Europe and propelled millions of immigrants to America, transforming it forever. In 1918, the Great War ended and a global influenza pandemic began. Assassinations of progressive leaders, protests against racism and the Vietnam War, and a narrowly decided presidential election in 1968 rattled the United States, and young Europeans mimicked 1848 with widespread protests of their own. In 1989, Chinese students defied their government in Tiananmen Square and the toppling of the Berlin Wall heralded the disintegration of the Soviet Union. In 2001, the World Trade Center in New York collapsed after being hit by jet planes hijacked by terrorists.

The events of those years still reverberate today. Then came 2020.

The year began with the news that another deadly disease, COVID-19, was spreading around the world. Several months later, a Minneapolis police officer killed a Black man named George Floyd. That murder, along with police killings of other African Americans across the country, touched off what some called "the largest protest movement in U.S. history" and sparked "a tectonic shift in the public debate over race, policing and criminal justice."[1] At the same time, mass shootings increased by 47 percent, and many states saw unprecedented increases in gun-related incidents. Likely factors were the COVID-19 pandemic and resulting economic downturn, a rise in drug use, an increase in gun ownership, and inequities in health care, education, housing, and employment.[2]

The pandemic was a trigger.[3] But in the background was a bitter presidential election campaign called "the most turbulent White House race in modern history."[4] Intermingled with the Floyd protests and campaign events were right-wing counterprotests and rallies challenging public health measures and the election result itself.[5]

Though turmoil in big cities dominated the news, protests and unrest spread to suburbs and smaller cities, too. As the new mayor of Wauwatosa, Wisconsin, a midsized, mostly White city bordered on three sides by the majority-minority City of Milwaukee—which *Newsweek* has called the "heartland of the heartland"[6]—I grappled with the impact of the pandemic, the economic crisis, a mass shooting, and yearlong racial protests, and my hometown played a quiet but crucial role in the outcome of the presidential election. Throughout 2020, the *New York Times*, the *Washington Post*, the *Wall Street Journal*, CNN, NBC News, the British Broadcasting Company, NHK Japan Broadcasting Corporation, and other news media covered events in Wauwatosa. We were a microcosm of a troubled and changing America.

In 2020, a perfect storm of stresses fueled anger, fear, frustration, and protests across the country and around the world. But an even deeper force was at work: America's perpetual refusal to tell the truth about itself. The stresses ripped our cities apart and challenged the country's mayors, unrelentingly, throughout the year and beyond.

PANDEMIC

IT SEEMS LIKE A BAD dream now. But here and there, years later, we see a reminder that the nightmare was real: a cautious person wearing a face mask in public.

As it fades into the past, the pandemic of 2020–21 might be remembered as a historical curiosity like the Black Death plague of the mid-1300s or the Spanish flu pandemic of 1918–19. Human nature tends to push fear and suffering to the back of the mind. But, like a veteran with a missing limb, a person wearing a mask jolts us back, uncomfortably, to a time we have tried to forget. Yet the pandemic did occur, and, like its antecedents, it shook and changed the world.

ULTRA VIRUS

On December 31, 2019, the People's Republic of China announced the discovery of a cluster of pneumonia cases in the city of Wuhan. On January 7, 2020, it revealed that the cluster was caused by a new coronavirus, labeled "COVID-19." The US Centers for Disease Control and Prevention (CDC) issued a health advisory the next day. The first American case was reported on January 20 in Everett, Washington. Ten days later, the World Health

Organization (WHO) warned that "all countries should be prepared for containment." The next day, the US declared a public health emergency.[1]

Though the virus had first been detected in Wuhan, it was not certain how it developed. The leading theory was that it had jumped from bats, birds, or animals in an open-air market and infected humans, but others believed it was developed in a Chinese government laboratory and inadvertently spread into the market nearby. This dispute had political repercussions later.[2]

The CDC observed a wide range of reactions to COVID, usually respiratory complaints that felt like a cold, the flu, or pneumonia, but reported symptoms also included coughs, sore throats, congestion or runny noses, fevers or chills, headaches, muscle or body aches, shortness of breath or difficulty breathing, fatigue, loss of the sense of smell or taste, nausea or vomiting, and diarrhea. The length and severity of symptoms varied from person to person. Some of those infected had no symptoms at all.[3] But especially in the first year, many died.

The first confirmed American COVID death occurred in California on February 6. As cases spread, state and federal agencies prepared for a surge of patients by setting up overflow sites in case hospitals became overwhelmed. The US military and National Guard were mobilized to help build the emergency facilities. On March 6, President Donald Trump signed a bill providing emergency funding for federal agencies to respond to the outbreak.[4]

By March 11, the virus had spread to 110 countries. The WHO declared a pandemic, defined as "an epidemic occurring worldwide, or over a very wide area, crossing international boundaries and usually affecting a large number of people."[5] That day, confirmed US COVID cases totaled 125,000, with fewer than 5,000 reported deaths; the National Basketball Association suspended its season; and actor Tom Hanks, filming the Baz Luhrmann movie *Elvis* in Australia, announced that he and his wife were infected. That evening, Trump announced restrictions on travel from Europe that touched off a trans-Atlantic scramble.[6]

Dr. Anthony Fauci, the director of the National Institute of Allergy and Infectious Diseases, said that deaths from the virus were 10 times higher than from the common flu. The CDC warned that large numbers of new patients would overload health-care facilities nationwide. The White House advised against gatherings of more than 10 people, and the State Department advised US citizens to avoid international travel. In late March, Trump invoked the Defense Production Act of 1950 to direct industries to produce ventilators and other medical equipment needed to combat the pandemic.[7]

The earliest significant US outbreak occurred in Washington. That state announced its first death from COVID on February 29; officials later reported that two deaths on February 26 were also due to COVID. The virus spread quickly. Thirty-seven deaths occurred among residents in a nursing home in the Seattle suburb of Kirkland. Governor Jay Inslee declared a state of emergency on February 29, followed by a statewide stay-at-home order on March 23. At a Skagit County community choir's practices in early March, one infected person spread the virus to 53 others in the group of 61 singers, and two died. "Transmission was likely facilitated by close proximity (within 6 feet) and augmented by the act of singing," the CDC later concluded. Washington had the highest number of confirmed COVID cases, and the highest number per capita, of any state in the country until New York State surpassed it on April 10.[8]

New York City's first COVID case was confirmed on March 1, though it was later discovered that the virus had been circulating there since January. On March 3, Governor Andrew Cuomo announced that New York State's first case of person-to-person spread had occurred in a lawyer who worked at a Manhattan firm. Six days later, there were 21 confirmed cases in New York City.[9]

By March 30, the city had more than 36,000 confirmed cases. A US Navy hospital ship, *Comfort*, arrived that day with 1,200 medical personnel on board. Field hospitals were set up across the city. Refrigerator trucks were parked outside hospitals to accept the overflow of dead bodies. Other bodies were picked up from homes by the US Army, National Guard, and Air National Guard. Cuomo called for nurses and doctors across the country to help New York. On April 4, President Trump announced that 1,000 additional federal medical personnel would be sent to the city. Two days later, the city had nearly 25 percent of the country's total COVID deaths and more confirmed cases than China, Iran, or the United Kingdom.[10]

By April, mirroring circumstances elsewhere in America, hundreds of thousands of New Yorkers were out of work, with lost tax revenues estimated to run into the billions of dollars. The city's many museums were closed. Low-income jobs in the retail, transportation, and restaurant sectors were especially affected, though the city allowed restaurants to create open-air dining rooms on the streets in front of their businesses.[11]

The virus swept across the country in ripples and waves. By mid-March, among states Louisiana ranked third per capita in cases, behind Washington and New York, and New Orleans ranked second among big cities behind Seattle. At that time, Seattle had 53 cases per 100,000 people, New Orleans 20 cases per 100,000, and New York 5.3 per 100,000.[12]

The Army Corps of Engineers reviewed more than 100 facilities nationwide that could be converted for medical use, such as the Century Link Stadium in Seattle and Sleep Train Arena in Sacramento. Illinois converted North America's largest convention center, Chicago's McCormick Place, into a facility for up to 3,000 COVID patients. Governor J. B. Pritzker activated 30 National Guard airmen to assist with general labor on the project. The Federal Emergency Management Agency (FEMA) provided $15 million to support the construction. At that time,

Illinois had 5,057 COVID cases, including 73 deaths. But that was an undercount. "The cases that I report do not capture all of the cases in Illinois of COVID-19," said Dr. Ngozi Ezike, director of the Illinois Department of Health. "We know that we're not testing everyone."[13]

By mid-March, city, county, and state governments across America were trying to stop the virus from spreading by imposing mask mandates, stay-at-home orders, and school closures and prohibiting gatherings like festivals, sporting events, and church services.[14] Forty-one states closed their schools for the rest of the academic year. Forty states issued stay-at-home orders in March and early April. The response was bipartisan: the earliest closures were announced in mid-March by 18 states, 9 with Democratic governors and 9 with Republican governors.[15]

Wisconsin governor Tony Evers, a Democrat, declared a statewide public health emergency on March 12 and ordered all schools to close by March 18. The first COVID case in my hometown of Wauwatosa was confirmed on March 15. The next day, the Milwaukee County Executive, Wauwatosa mayor Kathy Ehley, and the county's 18 other mayors and village presidents issued a 60-day emergency order mandating the wearing of face masks to prevent the spread of the virus.[16] The order was extended several times.[17] By the time I succeeded Ehley as mayor on April 21, Wisconsin's largest medical complex, the Milwaukee Regional Medical Center (MRMC) in Wauwatosa, had become clogged with COVID patients and, like other medical centers nationwide, had begun deferring elective surgeries.[18] Wauwatosa's schools began holding virtual classes, the city canceled its Memorial Day ceremony and July 4 parade, and the Tosa Tonight outdoor concert series went dark for the first summer since it began in 2000.

On April 11, the US death toll became the world's highest when it topped 20,000. By May 27, four months after the virus reached the US, 100,000 Americans had died from COVID. A May 2020 study indicated that the true number of COVID cases exceeded the number of confirmed cases, with infections at some locations 6 to 24 times higher.[19]

A second surge of infections began in June 2020 after several states relaxed restrictions following a decline in cases. A third surge began in October, initially driven by students returning to college campuses, with cases reaching 100,000 a day by month's end. Wisconsin's seven-day average of new cases was the third worst in the US. In Wauwatosa, a city of 49,000 residents, 411 new COVID cases were reported in October, up from 183 the month before. The State of Wisconsin opened a field hospital at State Fair Park in West Allis, two miles from the MRMC, to handle the surge.[20]

On November 8, total COVID infections in the US surpassed 10 million; on December 8, 15 million. Six days later, on December 14, the US passed 300,000 deaths, an average of about 961 deaths per day since the first known death on February 6, 2020.[21]

On January 19, 2021, the US passed 400,000 COVID deaths, five weeks after passing 300,000. Five more weeks later, it passed 500,000.[22] In May 2021, the WHO reported that COVID-related deaths were probably two to three times greater than countries had counted; by that time, it was estimated that 6 to 8 million people might have died from COVID worldwide, compared with 3.4 million deaths in official reporting.[23]

In 2020, COVID was the third-leading cause of death in the US behind heart disease and cancer. From 2019 to 2021, national life expectancy dropped by 2.1 years, the largest decline since World War I, partly the result of COVID but also from other factors such as drug abuse.[24] It dropped by 1.2 years for Whites, 2.9 years for African Americans, and 3.0 years for Hispanics. In 2021, US COVID-related deaths exceeded those in 2020, and life expectancy continued to fall. By mid-2022, the COVID pandemic had resulted in more than 103 million confirmed cases and 1,127,152 deaths in the US, the most of any country.[25] Worldwide through mid-October 2023, almost seven million people had died directly from COVID, 0.09 percent of the global population, but the WHO estimated that the pandemic's full direct or indirect death toll (described as "excess mortality" or "excess deaths") in 2020 and 2021 alone was almost 15 million.[26]

PANDEMIC POLITICS

Science was ready for the pandemic, but human nature was not. Many people wanted to go on with business as usual, acting as if the virus and its consequences were not real.

On March 10, 2020, just as city, county, and state governments were beginning to impose mask mandates, stay-at-home orders, school closures, and bans on large gatherings to stop the virus from spreading, a right-wing political commentator, Candace Owens, tweeted, "One day, we will look back and study the impact of the coronavirus. Not the virus itself of course, but the mass global mental breakdown that it inspired. Because people think it's novel that 80 year olds are dying at a high rate from a flu. This tweet will age well."[27]

It did not. She was wrong to call COVID a flu and minimize its impact, but she was correct about a mental breakdown: fear, denial, and right-wing resistance to vaccines and public health measures like mask wearing, crowd limitations, and social distancing led to preventable deaths and increased the pandemic's length and severity in the US.[28]

We had been down this road before. Beginning in 1918, the Spanish flu pandemic took 675,000 US lives and 50 million more around the world—between 1.3 and 3.0 percent of the global population.[29] Hardest hit in America were soldiers and sailors, 20–40 percent of whom were infected; this affected our country's ability to fight World War I, which was then raging in Europe. Flu and pneumonia killed more service members than enemy weapons.[30]

As Dr. Nancy Tomes recounted in *Public Health Reports*, "Despite unprecedented efforts at mass education and coercion designed to halt it, the disease spread with lightning speed. After decades of remarkable progress in controlling communicable diseases, the influenza pandemic raised troubling questions about the efficacy of modern public health methods. Perhaps the most important 'lesson' taught by the [Spanish flu] pandemic was the realization that those measures that worked the best to control a highly infectious disease—bans on public gatherings, school closures, and strict quarantine and isolation—were precisely the ones most difficult to implement in a modern mass society" featuring "mass transportation, mass media, mass consumption, and mass warfare."[31]

In 1918 and 1919, large numbers of Americans cooperated with public health authorities to combat the disease. Many, however, did not. Across the country, public health authorities promoted the wearing of gauze masks to allow cities to function while minimizing the spread of influenza. If cities allowed public gatherings, they often required that people wear masks. Mask wearing gained popularity as a sign of public-spiritedness and discipline. But not everyone joined in.[32]

The western US in particular resisted mandates. As University of Michigan medical historian J. Alexander Navarro has recorded, the Portland and Los Angeles city councils refused to require residents to wear masks. In other places, people defied mask orders because they claimed that masks were uncomfortable or the mandates violated their civil liberties. "One Denver salesperson refused because she said her 'nose went to sleep' every time she put one on," Navarro wrote. "Another said she believed that 'an authority higher than the Denver Department of Health was looking after her well-being.'" Denver's streetcar conductors threatened to strike over the city's mask order, and Seattle's conductors refused to turn away unmasked passengers. When Sacramento's police chief told officers to round up people who were not wearing masks, police stations filled with offenders within 20 minutes. In San Francisco, judges and police worked nights and weekends on prosecutions of mask scofflaws. When the city reinstated its mask ordinance after a flu spike in January 1919, 2,000 members of the Anti-Mask League, including prominent doctors and a city council member, attended a rally to resist the mandate.[33]

Similar resistance arose when cities closed churches, schools, saloons, movie theaters, sporting events, and other places where mass gatherings occurred. As in 2020, the question became what was essential versus nonessential. Some businessmen resisted closures of businesses and mass transit, arguing that the closures caused economic hardship for owners and workers. Churches complained that stores were allowed to remain open, but their congregants could not exercise their constitutional right to worship together.[34]

But then, as in 2020 and 2021, social distancing was needed to prevent the virus from spreading. In studies of the Spanish flu pandemic published in 2007 in the *Journal of the American Medical Association* and the *Proceedings of the National Academy of Sciences*, researchers reported that cities that banned public gatherings (and sustained the bans) in 1918 and 1919 had lower death rates. Kansas City, Milwaukee, St. Louis, and San Francisco instituted the earliest and most effective measures, curbing virus transmission rates by 30 to 50 percent compared to other cities. By contrast, on September 28, 1918, Philadelphia, whose public health director was skeptical of the pandemic, allowed 200,000 residents to watch a Liberty Bond Parade held to support the nation's war effort. Within 72 hours, every hospital bed in the city was filled. On one day, 759 people died. Twelve thousand more died in the following weeks.

Many cities that lifted their bans in response to public pressure had to reimpose them after flu deaths resurged. That should not have been a surprise. The authors of the National Academy of Sciences report concluded that social distancing and other measures "can significantly reduce influenza transmission, but . . . viral spread will be renewed upon relaxation of such measures."[35] They and other experts cautioned against removing social distancing too soon during an epidemic. Two of them, Dr. Navarro and Dr. Howard Markel of the University of Michigan, noted that an epidemic ends when a community reaches sufficient overall immunity through vaccination or antibody reaction from infection, but social distancing can "flatten the curve" of infections until that "herd immunity" is reached.[36] Those lessons from the Spanish flu pandemic were not fully heeded when COVID struck.

In 2020 and 2021, the goal was to sustain public support for social distancing and other preventive measures long enough to develop and distribute an effective COVID vaccine. As the pandemic began, majorities of Republicans, Democrats, and independents all favored slowing the spread of the virus rather than prioritizing the economy. On March 29, 2020, President Trump extended through April 30 the White House's recommendations regarding social distancing and closures of nonessential businesses.[37] But the economy staggered as governments imposed lockdowns and businesses closed. Early on, the nation's gross domestic product fell by 9 percent, the deepest recession since World War II, but it quickly bounced back as the federal government pumped money into the economy through such relief measures as the Coronavirus Aid, Relief, and Economic Security (CARES) Act passed by Congress in March.[38]

Nevertheless, rallies, encouraged by Trump and conservative organizations, were held across the nation to challenge lockdowns. The largest protests were in Michigan.[39] On March 23, Governor Gretchen Whitmer issued a stay-at-home order that limited nonessential travel; closed schools, bars, restaurants, and entertainment venues; and banned gatherings of more than 50 people.[40] By April 15, Michigan had 28,059 confirmed COVID cases—the third-highest number in the US—and 1,921 deaths attributed to the virus.[41] That day, 20,000 people surrounded the State Capitol in an eight-hour protest called "Operation Gridlock" organized by the Michigan Conservative Coalition. They complained about being out of work and claimed that Whitmer's orders violated their civil liberties.[42] On April 30, hundreds of protesters, organized by the right-wing American Patriot Council, gathered at the Capitol. Many carried nooses, guns, Confederate flags, and Nazi signs, and some compared Whitmer to Adolf Hitler.[43] On May 14, more heavily armed protesters gathered at the Capitol.[44] The legislature adjourned for several days to avoid another armed confrontation inside the chamber.[45] Despite the pushback, a poll showed that 71 percent of Michigan residents approved of Whitmer's COVID response.[46] Notwithstanding that support, 13 men were charged with plotting to kidnap and execute Whitmer and overthrow several state governments they believed were violating the Constitution.[47]

Some of the acts in furtherance of that conspiracy took place in my home state. One of the nation's largest protests occurred at the Wisconsin State Capitol on April 24, where a few thousand people, dressed in Tea Party and Trump campaign attire and carrying guns and American flags, protested stay-at-home orders. That day, the Wisconsin Department of Health Services announced 304 new COVID cases, the most in the state since the pandemic began.[48]

The question was whether the "freedom" demanded by the protesters was really just another word for selfishness. Nobel Prize–winning economist Joseph Stiglitz, writing in the *Washington Post*, observed that some people "often fail to recognize that one person's freedom is another's unfreedom.... Freedom to carry a gun might mean death to those who are gunned down in the mass killings that have become an almost daily occurrence in the United States. Freedom not to be vaccinated or wear masks might mean others lose the freedom to live."[49]

Wauwatosa took the health and economic disruptions seriously. In May, while our health department was working around the clock on curbing the pandemic, I asked department directors and the Common Council to expedite the city's permitting processes. (In Wisconsin, city councils are called "common councils.") Through the Tosa Restarts program, restaurants and other businesses were allowed to hold sidewalk sales and locate food trucks and outdoor dining sites in new locations. These activities usually require lengthy approvals, but under the program, city staff reviewed and approved applications within 72 hours. Tosa Restarts also helped small businesses retain employees and cover reopening expenses with working capital, low interest rates, and deferred repayments; the Wauwatosa Revolving Loan Fund Corporation and Community Development Authority provided financial assistance for over 100 small businesses; and our Small Business Forgivable Loan Program extended loans to businesses that met job creation and retention requirements.[50]

In the meantime, political pressure was building to undo public health restrictions. Trump, who had initially urged patience, became increasingly concerned about the damage to the economy—and his reelection prospects—caused by Americans staying home from work, school, stores, and restaurants. His inclination was always to downplay the risk. For example, on January 30, the day before the US declared a public health emergency, he said, "We have very little problem in this country at this moment—five. And those people are all recuperating successfully." At a White House meeting on February 27, he said, "It's going to disappear. One day—it's like a miracle—it will disappear."[51] In March, he expressed his belief that restrictions could be relaxed by Easter, observed on April 12 that year. "America will, again, and soon, be open for business," he said. "Very soon. A lot sooner than three or four months that somebody was suggesting. Lot sooner. We cannot let the cure be worse than the problem itself."[52]

As German Lopez observed on Vox, Trump's push for an early reopening seemed more wishful than medical. Easter "is a beautiful time," Trump said. "It would be a beautiful timeline." But

Dr. Fauci, the country's top infectious disease expert, told the Associated Press that Trump's goal was "overly optimistic" and the US did not yet have the tests and contact tracing needed to reopen the economy. "I'll guarantee you, once you start pulling back there will be infections," he cautioned. "It's how you deal with the infections that's going to count." In any event, though the White House and CDC created guidelines for dealing with COVID, most public health measures are imposed at the state and local levels, not by the federal government.[53]

Many Americans, especially conservatives, fretted that the restrictions were unduly burdening the economy, education, and social and community life. They became less supportive as time went on.[54] Some denied the existence of COVID at all or pushed back on public health measures in court. Several Republican members of the US House of Representatives refused to wear masks and lost a legal challenge to a House mask requirement.[55]

Around the country, numerous lawsuits were brought to challenge state pandemic responses.[56] Six were brought in Wisconsin, where many of the nation's most consequential political and legal battles have been fought in recent years. On May 13, Wisconsin became the first state to have a stay-at-home order overruled when the conservative majority of the state Supreme Court held 4–3, in a lawsuit brought by the legislature's Republican majority, that the Wisconsin Department of Health Services secretary exceeded her authority when she extended the statewide stay-at-home order on behalf of Governor Evers. At the time, a Marquette University Law School poll showed that 69 percent of Wisconsinites approved of the order, which was similar to orders in 42 other states.[57] In March 2021, the court again held 4–3 that Evers did not have the power to declare multiple 60-day emergencies in response to a single crisis.[58]

Whatever the legal merits of the court's rulings were, the practical effect was to restrict the state's ability to limit the pandemic's impact on its residents, a stark illustration of the politicization of public health. Considering that emergency health orders were being imposed at the local level under similar state statutes, it caused confusion in Wauwatosa and other Wisconsin communities about whether we could take measures to protect our residents. (Other mayors and I invoked the same emergency statutes in 2020 to declare curfews as protests over police killings of African Americans occasionally turned destructive.)

As the political winds shifted, Fauci became the target of COVID deniers because he sometimes publicly disagreed with Trump about COVID restrictions and would-be cures. On the far-right website Big League Politics, a podcaster tweeted an article headlined "Dr. Fauci Wants America to Become a Police State Like China in Order to Stop Coronavirus." An article depicting Fauci as an agent of the "deep state" gained 25,000 likes, comments, and shares on Facebook when it was posted to groups like Trump Strong and Tampa Bay Trump Club. In *Politico*, Tina Nguyen observed that "it's the right-wing fringe that has been going after Fauci, largely due to the fact that he tamps down Trump's excitement over quick-fix solutions, such as the antimalarial drug hydroxychloroquine, his desire for stringent restrictions on gatherings and his publicly dire predictions about the potential death toll that are at odds with Trump's more optimistic outlook." The US Department of Health and Human Services assigned a security detail to protect Fauci as he began receiving threats to his personal safety.[59]

"Anti-intellectualism (resentment, hostility, and mistrust of experts) has become a growing concern during the pandemic," wrote National Institutes of Health researchers in a study of the social media attacks on Fauci. "Based on the theoretical framework of science-related populism, we identified three anti-intellectual discursive elements in anti-Fauci tweets: people-scientist antagonism, delegitimizing the motivation of scientists, and delegitimizing the knowledge of scientists. Delegitimizing the motivation of scientists appeared the most in anti-Fauci tweets. Politicians, conservative news media, and non-institutional actors (e.g. individuals and grassroots advocacy organizations) co-constructed the production and circulation of anti-intellectual discourses on Twitter."[60]

Taking their cue from Trump, some courts, and public sentiment, all 50 states began easing their restrictions. As predicted, COVID infections resurged. Some states and localities reimposed limits on public gatherings, businesses, and other activities.[61] It was clear that a return to pre-2020 normality would have to wait until the country developed herd immunity, which would require at least 75 percent of the population to be COVID-resistant.[62] But vaccines were not available in 2020, and many people died before they could develop immunity.

The return to social distancing restrictions took a major economic toll on southeastern Wisconsin. Milwaukee was scheduled to host the Democratic National Convention from July 13 to 16, 2020, the first time the city would have hosted such an event since the Socialist Party convention in 1932 and the first time since 1916 that any midwestern city other than Chicago would have hosted the DNC. It was not to be. Because of the health risks, the DNC held a virtual convention, and metropolitan Milwaukee lost an anticipated $150–$250 million economic boost.[63] Among the losers was Wauwatosa, where multiple state delegations had been expected to fill hundreds of hotel rooms and restaurant tables each day of the convention.

VACCINATION

The battle over the wisdom of closing schools and businesses intensified as the year went on and merged into a partisan fight over the safety and effectiveness of COVID vaccines.

On May 15, 2020, President Trump announced a public-private partnership, dubbed Operation Warp Speed (OWS), to facilitate and accelerate the development and distribution of vaccines.

Initially funded with $10 billion from the CARES Act passed in March, OWS brought private companies together with federal agencies, including the CDC, Department of Health and Human Services, National Institutes of Health, Defense Department, Agriculture Department, Energy Department, and Department of Veterans Affairs, among others. The partnership's goal was to produce and deliver 300 million doses of safe and effective vaccines by January 2021.[64]

A German company, BioNTech, had started its own Project Lightspeed in January 2020 to develop a novel messenger RNA (mRNA) vaccine shortly after the genetic sequence of the COVID virus was made public. It partnered with an American company, Pfizer Inc., to develop and produce the vaccine. In July, OWS placed a $2 billion order with Pfizer to produce 100 million doses when and if the Food and Drug Administration (FDA) found the vaccine to be safe and effective.[65]

Pfizer and BioNTech announced positive results from their vaccine trial on November 9. On December 2, the United Kingdom authorized use of the vaccine on an emergency basis. Shortly thereafter, the FDA authorized the Pfizer-BioNTech vaccine and another mRNA vaccine made by the US start-up Moderna.[66] The vaccines were desperately needed. Columbia University researchers estimated that by year's end, 31 percent of Americans had been infected, including 42 percent in Miami, 44 percent in New York City, 48 percent in Chicago, 52 percent in Los Angeles, and more than 60 percent in parts of the Dakotas, Minnesota, Wisconsin, and Iowa.[67]

New York was the first state to administer the vaccine. Sandra Lindsay, the director of critical-care nursing at Long Island Jewish Medical Center in Queens, received the first shot on December 14.[68] On December 23, the US government ordered another 100 million doses from Pfizer.[69] It sent the vaccines to pharmacies nationwide, which then sent pharmacists to conduct mass vaccinations at care facilities like nursing homes.[70]

On January 20, 2021, Joseph Biden was sworn in as the forty-sixth US president. He set a goal of 100 million vaccinations in his first 100 days in office. The goal was reached on March 19. He then raised the goal to 200 million in his first 100 days. That was met on April 21. By then, the seven-day average of new COVID infections was decreasing, but the CDC estimated that 35 percent of Americans had been infected, four times higher than the official reported numbers.[71]

Public health experts feared that the name Operation Warp Speed and the short development timeline would encourage vaccine hesitancy. Their concern was justified. A September 2020 survey by the Pew Research Center found that 75 percent of adults were afraid that vaccines would be administered before being adequately tested, and 50 percent said they would not accept a vaccination. A majority of Americans feared that Trump would rush out a vaccine to help his reelection campaign.[72] In time, however, the COVID vaccines proved safe and effective.[73] Their rapid development saved many lives and was the first Trump term's greatest success. "In fact," observed the *Washington Post*, "the lightning-fast development of two leading coronavirus vaccines happened both because of and despite Trump—perhaps the most anti-science president in modern history, who has previously flirted with anti-vaccine views and savaged those who cited scientific evidence to press for basic public health measures in response to the pandemic."[74]

But just as some had denied the pandemic's existence, disputes over vaccination took on a partisan cast, with Democrats generally in favor of strong government action and Republicans generally resisting vaccines, mask requirements, and other government-sponsored public health measures as unconstitutional infringements of their civil liberties.[75] This resistance was initially fed by messages from the Trump White House that conflicted with guidance from the CDC and public health experts. Though Trump himself was vaccinated, his initial labeling of COVID as a "hoax," refusal to wear a mask and mocking of those who did, support for remedies not approved by the FDA as COVID treatments (like the antimalarial drug hydroxychloroquine and ivermectin, a drug used to treat parasitic roundworm infections), and on-again, off-again statements about vaccines and social distancing undermined masking and vaccine acceptance. (To the horror of doctors and the manufacturer of Lysol, in April 2020 Trump also proposed injecting COVID sufferers with disinfectants to knock out the virus. He walked back his suggestion the next day, claiming he had been sarcastic.)[76] By November 2021, when Biden announced vaccination mandates for federal employees and people working for large companies, 86 percent of Democrats supported the policy and 79 percent of Republicans opposed it.[77]

Mimicking earlier rallies against stay-at-home orders, anti-vaccine rallies spread across America. "Anti-vaxxers" like Robert F. Kennedy Jr., Green Bay Packers football star Aaron Rodgers, and Congresswomen Lauren Boebert (R-CO) and Marjorie Taylor Greene (R-GA) rose up to spread misinformation and hostility. An appalled reviewer noted that, in a 2022 book, conspiracy theorist Naomi Wolf contended that "vaccines and other public health measures were a plot by a 'transnational group of bad actors' to sterilize people, turn children into drones and undermine the Constitution, among many other unhinged assertions."[78]

As Vera Bergengruen reported in *Time* magazine in early 2022, "opposition to vaccine and mask mandates has become a purity test for Republican officials, as well as a key part of their agenda ahead of this year's midterm elections."[79] A Supreme Court justice contributed to the paranoia. In a 2023 opinion, Neil Gorsuch (who had been appointed by Trump) referred to lockdowns and vaccination mandates in the workplace and for US military members and wrote, "Since March 2020, Americans may have experienced the greatest intrusions on civil liberties in the peacetime history of this country." That ignored the real health impacts of the pandemic and the Spanish flu pandemic's lessons about military readiness. For decades, US military personnel have been required to be vaccinated against a variety of diseases.[80]

Public health officials worried that mixed messaging by Republicans would increase vaccine hesitancy. Their fears were realized.[81] Often, GOP officials declared support for vaccines while winking at the concerns of skeptical voters. In December 2021, on the same day that former President Trump was booed at a meeting in Texas for saying he had received a booster shot, another 2024 GOP presidential contender, Florida governor Ron DeSantis, acknowledged having been vaccinated and encouraged others to be vaccinated, too. But his position shifted as his campaign went on. In September 2023, he said, "I will not stand by and let the FDA and CDC use healthy Floridians as guinea pigs for new booster shots that have not been proven to be safe or effective." On a conservative talk show the next day, he alleged, in a moment of projection, that federal health authorities had been "corrupted by ideology."[82] He petitioned for a state grand jury to investigate alleged wrongdoing related to vaccines, and Florida's health department issued a vaccine safety "health alert" much criticized by medical experts.[83] DeSantis also signed legislation prohibiting school districts from requiring face masks and forbidding employers, schools, and governmental entities from requiring employees and students to be vaccinated.[84] Meanwhile, GOP-dominated Tennessee's health department homepage discussed the flu, vaping, and cancer screening but did not mention COVID or COVID vaccines, and in 2023, Texas legislators passed a budget forbidding health departments and other state-funded organizations to advertise, recommend, or list COVID vaccines apart from other vaccines.[85]

In a national survey published in March 2023, University of South Florida researchers found that 88 percent of Democrats, but only 49 percent of Republicans, said they were "very" or "somewhat confident" that COVID vaccines were safe. This had deadly consequences. A *Washington Post* analysis of CDC data from April 2020 through the summer of 2022 found that early in the pandemic, people of color, especially Black people, suffered a disproportionate number of COVID-related deaths. But by mid-October 2021—when 90 percent of Democrats, but only 61 percent of Republicans, had received at least one shot—the death rate for White Americans, who comprise the majority of GOP members, sometimes exceeded that of other groups.[86] A 2022 study from the University of Maryland and the University of California at Irvine published in *Health Affairs* concluded that Republican-majority counties experienced nearly 73 more deaths per 100,000 people through October 2021 than Democratic counties.[87]

How this occurred was illustrated in a *Lancet Regional Health—Americas* report in December 2022 on a Harvard University study. Researchers compared data on COVID death rates in all congressional districts from April 2021 to March 2022 to the overall voting records of members of Congress, how the members voted on COVID relief legislation, and whether one party controlled the state's legislature and governor's office. The study found that the more conservative the voting records of a state's legislators and members of Congress were, the higher was that state's COVID death rate for working-aged people. COVID death rates were 11 percent higher in GOP-controlled states and 26 percent higher in conservative districts.[88]

A Yale University report published in *JAMA Internal Medicine* in July 2023 found similar results. The study examined the deaths of 538,139 people 25 years and older in Florida and Ohio from 2018 through 2021. The excess death rate for Republicans and Democrats—their affiliations were gleaned from party registration records—was about equal from the start of the pandemic until vaccines became widely available. After April 2021, the Republican excess death rate was 7.7 percent higher than that for Democrats. That meant a 43 percent increase in excess Republican deaths. The gap was larger in counties with lower vaccination rates.[89]

THE PANDEMIC ENDS

As the US developed widespread resistance to COVID through vaccinations and acquired immunity, the country began to see light at the end of the long, dark, frightening tunnel. On May 13, 2021, the CDC announced that fully vaccinated individuals could resume activities without wearing masks or physically distancing, except where required by federal, state, or local laws, rules, and regulations. The nation began relaxing its pandemic-related restrictions.[90]

Wauwatosa's mask mandate expired in June. By that time, 64 percent of Wauwatosa residents ages 18 and older had received at least one dose of the vaccine. The health department's goal was to vaccinate 80 percent by the end of 2021.[91] I proposed that we use some of the $25 million we had received from the federal government's recently-passed American Rescue Plan Act to give incentives to residents and city employees to get vaccinated, in the form of $50 or $100 gift cards that could be used in Wauwatosa stores and restaurants. The goal was to encourage vaccinations while supporting struggling local businesses.[92]

Similar ideas were tried elsewhere. Some North Carolina counties offered $25 gift cards for those who got vaccinated, West Virginia offered $100 savings bonds for vaccine recipients ages 16–35, and Ohio governor Mike DeWine created a $1 million lottery for residents who received their initial vaccines. The number of Ohioans who received vaccines jumped 33 percent in the week after the lottery was announced, and one-third of unvaccinated people surveyed said a cash payment would encourage them to be vaccinated.[93] The University of Wisconsin System sponsored a "70 for 70" lottery to encourage 12 public universities to achieve a 70 percent student vaccination rate by October 15, 2021, by offering 70 $7,000 tuition reimbursement awards. Eleven campuses exceeded 70 percent, and 70 vaccinated students received $7,000 awards for the 2021–22 academic year.[94] The Wauwatosa Health

Department held gift-card drawings while promoting vaccinations through community outreach, mobile vaccine units, digital advertising, social media, and radio and TV commercials. In August 2021, the drawings stopped because 74.4 percent of residents were fully vaccinated and 78.8 percent had received at least one dose, one of Wisconsin's highest community vaccination rates.[95]

In the fall 2021 edition of a local magazine, *Tosa Connection*, I celebrated the return of in-person classes in our schools and urged everyone to get vaccinated and, if asked by businesses and schools, to wear a mask. "Just as Americans did when we defeated the Spanish flu 100 years ago," I wrote, "we will demonstrate our patriotism, show love for our friends and neighbors, and defeat the coronavirus if we all follow the advice of our health professionals."[96] This statement drew praise, but one resident called to complain that it was "divisive" because the vaccines were "experimental." I replied that they were not experimental because the CDC had approved them. He grumbled and hung up. Eventually, 81 percent of Wauwatosans received at least one dose and 53 percent at least one booster shot, well above national averages.[97] Still, because some people refused to be vaccinated, about 100 of our residents died from COVID—more than 2 per 1,000.

By 2022, more than 70 percent of Americans had contracted the virus.[98] Not all became sick, but in May, the US government announced that more than one million Americans had died from COVID.[99] By this time, however, 75 percent of US adults had been vaccinated.[100] That spring, I fell ill with COVID for a week, suffering a sore throat, deep fatigue, and a 102-degree fever. Had I not been vaccinated, it could have been far worse: nearly 9 out of 10 COVID-related deaths occur in people who, like me, are age 65 or older.

Though the end of COVID was nowhere in sight, vaccines had allowed America to move on.[101] In September 2022, President Biden declared the pandemic "over," a statement for which some public health experts criticized him, but he was speaking less from a public health perspective and more from the fact that Americans had tired of the restrictions placed on their lives and felt assured by vaccines that they could return to their normal pre-COVID activities.[102]

At the height of the pandemic, the number of US excess deaths from any cause was 30 percent higher than normal, because of COVID but also because of the disease's indirect effects, like vehicle crashes, gun deaths, and deaths from deferred medical care. In July 2023, the *New York Times* reported that the number of excess deaths was no longer historically abnormal. Finally, it seemed, the pandemic really was over. Deaths had been reduced to their historical averages because 97 percent of American adults had received at least one vaccine shot or gained natural immunity from having been infected with COVID or both.[103]

"Nearly every death is preventable [now]," former White House COVID advisor Dr. Ashish Jha told the *Times*. "We are at a point where almost everybody who's up to date on their vaccines and gets treated if they have COVID, they rarely end up in the hospital, they almost never die." This included people at high risk, like people with compromised immune systems. Age continued to be the leading factor for death from COVID, but victims were also more likely to be Republican and White, because so many members of that group resisted vaccination.[104]

On October 2, 2023, the Nobel Prize in Physiology or Medicine was awarded to Dr. Katalin Karikó and Dr. Drew Weissman, whose mRNA research at the University of Pennsylvania enabled COVID vaccines to be developed quickly to avoid millions of deaths and end the pandemic.[105] Despite the dangers that COVID still posed, science had prevailed.

Earlier that year, 34 experts published a book, *Lessons from the Covid War: An Investigative Report*,[106] to share their conclusions about what had happened during the pandemic and how we might do better when the next pandemic occurs. *New York Times* science writer David Wallace-Wells summarized what the authors identified as hampering the US response: bickering by Trump and Biden during a bitter presidential campaign; exhaustion and partisan wrangling over social isolation and shutdowns of schools and businesses; "normalization of mass death"; vaccination, which should have been celebrated as a way to end the pandemic but instead increased polarization; and vaccine mandates, which created more political division. "There is a common view that politics, a 'red response' and a 'blue response,' were the main obstacle to protecting citizens, not competence and policy failures," the experts wrote. "We found, instead, that it was more the other way around. Incompetence and policy failures, including the failure of federal executive leadership, produced bad outcomes, flying blind, and resorting to blunt instruments. Those failures and tensions fed toxic politics that further divided the country in a crisis rather than bringing it together."[107]

"What was unique to the United States," Wallace-Wells found, "was the intensification of pandemic partisanship that followed the arrival of vaccines. . . . The United States was unusual among the world's wealthy countries for having a deadlier 2021 than 2020."[108]

Partly due to the politicization of COVID vaccines, the number of kindergartners receiving vaccines for such diseases as measles, mumps, rubella, tetanus, and chicken pox dropped in the 2021–22 school year. Support for leaving vaccination choices to parents rather than mandating them increased, mostly due to reduced vaccine support among Republicans. Under pressure from right-wing activists, some states even considered rolling back vaccine mandates for children.[109]

The anti-vax movement intensified. A University of Pennsylvania survey in late 2023 found that faith in vaccines had dropped by 6 percent over the previous two years, with only 71 percent of Americans trusting their safety and 16 percent regarding them as unsafe.[110] This led to another public health challenge. In early 2024, the US experienced a massive outbreak of measles, which is one of the most contagious human viruses, even more than COVID.

The cause of the outbreak was easy to determine. The *Washington Post* explained that "measles can be prevented with the measles, mumps and rubella vaccine; two doses are 97 percent effective. . . . Unfortunately, vaccination rates are falling. The global vaccine coverage rate of the first dose, at 83 percent, and second dose, at 74 percent, are well under the 95 percent [herd immunity] level. Vaccination coverage among U.S. kindergartners has slipped from 95.2 percent during the 2019–2020 school year to 93.1 percent in the 2022–2023 school year, according to the CDC, leaving approximately 250,000 kindergartners at risk each year over the past three years." The anti-vax madness had put a generation of children at risk of prolonged hospitalization and even death.[111]

Additional risks emerged following the 2024 presidential election, imperiling our ability to cope with another pandemic. In a remarkable comeback, on November 5, 2024, Donald Trump was elected to a second term as president, avenging his 2020 defeat. Soon after, he nominated Robert F. Kennedy Jr. to be secretary of the Department of Health and Human Services, even though Kennedy had continued to insist that certain vaccines—including those for COVID and polio—were unsafe.[112]

Then, on his first day back in office in January 2025, Trump signed an executive order to withdraw the US from the World Health Organization. As CNN reported, he first tried to leave WHO during his first term in 2020, accusing it of "severely mismanaging and covering up" the spread of COVID. During his 2024 election campaign, he called WHO "nothing more than a corrupt globalist scam" which "disgracefully covered the tracks of the Chinese Communist Party" in concealing COVID's alleged origin in a laboratory in Wuhan, China, which Beijing has denied. Despite Trump's accusations, WHO itself called for China to be more transparent to help public health officials understand how the pandemic began. Devi Sridhar, chair of global public health at the University of Edinburgh, Scotland, told CNN that "the US would be weaker in its national security imperatives if it wasn't part of WHO, given it wouldn't have this cooperation with other countries to know what's happening in terms of outbreaks and in helping manage response."[113]

Once again, as in 1918 and 2020, politics and denial had triumphed over science. The loser was public health.

—‹›—

A LONG, HOT SUMMER

BEFORE 2020, MINNEAPOLIS-ST. PAUL, SEATTLE, and Portland were America's north stars, liberal havens blessed with progressive leadership and innovative businesses. Minneapolis was the home of "Mary Richards," the beloved heroine of television's *The Mary Tyler Moore Show*; Seattle was the home of Microsoft, Eddie Bauer, and fussy TV psychiatrist "Frasier Crane"; and the *New York Times* dubbed Portland the "capital of West Coast urban cool," while the TV series *Portlandia* affectionately poked fun at the city's quirky hipness.[1]

All that changed in 2020. As the COVID pandemic and presidential campaign simmered nationwide, an incident in Minneapolis caused tensions to boil over there—and everywhere.

On May 25, 2020, Minneapolis police officers arrested an African American man for allegedly trying to buy cigarettes at a corner store with a counterfeit $20 bill. While other officers watched, Derek Chauvin suffocated George Floyd by kneeling on his neck for almost 10 minutes while he gasped and cried for help and onlookers begged Chauvin to stop. The slow-motion murder, captured on a citizen's cell phone video and circulated online, ignited protests in Minneapolis, across America, and around the world. People poured into the streets to express their outrage against police killings of Floyd and other Blacks.[2]

The incident started what has been called "the largest mass protest movement in U.S. history." In just the five weeks after Floyd died, calculated the *New York Times,* as many as 26 million Americans participated in more than 4,700 protests—about 140 each day—in 2,500 large cities and small towns across the country.[3] The protests continued throughout 2020. By the end of November, protests had occurred in almost 4,500 cities worldwide in more than 60 countries and in all US states and territories. Although the international protests were linked to US racial problems, they were also aimed at issues in their own countries.[4] For example, demonstrations in the United Kingdom protested racism in that former empire, which is still struggling to come to terms with postcolonialism and its past involvement in the international slave trade.[5]

That the Floyd murder occurred in Minneapolis was a shock to many Americans. Minneapolis, observed Harvard University professor Khalil Gibran Muhammad, was "a city once considered a national model of racial liberalism, in a state whose citizens are thought to be 'Minnesota Nice.'"[6] Known for gleaming skyscrapers, beautiful lakes, and the University of Minnesota and bolstered by its partnership with the state capital of St. Paul across the Mississippi River, Minneapolis seemed to have escaped the Rust Belt declines and racial issues of other, more industrialized midwestern cities. Smug in that success, Minneapolis hid its rank of ninety-ninth—second worst—of America's 100 largest metropolitan areas in the gap between Black and White earnings and its police department's pattern and practice of discrimination against Blacks and Native Americans.[7] But after the murder of George Floyd, said Muhammad, "Minneapolis may be the city most notorious for anti-Black police violence in the world."[8]

It was hardly alone. America and its cities have a long history of violence against African Americans, dating back to the institution of slavery in the 1600s. The Thirteenth Amendment to the US Constitution (ratified in 1865) prohibited slavery, but after Reconstruction ended in 1877 and federal troops pulled out of the South, lynchings and other brutality against Blacks became common in the North as well as in the South. The brutality has persisted. Sometimes it has been inflicted by police officers, such as in the 1965 riots in the Watts neighborhood of Los Angeles, which resulted in 34 deaths. Riots erupted in Los Angeles again in 1992 after officers were acquitted for beating a Black man named Rodney King. In 2014, protests and unrest followed the police shooting of Michael Brown in Ferguson, Missouri, and the death of Eric Garner, whom New York City police killed with a chokehold for selling contraband cigarettes.[9]

In April 2015, Baltimore erupted in riots following the police killing of Freddie Gray, sparking the birth of the Black Lives Matter (BLM) movement. In June that year, a White supremacist killed nine Black worshippers at Mother Emanuel AME Church in Charleston, South Carolina. In July, a Black woman, Sandra Bland, was found hanged in a Texas jail cell after being arrested for failing to signal a lane change while driving her car. Soon after, two incidents in Minneapolis-St. Paul foreshadowed the George Floyd murder. In November 2015, Minneapolis police killed Jamar Clark, sparking 18 days of BLM protests, and in July 2016 a police officer shot and killed Philando Castile during a traffic stop in the St. Paul suburb of Falcon Heights.[10]

These were just a few of the many such incidents since the end of Reconstruction. In my hometown of Wauwatosa, a police officer killed three men of color over a five-year period, most recently on February 2, 2020. Months of protests challenged our community throughout the year.

In 2020, other shootings of Blacks stoked outrage. On February 23, three White men in a pickup truck chased a 25-year-old Black man, Ahmaud Arbery, and shot him to death for doing nothing more than jogging through a White neighborhood in

Satilla Shores, Georgia. On March 13, police in Louisville, Kentucky, killed 26-year-old Breonna Taylor as they tried to serve a warrant on her boyfriend at her apartment. On June 12, an Atlanta officer fatally shot 27-year-old Rayshard Brooks, who had been asleep in his car in a restaurant parking lot, as Brooks tried to run away. On August 23, a police officer in Kenosha, Wisconsin, shot 29-year-old Jacob Blake while serving a warrant for his arrest. These incidents rocked a nation already reeling from the pandemic and unrest.[11]

Videos recorded on cell phones often made it possible for people to see Floyd's murder and other police violence for themselves.[12] The incidents fueled growing resentment of police departments. When Floyd was killed, his desperate plea "I can't breathe" was chanted during protests against police brutality, as it had been in 2014 when Eric Garner used the same words to plead for his life before being killed by NYPD officers.[13]

Though there is a long history of protests against the brutality toward African Americans, the "racial reckoning" in 2020 was more intense and widespread than anything since the civil rights movement of the 1950s and 1960s. In a *New York Times* op-ed, Columbia University professor John McWhorter asked why. As an African American, he did not minimize the terrible events that had afflicted people of color through the years, but he noted that those events had not had the impact of the Floyd murder. "Tragically, hideously, Americans learn of Black people dying under appalling circumstances, involving police officers, quite often," he wrote. "Think of Sandra Bland, Philando Castile, Breonna Taylor, Eric Garner—whether these circumstances lead to criminal convictions, or charges, which they often don't." Something besides Floyd's murder had caused the surge of demonstrations nationwide, he concluded: "the fact that we had been in pandemic isolation for two months and that around that same time it was becoming clear that conditions were not going to change anytime soon."[14]

The Center for Disaster Philanthropy had a similar take, noting that protests and rallies connected to the pandemic and the upcoming presidential election also heightened the tension, as did counterprotests and rallies by White supremacy groups.[15] To this could have been added the long-standing segregation of African Americans in housing and schools and a lack of equal economic opportunity.[16] But, whatever the reason, immediately after the Floyd murder America erupted in protest. It was estimated that for most of 2020, more than 90 percent of the protests were peaceful, but some included rioting, looting, and arson, and deaths, serious injuries, and property damage occurred in hundreds of cities.[17]

For three nights following the Floyd murder, the twin cities of Minneapolis and Saint Paul collapsed into chaos. It quickly became the second-costliest civil disturbance in US history after the 1992 Los Angeles riots, with hundreds of people arrested and hundreds of millions of dollars of damage to hundreds of properties.[18] Widespread looting and destruction occurred, including a police station being overrun by demonstrators and set on fire. The chaos did not diminish until Governor Tim Walz activated the Minnesota National Guard on May 28.[19]

President Trump heightened tensions the following day when he called the protesters "thugs," suggested that the military could be used to stop the violence in Minneapolis, and fired off a partisan criticism of the city's Democratic mayor. "I can't stand back & watch this happen to a great American City," Trump tweeted. "A total lack of leadership. Either the very weak Radical Left Mayor, Jacob Frey, get his act together and bring the City under control, or I will send in the National Guard & get the job done right."[20]

That day, Governor Walz, Mayor Frey, St. Paul mayor Melvin Carter, and other leaders imposed a week of curfews in the Twin Cities area.[21] "What started as largely peaceful protests for George Floyd have turned to outright looting and domestic terrorism in our region," Frey tweeted. "We need you to stay home tonight." He later added, "We are now confronting white supremacists, members of organized crime, out-of-state instigators, and possibly even foreign actors to destroy and destabilize our city and our region."[22]

Among the outside agitators was Ivan Hunter, a member of the right-wing Boogaloo Bois group of antigovernment extremists, who was accused of traveling from Texas to Minneapolis to meet other Boogaloo Bois and engage in violent acts during the riots following Floyd's death. He was charged with participating in a riot after he allegedly shot 13 rounds from an AK-47 assault rifle into a Minneapolis police station. Afterward, he bragged on Facebook: "I helped the community burn down that police station in Minneapolis" and "I didn't protest peacefully Dude. . . . Want something to change? Start risking felonies for what is good."[23]

On June 1, Floyd's brother, Terrence, came from his home in Brooklyn, New York, to visit the site of his brother's death. The *New York Times* reported that he pleaded with the Minneapolis crowd to stop the violence and destruction. "If I'm not over here wilding out, if I'm not over here blowing up stuff, if I'm not over here messing up my community, then what are y'all doing? What are y'all doing?" he said. "Do this peacefully, please."[24]

By early June 2020, Wikipedia noted, at least 200 cities had imposed curfews, and more than 30 states and Washington, DC, had activated the National Guard to deal with the unrest.[25] By the end of that month, at least 14,000 people had been arrested at protests, mostly for low-level offenses like curfew violations.[26] But according to a September 2020 estimate by Property Claim Services (which tracks insurance claims related to civil disorder), arson, vandalism, and looting related to the nationwide protests caused $1–2 billion in insured damage in the two weeks between May 26 and June 8, making it the civil disorder event with the highest recorded damage in American history. Seth G. Jones, director of the Transnational Threats Project at the Center for Strategic and International Studies, told the *Washington Post* that most of the violence was committed by "local hooligans, sometimes gangs, sometimes just individuals that are trying to take advantage of an opportunity." This was seconded by an internal US Department of Homeland Security report, which stated that "most of the violence appear[ed] to have been driven by opportunists."[27]

Unrest visited smaller cities and suburbs, too. For example, protests sprung up in wealthy California communities such as Danville, Irvine, Redlands, Temecula, and Walnut Creek,[28] and a number of southern and western suburbs of Chicago declared curfews on Sunday, May 31, following a weekend of protests and looting after the Floyd murder. Curfews were imposed in the southern Chicago suburbs of Alsip, Blue Island, Calumet City, Calumet Park, Chicago Ridge, Country Club Hills, Evergreen Park, Oak Lawn, Orland Park, and Tinley Park and in the western suburbs of Bartlett, Berwyn, Brookfield, and Oak Park. In Aurora, the mayor declared a state of emergency and a curfew, and drivers had to show residential or employment identification to enter from the Interstate 88 ramps to the city.[29] In Wauwatosa, 100 miles north of Chicago, the unrest compelled me to impose three nights of curfews, too, on May 30–31 and June 1.[30]

A few days after Floyd died, Seattle and Portland erupted. Chaotic protests were nothing new in Seattle. During the World Trade Organization conference in 1999, hundreds of people converged there to protest economic globalization in what became known as the "Battle of Seattle." After vandalism and violence broke out during nonviolent protests and offenders eluded capture by escaping into crowds, the city imposed an order temporarily barring most public access to parts of downtown Seattle. Federal courts later upheld that order.[31]

But the extent of the 2020 protests was something new. As the *Seattle Times* recounted at the year's end,

> the protests—sometimes involving tens of thousands of demonstrators—have given voice and momentum to an emerging social movement that has been embraced here in Seattle and neighboring Portland with an urgency and passion that made the Pacific Northwest a poster child for both ends of the political spectrum. Seattle saw the birth of the Capitol Hill Occupied Protest, or CHOP, an eclectic police-free zone with an abandoned precinct house at its heart, that was ultimately dismantled by the city after two fatal shootings. Portland saw massive crowds nightly and growing violence between police, protesters and emboldened adherents to armed alt-right and quasi-racist movements such as Patriot Prayer and the Three Percenters. Both cities saw repeated incidents of vandalism and violence, spurring debate about protest tactics as some smaller groups of demonstrators continued to damage property for weeks on end. . . . The turmoil's fallout prompted [Seattle]'s police chief to retire and almost certainly influenced Mayor Jenny Durkan to not seek a second term.[32]

Protesters established CHOP on June 8, 2020, in Seattle's Capitol Hill neighborhood as a so-called autonomous zone and, because the police were excluded, allowed private groups to provide security. It became what some described as a "war zone." On June 20, CNN reported that a crowd had prevented police from reaching two shooting victims inside CHOP. Police body camera video showed protesters confronting police as they arrived. An officer said, "Please move out of the way so we can get to the victim. All we are trying to do is get to the victim and provide them aid." A bystander yelled, "You don't belong here, they're gone, the victim is gone." Another said, "Put your f*cking guns down." As the police left, some bystanders continued to yell while other protesters held them back. Finally, Mayor Durkan, who had first compared CHOP to a "block party," ordered the police to clear out the zone on July 1. "As I have said, and I will say again, I support peaceful demonstrations," said Carmen Best, Seattle's African American police chief. "Black Lives Matter, and I too want to help propel this movement toward meaningful change in our community. But enough is enough. The CHOP has become lawless and brutal."[33]

The protests in Portland went on every day during the summer. Taking their cue from CHOP, in June, on the twenty-first day of protests after the Floyd murder, Portland protesters created the "Patrick Kimmons Autonomous Zone," named after a man killed by Portland Police Bureau (PPB) officers in 2018 near the condominium tower where Mayor Ted Wheeler lived. In most places, forming special districts requires approval from officials elected by voters. By creating "autonomous zones" without input from residents or officials, the protesters acted in the dictatorial fashion of which they accused the mayors of Seattle and Portland, who at least were elected democratically. Unlike Seattle, however, which allowed CHOP to exist for several weeks, the PPB cleared the Portland zone, which was barricaded with dumpsters and wooden pallets, the next morning and arrested 19 of the more than 200 people there.

The *Oregonian* reported that some were accused of rioting, one was charged with trying to assault an officer, two faced first-degree criminal mischief charges, two were accused of carrying concealed weapons (including knives and at least one expandable baton), and eight were charged with disorderly conduct and interfering with a peace officer. But a television news reporter also videoed an officer beating a protester before other officers took the person into custody, and police arrested another person, allegedly for interfering with their work, who was filming another video of the protests.[34] This did not stop the unrest, which went on for months and devastated the city.

On August 29, Michael Forest Reinoehl, a 48-year-old self-described anti-fascist, allegedly shot and killed Aaron "Jay" Danielson, a pro-Trump demonstrator and supporter of the right-wing group Patriot Prayer. Danielson died soon after most cars in a caravan of Trump backers drove through downtown Portland. A federal task force began a manhunt that ended on September 3, when officers found Reinoehl at an Olympia, Washington, apartment complex and killed him after he initiated an exchange of gunfire.[35]

On August 31, on Mayor Wheeler's birthday and the ninety-sixth consecutive night of protests in Portland, more than 200 people came to his condominium tower to demand his resignation. Wheeler was under additional stress because he was not just mayor but also, under Oregon law, the PPB commissioner. Wearing party hats and singing "happy tear gas to you" to the tune of "Happy Birthday," the protesters denounced the PPB's use of tear gas to disperse protesters. Some lit a fire in the street, smashed windows, broke into a dental office, and stole office supplies and a chair, which they threw in the fire. Shortly after 11:00 p.m., they threw burning newspapers into a store. Police arrived, declared the gathering a riot, and ordered protesters to disperse. Nineteen people were arrested. Eight were charged with disorderly conduct and interfering with a peace officer. Some were accused of rioting, two of carrying concealed weapons, and one of trying to assault an officer. Two others were charged with first-degree criminal mischief. Some of those arrested had knives and an expandable baton.[36]

Appropriately, President Trump denounced the violence in Portland, but noted Oregon Public Broadcasting, did not denounce his supporters who participated in the violence. Chad Wolf, secretary of the US Department of Homeland Security (DHS), parroted Trump's earlier reaction to the Minneapolis violence by claiming that Portland mayor Wheeler's "inaction . . . fostered an environment that . . . fueled senseless violence and destruction night after night." He urged Wheeler to "request federal assistance to restore law and order in Portland," but federal intervention had already occurred: starting on June 4, DHS had begun sending officers to protect federal buildings in Portland in what it called "Operation Legend."

That stirred pushback. On July 22, the Portland City Council voted to forbid the PPB from cooperating with the DHS officers because those officers had tear-gassed and fought with protesters throughout the summer. Eventually, DHS deployed 755 officers from the Federal Protective Service, the Border Patrol, the Secret Service, and Immigration and Customs Enforcement, among other agencies, at a cost of over $12 million. Months later, a report from DHS's Office of Inspector General criticized Operation Legend for having few officers trained in riot and crowd control, for not having a coherent strategy for working with state and local agencies, and for not using consistent tactics when responding to the protests. US senator Ron Wyden (D-OR) praised the report but not the DHS officers' actions. "Paramilitary officers dispatched by the Trump administration into my hometown with incomplete weapons training, inconsistent tactics, and a shadowy mission added up to a toxic mix that inflamed the situation instead of managing it," he said.[37]

The consecutive nights of protest in Portland ended at 100 because of massive wildfires nearby, but protests continued. "Direct action" marches targeted different police buildings each night and then expanded to different "capitalist" targets throughout 2020. Protesters claimed victories when the city council cut the PPB's budget, the transit authority made cuts to transit police, the district attorney reduced the number of protest-related prosecutions, and the Portland Public Schools eliminated school resource officers. The protests continued into 2021, but some of the changes were reversed.[38]

The protests caused Portland and Seattle to suffer in lasting ways. Portland had long and proudly proclaimed its tolerance and livability, but the pandemic, the ongoing protests and destruction, a growing homelessness crisis, and a permissive scheme to deal with drug users combined to make residents despondent. In 2022, Earl Blumenauer, a liberal Democrat who had served 14 terms in the US House of Representatives as a staunch promoter of his hometown, announced his reelection bid with the words "Portland is broken." Just as Minneapolis had become the poster child for America's racial problems, Portland had become synonymous with urban chaos and, some believed, a liberal city that had swung too far to the left. Oregon Public Broadcasting reported that an April 2022 survey of residents of Multnomah County (which includes Portland) found that 82 percent were either somewhat or very worried about the future of their part of the state. In another survey, only 8 percent of voters said Portland was headed in the right direction. Both Democrats and Republicans shared that pessimism.[39]

Similarly, a May 2023 survey by EMC Research found that 65 percent of Seattle voters believed that "things ha[d] gotten pretty seriously off track." About 77 percent believed that the city's hands-off approach to people using illegal drugs in public was contributing to street crime and making it harder for the downtown to recover, and 73 percent were going downtown less often due to fears about crime and safety.[40]

While protests roiled Minneapolis, Seattle, and Portland, Louisville experienced ongoing protests related to the police shooting of Breonna Taylor. Though that shooting had occurred on March 13, protests over her death did not begin until May 26, the day after George Floyd died. The Louisville protests lasted into August and erupted again on September 23, after a grand jury decided to not charge any police officer in Taylor's death, though one was indicted on three counts of "wanton endangerment" for recklessly firing a gun during the raid on her apartment. Protests over the grand jury decision also occurred in Chicago, Dallas, Los Angeles, Memphis, Milwaukee, Minneapolis, New York, Seattle, and Portland as well as in smaller cities like Norfolk, Virginia, and Portland, Maine.[41]

Other incidents in the Midwest infused new energy into protests nationwide. On August 26, a riot, vandalism, and looting broke out in downtown Minneapolis after an African American man named Eddie Sole Jr. died. Police were seeking Sole during a manhunt for a murder suspect. Protesters believed that police officers shot him, but surveillance video showed that he had shot himself in the head.[42] Another two-night curfew was imposed again on August 27, and Governor Walz redeployed the National Guard. "It is absolutely possible to hold the idea that we need to do better on systemic racism," Walz said. "But we can also say, we can't live in a society where lawless, reckless behavior puts people and businesses at risk."[43]

(Several months later, restaurant owners sued Mayor Frey and the City of Minneapolis for allegedly not acting decisively to protect business owners and residents from vandals that looted and destroyed property and livelihoods following the Floyd murder. They sought $4.5 million in damages for their losses, which included their building, revenues, and future income. The lawsuit was later settled for $10,000. In January 2024, the Illinois Casualty Company sued Minneapolis for negligence, alleging that Frey had failed to properly implement the city's emergency plan and the police chief had failed to respond appropriately to the crisis. The insurance company also alleged that the city was "vicariously liable" for the actions of the police officers who killed Floyd, which it alleged "were a direct cause of the civil unrest and resultant damage to the insureds' businesses.")[44]

While Seattle, Portland, and Minneapolis were convulsing, an incident in Kenosha, Wisconsin, attracted most of the attention in late August. A city of 100,000, 67 percent White, 17 percent Hispanic, and 11 percent Black, Kenosha lies in the middle of a megalopolis of 12 million people along Lake Michigan's western shore, bracketed by Milwaukee 40 miles to the north and Chicago 66 miles to the south. The corridor's communities are connected by Amtrak, Interstate 94, and similar ethnic migrations.[45] They are also some of America's most racially segregated metropolitan areas and, since the Midwest's deindustrialization began in the 1980s, communities struggling with large pockets of poverty.[46]

Before August, Kenosha had not seen major protests. That changed on August 23, when a police officer shot Jacob Blake in the back, paralyzing him from the waist down. For seven days and nights, protests gripped the city. They included peaceful rallies and marches but also, mostly at night, property damage, arson, and clashes with police. Local and outside protesters were confronted by White supremacists from out of state, and deaths, serious injuries, and widespread property damage occurred. The unrest was quelled only when a curfew was imposed and Governor Tony Evers sent in the Wisconsin National Guard.

Weeks earlier, a warrant had been issued for Blake's arrest on charges of third-degree sexual assault, criminal trespass, and disorderly conduct. On August 23, the woman who had filed the complaint called 911 to report that Blake was at her home. When the police arrived, they said he was holding a knife, which was later found on the driver's side of his car. Officers claimed he resisted arrest, fought with officers, and ignored orders to drop the knife. They twice tried to use a Taser on him before Officer Rusten Sheskey shot him seven times in the back as he tried to enter the car. Blake denied he was carrying a knife and said he had only been trying to break up a dispute between two women. A neighbor recorded the incident on a cell phone.[47] After being shot and paralyzed, Blake was transported on a Flight for Life helicopter to the Milwaukee Regional Medical Center in Wauwatosa.

Protests flared immediately. Kenosha County declared a state of emergency at 10:15 p.m. that night and blocked streets with garbage trucks near the county courthouse and other government buildings. At 11:05 p.m., police began using tear gas and rubber bullets to disperse crowds. Near midnight, protesters lit a fire in front of the courthouse and set fire to a streetcar and several garbage trucks as well as to a truck in a used-car dealership. The blaze spread to most of the 100 other cars on the lot. Downtown businesses were torched and looted. Windows were smashed in the post office, a high school, a museum, and the Kenosha County Administration Building. An armored personnel carrier was damaged, and an officer was knocked out with a brick.[48]

The next day, August 24, Kenosha County imposed an 8:00 p.m. curfew and closed local exits for I-94. The Chicago commuter rail network, Metra, which extends to Kenosha, suspended service north of Waukegan, Illinois. Governor Evers activated the National Guard to protect firefighters and infrastructure, over the objections of the American Civil Liberties Union's Wisconsin chapter. Peaceful protests occurred during the day, but as darkness fell, protesters broke a door off its hinges at the Kenosha Public Safety Building before being repelled by pepper spray. At 8:30 p.m., police used tear gas to disperse crowds near the courthouse as fireworks were launched at officers. Protesters looted a car dealership, pulled down streetlights, and set fire to a garbage truck, a furniture store, state offices, the Danish Brotherhood Lodge, apartment buildings, and several homes.

On August 25, Sheriff David Beth said that most of the damage had been done by individuals from outside Kenosha County. The Kenosha County Board asked Evers to send 2,000 more National Guardsmen. He declared a state of emergency for the region and sent in 250 more soldiers. Around 11:15 p.m., a protester started a fire in a rolling dumpster at a gas station and called for others to pour in more flammable liquids before pushing the trash bin into Sheridan Road, a major north-south thoroughfare, in the path of police. Shortly before midnight, a crowd clashed with officers and was expelled from Civic Center Park. Police erected an eight-foot-high fence to protect the courthouse. All night, protesters tried to breach the fence but failed.[49]

Large numbers of armed civilians roamed the streets. The previous day, a militia group founded by a former member of the Kenosha Common Council had created an "Armed Citizens to Protect Our Lives and Property" Facebook page and hosted a gathering for members to choose locations to protect. Both Mayor John Antaramian and County Sheriff Beth said the civilians patrolling the streets were not helpful. However, cell-phone videos showed police thanking the vigilantes and giving them bottles of water. The officers, Beth admitted, were "very wrong" to do so.

Among the vigilantes was 17-year-old Kyle Rittenhouse from nearby Antioch, Illinois. He and a friend armed themselves with assault rifles and went to a Kenosha car dealership that had suffered $1.5 million in arson damage the night before. At 11:45 p.m. on August 25, he shot three BLM protesters. He killed Joseph Rosenbaum of Kenosha and Anthony Huber of Silver Lake, Wisconsin, and shot and severely wounded Gaige Grosskreutz of West Allis, Wisconsin, after Grosskreutz pointed a handgun at him. Police arrested him the next day.[50]

Rittenhouse's killings mimicked an event in Austin, Texas, the previous month. There, Daniel Perry, a US Army sergeant, drove toward a crowd of BLM protesters and was confronted by Air Force veteran Garrett Foster, a protester who was wearing a bandanna on his face and carrying an AK-47 rifle. Perry, who had a history of making racist comments online, shot and killed Foster, claiming that Foster had pointed his gun at him. Perry was arrested for murder.[51]

Apparently because of the Rittenhouse shootings the previous night, on August 26 the Kenosha protests were smaller and quieter. Protesters rallied peacefully in Civic Center Park and then held a march, and militia members stayed away from them. Law enforcement officials praised the protesters for remaining peaceful, but the Kenosha County Board sent a second letter to Governor Evers asking for 1,500 more soldiers. Evers increased the number to 500.[52]

The Blake shooting, like the earlier Floyd murder, sparked nationwide protests. Led by the National Basketball Association's Milwaukee Bucks, athletes from the NBA, the Women's NBA, major league baseball, and major league soccer expressed their resistance to racism and police brutality by refusing to play.[53] Demonstrations broke out in Atlanta, Los Angeles, Madison, Minneapolis, New York, Oakland, Philadelphia, Sacramento,

San Diego, San Jose, and Seattle. Though Blake's mother called for peaceful protests and said her son would not be pleased with "the violence and the destruction,"[54] protesters attacked police officers in Atlanta, Oakland, and San Diego, and property damage occurred in Atlanta, Madison, Minneapolis, Oakland, Sacramento, and San Jose.[55]

In Oakland, more than a dozen people were arrested for crimes that included assault on a police officer, breaking windows, lighting off fireworks, and setting fires, as well as pointing lasers and throwing objects at officers. Firefighters there responded to at least two dozen fires, including two vehicle fires. In San Jose, protesters vandalized the mayor's home, and in Sacramento they damaged City Hall and the sheriff's and district attorney's offices.[56]

The day after Blake was shot, a flyer shared on social media called for protesters in Wisconsin's state capital, Madison, only 115 miles from Kenosha and 75 miles from Wauwatosa, to meet downtown to "Do what you want. F*ck shit up." According to Isthmus.com, the flyer also said, "No bad protesters. No good cops. F*ck Kenosha PD. F*ck Madison PD. F*ck Milwaukee PD. F*ck Chicago PD."

Some protesters followed the flyer's advice to "f*ck shit up." On August 25, about 1,000 protesters clogged downtown Madison. As darkness fell, some set dumpster and trash fires, broke windows, injured three police officers, and looted businesses, including office buildings on Capitol Square. On the nearby Wisconsin Manufacturers & Commerce building, reported WisPolitics.com, graffiti was scrawled: "You have stolen more than we could ever loot." Protesters poured gasoline inside one building and tried to set it on fire. Police used tear gas and pepper spray to disperse crowds so firefighters could stop buildings from igniting and made six arrests. Two men were later charged in federal court for committing arson. At a press conference, Fire Chief Steven Davis said, "What we witnessed last night, and what we responded to as a fire department, was in my 31 years probably the most destruction and damage I've seen in this city." Mayor Satya Rhodes-Conway added, "Our city honors the First Amendment and peaceful protests, but we draw the line at arson, theft and criminal damage to property damage that puts people's lives in danger. This behavior does not build a movement—it undercuts the movement, and in Madison, it divides a community that largely supports change."[57]

During the evening of August 26, Kenosha police received a tip that vehicles with out-of-state license plates had met in a remote lot. Police and US marshals followed a black school bus, a bread truck, and a minivan to a gas station, where they saw the occupants of the bus and truck try to fill multiple fuel cans. Suspecting that the occupants were preparing for criminal activity related to the unrest, the officers arrested them. The occupants of the minivan tried to drive away, but the police stopped and detained them, too. In the vehicles, the police found helmets, gas masks, protective vests, illegal fireworks, and suspected controlled substances.[58]

On August 27, a small group continued to protest in downtown Kenosha after the curfew went into effect at 7:00 p.m. Some of the protesters were arrested. By midnight, fewer than 50 protesters remained. That night, President Trump denounced the events in Kenosha in his speech accepting the Republican Party nomination for reelection.[59]

By August 28, Wisconsin had deployed 1,000 National Guardsmen and 200 federal agents in Kenosha, supplemented by National Guardsmen from Michigan, Arizona, and Alabama. Protests continued through Saturday, August 29, when about 1,000 people participated in a march and rally. The group marched to the courthouse chanting, "7 bullets, 7 days," "One Person, One Vote," and "No Justice, No Peace." Kenosha's curfew ended on September 2.[60]

Overall, rioters and arsonists had destroyed city property valued at $2 million, including garbage trucks, streetlights, and traffic signals. Damage to private property totaled $52 million. Eighty businesses were affected by the unrest; their losses were estimated at $25–$30 million. Forty buildings were destroyed and 100 other buildings were damaged. Five closed permanently. About 250 arrests were made, mostly for curfew violations, disorderly conduct, and looting. One man was charged with starting the dumpster fire on August 25.[61]

Two self-described militia members who had traveled to Kenosha from Missouri were arrested on federal gun charges. Prosecutors alleged that one of them had told a witness that he was going to Kenosha "with the intention of possibly using the firearms on people." Months later, a federal grand jury indicted four Minnesota men on charges related to the Kenosha riots. The complaint alleged that on August 24, Allen King, David Garner, and Kevin Martinez tried to set fires in a bar and looted and damaged a pharmacy and gas station. They were charged with conspiring to steal controlled substances and transport stolen goods. King and Garner were also charged with two counts of arson and conspiring to commit arson, while Martinez was charged with illegally possessing ammunition as a convicted felon. In a second case, Devon Vaughn was charged with arson after allegedly setting a fire at a furniture store.[62]

When the riots broke out, Sue Moniz and her husband, owners of the Mattress Shoppe in Kenosha's Uptown neighborhood, saw their store go up in flames while finding a 70-year-old employee on the sidewalk with a broken jaw. "With a gun in one hand and the steering wheel in another," reported the *Milwaukee Journal Sentinel*, Moniz sped him to the hospital in their car. "My fear is the message of the peaceful protesters, who legitimately want and deserve change, I'm afraid their voices are not going to be heard because of the violence," she said. "Businesses can rebuild and buildings can be replaced. But the importance of that message is lost."[63]

—∾—

OUR TOWN

WHILE KENOSHA DOMINATED THE NEWS, a very different city, 45 miles northwest of Kenosha and also part of the Chicago-Milwaukee megalopolis, prepared for its moment of peril.

In his memoir, renowned film critic Richard Schickel described the community in which he grew up in the 1930s, 1940s, and 1950s: "Wauwatosa. Something inescapably comic in that soft tumble of vowels. But it was a serious place: a suburb of Milwaukee where many of the people who soberly, responsibly tended the larger city's business lived. The name is a corruption of a word borrowed from some local Indian dialect. . . . In high school the joke was that it meant 'strong middle class with delusions of grandeur.'"[1] In those years, the *Milwaukee Journal* noted, "Wauwatosa was the premiere residential community to the west [of the City of Milwaukee]." Over time, that changed as other suburbs developed.[2] The community's racial composition and political leanings began to evolve as well.

In 2020, Wauwatosa suffered through months of protests because one of our police officers, Joseph Mensah, had killed three men of color in the previous five years. In 2015, Mensah, who is Black, fatally shot Antonio Gonzales, a 29-year-old Hispanic man. In 2016, he killed Jay Anderson Jr., a 25-year-old Black man. On

February 2, 2020, 2½ months before I became mayor, he killed Alvin Cole, a 17-year-old Black teenager. Each time, Milwaukee County district attorney John Chisholm found that Mensah had acted in self-defense and declined to prosecute him.[3]

Long before these incidents, Wauwatosa had been a racial tinderbox. With a nighttime population over 49,000, it is Wisconsin's fourteenth-largest city, but the fourth-largest (after Milwaukee, Madison, and Green Bay) each workday, when more than 105,000 people work or receive care at the state's largest medical center, shop or work at the state's busiest retail mall, work at Briggs & Stratton and Harley-Davidson and in large research parks, or teach or attend classes at several college campuses.[4] This churn of humanity in an affluent, mostly White suburb bordered on three sides by the majority-minority City of Milwaukee makes Wauwatosa ground zero for racial interactions and friction.[5]

Its history compounded the problem. Though settled in the mid-nineteenth century by Yankee abolitionists who made it a stop on the Underground Railroad,[6] early in the twentieth century Wauwatosa, like hundreds of American cities and towns, enacted a "sundown law" prohibiting non-Whites from remaining in the city after dusk.[7] Restrictive covenants in deeds also prohibited non-Whites from renting, owning, or occupying homes in many Wauwatosa subdivisions and across metropolitan Milwaukee.[8] From the 1920s into the 1950s, signs at the city limits announced, "ENTERING WAUWATOSA / CITY OF HOMES / RESTRICTIVE ZONING." They expressed a dual message: Wauwatosa protected its graceful neighborhoods from encroachment by industry but did not welcome non-Whites.[9]

Wauwatosa's first Black family arrived in 1955. That year, World War II veteran Zeddie Hyler applied for a permit to build a home on 113th Street. Overcoming vandalism, numerous threats, and impediments created by the Common Council, Hyler built his home and stayed. Nevertheless, in 1956 the director of the Milwaukee Urban League was denied a permit to build a home in

Wauwatosa. In 1959, two officials on the city's building board sought to require Black homeowners to meet higher aesthetic standards than Whites.[10] Such hostility deterred Blacks from residing in what was then called the "City of Homes and Churches."

For 11 days in August 1966, members of the Milwaukee chapter of the National Association for the Advancement of Colored People, led by Catholic priest James Groppi, picketed at the Wauwatosa home of Judge Robert Cannon to protest his membership in the all-White Milwaukee Eagles Club. On the first night, 12 people picketed. The next night, counterprotesters appeared. On the third night, Ku Klux Klan members arrived. Eventually, thousands of people, most of them outsiders, converged on the site. The Wauwatosa police, Milwaukee County sheriffs, and the Wisconsin National Guard kept the crowds under control.[11] But Wauwatosans were bewildered that the cares of the outside world had intruded on their community.

By this time, the civil rights movement had begun to change America. Congress passed the Civil Rights Act of 1964, the Voting Rights Act of 1965, and the Fair Housing Act of 1968 to enforce the Fourteenth, Fifteenth, and Nineteenth Amendments to the US Constitution, which on paper but not in practice had provided everyone "equal protection under the laws" and all citizens the right to vote. Over time, Wauwatosa became more welcoming and diverse. But progress was hampered in the late 1980s when some police officers held a party mocking slain civil rights leader Dr. Martin Luther King Jr.[12]

Such incidents made Wauwatosa the poster child for racial discord in metropolitan Milwaukee. But other area communities were little better: the 2020 US Census found that Milwaukee had the lowest percentage of suburban Black residents of any metropolitan area and remained the nation's leader in residential segregation,* just ahead of New York, Chicago, Cleveland, Detroit,

* In February 2022, an ABC *Nightline* segment about the impact of segregation focused on metropolitan Milwaukee. By happenstance, my

St. Louis, and Buffalo.[13] Blacks have remained largely confined to substandard housing and lack of economic opportunity on Milwaukee's North Side. The industrial jobs once plentiful in what some have called the "Selma of the North" left for other countries in the 1970s and 1980s, and prosperous Milwaukee, once more flatteringly called the "Star of the Snowbelt" by the *Wall Street Journal*, became one of America's most impoverished cities.[14] In 2024, Wisconsin's racial wealth gap ranked third highest behind Washington, DC, and North Dakota.[15]

Despite Officer Mensah's shootings, there were no ongoing protests in Wauwatosa until George Floyd was murdered in Minneapolis on May 25. Immediately afterward, deaths, injuries, and property damage occurred in nearby Milwaukee and Madison. On Milwaukee's North Side, protests turned violent. Walgreens and Boost Mobile stores were vandalized and looted. A police officer was shot on May 30, and the following night a fire was set in the middle of an intersection.[16] That night in Madison, only 75 miles from Wauwatosa, peaceful protests also turned violent. Vandals smashed downtown windows, looted stores, and set a police car on fire. Mayor Rhodes-Conway imposed a two-night curfew and Governor Evers activated the National Guard.[17] The unrest spilled over into Wauwatosa. Like mayors across the region and around the country, I declared curfews on May 30 and 31 and again on June 1 because of unrest and because people were driving cars at 100 miles per hour on major thoroughfares on our West Side.[18]

On June 3, I joined a rally sponsored by a local group, Tosa Together, outside City Hall.[19] Two days later, I apologized for Wauwatosa's history of racism—the first mayor to do so—and expressed the city's commitment to positive change.[20] On June 10, the Common Council held a special meeting to consider a

---

street appeared in the segment, though Black families do reside in my neighborhood.

response to the issues raised by the Floyd murder and by events in Wauwatosa.[21]

Soon thereafter, the council allocated $760,000 to the Wauwatosa Police Department (WPD) for body cameras and banned the police from using chokeholds, which were already against WPD policy. We joined the national Government Alliance on Race and Equity; the Health Department declared racism a public health emergency and hired a social worker, a substance abuse specialist, and a youth social worker to focus on challenges in our underserved populations; and we added a specialist to the Human Resources Department to oversee culture, training, and other equity-and-inclusion initiatives in all departments and scheduled additional implicit-bias training for city staff and elected officials. The city also declared Juneteenth Day a paid holiday for its employees and became the first governmental entity to adopt the Metropolitan Milwaukee Association of Commerce's "Region of Choice" pledge to increase diverse hiring in management and employment.[22] These initiatives did not bring peace.[†]

On June 11, Alvin Cole's family and its attorney, Kimberley Motley, met with District Attorney Chisholm to discuss the evidence that Chisholm would assess in deciding whether to charge Mensah criminally for killing Cole.[23] A week later, Jay Anderson's family, also represented by Motley, filed a complaint with the Wauwatosa Police and Fire Commission (WPFC) seeking to have Mensah fired.[24] Under Wisconsin law, only the WPFC, not the mayor or Common Council, has the authority to hire, fire, or discipline Wauwatosa police officers or chiefs.[25]

Later that month, after weeks of peaceful demonstrations, Madison protesters assaulted a Democratic state senator and

† "How did you get those measures passed?" the previous mayor asked. "I tried for years to get the Common Council to agree to them." "Kathy," I replied, "I had the advantage of a crisis."

toppled two statues on the State Capitol grounds, one of a woman with her arm extended in an echo of the state motto "Forward" and the other of a Wisconsin abolitionist, Hans Christian Heg, who fought for the Union in the Civil War. Police used pepper spray to thwart a Capitol break-in. Rioters smashed windows in the City-County Building and threw a Molotov cocktail inside. They also broke windows and looted stores on State Street, a major commercial street stretching from the Capitol to the University of Wisconsin campus.

The *Milwaukee Journal Sentinel* reported that the rioting—which followed the arrest of a Black activist who later pleaded guilty to a federal extortion charge for threatening business owners with vandalism and violence unless they gave him and friends free food and beer—severely affected downtown Madison businesses, which were already struggling with shutdowns and layoffs caused by the pandemic. One was a tavern that had closed for 10 weeks and reduced its staff from 76 to 25. Even with boards on the building, protesters smashed the tavern's windows. Like many others in Wisconsin's most liberal city, the tavern's general manager supported the effort to end racism, but he told the *Journal Sentinel*, "It was heartbreaking to see the protests be manipulated. The protests were good to see, but it was hard to see fellow businesses being hurt."

One was a State Street jewelry shop. After being closed for two months because of the pandemic, it closed for another two months after protesters smashed its windows and display cases. When the store reopened, the boarded-up windows and lack of foot traffic hurt its sales. Eventually, one of the protesters, Kelsey Nelson, was sentenced to six months in jail and ordered to pay $5,000 to the jewelry store he had looted (a cost shared with two other people) and $2,500 to the state for damaging the Heg statue (a cost shared with four others). "I was just a person who woke up and saw the injustice done to a man named George Floyd. Am I going to say what I did was right? I am not," Nelson apologized.[26]

America had experienced such unrest before. During the 1960s, frustration with discrimination caused some African Americans to express that frustration in violence. Unrest swept cities nationwide. Decades of racist housing policies and police brutality fueled outrage in Milwaukee's Black neighborhoods. Fires and looting broke out in the summer of 1967, and the National Guard was sent in to restore peace. Milwaukee mayor Henry Maier declared a curfew that lasted for several days. When the riots were over, 4 people had been killed, 100 were injured, and 1,740 had been arrested. Apart from the deaths and injuries, a thriving neighborhood was heavily damaged. Third Street (now Martin Luther King Drive), which extends from Milwaukee's downtown north into its Black community, had been one of the city's premier shopping districts. Rioting destroyed many businesses there.[27]

As a teenager, I was acutely aware of the unrest because my parents, reporters for Milwaukee's daily newspapers, were allowed to travel to and from downtown Milwaukee for work during the riots. Other incidents during my teenage years also profoundly affected me. In 1968, my mother covered the Democratic National Convention in Chicago for the *Milwaukee Sentinel*. That gathering descended into chaos as protesters and police engaged in pitched battles and resulted in my mother having her ankle broken by Chicago police and, ultimately, GOP candidate Richard Nixon winning the presidential election as voters recoiled from what was perceived as the Democrats' inability to maintain law and order. In 1970, three anti–Vietnam War protesters bombed Sterling Hall at the University of Wisconsin–Madison. Opposition to a misguided war overwhelmed the protesters' common sense and led to the murder of a man—a husband and father—who was doing research in that building when the bombing occurred.[28] When speaking to people who claim to love peace and justice, I have asked them—sometimes in vain—to understand that violence and destruction are not a viable path forward, morally or politically.

In recent times, MLK Drive near downtown Milwaukee has experienced a renaissance, but farther north, more than 50 years later, that strip still has not recovered. Sadly, during the 2020 protests, stores there were destroyed and looted again.[29] A similar history could be written about other cities.[30]

On June 30, 2020, so many issues regarding the WPD had arisen that the Wauwatosa Common Council created an ad hoc committee of four alderpersons, two residents, and two Milwaukee residents to "address policing and systemic inequities." The committee was expected to meet regularly through the council's August recess to decide how to foster dialogue with the community and drive action through the council. It was instructed to make timely recommendations concerning topics already being considered, such as body cameras for WPD officers, remediation of racial disparities, demographic data regarding detentions and traffic stops, a proposed ordinance prohibiting the use of no-knock warrants by the WPD, and implicit-bias training for police and Common Council members. Because the committee could not coordinate its members' schedules and its leadership was ineffective, it drifted out of existence months later, having accomplished little. The council had moved on without it.[31]

The challenges facing our community were daunting, but I felt prepared. With degrees in journalism, public administration, and law as well as decades of experience in local, state, and federal government as an intern, employee, volunteer, and elected official, I was comfortable in the mayor's chair. I hoped the community would cut me slack because of my background as a civil rights lawyer. For 24 years before becoming mayor, I had litigated cases for the U.S. Equal Employment Opportunity Commission on behalf of people who had suffered job discrimination because of their race, color, religion, sex, age, or disability, including a race discrimination class action that established important national precedents[32] and another involving undocumented female workers at agricultural plants in Iowa who had been sexually assaulted at work,[33] for which I was interviewed for a PBS *Frontline* episode, "Rape in the Fields," that aired nationally in 2013.[34] In 2019, I also applied to have Wauwatosa designate the home of its first African American family as a landmark and enlisted the current owner, Zeddie Hyler's nephew Gerald Williamson, as a coapplicant. The Common Council unanimously approved our application. Later that year, I advocated for the creation of a Wauwatosa Equity and Inclusion Commission. I gave the new commission a presentation on the history of race relations in our community, taken from an article I had written for the Wauwatosa Historical Society newsletter 13 years earlier.

But, as was true for Jacob Frey, who worked as a civil rights attorney before becoming mayor of Minneapolis, BLM advocates were not inclined to give me the benefit of the doubt.[35] My lifetime of advocacy for justice, the fact that I was not mayor when Mensah killed his three victims, and my lack of legal authority to give the protesters what they wanted—having Mensah and our police chief fired—did not matter; what mattered was that I was mayor, the White face of the system at which they were directing their anger and demands for change. That realization was frustrating and saddening. For the protesters, emotion, however understandable, quickly overtook reason.

The local protests attracted national attention. On June 24, a *Wall Street Journal* article—"Outside Milwaukee, Protests over One Officer's Three Killings: Alvin Cole, 17, Was Shot Five Times by Officer While Fleeing Police in February"—described the tense atmosphere in Wauwatosa.[36] The same day, a new Milwaukee-area group called The People's Revolution (TPR) shut down Wisconsin's busiest shopping center, Mayfair Mall in Wauwatosa, where Cole was killed, holding signs and marching through the mall.[37]

On July 2, rapper Jay-Z's social justice organization, Team ROC, and two national activist groups, Until Freedom and Gathering for Justice, published a full-page advertisement in the *Journal Sentinel* demanding that Mensah be fired and decertified as a police officer and calling on the district attorney to prosecute him. "If you fail to prosecute Mensah," said the ad, "you're doing a disservice to the legacies of Alvin Cole, Antonio Gonzales and Jay Anderson, ignoring the lives of black, brown and LGBTQ citizens in your county, and essentially allowing for the possibility of a future catastrophe."[38] The Jonas Brothers rock band tweeted, "@DAJohnChisholm: How many more people must die at the hands of Officer Joseph Mensah?"[39]

Also on July 2, TPR members packed into a chain restaurant, the Cheesecake Factory, at Mayfair Mall near where Mensah killed Cole and shut it down for an hour, using loudspeakers to shout about the case. No protesters were arrested or ticketed because the WPD was trying to deescalate the situation.[40] The following Monday, July 6, City Administrator Jim Archambo and I met with WPD chief Barry Weber, two police captains, and Mayfair's general manager and security chief to discuss TPR's tactics. The general manager said he was willing to allow protests in the Mayfair parking lot—shopping malls are private property and can decide which activities will be allowed there[41]—but asked for help to keep businesses open. I instructed the police to enforce the law without prejudice: if protesters were peaceful, their constitutional right to protest should be protected, but if they broke the law, they should be given tickets or arrested.

Midday on July 7, Archambo and I met at City Hall with TPR leader Khalil Coleman to try to find common ground. We appeared to be making headway. As the meeting ended, however, he announced that he was leaving to lead another protest at the Cheesecake Factory and shut it down. "What have we been talking about for the past two hours?" I replied in frustration. "Don't do it. If you shut down the restaurant, you'll be arrested." He said he had no choice, because he had already committed to that plan. Meeting with him had been a waste of time.

What we did not know at the time was that Coleman, a Milwaukee resident whom the *Journal Sentinel* later called "the key organizer of the largest local daily demonstrations" in Milwaukee and Wauwatosa in 2020, had alleged ties to the Gangster Disciples and a criminal history dating back a decade. In 2021, he was arrested for trying to rob a drug house in Kentucky and then sentenced to 10 years in prison.[42]

After he left our meeting on July 7, TPR again shut down the Cheesecake Factory. This time, the WPD arrested and ticketed protesters for assaulting restaurant employees and other violations. That night, Coleman led about 100 protesters into City Hall and tried to shut down our Common Council meeting. For 45 minutes, they kept us from proceeding, chanting, "No justice, no peace!" and "If we don't get what we want, shut it down!" Despite a posted ban on guns, some were armed. One protester was stopped from hurling a full water bottle at me. Coleman and a Cole family lawyer commandeered a table and microphones in front of the council and demanded that we discuss police shootings and reform.

I responded that because those topics were not on the night's agenda, discussing them would violate the Wisconsin Open Meetings Law, which requires agenda items to be posted at least 24 hours before meetings, and that we take public comments at council committee meetings but not at full council meetings. Finally, I said, under Wisconsin law, mayors and common councils have no role in the discipline of police officers, but the WPFC would address the Mensah complaints at its July meeting. The protesters booed. One shouted, "You're not listening to us!" I appealed to Coleman to control his followers, but he continued to incite them. The yelling and chanting persisted. Fearing a melee, I did not want to call in the police to clear the chamber, so I asked the council to approve all the night's business with a single motion. The motion was made, the vote was unanimous, and the meeting ended.[43]

TPR's attempted shutdown of our council meeting was similar to the insurrection six months later by militia members and other

Trump loyalists in Washington, DC. Though the January 6, 2021, insurrection was far more serious, both were antidemocratic attempts to keep a governmental body from doing business.[44]

Following the July 7 meeting, the joint leader, with Coleman, of TPR's Wauwatosa protests, Brian Anderson, sent a letter from TPR to the council and me proudly admitting that the protesters had been "disruptive" there. Anderson, a White resident of Wauwatosa, had a troubled past, having been convicted several times for burglary. Three months after sending the letter, in October 2020, he was sentenced to 12 months in prison and five years of probation for another burglary and theft.[45] His long criminal history did not deter him from lecturing us on morality. The TPR letter said, "At this time, there will be no business as usual in Wauwatosa," and promised that TPR would continue to disrupt and shut down our meetings until we met 10 different demands.[46] The demands were unrealistic, and because of pandemic-related health concerns, the July 7 meeting was the last council meeting held in person until January 2022. In the interim, we conducted meetings, without disruption, on Zoom.

On July 8, seeking peace, Archambo, City Attorney Alan Kesner, and I met via Zoom with two Democratic state representatives from Milwaukee, David Bowen and Jonathan Brostoff. Bowen demanded that we rescind the July 7 arrests and tickets and insisted that protesters had the right to break the law because they were engaging in "civil disobedience." I replied that the police would comply with the US Constitution and Wisconsin law: if protesters were peaceful, their right to protest would be protected, but if they broke the law, they would be ticketed or arrested. I urged the protesters to follow the ACLU's protest guidance.[47] The legislators insisted that I fire Mensah. I reminded them that only the WPFC can fire a police officer and if they did not like that, as state legislators they should change the law. Bowen responded that they could not do so because the Republican Party controlled the legislature. "That's your problem, not mine," I replied. "In the meantime, as a local official, I have to comply with the law as the legislature has enacted it." The meeting ended with their vow that protests would continue as before. The lawmakers did not intend to follow the law they had taken an oath to uphold. I did.‡

In closed session on July 14, the Common Council and I drafted a resolution directing Chief Weber and City Administrator Archambo "to facilitate [Mensah's] transition" from the WPD. In open session, the council approved the resolution with a 14–1 vote.[48] The next day, in an unrelated action—though the police union, the Wauwatosa Peace Officers Association, believed otherwise—the WPFC, chaired by a retired WPD lieutenant, unanimously voted to suspend Mensah with pay and to retain Steven Biskupic to investigate the Anderson family's complaint. As the US attorney for the Eastern District of Wisconsin, appointed by a Republican president, George W. Bush, Biskupic had won convictions of seven Milwaukee police officers for beating a Black man, Frank Jude Jr., in 2004.[49] His sister, Joan, has covered the US Supreme Court since 1989 for the *Washington Post*, *Congressional Quarterly*, and Reuters News Service and currently serves as CNN's Supreme Court analyst.

Responding to demands from some residents that elected officials hear the protesters' grievances, the Common Council sponsored a "listening session" on July 21 in the city's Hart Park

‡ The two legislators also protested at my home that summer. Two years later, at a political gathering, Brostoff apologized. "The pandemic drove us all a little crazy," he told me, admitting that he had gone too far in 2020. "You're doing a great job as mayor," he added, and expressed his hope that we could work together in the future. I accepted his apology. Like many others in the Milwaukee community, I was shocked and saddened when he took his own life in November 2024, allegedly because of bullying (including protests at his home) he suffered for his support of Israel during the Gaza conflict, though he had also struggled with mental illness for many years.

stadium. The council insisted that, as mayor, I should moderate. Nothing about the session was moderate. At 7:00 p.m., TPR members led by Coleman marched in brandishing guns and playing music on a boombox, and they spent most of the session shouting generalized grievances and vulgarities into a microphone only 15 feet from me. Four hours later, the TPR members marched out, again to music.[50] The session generated heat but no light; it did nothing to calm the community. It did inflame the Wauwatosa Peace Officers Association, which believed the council and I had pandered to TPR.

Throughout the summer and into the fall, TPR staged 98 days and nights of protests in Wauwatosa, including 40 nights at my home. Protesters blocked busy intersections for hours, obstructed traffic by driving cars on both sides of streets while honking their horns, screamed profanities, wrote obscenities on sidewalks, placed vulgar signs on lawns, played extremely loud music, shined strobe lights into house windows and the eyes of police officers, threw trash on lawns, carried AR-15s and other guns, drove cars on lawns and sidewalks, and engaged in shoving matches with police.[51] I observed all these things happening outside my home and on my street, repeatedly.

On a Saturday night, August 8, the protests turned even uglier. Scores of TPR protesters gathered at a Wauwatosa home occupied by Mensah, his fiancée, and the fiancée's two young daughters. Protesters spread toilet paper throughout the yard and discharged firecrackers. Mensah's fiancée ran outside as someone tried to flatten the tires on her car. When protesters surrounded her, Mensah came out, and a protester struck him in the head with a bullhorn. As he retreated inside the house, a protester fired a shotgun at the rear door, missing him by inches.[52]

The day after the incident, I released a statement: "The City of Wauwatosa has always supported and protected the right to peaceful protest. Last night's event was not a peaceful protest; it was criminal behavior. If the perpetrators of this criminal behavior are identified, they will be prosecuted to the fullest extent allowed by law." I stressed that Mensah had the right to due process under the US and Wisconsin Constitutions and that, under state law, only the WPFC could decide whether he would be fired.[53]

District Attorney Chisholm charged three men with felonies arising from the incident.[54] Also at the melee were Khalil Coleman, Representative Bowen, and Tiffany Henry, the director of US senator Tammy Baldwin's Milwaukee office. They were not arrested or charged, though Coleman was believed to have been the man who struck Mensah with a bullhorn.[55]

On August 11, Archambo, Weber, and I participated in a telephone conference with Governor Evers's chief of staff, Maggie Gau, and General Paul Knapp of the Wisconsin National Guard to discuss options for protecting protesters and residents if violence occurred after Chisholm announced whether he would charge Mensah with a crime in the Cole shooting. While we were in the meeting, Congressman Jim Sensenbrenner (R-WI) sent me—and the media—a letter lamenting the violence at Mensah's home and offering to "contact federal law enforcement agencies and bring them to Wauwatosa in order to bring peace and tranquility back to the community." The letter was an obvious ploy to support President Trump, who was threatening to send federal agents to cities experiencing unrest as part of his "law and order" reelection campaign. After I came out of my meeting and learned of the letter, I fired off a terse response to the congressman's chief of staff: "Please inform Rep. Sensenbrenner that we do not need federal intervention in Wauwatosa. We can manage without it, and federal intervention would only exacerbate the tensions in our city." My message echoed the sentiments of the mayors of Atlanta, Chicago, Kansas City, Portland, Seattle, and Washington, DC, who sent letters asking Trump not to send federal forces to their cities and Congress to investigate the deployments.[56]

Right-wing residents and commentators criticized me for not accepting Sensenbrenner's "offer" and not responding to protests more forcefully,[57] while left-wing residents were upset that the police were trying to restore order amid unruly protests. Middle ground was a lonely place, and no elected official supported me in public but emails, calls, and comments suggested that roughly 15 percent of residents opposed and complained about the unrest, 15 percent supported the protests and complained about the police, and 70 percent were somewhere in the middle but did not like how protests were being conducted and were weary of the turmoil.[58]

On August 13, I issued a statement reiterating that although Wauwatosa would continue to support protests, the US Supreme Court has made it clear that protests must be peaceful and that communities may impose reasonable "time, place, and manner" restrictions on them. Though some protests had been peaceful, I said, increasingly some activities violated the law. For that reason, going forward the WPD would enforce the law in full measure. I called on the Wisconsin Legislature to work with us to create the lasting change we need to correct inequities in Milwaukee and surrounding communities. Despite that balanced approach, my statement drew a negative response from the ACLU of Wisconsin, which had done nothing to ensure that protesters followed its own protest guidelines.[59] It was astonishing to receive such criticism after protesters had fired a shotgun at Mensah's home, but, as we learned a few weeks later when Jacob Blake was shot in Kenosha, the ACLU also opposed the governor's efforts to stop the rioting there.

That night, a honking 25-car TPR convoy arrived at my home. As before, protesters blocked intersections, threw toilet paper in my trees, played loud music, made speeches over a bullhorn, shined strobe lights in my windows, chalked "f*ck you" on the sidewalk, and laced my bushes with police caution tape. They stayed until 2:00 a.m. The next night, Friday, August 14, an even uglier protest erupted. For several hours, more than 100 marchers clashed with police a block north of my home. "What began as a push against a single officer . . . evolved into a battle of wills between marchers and the police," reported the *Wisconsin Examiner.* WPD officers were joined by police from nearby suburbs, many in riot gear and carrying shields, and blocked off surrounding streets. Multiple protesters were arrested or received tickets for disorderly conduct. John Larry, the nonelected chair of the Common Council's ad hoc committee on policing issues, was ticketed after he threatened officers and shouted at a WPD lieutenant that he would "knock you the f*ck out" and "slap the shit out of you." Eventually, the police steered the marchers away from my home. That night, as on many nights that year, it was not safe for my wife or me to venture outside.[60]

Throughout the summer, Archambo and I met with TPR leaders and representatives of Tosa Together, Indivisible Tosa, and Tosa Moms Tackling Racism searching for a path to peace. Each time, they demanded that we immediately fire Mensah, bring charges against Chief Weber, and reform the WPD. Each time, I reminded them that only the WPFC can discipline police officers and asked them to tone down the protests and work with us on reform. They never offered suggestions for a path forward. Instead, they complained that the city was interfering with "peaceful" protests. Their definition of peace could not be found in any dictionary. And no change in approach was suggested when Archambo, Weber, WPD captain Luke Vetter, Common Council president Kathy Causier, and I met with the Common Council committee chairpersons on August 27 and September 3 to discuss the ongoing protests.

The unrelenting protests sparked a backlash. In mid-August, a few residents put up yard signs that said, "For Sale, Unless Politicians Keep Tosa Safe. (Paid for by Tosa Taxpayers fed up with Mayor and City Council)." On August 26, those residents received letters from unidentified "Whites of Wauwatosa," which said, "We must keep Wauwatosa free from Blacks. Together we can keep Wauwatosa white. Together we can keep Wauwatosa safe." The letter, addressed to "White Wauwatosa Resident," made other racist statements, too. I responded on September 1: "Anyone who believes that 'Wauwatosa should be for whites only' should leave Wauwatosa now. Your statement is racist, immoral, unconstitutional, and un-American." Outside City Hall two days later, I appeared with a Black community activist, Tracey Dent, to denounce the signs and letters. I said they "do not reflect Wauwatosa. It's a very simple message: If you believe Wauwatosa or any part of America is for whites only, we invite you to leave now."[61]

That day, a British Broadcasting Company producer sent me an email asking for an interview about the "'White Wauwatosa' letter and the wider situation in Wisconsin" on "the late news show here on Radio 5, one of the BBC's national speech stations here in the UK." I thought it was a prank. It was not. That afternoon, I was on the telephone with *Up All Night* host Dotun Adebayo.[62] America's heartland was in turmoil, and the world wanted to know why.

Despite our best efforts, residents at the far ends of the political spectrum were not listening. The right wing wanted to ban all protests and the left wing wanted protesters to operate unimpeded. Continuing frustration about the pandemic, anger over the killings of Blacks, and political polarization amid a contentious presidential campaign made it impossible to restore a peaceful equilibrium in Wauwatosa. Tensions rose as everyone nervously awaited the district attorney's decision on whether to charge Mensah with a crime for shooting Alvin Cole.

Wauwatosans feared that their homes and businesses would not be safe if Chisholm declined to charge Mensah. Jittery residents called to ask me when he would issue his decision and begged for protection. One had called weeks earlier to express support for the protests. In September, after the Kenosha riots ended, he called again. He reiterated his support for the BLM movement, but feared that his business on North Avenue, a major commercial street linking Milwaukee and Wauwatosa on which TPR often marched, would go up in flames. He implored me to keep the city safe, saying that his family's livelihood depended on it. Other proprietors in our historic Village and North Avenue business districts begged for protection, too. I assured them we were prepared, but they were already boarding up their buildings. A fire ignited by a Molotov cocktail could level those buildings, some of which are over 100 years old. During our emergency planning, our fire chief said he could not send his crews in to fight fires in the three paint stores on North Avenue. Fighting a fire in a paint store, he warned, is like trying to suppress a blaze in a nuclear power plant.

The Kenosha riots motivated another call from Governor Evers's chief of staff, Maggie Gau. During our previous discussion in August, before Kenosha erupted, the National Guard was only considered a last resort, and we were told that if we needed the Guard it would take 12 to 14 hours for soldiers to arrive—from the Kenosha armory, ironically. Now, on September 17, only 2½ weeks after the Kenosha riots ended, Archambo, Weber, and I discussed with Gau, two National Guard generals, and the director of the Wisconsin Department of Emergency Management how to protect Wauwatosa following Chisholm's decision. Gau said Evers would pre-position soldiers at key Wauwatosa sites. After having been criticized for not sending the Guard to Kenosha sooner, Evers was not going to leave Wauwatosa unprotected.[63]

A week later, in an echo of Congressman Sensenbrenner's August 11 letter, a state senator and a state representative, both Republicans, sent me a letter insisting that we request National Guard and federal law enforcement assistance. As before, I rejected the attempt to politicize the tense situation, saying we were "prepared to protect the lives and property of all residents and businesses while continuing to protect the First Amendment rights of citizens to engage in peaceful protests. . . . How the City of Wauwatosa deals with unrest will not be dictated by politics or emotion, but by a respect for the U.S. Constitution and a concern for the well-being of all residents." I offered to discuss our planning with them, but they never responded.[64]

Rumors continued to spread. One was posted on Facebook by the Cole family: they would be meeting with Chisholm at the Milwaukee County Courthouse on October 7.[65] We did not know if that was accurate, but we took it seriously. City Attorney Alan Kesner circulated a draft "Proclamation of Emergency" to Archambo, Weber, and me. It stated that based on experience with protests concerning Mensah and on community responses to decisions and actions regarding police officers nationwide, most recently in Kenosha and Louisville, Chisholm's announcement would raise an imminent threat of a riot or civil unrest that could impair transportation and fire, health, and police protection. For that reason, pedestrian and vehicular traffic would be prohibited on city streets between 7:00 p.m. and 6:00 a.m. each night between October 7 and 12, 2020, except for government officials, social service workers, people going to or from work, and credentialed members of the press.[66]

The order was based in part on advice from Kenosha officials. They urged us to deny access to flammable materials during curfew hours to prevent the widespread arson that had occurred there. For that reason, during curfew hours, the order closed gasoline stations, prohibited the sale of flammable materials at hardware and home improvement stores, and limited the sale, use, or transportation of containers that could be used to transport and dispense such materials.

The possibility of arson was real. In Minneapolis, buildings had burned down during the rioting following George Floyd's death.[67] The same week in Milwaukee, protesters looted, vandalized, and burned dozens of businesses.[68] Of course, in Kenosha, just down the road on I-94, blocks of buildings had burned down in late August. And on September 23, Cole's sister, Taleavia, posted a Facebook video in which a friend said that protesters would shut down the Cheesecake Factory at Mayfair Mall the following day, and Taleavia chanted, "Burn it down!" and "That's what needs to happen!"

We also were concerned about the criminal histories of the leaders of TPR's Wauwatosa protests, Coleman and Anderson, and of two other TPR participants, Whitney Rise Roberson and Vaun Mayes, who were awaiting trial on arson charges. In 2019, Roberson was charged with trying to set fire to her Wauwatosa apartment. She committed suicide in 2022 before her case came to trial.[69] In 2018, Mayes was charged with plotting to firebomb a police station and intimidating a witness after a police shooting in Milwaukee in 2016. He was active in protests in Milwaukee and Wauwatosa in 2020 while awaiting trial. In October 2024, he pled guilty to promoting and encouraging a riot in exchange for having his firebombing charge and other charges dropped.[§70]

On September 30, 2020, I signed the emergency proclamation under authority granted by state law.[71] I would issue it only if circumstances required. But I signed it then because I was told that, under the law, Governor Evers needed the mayor to issue an emergency proclamation before he could send the National Guard to Wauwatosa.

On Wednesday, October 7, after meeting with Cole's family and their attorney, Chisholm announced that he would not charge Mensah for shooting Cole. Chisholm and the WPFC's outside investigator, former US attorney Biskupic, then released

---

§ In November 2021, Darrell Brooks drove his SUV into the Christmas parade in Waukesha, Wisconsin, 15 miles west of Wauwatosa, killing 6 people and injuring 61 more. He was later convicted on 6 counts of first-degree intentional homicide, 61 counts of recklessly endangering safety, and 6 counts of hit-and-run involving death. This carnage did not deter Mayes from posting a video on Facebook Live the day after the parade in which he said the incident signaled that the "revolution" may have begun. He did not say what he meant by the "revolution."

statements. Cole, they found, was shot after police responded to a report of a man displaying a gun during an argument at Mayfair Mall. As officers chased him through a parking lot, Cole pulled out a (stolen) handgun, which accidentally fired, striking him in the arm. Officers ordered him to drop the gun. Instead, he pointed it at Mensah, who shot and killed him. Chisholm noted that Cole may have fled because he was forbidden to have a gun due to his age and several prior felony convictions. That Cole aimed his gun at the officers, he said, was "sufficient evidence that Officer Mensah had an actual subjective belief that deadly force was necessary and that belief was objectively reasonable. I do not believe that the State could disprove self-defense or defense of others in this case and therefore could not meet the burden required to charge [him]." Biskupic agreed. Nevertheless, he recommended that Mensah be fired. "The risk and ensuing consequences to the Wauwatosa Police Department and the City of Wauwatosa of a fourth shooting by this Officer are too great for [the WPFC] to find otherwise," he wrote.[72]

After Chisholm and Biskupic released their findings, I issued my emergency proclamation announcing a curfew for five nights.[73] We closed City Hall and the library for the rest of the week. The Wauwatosa School District shifted to virtual learning. Mayfair Mall closed early.[74] Milwaukee County Executive David Crowley, who is Black, closed the County Courthouse at 2:00 p.m. to give "time for reflection and self-care, but also help prevent the escalation of the anticipated peaceful vigils and protests in the downtown area this evening."[75]

I also issued a statement. "Given recent events in Kenosha, Louisville, and other cities around the country, it should be clear that we all must do everything we can to keep our community peaceful," I said. "Violence is not the answer; it only impoverishes communities and brings more pain and despair." I promised that the police would "protect the lives and property of all residents and businesses while continuing to protect the constitutional rights of people to engage in peaceful protests." Regardless of anyone's opinion about Chisholm's decision, the wheels of government and law would continue to turn. I asked everyone to remain peaceful.[76]

Tosa Together, Indivisible Tosa, and Tosa Moms Tackling Racism also called for peace but added, "It is with great disappointment that we see our city being closed down out of fear and distrust of what might happen. Outside agitators are a concern, but the expected sharp escalation in militarized policing practices is vastly disproportionate. Our mayor has decided to take actions this week that show how much control the police have. They also show the escalatory tactics that our police department utilizes when controlled by fear and implicit bias against people of color. We expected more of our city leaders."[77]

That statement was stunningly naïve. Violence had occurred in earlier protests, and as October 7 approached, police observed out-of-state vehicles owned by Kenosha rioters being driven in the Milwaukee area.[78] During the Wauwatosa curfew period, Kenosha mayor John Antaramian called to express support. He asked if we were seeing outsiders. I replied that protesters and counterprotesters had come from Illinois, Texas, Washington, and other states. "It was outsiders who caused all the trouble in my city," he said. I asked whether it was prudent to have the National Guard in Wauwatosa. Without hesitation, he replied, "Absolutely." After what had happened in Kenosha, he said, it would have been foolish not to prepare as we did.**[79]

During the five curfew nights, I watched Facebook streams and drone footage of marches, standoffs, and clashes between

** We were reminded of the threat of outsider violence in 2022 when a man murdered 7 people and wounded 40 more at the July 4 parade in Highland Park, Illinois, and then drove to Madison, contemplating another attack there. Highland Park is 150 miles from Madison but only 70 miles from Wauwatosa. It would have been easier for the murderer to travel to Wauwatosa to make another attack during our parade the same day.

protesters and police in real time in an emergency operations center set up in an insurance company building in Wauwatosa. Sitting with me at tables facing large screens were our city administrator, city attorney, police chief, and fire chief, state and county emergency officials, and a Milwaukee Regional Medical Center liaison. From time to time, General Knapp came in to confer with us. Down the hall, our deputy city administrator and communications director worked with WPD and National Guard public information officers to provide information to the media.

During the curfew period, the WPD urged me and WPFC members to vacate our homes in case protesters besieged us, saying, "We don't want to have to extract you from your home." My wife and I spent several nights with relatives in nearby suburbs. While we were gone, the police received reports of an explosion, shots fired, and placement of suspicious materials at our home. On the emergency operations center screen, I did watch protesters advance on my home, but the police found no damage, and no injuries were reported.[80]

Police officers and soldiers were pre-positioned at City Hall, Mayfair Mall, and other key sites and deployed based on intelligence and protest group size. The goal was to deter violence and vandalism with a visible law enforcement presence. Police officers from 72 different agencies around the state provided support, coordinated by the Wisconsin Department of Emergency Management. They assisted the WPD with security, crowd control, investigations, surveillance and intelligence, service calls, and prisoner transport and processing. About 500 soldiers provided security, security escorts, and assistance with crowd control. Each National Guard unit was assigned a police escort because, under law, soldiers cannot take police action.[81] Although some residents later complained they saw the Guard in tanks, they did not; the Guard drove Humvees and transport trucks. Still, it was heartbreaking to see military vehicles on our streets.

Each day, life in Wauwatosa seemed strangely normal, except for the boarded-up windows on some businesses. Enjoying the unseasonably warm autumn weather, people sat outside boarded-up restaurants, ate lunch, and sipped coffee. Each night, protesters gathered at City Hall, and others massed in Milwaukee and waited until 7:00 p.m. to cross the boundary into Wauwatosa in defiance of the curfew.[82] Media outlets as far away as India and Taiwan reported on the events.[83] On the first night, October 7, at least 100 protesters gathered in the busy intersection outside City Hall. The police repeatedly ordered them to disperse.[84] They refused. At 7:45 p.m. the police advanced. Most of the protesters departed, but a few were arrested. Some drove their cars over the lawn at Longfellow Middle School across North Avenue from City Hall. The police deployed "stop sticks" to puncture their tires.

A group of protesters eluded the police and marched west on North Avenue toward Mayfair Mall, breaking windows in 11 stores and two residences. On a live Facebook feed, we watched a protester pull a pipe from his backpack and calmly walk along smashing windows in a pharmacy, a wallpaper store, and apartment buildings about a mile from City Hall. A few protesters drove motorcycles on lawns. Near Mayfair, a police line stopped the protesters, some of whom threw rocks, bricks, and bottles at officers. Others fled several blocks north into Milwaukee, smashed windows in a café, and looted businesses. Milwaukee police arrested many of the looters.[85]

On the morning of Thursday, October 8, Governor Evers called me to ensure that we had enough resources to deal with the unrest. I said we did. That night, police arrested 24 protesters who did not depart when ordered. Stop sticks were deployed, and cars were towed. Because WPD booking rooms were full, some protesters were booked in the adjacent suburb of West Allis. On a live video stream, we saw a standoff develop between armed protesters and counterprotesters outside the police station there.

General Knapp quickly dispatched National Guard soldiers to keep a gun battle from breaking out.

Among those arrested that night were Alvin Cole's mother, Tracy, and her three daughters. Though they shouted, "Do you know who we are?!" the police did not know who they were before pulling them out of their car, which was part of a small convoy traveling near Lincoln Elementary School 6 blocks south of City Hall. Their family status did not exempt the Coles from the curfew, but they were not given tickets. Mrs. Cole sustained minor injuries when she resisted being removed from her car. She was taken to a hospital and released shortly thereafter.[86]

On Friday, October 9, the WPD arrested 28 people and turned 9 others over to Milwaukee police. Shortly before 7:00 p.m., officers ordered two women holding a long banner to stop blocking traffic on North Avenue in front of City Hall and arrested them when they refused. A large crowd gathered. After giving multiple orders to disperse over a 52-minute period, the police advanced. Many protesters ran away, but some threw rocks and water bottles before being arrested. Several blocks away, protesters pushed restaurant dumpsters into North Avenue and tried to set them on fire. A man carrying materials used to make Molotov cocktails was arrested. After the crowd finally dispersed, police discovered other flammable liquids in containers on the lawn outside City Hall.

After that, the lawlessness diminished. On Saturday, October 10, after repeated warnings were given, the protesters dispersed on their own, but stop sticks had to be deployed to stop reckless driving. The WPD made eight arrests. The next day, October 11, it made four arrests. When officers ordered protesters to disperse, they generally complied. The curfew ended on Monday morning.

Each night of the protests, some protesters carried guns. On two nights, police deployed pepper spray, tear gas, and smoke canisters and fired small beanbags when protesters refused to disperse, pushed back, and threw rocks, bricks, and bottles at them.[87] This was distressing, but, as US district judge Lynn Adelman later held while dismissing a lawsuit challenging the curfew and police actions, "no case suggest[s] that the [Constitution] forbids law enforcement from [using tear gas and less-lethal projectiles] to disperse a crowd that has assembled in violation of a curfew and has started to throw objects."[88] The police would not have deployed those items if the protesters had not resisted. Though my curfew order forbade protesting for five nights, Adelman and another federal judge later noted that it did not prevent protests during the day or on weekends.[89] If the protests had occurred at those times, no one would have been arrested for curfew violations. And the right to protest does not shield from prosecution people who smash windows or set fires in dumpsters.

In all, police arrested 78 people—36 Whites, 32 Blacks, 8 Hispanics, and 2 of unknown race. Forty-seven were from Milwaukee, 7 from Wauwatosa, 19 from other Wisconsin cities, and 5 from out of state. Among those arrested was Gaige Grosskreutz, whom Kyle Rittenhouse had shot during the Kenosha riots a few weeks earlier. Two protesters were arrested for carrying concealed weapons, two for possessing flammable liquids, and three for looting a Milwaukee store. Six were ticketed for resisting arrest, including 2 who injured police officers. Jay-Z and his social justice group, Team ROC, paid court fees and posted bond for Tracy Cole and her three daughters, along with several others who were arrested.[90]

Because of our preparations, damage was minor—an estimated $16,000, mostly from broken windows. A police vehicle was vandalized, and a car was stolen but recovered. Other minor damage occurred in Milwaukee during the looting.[91] Unlike in Kenosha, no one was killed or seriously injured in Wauwatosa, and no buildings were burned. The unrest cost the city hundreds of thousands of dollars for police and fire overtime and other expenses, however.

On Monday, October 12, the day the curfew ended, Chief Weber and I held a press conference at the request of local and national media.[92] The following night, as required by the Wisconsin Statutes, the Common Council held a special meeting to discuss my emergency proclamation. Under law, it could ratify, alter, modify, or repeal that order, but no action taken would affect the proclamation's legality.[93] The council voted to place the matter on file.

A day or two after the special meeting, Bishop Tavis Grant, national field director of Reverend Jesse Jackson's Rainbow Push Coalition in Chicago, called me to set up a meeting with the Cole family to try to restore peace. We met on October 20.[94] I expressed my condolences to Mrs. Cole for the loss of her son, saying I have a son, too, and losing him would be devastating. She did not respond. Attorney Motley engaged in grandstanding, and Taleavia Cole was hostile. (In addition to her earlier threat to burn down Mayfair, in another Facebook post Taleavia accused my niece and me of being members of the Proud Boys, a White nationalist group.) It was not clear what the family's goal was. The meeting ended without progress.

To a reporter afterward, Motley again publicly demanded that I direct the WPFC or Chief Weber to fire Mensah.[95] As a lawyer, she knew better; all year we had reminded her that only the WPFC can discipline police officers. Firing Mensah without due process would have exposed the city to huge legal and financial liability. We continued to negotiate with him quietly. On November 17, the Common Council approved a separation agreement. Mensah agreed to resign in return for $125,065.44, representing his salary through 2021, overtime and vacation pay, a payment to his deferred compensation plan, and a settlement amount. (This was a bargain. By comparison, in 2024, the City of Tacoma, Washington, paid three police officers $500,000 each to resign after they were acquitted of murder and manslaughter charges for a 2020 incident in which a Black man died after they put him in a chokehold and placed a hood over his head.)[96]

On January 5, 2021, the Kenosha County district attorney announced he would not charge the police officers who shot Jacob Blake. Governor Evers deployed the National Guard in advance. No one was hurt, and no property damage occurred.[97] A few weeks later, Mensah was sworn in as a deputy sheriff in Waukesha County, just west of Milwaukee County. His hiring there made national news and drew criticism from the ACLU and others.[98]

In the end, though the earlier unrest had created urgency, the October protests were futile. The City of Wauwatosa had no role in Chisholm's decision not to charge Mensah, and those protests had no impact on the WPFC's review of Mensah's employment or on our long, behind-the-scenes effort to negotiate his departure. They only further divided the community and further diminished support for the BLM movement.

TPR engaged in sporadic protests after the curfew period ended in Wauwatosa, but those events and the number of protesters dwindled. Cold weather, the distractions of life, and the criminal problems facing TPR leaders caused most people to move on. Any lingering energy moved into courtrooms as participants in the October 2020 protests sued the city and me in state and federal court.

—⁓—

TIME, PLACE, AND MANNER

ACROSS AMERICA, THOUSANDS OF PEOPLE peacefully protested George Floyd's murder. At times, however, riots, vandalism, looting, and arson occurred.[1] Many cities imposed curfews, and a number of states and the District of Columbia activated the National Guard.[2] Immediately, protesters began filing what the *Los Angeles Times* termed a "mountain of litigation."[3]

Some lawsuits challenged arrests for curfew violations. Others, which alleged police brutality, sought monetary damages and bans on the police using tear gas, rubber bullets, and other crowd control tactics. Kneeling protesters in Oakland alleged that officers tackled them and "forced [them] into lying in a pile on the ground," a woman with spinal injuries riding a knee scooter alleged that Seattle police twice tear-gassed her, and Portland protesters alleged that police targeted and shot them with rubber bullets.[4]

By the end of May 2023, 19 cities had already paid more than $80 million to settle lawsuits arising out of the 2020 protests, with many lawsuits still pending.[5]

In March 2021, Minneapolis agreed to pay $27 million to Floyd's family.[6] In early 2022, to settle lawsuits arising from the firing of foam projectiles by police during 2020 protests, it also paid $2.4 million to a man who was partially blinded, $1.8 million to two women who were struck in the eyes, and $600,000 to a photographer who lost sight in her left eye. In October 2022, it agreed to pay over $700,000 to more than a dozen protesters who alleged that the police had used excessive force and chilled their First Amendment rights to free speech and peaceful assembly. In addition, noted the ACLU, the settlement agreement "prohibit[ed] the city from arresting, threatening to arrest, or using physical force including but not limited to chemical agents, flash bang/concussion grenades, and foam-tipped bullets against people engaging in lawful protests, assemblies, or demonstrations." Minneapolis also agreed that officers at protests would wear body cameras and first give orders and reasonable time for people to leave before they used chemical agents to disperse crowds acting unlawfully.[7]

In November 2022, the first of the more than 50 lawsuits arising from the 2020 protests in Portland went to trial. In that case, Erin Wenzel alleged that at an August 2020 protest, an officer "ran at her and violently slammed into her with a nightstick" and another officer pushed her while she was following orders to disperse. Medical experts confirmed she suffered post-traumatic stress disorder and a broken arm. Wenzel asked for $450,000. The jury decided that the police had used unreasonable force, but only awarded her $40,272. The following month, Portland settled a lawsuit filed by the Don't Shoot Portland advocacy group and five protesters. Each of the five received $50,001. The settlement required the Portland Police Bureau (PPB) to follow state law and its own policies, not federal dictates, when using tear gas, pepper spray, long-range acoustic devices used to disperse crowds, and less-lethal launchers that fire projectiles meant to cause pain but not break the skin. The PPB will no longer use "rubber ball distraction devices," which create a loud noise, a flash of light, and the projection of rubber balls.[8]

By March 2023, Portland had settled 71 bodily injury claims totaling more than $3 million. More had yet to be resolved. Many of the claims alleged that crowd-control tactics caused injuries to lawful protesters. Other plaintiffs alleged that police struck protesters with batons or pinned protesters to the ground and repeatedly punched them.[9]

Seattle was sued repeatedly, too. In February 2023, it agreed to pay more than $3 million to residents and businesses disrupted during the Capitol Hill Organized Protests (CHOP). Clashes between protesters and police had led the city to withdraw officers from an eight-block section of Capitol Hill from June 8 to July 1, 2020. Businesses complained that they were cut off from customers and that their rights were violated by the city's decision to provide street barricades and sanitation stations and not disband the protest zone. While the zone existed, vandalism and two fatal shootings not directly related to the protests occurred, including a 16-year-old who died as the result of a stolen-vehicle incident and a 19-year-old who bled to death after being taken to a hospital in a pickup truck when police and firefighters refused to respond. The city paid the 19-year-old's father $500,000 in settlement and was later sued by the 16-year-old's father for the failure by police to pursue the case. Allegedly, it took several hours after the death for police detectives to arrive and begin their work, and the murder was never solved.[10]

In February 2022, a grand jury indicted 19 Austin, Texas, police officers for using excessive force. The same day, the city agreed to pay $10 million to two men who were injured during the 2020 protests.[11] That year, a jury awarded $14 million to 12 others who were injured during demonstrations in Denver, and in separate settlements, that city agreed to pay $1.6 million to seven injured protesters and $4.7 million to 300 others.[12]

In March 2023, Philadelphia agreed to pay $9.25 million to 343 plaintiffs who sued over the police response to the 2020 protests. Those protests included multiple clashes with police, the burning of police cars, looting, and vandalism of businesses, but videos also showed police firing tear gas at dozens of protesters trapped on Interstate 676 by SWAT team officers, and plaintiffs alleged that police used excessive force in Black neighborhoods, too.[13]

In the same month, New York City agreed to pay at least $21,500 each to 320 protesters who alleged that on June 4, 2020, NYPD officers surrounded them in the Bronx and then ran at them swinging batons and using pepper spray. In July 2023, New York agreed to pay another $13.7 million to settle a class action lawsuit brought by 1,380 people who were arrested or subjected to force by NYPD officers during marches in Manhattan and Brooklyn between May 28 and June 7, 2020. The NYPD said squad cars were burned and looting occurred in various neighborhoods, especially in Manhattan's SoHo district, where people plundered luxury shops. But *New York Times* reporters also saw officers, unprovoked, repeatedly charge at protesters out after curfew, shove them onto sidewalks, and hit them with batons. Police body-camera and helicopter videos allegedly showed the police indiscriminately using pepper spray and batons and preventing protesters from leaving by "kettling" them between police lines. Videos posted on social media also showed police SUVs ramming a crowd in Brooklyn and people in Manhattan screaming and fleeing from an officer who was holding a pistol. The total of the NYPD misconduct payouts was expected to reach up to $50 million, including attorney fees.[14]

Also in March 2023, a woman received $10 million after she lost vision in one eye and was placed in a medically induced coma when La Mesa, California, police shot her in the head with a beanbag during the 2020 protests. Later in 2023, San Jose, California, paid a man $2.9 million after he lost an eye when an officer shot him with a hard projectile, and paid a total of $450,000 to four others for lesser injuries, while six plaintiffs had their claims dismissed.[15]

In January 2024, Seattle agreed to pay another $10 million to 50 demonstrators who suffered injuries during protests in 2020. The plaintiffs alleged that the police use of pepper spray, tear gas, and other crowd-control devices had caused cardiac arrest, hearing loss, broken bones, concussions, severe bruises, post-traumatic stress syndrome, and other serious injuries.[16]

CURFEW LITIGATION

People arrested for curfew violations in 2020 challenged the arrests as invalid under the First Amendment to the US Constitution, which states: "Congress shall make no law . . . abridging the freedom of speech, or of the press; or the right of the people peaceably to assemble, and to petition the Government for a redress of grievances." Through the Fourteenth Amendment, these rights also bind state and local governments.[17] But they are not absolute.

The US Supreme Court has long held that "the First Amendment does not guarantee the right to communicate one's views at all times and places or in any manner that may be desired"[18] and that thus First Amendment rights are subject to "time, place, and manner" restrictions. These can include limits on noise levels, the number of protesters who can assemble, the hours of protests, and if and how protesters can march through residential areas and picket a person's house.[19] To survive constitutional challenges, such limits must satisfy a test stated in 1989 by the Supreme Court in *Ward v. Rock Against Racism*: restrictions must be "content neutral" (not favoring one viewpoint over another), be "narrowly tailored to serve a significant governmental interest," and provide ample alternative ways to communicate the speaker's message.[20] If this test is met, the government does not need to choose the least restrictive alternative in imposing time, place, and manner restrictions on speech and assembly.[21]

Challenges to 2020 curfew orders were less successful than injury cases, unless the curfews were unreasonably long. On June 5, 2020, facing federal lawsuits, the mayors of Cleveland and Columbus, Ohio, rescinded curfew orders imposed on May 30 because the vandalism that led to the orders had stopped.[22] Elsewhere, plaintiffs were on shakier legal ground. In another lawsuit, the ACLU sued Los Angeles County and the cities of Los Angeles and San Bernardino to end curfews that extended from May 30 to June 4, 2020. As in the Ohio cities, after several nights the curfews were probably unnecessary. (Wauwatosa's initial curfew lasted three nights, from May 30 through June 1, 2020.)[23] But the ACLU argued against any curfew at all, stating, "The curfews' extraordinary suppression of all political protest in the evening hours plainly violates the First Amendment to the U.S. Constitution, and their blanket restrictions on movement outside working hours violate the Constitution's protection of freedom of movement."[24]

The ACLU's argument was weak. The Supreme Court has repeatedly held that "even protected speech is not equally permissible in all places and at all times."[25] As lawyer and *New York Times* columnist David French has explained with reference to protests on university campuses, "There are times when universities inhibit free speech to prevent harassment, and there are times when universities wrongly permit harassment in the belief that they're protecting free speech. But there are ways to parse the difference. If an administrator receives a complaint that is primarily related to the content or viewpoint of the speech ('I don't like what he said'), then in a vast majority of circumstances, the administrator has an obligation to protect the speech and to teach the student how to handle exposure to difficult or offensive ideas. If, however, the complaint is related to conduct—like blocking access to class or making loud noises that prevent study or sleep—or is related to the time, place or manner of the speech (you can chant in the quad but not in the dorm at 3 a.m., or you can protest in the quad, but you can't seize it so others are prevented from using the space), then universities often have to react."[26]

In the wake of divisive protests, some universities are prohibiting encampments (which resemble the "autonomous zones" created in Seattle and Portland in 2020) and requiring prior approval of temporary structures, banning protests within 25 feet of building entrances, prohibiting protesters from blocking access to driveways and other facilities, requiring protesters to obtain advance approval to use bullhorns or other sound equipment and limiting their hours of use, banning all protests after 5:00 p.m. and during the final two weeks of each semester, and implementing measures to keep outsiders from stirring up trouble. Approving of these restrictions, which balance the rights of protesters and nonprotesters, the *Washington Post* editorial board advised that universities, like cities, "can and should follow the constitutional framework the Supreme Court has set down: They may not police content unless it is threatening or harassing, but they may regulate protests' time, place and manner to preserve public order. Over the decades, this framework has proved capable of balancing the right to free speech and the imperative of public order."[27]

In 2020, where curfews were reasonable in scope and duration and emergency conditions existed, cities prevailed in court. On May 31, Washington, DC, mayor Muriel Bowser imposed a curfew from 11:00 p.m. until 6:00 a.m. the following day. During those hours, no one, other than designated persons, was allowed to "walk, bike, run, loiter, stand, or motor by car or other mode of transport upon any street, alley, park, or other public place within the District." The order signed by Bowser, who is African American, recognized the "outrage" that people felt following the Floyd murder, along with grief over "hundreds of years of institutional racism," but also described the vandalism and other crimes that had occurred over several previous nights: in downtown DC, "numerous businesses and government buildings were vandalized, burned, or looted," and officials observed a "glorification of violence, particularly during later hours of the night." The order stated that these actions threatened and endangered the health, safety, and well-being of people. It also invoked the need to protect public health during the COVID-19 state of emergency then in place, noting that many protesters were not wearing masks or observing distancing requirements.

On June 1, after another night of destruction, Bowser renewed the curfew for two more nights, but starting at 7:00 p.m. instead of 11:00 p.m. According to the new order, "numerous businesses, vehicles, and government buildings" had been "vandalized, burned, or looted" and more than 80 people arrested, most of them charged with felonies. Despite the previous night's curfew, the order stated, looting and vandalism had occurred throughout the city, not just downtown, and "vandals smashed windows in Northeast DC, upper Northwest DC stretching to Georgetown, and caused extensive damage in the Golden Triangle Business Improvement District, Downtown DC Business Improvement District, and Mount Vernon Triangle Community Improvement District." The order stated that "rioting and looting affected the operations of District government agencies" and that gatherings of more than 10 people violated the District's COVID-19 emergency declaration then in place. Violators could face misdemeanor penalties of up to $300 or 10 days' imprisonment. The order did not require police officers to give people an opportunity to disperse before arresting them for violating the curfew.

At 11:00 p.m. on June 1, Devon Tinius and others stood near the White House protesting the treatment of African Americans by police. They were arrested for violating the curfew order, jailed overnight, and released after arraignment the next morning.[28] Several months later, DC dismissed the charges against them.

In 2021, Tinius and six others sued the arresting officers in federal court under 42 U.S.C. § 1983, alleging that the arrests during a peaceful protest violated their First Amendment rights to freedom of speech and assembly and their Fourth Amendment right to be free from excessive force. Section 1983 states: "Every person who, under color of any statute, ordinance, regulation, custom, or usage, of any State or Territory or the District of Columbia, subjects, or causes to be subjected, any citizen of the United States or other person within the jurisdiction thereof to the deprivation of any rights, privileges, or immunities secured by the Constitution and laws, shall be liable to the party injured in an action at law, suit in equity, or other proper proceeding for redress." In *Monroe v. Pape*, 365 U.S. 167 (1961), the Supreme Court listed three uses for the statute: overriding state laws, providing remedies where state laws are inadequate, and providing federal remedies where state remedies are available in theory, but not in fact. Since then, courts have applied Section 1983 to lawsuits against police officers, correctional officers, state and municipal officials, municipalities, and private parties acting under color of law.

US district judge Amy Berman Jackson dismissed the *Tinius* case, holding that the DC curfew complied with the First Amendment because it was content neutral and narrowly tailored to serve significant government interests and left open the alternative of daytime protests.[29] The plaintiffs appealed the dismissal to the US Court of Appeals for the District of Columbia Circuit. The court affirmed Jackson's decision, holding that the District's public safety and public health interests were significant and that the curfew order was narrowly tailored to achieve those interests. It further held that the order was a content-neutral time, place, and manner restriction that allowed ample alternative channels of communication, such as protesting during the day or at night after the curfew expired.[30] "Our Constitution provides for ordered liberty," the court wrote. "Even though the June 1 Order limited some valuable opportunities for public speech and association, the public interest in keeping the peace by responding effectively to a surge in vandalism, arson, and looting was not directed at the suppression of expression, and it justified the June 1 Order's temporary restriction on nighttime activity in public spaces."[31]

On October 7, 2020, I issued a "Proclamation of Emergency" in Wauwatosa that mirrored the language in the order issued by Mayor Bowser in DC. My order stated that based on our experience with protests in 2020 and community responses to decisions and actions regarding police officers nationwide, the Milwaukee County district attorney's announcement that he would not charge Officer Mensah for shooting Alvin Cole raised an imminent threat of a riot or civil unrest, especially because of the violence that had occurred only five weeks earlier in Kenosha. Like the DC order, my proclamation prohibited pedestrian and vehicular traffic on city streets between 7:00 p.m. and 6:00 a.m. each night.[32]

After our curfew ended, multiple protesters sued the city and me. In the *Tinius* case, the plaintiffs argued that it violated their First Amendment rights because they were "engaged in peaceful public expression."[33] They did not dispute that the DC order was "content neutral." The Wauwatosa plaintiffs made both arguments.

In November 2020, two protesters filed a federal lawsuit, *Knowlton v. City of Wauwatosa* (E.D. Wis.), under Section 1983 seeking to enjoin the city and me from issuing "unlawful" emergency orders and Chief Barry Weber from "issuing and enforcing unlawful policies including dispersal orders to peaceful passersby based on alleged unlawful assembly or other group misconduct by others."[34] Though they alleged the pre–October 7 protests were "largely peaceful," they admitted "some people disturbed neighbors at night and a few engaged in illegal acts."[35] Subsequent amended complaints increased the number of plaintiffs to more than 60.

A few months later, another protester filed a federal lawsuit, *Paige Radke v. City of Wauwatosa* (E.D. Wis.), alleging that the October 2020 curfew violated her First Amendment rights. *Radke* was decided before *Knowlton*. In August 2022, US district judge Lynn Adelman, generally regarded as the most liberal judge in the US District Court for the Eastern District of Wisconsin, ruled that my proclamation satisfied the time, place, and manner test.[36]

First, he held that it was content neutral because it did not refer to anyone's viewpoint but instead "focuse[d] on the safety concerns that could have arisen if conditions like those that had been experienced in municipalities such as Kenosha materialized in Wauwatosa."[37] Second, though Radke argued that the curfew was not constitutional because it was imposed before a riot or disaster occurred, she did not cite any case holding that a city had to wait before acting to protect public safety or that a city cannot rely on the experience of other cities when deciding if a curfew is needed. For these reasons, Adelman held that the curfew served a significant governmental interest.[38] Third, Radke did not "identify any alternative to the curfew that would have allowed Wauwatosa to achieve with equal effectiveness its interest in preventing demonstrations from turning into riots." Instead, she argued that the city had not given her other outlets for protest. But Adelman held, as the DC Circuit had in *Tinius*, that protesters had alternatives: although the curfew barred protests for five nights from 7:00 p.m. to 6:00 a.m., it did not do so during daytime hours or on weekends.[39]

Historically, most of the violence in protests occurs after dark. "The curfew began at 7:00 p.m. and ended at 6:00 a.m.," Adelman noted. "I take judicial notice that, during early October in Milwaukee County, the sun sets at about 6:30 p.m. and rises at about 7:00 a.m."[40]

With this, Adelman dismissed Radke's First Amendment challenge to my proclamation. He also rejected her claim that the police violated her Fourth Amendment right to be free from excessive force when officers allegedly injured her by releasing tear gas and shooting her in the foot with a small beanbag. (The Wauwatosa police fired small beanbags rather than rubber bullets because they are less harmful.) She seemed to argue that the police should have just allowed the crowd to remain on the street but did not identify a lesser form of force that could have been used or cite any case suggesting that the Constitution forbids police from dispersing a crowd that is violating a curfew and throwing objects. Accordingly, Adelman held that she had not proved that using tear gas and nonlethal projectiles violated her rights.[41]

In March 2023, relying on *Radke* and Supreme Court cases, US Magistrate Judge Nancy Joseph, a Black woman who had previously served as a public defender, dismissed the First and Fourth Amendment claims in *Knowlton*.[42] Though Radke did not appeal the dismissal of her case, the *Knowlton* plaintiffs did. Based on the decisions by Judge Adelman and Judge Joseph and the DC Circuit's decision in *Tinius*, we expected the US Court of Appeals for the Seventh Circuit to affirm the dismissal of the plaintiffs' claims. In October 2024, it did just that. It noted that the facts suggested that we "enacted the curfew to ensure public safety, and not because of disagreement with any specific message" of the protesters or counter-protesters and emphasized that a city "need not wait to act until violence or harm materializes. Indeed, the government has an interest in preventing emergencies and threats to public safety, not merely responding to them after they transpire."[43]

Private civil lawsuits by the families of Mensah's shooting victims continued against Officer Mensah, Chief Weber, and the City of Wauwatosa, alleging that the defendants had violated the victims' constitutional rights when Mensah killed them, but the outcomes of the *Knowlton* and *Radke* cases and of other litigation made it unlikely that the families' lawsuits would succeed. In March 2024, Judge Adelman dismissed the Gonzales and Anderson families' lawsuits but allowed the Cole family's lawsuit to proceed because he said it was not clear whether Cole had pointed a gun at Mensah or other officers. It would be up to a jury, at a trial in mid-2025, to decide if Mensah had behaved as an objectively reasonable officer under the circumstances.[44] But this was not a criminal matter; even if the jury decided against him, it would only award monetary damages to the Cole family. That outcome did not seem likely.

Meanwhile, in July 2021, while the *Knowlton* case was being litigated, the plaintiffs' attorney, Kimberley Motley, sought to apply political pressure on the city for leverage in her legal case, by asking Senator Tammy Baldwin (D-WI) and Congresswoman Gwen Moore (D-WI) to have the US Department of Justice (DOJ) investigate the Wauwatosa Police Department. Without seeking input from the city, Baldwin and Moore asked DOJ to "thoroughly and deliberately consider" that request, which, they said, had "put forward serious allegations of misconduct, including policing practices that allegedly targeted individuals because of their race and/or their engagement in activities protected by the First Amendment." Perhaps they were not aware, but their letter did not say that the director of Baldwin's Milwaukee office, Tiffany Henry, had participated in protests in Wauwatosa in 2020. In January 2022, Henry filed a lawsuit alleging she had been defamed by being included on an internal WPD list of names, addresses, telephone numbers, dates of birth, vehicle information, and driver's-license photos of people who protested in Wauwatosa in 2020. But to be defamatory, a statement must be untrue and intentionally or negligently communicated to someone other than the person defamed. Henry did not deny taking part in the protests, and the WPD list became public only because protesters and media outlets received it through open-record requests. Her lawsuit was dismissed in June 2022.[45]

In any event, asking DOJ to consider a request is not the same as a demand that it undertake an investigation. As the *Knowlton* and *Radke* decisions indicated, the city's legal position was strong. We never heard from DOJ. Other cities did. In April and May 2021, DOJ announced civil rights investigations of the Louisville and Minneapolis police departments, triggered by the killings of Breonna Taylor and George Floyd.[46] In both cases, it found that the departments had engaged "in a pattern or practice of conduct that deprives people of their rights under the Constitution and federal law."

In March 2023, DOJ released a report stating that the Louisville Metro Police Department (LMPD) used excessive force; conducted searches based on invalid warrants; unlawfully executed search warrants without knocking and announcing; unlawfully stopped, searched, detained, and arrested people during street enforcement activities; unlawfully discriminated against Black people; and violated the rights of people engaged in protected speech critical of police. DOJ identified deficiencies in LMPD's investigations of domestic violence and sexual assaults, including its responses to allegations that LMPD officers engaged in such activity. It also found that LMPD and the Louisville/Jefferson County Metro government discriminated against people with behavioral health disabilities when responding to calls for assistance. DOJ negotiated a settlement agreement with LMPD and Louisville Metro to address its findings.[47]

Similarly, in June 2023, DOJ found that the Minneapolis Police Department (MPD) used excessive force, violated the rights of people engaged in protected speech, and unlawfully discriminated against Black and Native American people, including in its use of force following stops. It also found that the MPD and City of Minneapolis discriminated against people with behavioral health disabilities when responding to calls for assistance. It identified deficiencies in the MPD's accountability systems, training, supervision, and officer wellness programs that contributed to the violations. These patterns, US attorney general Merrick Garland said, "made what happened to George Floyd possible." DOJ recommended a variety of remedial measures, including enhanced training, accountability measures, and data collection, and negotiated a settlement agreement with the city and MPD.[48]

The DOJ report followed a similar report issued by the Minnesota Department of Human Rights (MDHR) in April 2022 after a two-year investigation. Like DOJ, the MDHR found disparities in how officers interact with people of color compared with Whites. The report said that the MPD had engaged in a pattern of race discrimination for more than 10 years and that its officers "receive deficient training, which emphasizes a paramilitary approach to policing that results in officers unnecessarily escalating encounters or using inappropriate levels of force." After the report was released, city and state officials began negotiating a consent decree to resolve the issues in the report as well as a lawsuit that MDHR filed against the city shortly after the Floyd murder. At that time, the court imposed a preliminary injunction that compelled the city to address systemic racism in the MPD, including banning chokeholds and neck restraints and requiring officers to try to stop other officers who they believe are using improper force.[49]

Despite the protests and unrest in Seattle and Portland in 2020, DOJ did not open investigations of the Seattle Police Department or Portland Police Bureau. Those departments were already operating under settlements negotiated after earlier DOJ investigations.[50]

MEDIA RIGHTS

First Amendment rights and time, place, and manner restrictions apply to observers as well as to protesters.

When protests erupted in Des Moines, Iowa, following the Floyd murder, the police arrested *Des Moines Register* reporter Andrea Sahouri, and the Polk County attorney John Sarcone charged her with "failure to disperse" and "interference with official acts" for conducting interviews, taking photos, and recording what was happening. If convicted, she would have had a criminal record, served up to 30 days in jail, and paid a fine of

$625 for each offense. This was outrageous. As stated in a *Register* editorial, "When reporters are arrested, assaulted or otherwise prevented from doing their jobs, it's not an attack on just a single journalist or a media company. It's an attack on everyone's rights to be informed and to hold those in power accountable for their actions. Sarcone needs to do his job and dismiss these charges, which clearly violate free press rights." That did not happen, but at Sahouri's trial in March 2021, the jury acquitted her after deliberating for less than two hours.[51]

In her curfew orders of May 31 and June 1, 2020, DC Mayor Bowser prohibited people from being on any District street, alley, park, or other public place during the stated hours. "Individuals performing essential duties as authorized by prior Mayor's Orders, including working media with their outlet-issued credentials and healthcare personnel," were exempted.[52] Similarly, in July 2020, a federal judge ordered that the City of Portland exempt credentialed journalists and legal observers from arrest or threat of arrest by police after officers issued an "unlawful assembly" or "riot" declaration.[53] Likewise, in the emergency proclamation issued on October 7, 2020, I declared a curfew for five nights "except for persons who are going to or from work and government officials, social service workers, and credentialed members of the press acting in their official capacities."[54] We later added ACLU legal observers to that list.

During protests, especially in this social media age, many people claim to be reporters but really are just individuals. The court order in Portland said that journalists could be identified with a press pass, a press badge, or distinctive clothing that identified the wearer as a member of the press. Legal observers could be identified with distinctive hats or vests.[55] Reporters for television and radio stations and for newspapers like the *Des Moines Register, Washington Post,* and *Milwaukee Journal Sentinel* carry identification cards; do-it-yourself bloggers and podcasters typically do not. (As a journalism school graduate and son of two former newspaper reporters, I am well aware of these distinctions.) In Wauwatosa, ACLU observers wore blue vests and carried identification. Without credentials, everyone could defy a curfew by saying they are reporters or legal observers. For this reason, during the 2020 curfew period in Wauwatosa, the police arrested a few self-proclaimed journalists, who did not have credentials, for curfew violations.[56]

In a different context, federal courts have provided guidance on this issue. In 2019, the MacIver Institute, a right-wing Wisconsin think tank and advocacy group, sued Governor Evers, a Democrat, claiming that he had excluded MacIver's "reporters" and "news director" from press conferences because of the group's political affiliation. A federal district court judge in Madison rejected the suit and found that Evers's staff had excluded MacIver based on its media access policy, which limits access to "organizations whose principal business is news dissemination." Judge James Peterson wrote: "Evers has reasonably concluded that MacIver is not a bona fide news organization. MacIver publicly brands itself as a think tank committed to ideological principles. It engages in policy-driven political advocacy, including advocating for specific initiatives and policy approaches. It has a 'news' tab on its website, but it does not maintain a news-gathering organization separate from its overall ideological mission."[57]

On appeal, the Seventh Circuit unanimously held that Evers's media access policy used neutral criteria and that MacIver had not proved the policy was discriminatory. "The protections of the First Amendment extend not just to the traditional press embodied by newspapers, television, books, and magazines, 'but also humble leaflets and circulars,' which were meant to play an important role in the discussion of public affairs," the court's opinion stated. "Protecting the right of small, upstart, and non-objective media producers, however, does not mean that the Governor of Wisconsin must grant every media outlet access to every press conference. We cannot fathom the chaos that might ensue if every gubernatorial press event had to be open to any 'qualified' journalist with only the most narrowly drawn restrictions on who might be excluded. And no one's needs would be served if the government were required to allow access to everyone or no one at all."[58] The US Supreme Court declined to hear MacIver's appeal from that decision.[59]

If a governor can deny access to press conferences to people who do not meet a reasonable definition of journalist, a city must be able to bar self-proclaimed but uncredentialed "journalists" from being exempted from a curfew to "avoid the chaos that might ensue" if the city cannot control who is on its streets during an emergency. Otherwise, agitators could render a curfew meaningless merely by claiming to be reporters.[60]

But just as the government cannot discriminate against protesters and counterprotesters based on their viewpoints, cities cannot forbid real journalists from being present at protests based on what they are reporting.[61] In 2020, Wauwatosa, Portland, and the District of Columbia simply required that anyone who wanted to be exempted from a curfew as a journalist had to be credentialed. That served the important public interests of keeping public places clear during unrest while allowing the public to receive information it needed to assess whether its government officials had acted appropriately.

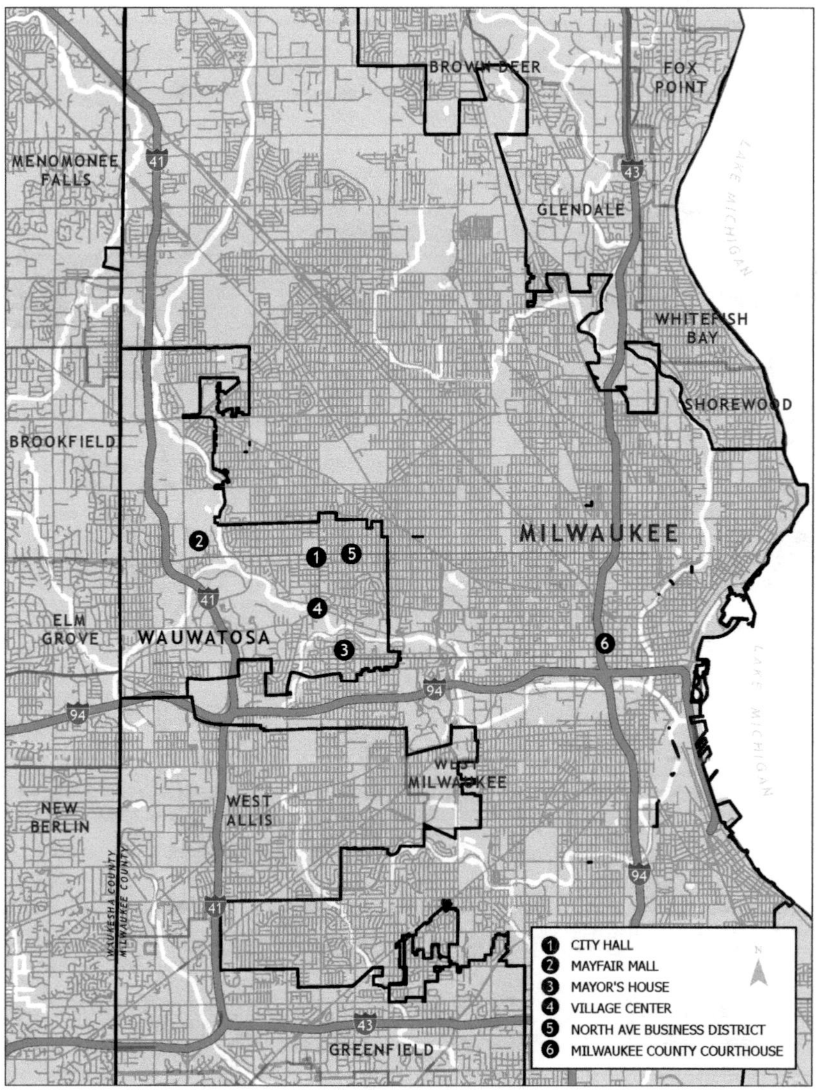

This map of the Milwaukee metropolitan area illustrates how Wauwatosa is seamlessly connected to the majority-minority City of Milwaukee, which borders it on three sides. (Paul Vepraskas map)

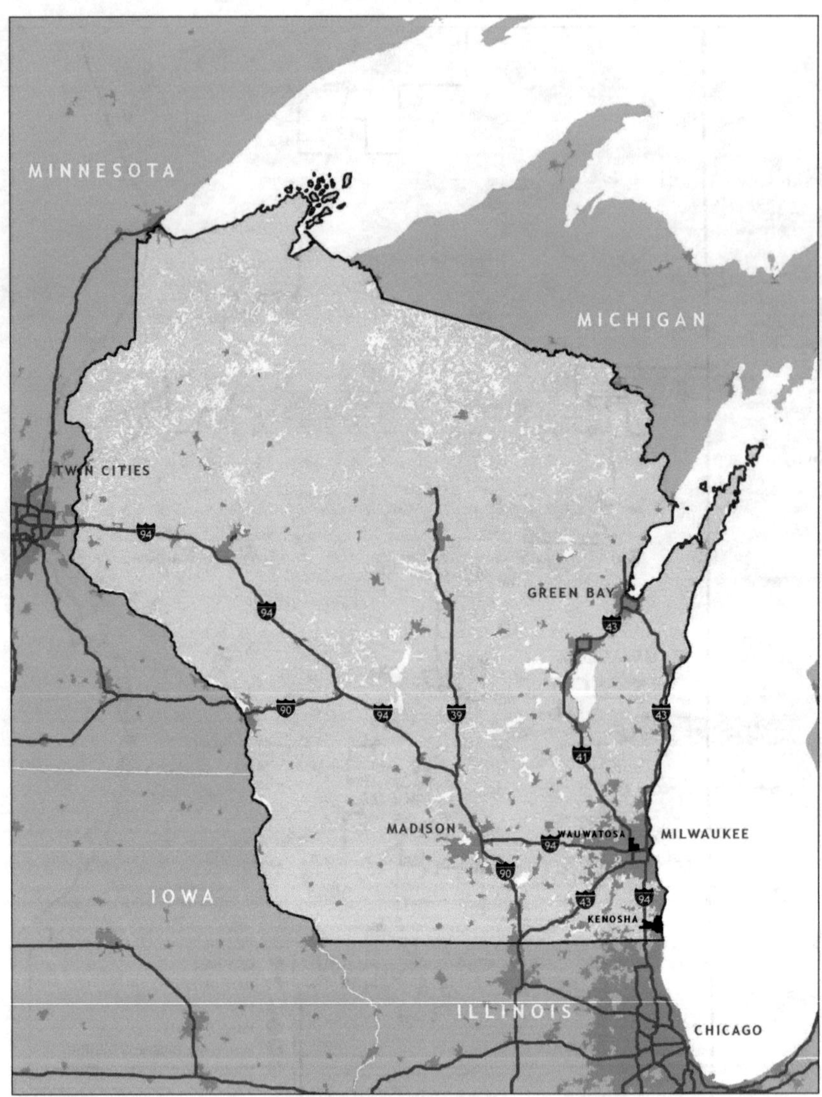

This map of Wisconsin, northern Illinois, and eastern Minnesota shows Wauwatosa's proximity to Chicago, Milwaukee, Madison, Minneapolis, and Kenosha, all cities where major protests and unrest occurred in 2020, both during and after protests and unrest in Wauwatosa. (Paul Vepraskas map)

From the 1920s into the 1950s, signs at the city limits announced "ENTERING WAUWATOSA / CITY OF HOMES / RESTRICTIVE ZONING." They expressed a dual message: Wauwatosa protected its graceful neighborhoods from encroachment by industry but did not welcome non-Whites. (From the Wauwatosa Historical Society Collections)

Former Wauwatosa police officer Joseph Mensah, whose fatal shootings of three men of color between 2015 and 2020 touched off months of protest in Wauwatosa in 2020. (Wauwatosa Police Department photo)

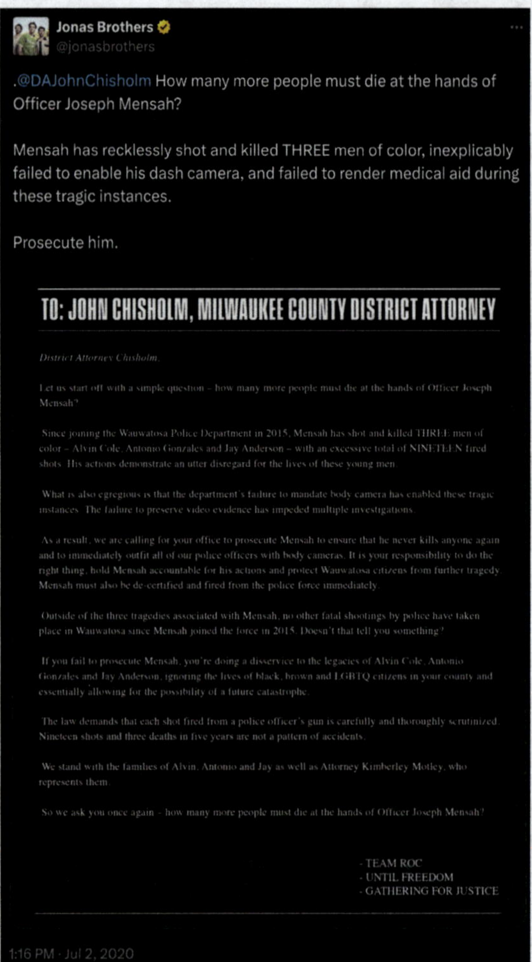

Jonas Brothers
@jonasbrothers

.@DAJohnChisholm How many more people must die at the hands of Officer Joseph Mensah?

Mensah has recklessly shot and killed THREE men of color, inexplicably failed to enable his dash camera, and failed to render medical aid during these tragic instances.

Prosecute him.

TO: JOHN CHISHOLM, MILWAUKEE COUNTY DISTRICT ATTORNEY

District Attorney Chisholm,

Let us start off with a simple question – how many more people must die at the hands of Officer Joseph Mensah?

Since joining the Wauwatosa Police Department in 2015, Mensah has shot and killed THREE men of color – Alvin Cole, Antonio Gonzales and Jay Anderson – with an excessive total of NINETEEN fired shots. His actions demonstrate an utter disregard for the lives of these young men.

What is also egregious is that the department's failure to mandate body camera has enabled these tragic instances. The failure to preserve video evidence has impeded multiple investigations.

As a result, we are calling for your office to prosecute Mensah to ensure that he never kills anyone again and to immediately outfit all of our police officers with body cameras. It is your responsibility to do the right thing, hold Mensah accountable for his actions and protect Wauwatosa citizens from further tragedy. Mensah must also be de-certified and fired from the police force immediately.

Outside of the three tragedies associated with Mensah, no other fatal shootings by police have taken place in Wauwatosa since Mensah joined the force in 2015. Doesn't that tell you something?

If you fail to prosecute Mensah, you're doing a disservice to the legacies of Alvin Cole, Antonio Gonzales and Jay Anderson, ignoring the lives of black, brown and LGBTQ citizens in your county and essentially allowing for the possibility of a future catastrophe.

The law demands that each shot fired from a police officer's gun is carefully and thoroughly scrutinized. Nineteen shots and three deaths in five years are not a pattern of accidents.

We stand with the families of Alvin, Antonio and Jay as well as Attorney Kimberley Motley, who represents them.

So we ask you once again – how many more people must die at the hands of Officer Joseph Mensah?

- TEAM ROC
- UNTIL FREEDOM
- GATHERING FOR JUSTICE

1:16 PM · Jul 2, 2020

On July 2, 2020, the Jonas Brothers musical group posted a message on Twitter (now known as X) reposting an advertisement funded by rapper Jay-Z that was published in the *Milwaukee Journal Sentinel* the same day and demanding that Milwaukee County district attorney John Chisholm charge Officer Mensah with a crime for shooting and killing three men of color. (@jonasbrothers)

On July 14, 2020, protesters from The People's Revolution wrote graffiti in chalk on the sidewalk in front of Mayor McBride's Wauwatosa home. TPR held at least 40 nights of protests there in 2020, almost always leaving such graffiti behind, along with signs and trash. (Dennis McBride photo)

Mayor McBride (in the blue shirt) and several members of the Wauwatosa Common Council listen to speakers from the community during a special council meeting at Wauwatosa's Hart Park Stadium on July 21, 2020, that addressed race, equity, and police issues. About 150 people attended the listening session, which occurred six days after the Wauwatosa Police and Fire Commission suspended Officer Mensah, who had fatally shot three men of color between 2015 and 2020. (@Mark Hoffman / *Milwaukee Journal Sentinel* via Imagn Content Services LLC; USATSI_14560577.jpg)

On August 14, 2020, protesters from The People's Revolution displayed an "Accomplice" sign with a photo of Mayor McBride in the front yard of his home. (Dennis McBride photo)

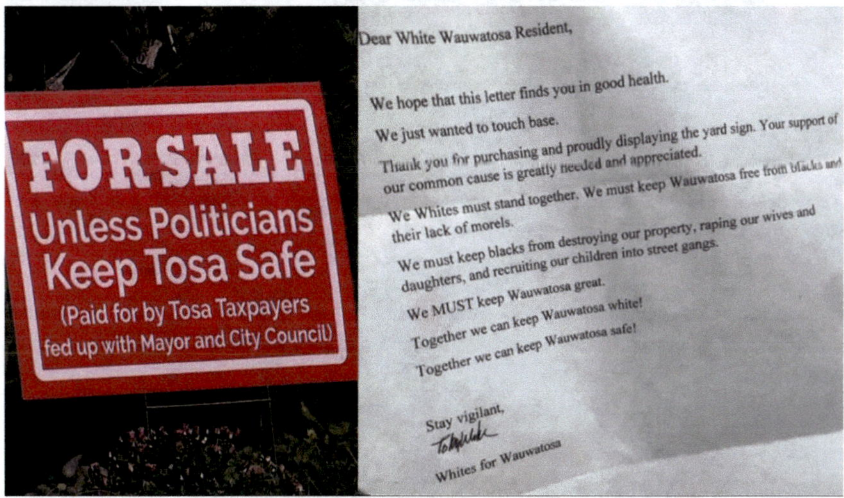

Dear White Wauwatosa Resident,

We hope that this letter finds you in good health.

We just wanted to touch base.

Thank you for purchasing and proudly displaying the yard sign. Your support of our common cause is greatly needed and appreciated.

We Whites must stand together. We must keep Wauwatosa free from blacks and their lack of morels.

We must keep blacks from destroying our property, raping our wives and daughters, and recruiting our children into street gangs.

We MUST keep Wauwatosa great.

Together we can keep Wauwatosa white!

Together we can keep Wauwatosa safe!

Stay vigilant,

Whites for Wauwatosa

In late August 2020, some Wauwatosa residents posted "For Sale" signs denouncing Mayor McBride and the Wauwatosa Common Council for not keeping them safe during protests by The People's Revolution. Those who posted the signs received a letter addressed to "White Wauwatosa Resident" and proclaiming that "Together we can keep Wauwatosa white." It is not known who wrote and sent the letters. (Fox 6/Milwaukee photo; https://www.fox6now.com/news/we-invite-you-to-leave-wauwatosa-mayor-condemns-racist-letters)

HVT

- Dennis McBride
  - Sanctioned violence against Mensah,
  - Alleged to have met privately with Coleman, Motley and Vishny and Brian Anderson.
  - Close connection to David Bowen, was willing to meet and provide an investigative update until stopped by City Attorney,
  - Continually provides outright lies and misleading information to the public,
  - Permitted the People's Revolution to run City of Wauwatosa meetings, has had discussions and Q&A sessions not outlined on meeting agendas, in violation of Open Meetings laws.
  - No PC for involvement in Mensah shooting...yet.

On September 1, 2020, a Wauwatosa detective created a PowerPoint slide describing Mayor McBride as a "high value target" of the Wauwatosa Police Department's investigation into a protester's discharge of a shotgun at Officer Mensah's Wauwatosa home on August 8, 2020. (Wauwatosa Police Department photo)

Presidential candidate and former vice president Joe Biden waves to a crowd of supporters after meeting with three voters, all mothers and teachers, at a home on North 71st Street in Wauwatosa on September 3, 2020. (@Mary Spicuzza / *Milwaukee Journal Sentinel* via Imagn Content Services LLC; USATSI_14875021.jpg)

Khalil Coleman, one of the leaders of the months-long protests by The People's Revolution in Wauwatosa in 2020, speaks as Gaige Grosskreutz of West Allis, Wisconsin, who was shot by Kyle Rittenhouse during the Kenosha riots on August 25, 2020, holds up his injured arm before a march in Milwaukee on September 5, 2020. In 2022, Coleman, who had a long criminal record, began serving a 10-year sentence for robbing a drug house in Kentucky at gunpoint the previous year. (@ Mike De Sisti / *Milwaukee Journal Sentinel* via Imagn Content Services LLC; US-ATSI_14883732.jpg)

A man who did not want to be identified walks with an assault rifle along with others from The People's Revolution as they march through the streets of Milwaukee on September 5, 2020. A man brandished a similar weapon during a TPR march in Wauwatosa on July 28, 2021. (@Mike De Sisti / *Milwaukee Journal Sentinel* via Imagn Content Services LLC; USATSI_14883745.jpg)

Dear Jessica McBitch, I mean McBride,

Im on your ass when I see you. Tell your uncle that. He might just get it to.

This is her with her racist MCBitch Family.
Your own Mayor McBride is in a picture full of KKKs.
Jessica by the way didn't you get divorced becuz you was sleeping with the chief of Police and your Husband who was a DA at the time left your Hoe azz.

Only McBrides mother had some sense. From my knowledge she fought against what McBride is supporting, A racist system.

Until you come to the conclusion that Black Lives matter then it will forever be Fuck you, your ugly ass fatherless daughter and your entire family.

Anyone have a problem with my post you better keep it to your Mfing self becuz I'm going in on every Mfingbody.

All these racist Mfing talking about my brother and my family.
You got the right mfa.

And guess what. God still loves me and knows my heart. I told him I'll talk to him tomorrow becuz today I'm on Tip.

I'm not looking for no likes no nothing I'm gone talk my shyt regardless.

On October 6, 2020, Alvin Cole's sister, Taleavia Cole, posted a message on Facebook denouncing Mayor McBride and his niece, Jessica McBride (who is a lecturer in journalism at the University of Wisconsin–Milwaukee and a contributor to a conservative website, Wisconsin RightNow), as "racists" and "KKKs." This was one of several such Facebook posts by Ms. Cole accusing the McBrides, without citing any supporting evidence, of being members of right-wing extremist groups.

Black Lives Matter supporters write chalk statements on the sidewalk near North 65th Street and West North Avenue in Wauwatosa while workers board up businesses on October 6, 2020, the day before Milwaukee County district attorney John Chisholm announced that he would not charge Officer Joseph Mensah with a crime in the February 2020 fatal shooting of Alvin Cole at Mayfair Mall. (@Rick Wood / *Milwaukee Journal Sentinel* via Imagn Content Services LLC; USATSI_15513655.jpg)

Protesters hold signs outside the Milwaukee County Courthouse on October 7, 2020, including one denouncing Wauwatosa police chief Barry Weber, Wauwatosa mayor Dennis McBride, and Milwaukee County district attorney John Chisholm as "co-conspirators" and demanding that they resign. (@Mike De Sisti / *Milwaukee Journal Sentinel* via Imagn Content Services LLC; USATSI_15035412.jpg)

Police officers and Wisconsin National Guard soldiers protect Wauwatosa City Hall on October 7, 2020, the first night of the curfew imposed by Mayor McBride after Milwaukee County district attorney Chisholm announced he would not charge Officer Mensah with a crime in the fatal shooting of Alvin Cole in February 2020. (@Rick Wood / *Milwaukee Journal Sentinel* via Imagn Content Services LLC; USATSI_15233097.jpg)

Wisconsin National Guard soldiers patrol at Mayfair Mall in Wauwatosa during the night of October 7, 2020. (@Angela Peterson / *Milwaukee Journal Sentinel* via Imagn Content Services LLC; USATSI_15037431.jpg)

Volunteers clean up broken glass on October 8, 2020, from windows that were broken the previous night in stores at the intersection of North Avenue and Swan Boulevard in Wauwatosa during unrest that erupted during protests following Milwaukee County district attorney Chisholm's announcement that he would not charge Officer Mensah with a crime in the fatal shooting of Alvin Cole in February 2020. (@Mark Hoffman / *Milwaukee Journal Sentinel* via Imagn Content Services LLC; USATSI_15039855.jpg)

Outside Wauwatosa City Hall on October 9, 2020, the third night of the curfew period in Wauwatosa following Milwaukee County district attorney Chisholm's announcement that he would not charge Officer Mensah with a crime in the fatal shooting of Alvin Cole, protesters began to depart when police discharged tear gas after the protesters hurled bottles at them. (Fox 6/Milwaukee photo; https://www.fox6now.com/news/protests-form-in-wauwatosa-for-3rd-night-after-mensah-decision)

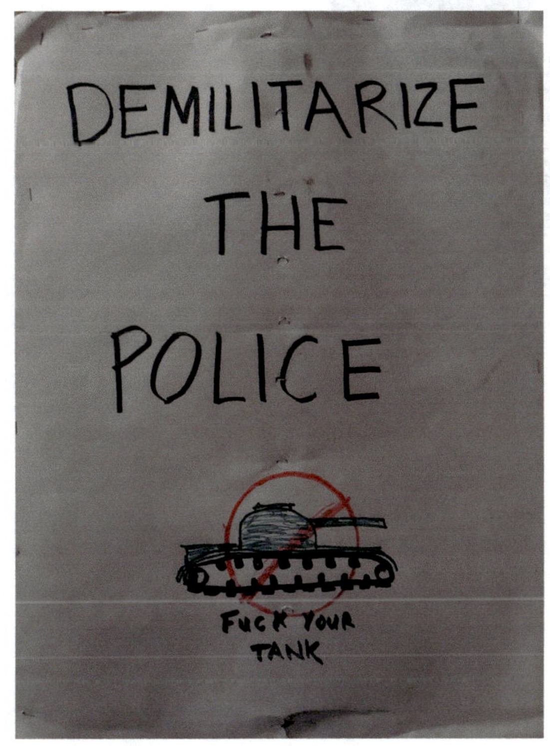

On December 15, 2020, protesters from The People's Revolution displayed a "Demilitarize the Police / F*ck Your Tank" sign in the front yard of Mayor McBride's Wauwatosa home. (Dennis McBride photo)

Sometime in 2020, someone shot a BB through a window in the enclosed front porch of Mayor McBride's Wauwatosa home. The hole was not discovered until later. (Dennis McBride photo)

—~—

UNCIVIL LIBERTIES

DRIVEN BY FEAR, STRESS, AND anger, Americans behaved badly in 2020—and beyond.

"During the pandemic, disorderly, rude, and unhinged conduct seems to have caught on as much as bread baking and [Netflix's Regency-era costume drama] *Bridgerton*," Olga Khazan observed in the *Atlantic* in 2022. "Bad behavior of all kinds—everything from rudeness and carelessness to physical violence—has increased. . . . Americans are driving more recklessly, crashing their cars and killing pedestrians at higher rates. Early 2021 saw the highest number of 'unruly passenger' incidents ever, according to the [Federal Aviation Administration]."

In an essay titled "Why People Are Acting So Weird," Khazan, with the help of psychiatrists, psychologists, sociologists, and other observers, identified likely causes: people were feeling "stressed or overwhelmed" by the pandemic and its impacts like mask mandates and staffing shortages, drinking more alcohol and using more drugs, buying and using more guns, and feeling more socially isolated. "The pandemic loosened ties between people: Kids stopped going to school; their parents stopped going to work; parishioners stopped going to church; people stopped gathering, in general," she wrote. "Sociologists think all of this isolation shifted the way we behave. 'We're more likely to break rules when our bonds to society are weakened,' Robert Sampson, a Harvard sociologist who studies social disorder, told me. 'When we become untethered, we tend to prioritize our own private interests over those of others or the public.'"[1]

A major impact was felt by America's schoolchildren. According to the National Center for Education Statistics of the US Department of Education, 87 percent of public schools reported that the pandemic, which had caused many schools to go to all-virtual classes during the 2020–21 school year, had negatively affected student socioemotional development the following year. Similarly, 84 percent of public schools agreed or strongly agreed that the pandemic had adversely affected student behavior. They reported increased classroom disruptions from misconduct (56 percent), rowdiness outside the classroom (49 percent), disrespect toward teachers and staff (48 percent), and prohibited use of electronic devices (42 percent).[2] The mental health of young people became an ongoing concern.

Describing an early 2024 poll by the Public Religion Research Institute of "Gen Z"—Americans under age 25—*Washington Post* columnist Jennifer Rubin noted that "Gen Z voters are less trustful of government, organized religion, news organizations, the criminal justice system and the police than older generations are."[3] In part, this suggests why 2020 protests were heavily populated with young people, frustrated with the seemingly slow response of society to those issues. The pandemic, political polarization, and changing demographics of America magnified the impatience often associated with young people.

But the pandemic threw people of all ages out of sorts. On the right, protesters objected to mask-wearing and vaccine requirements and equity and inclusion efforts, and on the left, protesters reacted in understandable anger to ongoing abuses of African Americans. Both sides fought over police reform and other hot-button issues.[4] Because emotions were running so high, during

2020 I warned my three adult children that "there is a non-trivial chance that someone will take a shot at me." This was not paranoia; government officials had been shot before, and have been since, by people unhinged by emotion and grievance. In fact, that year someone with a BB gun shot a hole through a window on our enclosed front porch. It was not clear who the shooter was or what his or her motive might have been.[5] In 2020 and for several years thereafter, I went about my regular activities, but always on guard.

In this cautiousness, I was not alone. Princeton University surveys of US municipalities with populations of 1,000 or more in 2023 and 2024 reported that "local elected officials experience pervasive worries about their well-being and safety."[6] A study by the Center for American Women and Politics at Rutgers University found that 95.7 percent of mayors serving cities with populations of 30,000 or more reported having suffered psychological violence ("acts likely to harm the psychological well-being of individuals by inducing fear or harm to their sense of self-worth or well-being"), an increase of 23 percent between 2017 and 2021, and that 13.9 percent of the mayors had suffered physical violence to themselves or their property in 2021, up from 9.2 percent in 2017.[7]

Death threats were repeatedly made to elected and election officials around the country.[8] In a University of Massachusetts poll, nearly half of former members of Congress said they had received threats somewhat often while in office.[9] A higher percentage of women and lawmakers of color reported such threats.[10] Even school board members faced death threats and online abuse, causing some to resign and move out of their communities.[11] During the pandemic, Minneapolis mayor Jacob Frey received death threats from right-wing extremists upset about pandemic restrictions; three years after the George Floyd murder, he was still receiving them from left-wing extremists.[12]

In July 2020, a man who intended to kill US district judge Esther Salas shot and killed her son at her front door in New Jersey and critically wounded her husband.[13] The following year, more than 9,600 direct threats and "concerning statements" were made against members of Congress, and federal judges received more than 4,500 threats and other inappropriate communications.[14] In 2022, a Maryland judge was killed in his driveway by a man angry about losing custody of his children;[15] an intruder chanting "Where's Nancy?" brutally beat the husband of the Speaker of the US House of Representatives, Nancy Pelosi, in their San Francisco home;[16] and a retired Wisconsin judge was killed by a man he had sentenced to prison 17 years earlier.[17] (Also on the Wisconsin murderer's hit list were Wisconsin governor Tony Evers [D], Michigan governor Gretchen Whitmer [D], and US Senate minority leader Mitch McConnell [R-KY].) Later that year, a New Mexico man fired bullets into the homes of the Speaker of the state House of Representatives, a state senator, and two election commissioners, all Democrats, because the Republican candidate for whom he volunteered had alleged that the results in his unsuccessful race for the state House were fraudulent.[18]

Thankfully, no mayor or mayor's family member was injured during 2020. But civility, common sense, and constitutional principles still took a beating. Left- and right-wing protesters did not need to travel far to protest at the homes of their local elected officials.

Angry militia-related crowds protesting COVID restrictions gathered at the home of Lauren McLean, the mayor of Boise, Idaho, every Sunday night in the summer of 2020. The mobs returned with torches and pitchforks that November. She and her family also received repeated threats to their well-being by mail and email and on social media. The Boise police assigned McLean a security detail, but she was no longer able to walk alone to work, ride her bike as she wished, or run on local trails as she had done for 24 years. She was dismayed that other elected officials had left office because of threats to them and their families, but she did not criticize them.

"I understand the decision to leave public office because I still feel intensely the fear, frustration, and helplessness of watching my two children quietly take in news of thwarted threats against me and learning that they, too, were being targeted and tracked online," she said in a March 2022 statement. "A parent's dearest wish is to keep their kids safe and sound and far away from the worst the world has to offer. . . . I understand the decision to leave public office because just weeks after the first of several family briefings and as people carrying torches stood just twenty feet from our living room window, I sat on our basement stairs to be sure my brave, supportive kids wouldn't see my face. Because, in that moment, I knew masking my fear from them was impossible." But courage had not left her. "I've decided, with my family, that we won't back down, and that I'll continue to serve this city I love, to encourage our kids to find careers of service, to support my staff in their own callings to serve their city," she said. "We won't let the threats designed to terrify and silence us win."[19]

Mayors became targets in the aftermath of the Floyd murder, too.[20] In June 2020, thousands of people protested at Los Angeles mayor Eric Garcetti's home, even though at a demonstration earlier in the day he had taken a knee, denounced the Floyd murder, and defended the right to protest.[21] Two weeks later, 100 people protested at the home of Miro Weinberger, the mayor of Burlington, Vermont. Deploying a sousaphone, drums, and loudspeakers, they blocked traffic and chanted, "Black lives matter!" and "Hey hey, ho ho, Mayor Weinberger's got to go!" They denounced his 2021 budget proposal, even though it would have left 12 police officer positions vacant and reduced the $17.4 million police budget by $1.1 million, and demanded that Burlington reduce its police force by 30 percent and spend the money on issues facing people of color.[22]

At 2:00 a.m. one morning at Mayor Libby Schaaf's home in Oakland, California, in July 2020, protesters spray-painted messages that included "Defund OPD!" (Oakland Police

Department), "homes 4 all," and "blood on your hands" on the garage, sidewalk, and wall and 30 to 40 people wearing masks shot projectiles and set off fireworks. In August, Chicago police blocked access to Mayor Lori Lightfoot's block to protect her and her wife, daughter, and neighbors after she received threats. That month, protesters and police also clashed outside Pittsburgh mayor Bill Peduto's home. It was not enough that Peduto had said he was "livid" over police tactics that had sparked earlier protests; he had already angered BLM protesters by tweeting—correctly, as a matter of law—that "the right to assemble is a guaranteed right, but the right to shut down public streets is a privilege."

After two nights of protests at his home, Peduto expressed support for the BLM movement but added, "What I cannot defend is any neighborhood in our city—and their residents and families—being disturbed through the night and morning, and a peaceful protest devolving into unacceptable conduct in which residents are being harassed and threatened." At 10:00 p.m. the second night, police told the protesters that their demonstrations violated the city's noise ordinance, declared the protest an unlawful assembly, and ordered protesters to disperse or face arrest. Police deployed tear gas after protesters continued to use bullhorns, sing, and chant.[23]

Likewise, a late August protest in San Jose, California, ignited by the shooting of Jacob Blake in Kenosha, turned ugly. Hundreds of protesters, mostly peaceful, demonstrated downtown, but some spray-painted expletives on Mayor Sam Liccardo's home and burned a flag outside. KGO-TV reported that Liccardo expressed gratitude for neighbors who helped remove the graffiti. "Many of these same neighbors' homes bear 'Black Lives Matter' signs, and they represent the true spirit of the movement, and of our San Jose community," he said. "They contrast sharply with the roughly hundred so-called 'protesters' who stood by silently—or even cheered—as a flag was burned and while 'f*ck you' and other messages were scrawled on our home."[24]

On August 31, protesters "celebrated" Portland mayor Ted Wheeler's birthday by rioting at his condominium tower and demanding his resignation. As previously described, they lit a fire in the street and in a store, smashed windows, broke into a dental office, and looted office supplies and a chair, which they threw in the fire. Police arrested 19 people. This was not the first time that protests had occurred at Wheeler's home. He refused to resign and was reelected a few months later.[25]

The incidents in other cities resembled the 40 days and nights of protests at my home during the summer and fall of 2020. The People's Revolution's actions at its Wauwatosa protests, described earlier—blocking intersections, driving cars on both sides of the street while repeatedly honking car horns, screaming profanities, writing obscenities on sidewalks, placing vulgar signs on lawns, shining strobe lights into house windows and into the eyes of police officers, throwing trash on lawns, brandishing guns, driving cars on lawns and sidewalks, shoving police officers, and discharging a shotgun at Officer Mensah's home—were defended by supporters as "peaceful" protesting or "civil disobedience." As one journalist observed, such protesting was exhilarating for young people, tired of being cooped up during the pandemic and understandably angry about Black people being killed, "both to save the world and to experience a nightly spurt of relief."[26] But it was disorderly or criminal behavior, and, like similar behavior in some other protests across the country, it hurt the cause of police reform for which people were rallying.[27]

After the Wauwatosa curfew period ended in October 2020 and criminal prosecutions sidetracked TPR's leaders, the group's protests became more peaceful. A notable exception occurred on July 28, 2021. That afternoon, TPR members spilled into Wauwatosa's streets after a Milwaukee County judge decided to appoint special prosecutors to determine whether Mensah should be charged in the killing of Jay Anderson Jr. Celebrating that temporary victory—the prosecutors later decided not to charge

Mensah—the protesters marched up the middle of Wauwatosa Avenue to City Hall and blocked several busy intersections. One of their leaders, who brandished an AR-15 assault rifle throughout the march, stopped a Black woman driving home with her three children and pointed his rifle into her car. When a police officer intervened, protesters surrounded him and tried to stop him from protecting the family. Our new police chief offered to show a video of the incident to Common Council and Tosa Together members who had claimed that every TPR protest was peaceful. They all declined, saying that watching the video would be "too traumatic."

Many of TPR's unpeaceful 2020 protests lasted for hours. Some happened as late as 2:00 a.m.[28] Such behavior occurred throughout Wauwatosa but was primarily directed at me and the citizen volunteers who serve on the Wauwatosa Police and Fire Commission (WPFC), including its then-chairman, who by chance lived on my block, demanding that we fire Mensah and Chief Barry Weber. During the protests, my wife and I were trapped inside our home and often awakened from a sound sleep by music blaring from large speakers mounted on trucks, by lines of cars honking their horns, and by crowds of protesters chanting, "Mayor McBride, come outside!"[29]

A Wauwatosa ordinance prohibits "picketing before or about the residence or dwelling of any individual."[30] That ordinance's language, approved by the Wisconsin Supreme Court in 1971,[31] was later adopted by the Town of Brookfield, Wisconsin, when protesters repeatedly picketed outside a doctor's home to pressure him to stop performing abortions. In *Frisby v. Schultz* (1988), the US Supreme Court upheld the Brookfield ordinance as a reasonable time, place, and manner restriction on the exercise of free speech.[32] It interpreted the ordinance as content neutral and allowing picketers to march through residential areas and assemble in public streets if they do not congregate around a specific house. It held that municipalities have the constitutional authority to ensure residential tranquility and protect listeners from unwanted speech while in their homes.[33]

In *Frisby,* the court noted that the picketers were not merely expressing their views to the public but were intruding on the homeowner's privacy.[34] Similarly, the picketing at my home intruded on my family's privacy to pressure me to fire Mensah and Weber. Because I had no such authority under law, TPR's protests at my home were as legally unsound as those that occurred at the homes of state and local election officials when Trump supporters demanded that the 2020 presidential election be overturned.[35] But such behavior had become common.

In September 2021, the *Washington Post* reported, "Protests that blur the boundaries between free expression and mob rule have taken aim at local and national officials of both parties," noting that protesters had defaced the San Francisco home of Congresswoman Nancy Pelosi (D-CA) with demands for $2,000 stimulus payments, demonstrated outside the Virginia home of Senator Josh Hawley (R-MO) to object to his challenge to President Biden's election victory, picketed the homes of Michigan governor Gretchen Whitmer's cabinet in opposition to COVID restrictions, and rallied at the home of Washington, DC, mayor Muriel Bowser on issues ranging from homeless services to defunding the police.[36]

The value of anti-residential-picketing ordinances seemed clear to liberals when "pro-life" extremists murdered three doctors and four workers at abortion clinics in the 1990s. They also seemed clear when Rusty Bowers, the Republican Speaker of the Arizona House of Representatives, resisted efforts to undo Trump's 2020 loss in that state and had his home picketed while his daughter lay dying inside, and when the FBI had to warn embattled Georgia poll worker Ruby Freeman, who had received death threats and racist messages, to vacate her home because it was about to be surrounded by angry Trump supporters.[37] On the other side, conservatives expressed outrage when pro-choice activists chanting slogans, using bullhorns, and banging drums picketed the homes of Supreme Court justices after the draft opinion was leaked in *Dobbs v. Jackson Women's Health Organization* (2022),[38] which overturned *Roe v. Wade* (1973)[39] and rejected a constitutional right to abortion.[40]

"It should be possible to find ways to express justified outrage at the conservative justices without terrorizing them and their families," wrote liberal *Washington Post* columnist Ruth Marcus. "Can we not at least manage that?" Two Democratic senators who opposed the *Dobbs* decision, Richard Durbin of Illinois and Patrick Leahy of Vermont, agreed. "We all know that you have to have a tough mental hide to be in this business," Durbin said at a Judiciary Committee hearing. "But it's absolutely unacceptable, from my point of view, to involve any major public figure's family or their home or to involve yourself in criminal trespass in the name of political freedom of speech." He and Leahy said that if people are not happy with a judge's or elected official's actions, they should express themselves through their votes or in a protest at a public building. For its part, the *Post* editorial board wrote, echoing Marcus's observation that picketing at homes of public officials makes those officials and their neighbors less likely to agree with the protesters, "Leave spouses, children and homes out of it. If that appeal for basic civility and decency isn't persuasive, those who engage in these reprehensible tactics should realize they are only hurting their cause when it is overshadowed by their tactics."[41]

Although the Wauwatosa ordinance banning residential picketing is constitutional, the Wauwatosa Police Department did not have enough officers to enforce the ordinance when hundreds of protesters massed at my home and at the homes of WPFC members. All the police could do was to try to maintain order. But we were still trapped and harassed in our homes.

In July 2020, the WPFC began considering a complaint filed against Officer Mensah by the family of Jay Anderson Jr.

Wisconsin law gives police and fire commissions sole authority over the hiring, firing, and discipline of police and fire chiefs, police officers, and firefighters so the commissions can carry out their duties without political pressure or interference from elected officials.[42] Section 62.13 of the Wisconsin Statutes spells out the procedures the commissions must follow; in short, officers and chiefs must receive due process of law. This requires that civil and criminal legal matters be resolved according to established rules and principles.[43] As a prominent DC lawyer has described, "Due process is the crown jewel of the rule of law; it embodies the idea that every person is entitled to a day in court and to be heard following a set standard protocol to ensure fairness."[44]

That protection is required not just by statute but also by the US and Wisconsin Constitutions, which provide identical due process safeguards.[45] Nevertheless, throughout 2020, TPR and its attorneys, Wauwatosa advocacy groups, state legislators from Milwaukee, and the people who protested at my home continually demanded that I fire Mensah and Chief Weber immediately.[46] That would have had harmful results.

While the WPFC dealt with Mensah, the Milwaukee Fire and Police Commission (MFPC) created a legal and financial mess in August 2020 when, bowing to community pressure, it demoted Police Chief Alfonso Morales to captain without giving him the due process required by Section 62.13. In December 2020, a state judge reversed the demotion.[47] Because of the MFPC's blundering, Milwaukee then had two chiefs—an interim chief and another reinstated by the court.

In February 2021, Milwaukee's inspector general concluded that the MFPC had disregarded Section 62.13 and its own complaint procedure when it demoted Morales. She wrote that "evidence suggests that . . . the [MFPC]'s decision to demote the chief was exclusively based on an apparent assertion by the City Attorney [Tearman Spencer] 'to do what needs to be done' with assurance that the [MFPC]'s decision would be supported and defended by the City Attorney's Office."[48] In July 2021, the city agreed to pay Morales $500,000 in damages and $127,000 in legal fees to resolve the case. Costs for mediation and the city's own legal fees drove up the total to $668,000.[49]

A puffed-up sense of moral certainty or a panicked response to community pressure can lead to "doing what needs to be done" without regard to legal rights or consequences. The Milwaukee fiasco illustrates what would have happened if the WPFC or I had denied Mensah due process by caving in to demands to "fire him immediately." After a certain legal battle, we would have been required to reinstate him and pay him hundreds of thousands of dollars in damages. Instead, while TPR's protests continued, we quietly negotiated with him for four months and reached a separation agreement at a fraction of that cost.[50] Despite the lessons that should have been learned from those patient negotiations and from Milwaukee's mistreatment of Morales, Kimberley Motley, the attorney who unsuccessfully sued Wauwatosa on behalf of the protesters arrested during the October 2020 curfew, still demanded that we fire Chief Weber even after he announced his retirement.[51] Had we done so, we would have sunk into the same legal and financial mire that Milwaukee stumbled into.

In 2020, Motley and others likewise demanded that Mensah be fired because "he's bad," ignoring that he had never been charged with or convicted of a crime and the law requires that police officers be given due process before they can be punished. When I refused to give in to such demands and fire Mensah "immediately," one dissatisfied resident accused me of "thinking too much like a lawyer." Guilty as charged. As Supreme Court justice Felix Frankfurter wrote in *McNabb v. United States* in 1943, "The history of liberty has largely been the history of the observance of procedural safeguards."[52]

In Mensah's case, the question was not one of morality, but of law. In 1966, *A Man for All Seasons* won the Academy Award for Best Picture for its depiction of the life and death of Thomas

More, the patron saint of lawyers, politicians, and public servants and the lord chancellor of England beheaded by King Henry VIII for opposing the Protestant Reformation.[53] In one scene, More's wife, daughter, and son-in-law demanded that More arrest a man for being "bad." Ever the lawyer, More answered that he would let the man go "if he was the Devil himself, until he broke the law." In a fit of performative piety, More's son-in-law proudly proclaimed that he would cut down every law in England to go after the Devil. "Oh?" replied More. "And when the last law was down, and the Devil turned 'round on you, where would you hide, the laws all being flat? This country's planted thick with laws from coast to coast—man's laws, not God's—and if you cut them down . . . do you really think you could stand upright in the winds that would blow then? Yes, I'd give the Devil benefit of law, for my own safety's sake."[54]

Even if Mensah had been prosecuted, under law—and morality—it would have been the duty of the district attorney, the WPFC, the Common Council, and me to provide him with due process, for his sake and for all other people charged with crimes or at risk of losing their jobs. We could not allow lawyers and politicians with personal agendas, or even citizens with good intentions, to trample on that constitutional right, whether we sympathized with their goals or not.

—~~—

BATTLEGROUND

WHILE THE PANDEMIC AND PROTESTS glowed red hot in 2020, the presidential campaign between President Donald Trump and former Vice President Joseph Biden raged on.

Though Trump lost the popular vote to Hillary Clinton in 2016, he won in the Electoral College by finishing ahead in the vote in key states, including the "Blue Wall" state of Wisconsin, which had not voted for a GOP presidential candidate since 1984 but in which presidential contests have been routinely decided by less than a percentage point.[1]

At the start of 2020, it was clear that for Electoral College purposes, most states remained firmly Democratic or Republican. Six closely divided battleground states—Arizona, Georgia, Nevada, and Wisconsin and the other Blue Wall states of Michigan and Pennsylvania—would be crucial to the outcome. The political parties waged yearlong legal battles in those states over voting qualifications, procedures, and outcomes that reached the state and US Supreme Courts. More than 250 election lawsuits spurred by the pandemic were filed. Election law expert Rick Hasen (then at the University of California at Irvine and later at the University of California at Los Angeles) called the 2020 race "almost certainly" the most litigated election in American history.[2]

On November 3, 2020, Biden won the election with 81,283,098 votes to 74,222,958 for Trump. With 51.3 percent, he received the highest share of the vote for a challenger of an incumbent president since Franklin D. Roosevelt defeated Herbert Hoover in 1932.[3] Though Biden won by 7 million votes, National Public Radio's Domenico Montanaro noted that "just 44,000 votes in Georgia, Arizona and Wisconsin separated Biden and Trump from a tie in the Electoral College."[4] CNN observed that "even a small tick toward the Republicans would have resulted in a very different outcome in 2020. Biden won the state that put him over the top in the Electoral College (Wisconsin) by less than a point."[5]

It could have been very different. As the BLM protests intensified nationwide throughout the summer, the question was whether they would sway the presidential election. For some voters, they did.[6] The riots that gripped Kenosha in late August seemed like a tipping point.

While that unrest was occurring, the Republican Party held its national convention.[7] On the convention's third night (August 26), Vice President Mike Pence, Trump's daughter-in-law, and other speakers seized on the unrest as they addressed the delegates. Accepting renomination, Pence said, "Let me be clear, the violence must stop—whether in Minnesota, Portland or Kenosha. We will have law and order on the streets of America." But in a *New York Times* article titled "With Wisconsin Unrest as Backdrop, Republicans Intensify Law-and-Order Message," Jonathan Martin and Alexander Burns wrote, "The intense focus on the rioting amounted to an acknowledgment by Republicans that they must reframe the election to make urban unrest the central theme and shift attention away from the deaths and illnesses of millions of people from the coronavirus." Similarly, the *Washington Post*'s Jacqueline Alemany observed, "Republican denunciations of 'violent mobs' in 'radical Democratic cities' didn't note that self-declared militia members and armed counter-protesters . . . contributed to and instigated such violence or acknowledge that by then more than 175,000 Americans had died from the coronavirus and that the economic fallout from the virus had thrown many people out of work." Pence was undeterred. "You won't be safe in Joe Biden's America," he asserted.[8]

Accepting renomination the following night, Trump likewise denounced "the rioting, looting, arson, and violence we have seen in Democrat-run cities like Kenosha, Minneapolis, Portland, Chicago, and New York."[9] Biden retorted, "Did Mike Pence forget Donald Trump is president? Is Donald Trump even aware he's president? These are not images from some imagined 'Joe Biden's America' in the future. These are images from Donald Trump's America today."[10] But the *Times*, *Politico*, and other media outlets reported that the riots were making Democrats nervous.[11]

Democratic Party leaders criticized Wisconsin governor Tony Evers, a Democrat, for not sending the National Guard to Kenosha sooner, even though he had declared a state of emergency and sent troops on the first night of the riots and doubled the number of soldiers the second night. *Politico* reported that Democrats feared that Evers had given the Republican presidential campaign a political advantage. Terry Rose, a county supervisor and former Kenosha County Democratic Party chair, said that Kenosha residents and business owners who lost their livelihoods, feared for their lives, or watched their city burn were angry. "This is about the public safety and the lifeblood of this community," said Rose. "Who has the governor really helped? I think he helped the Trump campaign, not the Biden campaign—unwittingly."[12]

The former mayor of Madison, Paul Soglin, agreed. "There's no doubt it's playing into Trump's hands," he told *Politico*. "There's a significant number of undecided voters who are not ideological, and they can move very easily from Republican to the Democratic column and back again. They are, in effect, the people who decide elections. And they are very distraught about both the horrendous carnage created by police officers in murdering

African Americans, and . . . for the safety of their communities." Soglin, a liberal and former leader of anti–Vietnam War protests at the University of Wisconsin–Madison, said he was concerned that Democrats were not paying enough attention to the business owners and residents who wanted protection. "The perception [that swing voters] have is that innocent people are the victims of the looters and the arsonists," he said. "They're watching small business people in their communities, seeing their stores trashed. Seeing jobs lost. And people already under stress from the pandemic don't have much patience for this politics of punishment—punishment of innocent people."[13]

"If Donald Trump wins, what's happening this week in Kenosha, Wisconsin, will be one reason," George Packer agonized in the *Atlantic* on August 28. "Maybe *the* reason. . . . In the crude terms of a presidential campaign, voters know that [Biden] means it when he denounces police brutality, but less so when he denounces riots. . . . Democratic leaders, from the nearly invisible mayor of Kenosha up to those on the presidential ticket, are reluctant to tarnish a just cause, amplify Republican attacks, or draw the wrath of their own progressive base. . . . So Democrats continue to mute their response to the violence and hope it will subside, even though it has persisted straight through the summer."[14]

In polls, Wisconsin voters' support for the BLM movement and BLM protests slid from 59–27 percent and 61–36 percent in June to 49–37 percent and 48–48 percent only six weeks later. But, noted Wisconsin political expert J. R. Ross in *Politico*, not all voters embraced Trump's law-and-order message. Most gave him low marks for his response to the protests. "Why?" Ross asked. "Because, to Wisconsinites, after such a tense, violent summer, the protesters might look bad, but Trump, and his law-and-order supporters, don't look much better."[15]

On September 1, Trump visited Kenosha and doubled down on his dark rhetoric. "These are not acts of peaceful protest but, really, domestic terror," he said. And he chastised Democratic officials for not always accepting his offers of federal enforcement assistance, claiming, "They just don't want us to come."[16] Biden visited Kenosha the next day. The following day, on a Wauwatosa backyard patio, he and his wife Jill spoke with three women who are educators and mothers about the challenges of sending children back to school during a pandemic. The *Milwaukee Journal Sentinel* concluded that the Wauwatosa visit was intended to blunt Trump's law-and-order appeal to suburban female voters.[17]

Five weeks later, because of what had happened in Kenosha, Governor Evers posted the National Guard in Wauwatosa in October 2020 to control the unrest expected to follow the district attorney's decision whether to charge Officer Mensah with a crime for killing Alvin Cole. That military activation and accompanying curfew were unpopular with some progressives. But what we did not hear was that a Democratic governor—or mayor—had allowed another city to burn down. The only murmur was an occasional television commercial run that October by a Republican candidate for a Wauwatosa seat in the Wisconsin Assembly, scolding her Democratic rival for not denouncing the violence in Wauwatosa.[18]

On November 3, Biden carried Wisconsin, but only by 20,682 votes out of 3 million cast.[19] The margins in Wauwatosa and Milwaukee's North Shore suburbs were critical to that victory.[20] Of Wauwatosa's 34,895 registered voters, 31,620 cast ballots, a 90.9 percent turnout. Biden received 20,880 votes, Trump received 10,104, and other candidates split the remaining 636. Thus, more than half of Biden's winning margin in Wisconsin came from Wauwatosa.[21] Not surprisingly, one commentator has called Wauwatosa "one of the most important cities on the political map in . . . Wisconsin."[22]

The *Journal Sentinel*'s national political reporter, Craig Gilbert, has observed that no community better illustrates the changing nature of Wisconsin politics than Wauwatosa, which Republican governor Scott Walker, who lived in Wauwatosa and ran for the GOP presidential nomination in 2016, won by 5 points in 2014 but lost by 16 points in 2018. Wauwatosa was the Wisconsin community with the biggest swing between the 2018 and 2022 midterm elections, from plus-16.2 points Democratic to plus-40.3 points Democratic. Only two Wisconsin cities gave Governor Evers a bigger vote margin in his 2022 reelection. "In 22 years," Gilbert wrote in 2022, "this Milwaukee suburb has gone from being one of the single most important sources of Republican votes to being one of the single most important sources of Democratic votes."[23]

Though it cannot be proved, the actions taken to preserve life, property, and order in Wauwatosa in October 2020 seem to have enabled Biden to win Wisconsin, and the overall election, a month later. Republican political commentator Charles Sykes observed, "In June, Biden led the Marquette University Law poll by six points [in Wisconsin], but he ended up winning the state by just 20,600 votes—well under 1 percentage point. Election analyst Jesse Richardson, who blogs on the Political Kiwi website, wrote that he found 'strong evidence that the rioting in Kenosha resulted in increased support for Donald Trump, and that if we'd seen a similar level of rioting in say, Milwaukee, it might've cost Joe Biden the state.'"[24] Thus, had Wauwatosa—in Milwaukee County—experienced Kenosha-like unrest, Biden's razor-thin victory in Wisconsin might have disappeared. The measures we took to keep Wauwatosa safe in October 2020 kept that from happening. A few Democratic Party officials later quietly acknowledged this to me.

After the election, Trump claimed without evidence that fraud had deprived him of victory. But Georgia held two recounts of its presidential election results, both affirming Biden's victory. A recount in Wisconsin confirmed Biden's victory, too.[25] This did not stop Trump from continuing to challenge the outcome, to the point of having false slates of Electoral College electors created in the six battleground states plus New Mexico.[26]

He and his supporters brought 62 lawsuits and lost them all, even though he had appointed some of the judges who dismissed the meritless cases. Nearly all the lawsuits were dismissed or dropped for lack of evidence.[27] "While there are many arenas—including print, television, and social media—where protestations, conjecture, and speculation may be advanced," US district judge Linda V. Parker later wrote in a Michigan case in which she sanctioned the plaintiffs' lawyers for "abusive" litigation practices, "such expressions are neither permitted nor welcomed in a court of law."[28]

The Arizona and Nevada Supreme Courts rejected or declined to hear Trump's appeals to overturn results in those states, while the Pennsylvania and Michigan Supreme Courts denied multiple lawsuits. The US Supreme Court rejected two cases that sought to overturn the election. In a one-sentence order on December 8, the court rebuffed a claim that the Pennsylvania legislature's expansion of absentee voting had violated the state constitution. Three days later, it rejected GOP-dominated Texas's challenge to the Georgia, Michigan, Pennsylvania, and Wisconsin results, holding that Texas lacked "a judicially cognizable interest in the manner in which another state conducts its elections."[29]

But one lawsuit could have profoundly disrupted the election and undermined our democracy. On December 14, an hour before Wisconsin's 10 Electoral College votes were cast for Biden, the Wisconsin Supreme Court narrowly rejected Trump's request to disqualify 221,000 absentee ballots in the state's two most Democratic counties, Dane (Madison) and Milwaukee. "Striking these votes now—after the election, and in only two of Wisconsin's 72 counties when the disputed practices were followed by hundreds of thousands of absentee voters statewide—would be an extraordinary step for this court to take," conservative Justice Brian Hagedorn wrote in a 4–3 decision joined by the court's three liberal justices. "We will not do so." The three dissenting conservative justices said the court should have decided the claims.[30]

That those justices voted to overturn the results in the state's most Democratic counties, without evidence of irregularities, was shameful.[31] More dangerously, such partisanship could have created chaos nationwide by casting doubt on a battleground state's election results and giving Trump his only legal victory.[32]

Chaos erupted three weeks later. On January 6, 2021, the 2020 election, democracy, and the rule of law fell under siege. Thousands of Proud Boys, Oath Keepers, and other Trump supporters, egged on by Trump's inflammatory speech on the Ellipse south of the White House, marched to the US Capitol and mounted an insurrection aimed at stopping Vice President Pence and Congress from certifying the election results. Only the heroism of Capitol and DC police and other law enforcement officers stopped the rioters from achieving their goals.[33]

In July 2022, eight prominent Republican attorneys, judges, and politicians published a 72-page report, *Lost, Not Stolen: The Conservative Case That Trump Lost and Biden Won the 2020 Presidential Election,* which examined the lawsuits filed by Trump and his supporters in Arizona, Georgia, Michigan, Nevada, Pennsylvania, and Wisconsin. They concluded that there was no evidence of election irregularities, that Trump's arguments were "woefully deficient," and that our election system had worked well. "Even now, twenty months after the election, a period in which Trump's supporters have been energetically scouring every nook and cranny for proof that the election was stolen, they come up empty," the Republican stalwarts wrote. "Claims are made, trumpeted in sympathetic media, and accepted as truthful by many patriotic Americans. But on objective examination they have fallen short, every time."[34]

The four closest states in 2020—Arizona, Georgia, Pennsylvania, and Wisconsin—were the only states with races for both governor and US Senate in the 2022 midterm elections. "Partisans who obsessively checked the poll results from those few states in 2020 have found themselves in a political *Groundhog Day,* scanning the *FiveThirtyEight* election-outcome probabilities on pretty much the same places two years later," the *Atlantic*'s Ronald Brownstein wrote in October 2022. "Two years from now, in the 2024 presidential contest, they are almost guaranteed to be fixated on the same states again." Similarly, Craig Gilbert observed, "'ground zero' in American politics in 2022 looks a lot like 'ground zero' in 2020. The Senate races in these battleground states will go a long way toward deciding control of that 50–50 chamber."[35]

Gilbert's prediction came true. The Democrats retained control of the Senate by winning races in Arizona and Georgia and added a seat to their slim majority by flipping a seat in Pennsylvania.[36] They narrowly failed to pick up a seat in Wisconsin—which a CNN analyst called "the nation's premier swing state" (underscored by the parties' selection of Milwaukee as the site of the 2020 Democratic National Convention and the 2024 Republican National Convention)—where GOP incumbent Ron Johnson accused Governor Evers and Lieutenant Governor Mandela Barnes, who was running to replace Johnson, of "inciting" the Kenosha riots in 2020.[37] In the end, the midterm results illustrated how closely divided our government and country were: Democrats controlled the Senate with a 51–49 majority, Republicans controlled the House of Representatives with a 222–213 majority, and a Democrat, Biden, occupied the White House.[38]

Though 2020 had been one of our country's most consequential elections, the stakes and potential for strife in 2024 seemed even higher. Biden and Trump were their parties' front-runners again before Biden dropped out in late July in favor of his vice president, Kamala Harris. It seemed clear that the same battleground states would decide the 2024 election, and perhaps over the same issues.[39] When Harris chose Minnesota governor Tim Walz as her running mate, a Trump surrogate, Florida governor

Ron DeSantis, accused Walz of "let[ting] Minneapolis burn" during the unrest of 2020, and GOP vice-presidential candidate J. D. Vance appeared in Kenosha to blame Democrats for the 2020 riots there.[40]

Ever since 2020, Republicans across the nation had been instituting measures to suppress voting in the name of preventing "voter fraud" for which there was little evidence. In closely divided and watched Wisconsin, where every vote mattered, conservative poll watchers descended on the Democratic-leaning Milwaukee suburb of Glendale and challenged every absentee ballot cast in a primary election in late July 2024. Police had to be called. Glendale mayor Bryan Kennedy, fearful that such actions, if repeated, would intimidate Democratic voters in the November presidential election, warned me to be on guard in Wauwatosa, too.

In an article looking ahead two months before the 2024 election, the *Christian Science Monitor* called Wisconsin "a microcosm of a broader struggle to restore confidence in a bedrock of U.S. democracy: the casting and counting of votes." In the article, I responded to Mayor Kennedy's warning. "Frankly, I expect problems in November," I said. "That's the story in America right now."[41] We were afraid for our nation and weary of being a battleground.

On November 5, 2024, Donald Trump broke through the Democrats' Blue Wall of Pennsylvania, Michigan, and Wisconsin again and was elected to a second term as president. For the fifth time in seven presidential elections, Wisconsin was decided by less than one percentage point. On election night, when the race was called for Trump, it was the state that put him over the top in Electoral College votes, just as Wisconsin had put Biden over the top four years earlier.[42] Our fears about interference with voting did not come true, but it appeared that Wisconsin would remain a political battleground for years to come.

Meanwhile, European Union countries pondered what a second Trump presidency would mean for them and the North Atlantic Treaty Organization. It seemed clear that they would have to steer a course less dependent on the United States. "We cannot leave the security of Europe in the hands of voters in Wisconsin every four years," said France's minister delegate for European affairs, Benjamin Haddad. "Let's get out of collective denial. Europeans must take their destiny into their own hands, regardless of who is elected president."[43]

MASS SHOOTING

IN 2020, WHILE MANY COMMUNITIES were under COVID lockdowns, protesters and counterprotesters were flooding the streets, and economic uncertainty and social isolation were deepening, Americans went on a shopping spree—for firearms. Some 22 million guns were sold that year, 64 percent more than in 2019. More than eight million were obtained by people who had never owned a gun, according to the industry's trade association, the National Shooting Sports Foundation. Firearm homicides increased that year as well, to 19,350 from 14,392 in 2019. The death count from guns, including suicides, rose to 45,222 in 2020 from 39,702 in 2019. The number of lives lost to guns rose again in 2021, to 48,830.[1]

The anger, fear, uncertainty, and disconnectedness felt by people of all ages, races, and demographics had manifested themselves in gun violence. A *Washington Post* headline said it all: "2020 Was the Deadliest Gun Violence Year in Decades."[2]

Since violent crimes spiked in the 1980s and early 1990s, America had experienced what was called "the great American crime decline." That changed in 2020, which saw a 47 percent increase in mass shootings as well as unprecedented increases in gun-related incidents.[3] Not only did firearm homicides increase by 35 percent from 2019 to 2020; the number of gun deaths in 2020 was the highest ever recorded by the US Centers for Disease Control and Prevention. On average, 124 people died every day that year from gun violence. Gun violence was the leading cause of death for Americans under age 25.[4]

More Americans bought guns in June 2020, the month after George Floyd was murdered, than any previous month in US history.[5] In a national survey, firearms retailers estimated that 40 percent of their sales came from first-time gun buyers, of whom 40 percent were women. Some buyers were fearful that they and their families would not be safe if the "defund the police" movement got momentum. On the other side, some bought guns in reaction to police brutality.[6] The lack of trust was deadly.

In 2020, the US experienced its biggest one-year increase in homicides ever, a spike that continued into 2021. Albuquerque, Des Moines, Indianapolis, Memphis, Milwaukee, and Syracuse recorded their highest homicide totals ever.[7] Homicide rates in large cities increased by more than 30 percent overall, but by 36 percent in Los Angeles, 72 percent in Minneapolis, and 82 percent in Portland. In Milwaukee, homicides increased by 95 percent, from 97 in 2019 to 189 in 2020. It set another record in 2021 with 205 homicides, more than twice the 2019 number.[8]

Experts interviewed by CNN, the *New York Times*, and the *Washington Post* offered a variety of explanations for the sharp uptick. Many pointed to the economic and mental stress caused by the pandemic, the limited availability of mental health counseling during quarantines, and the massive increase in gun ownership. Others suggested that the increase was caused by "de-policing"—reduced law enforcement related to low morale among officers as a result of the "defund the police" movement; officers being distracted from everyday police work by the need to staff protest sites; reduced numbers of officers on the street due to resignations or COVID-related illnesses; officers avoiding public contact for fear of contracting the COVID virus;

and the fact that COVID forced court systems to shut down or postpone or cancel proceedings to limit in-person interactions.[9] The deputy director of the Johns Hopkins Center for Gun Violence Prevention and Policy, Cassandra Crifasi, noted that the pandemic-related recession disproportionately affected low-wage and minority workers and kept them out of work longer than other Americans, the murder of George Floyd eroded confidence in law enforcement, and ensuing protests yielded more images of police brutality. Shani Buggs, an assistant professor with the University of California at Davis's Violence Prevention Research Program, agreed. "The pandemic exacerbated all of the inequities we had in our country—along racial lines, health lines, social lines, economic lines," she told the *Post* in 2021. "All of the drivers of gun violence pre-pandemic were just worsened last year."[10] Mayors saw the same factors at work.[11]

As the pandemic eased, nationwide rates of violent crime, including homicides, began to decline, too.[12] Nationwide, violent crimes dropped overall in 2022 and 2023, returning the US to the prepandemic level of 2019.[13] Milwaukee's homicide rate dropped by 21 percent in 2023, mirroring the US trend.[14] A 37-city study by the Council on Criminal Justice found that gun assaults, robberies, burglaries, larcenies, and aggravated assaults all fell in the first half of 2023 compared to the same period in 2022, but gun assaults, aggravated assaults, and robberies remained higher than in 2019. Homicides peaked in 2021, but 2023 levels were 24 percent higher than in 2019, and the 2019 rate was still 15 percent higher than in 2014, the lowest level recorded since World War II.[15] Though the reasons for the decline were not clear, experts theorized that reinvigorated policing and the end of pandemic-related isolation were responsible.[16]

What did not decline much were mass shootings. Such shootings—defined by the Gun Violence Archive as an incident in which at least four people other than the shooter are shot—averaged 1.67 per day nationwide in 2020. The numbers continued to rise. In 2019, there were 417 mass shootings overall; in 2020, 610; and in 2021, 690. Though the number dipped slightly to 647 in 2022 and 656 in 2023, those numbers remained far higher than the 273 recorded 10 years earlier in 2013.[17] The 499 mass shootings in 2024, though a significant improvement, still exceeded the 2019 total.[18]

A few mass shootings in 2020 were illustrative. On January 24, a man in Vanceboro, North Carolina, killed his wife and three children and then killed himself. On February 26, a man killed five coworkers at the Molson Coors brewery in Milwaukee before committing suicide. On March 7, 18 people in Cleveland were shot, including one fatally, after a fight broke out among motorcycle clubs late on a Saturday night. On June 21, three people were killed and 11 were injured at a block party in Charlotte. On July 18, five people were shot, one fatally, while standing on a Chicago sidewalk and street at 3:12 a.m. On December 26, a gunman killed three people and injured three others in a random attack inside a Rockford, Illinois, bowling alley.[19]

One mass shooting with a high number of victims in 2020 occurred in Wauwatosa on November 20. The holiday season was approaching, and the night before our Police and Fire Commission had accepted Officer Mensah's resignation. Finally, it seemed, our community could begin to heal. But that had to wait.

At 2:49 p.m. that day, a Friday, Xavier Sevilla shot eight people at Mayfair Mall, Wisconsin's busiest shopping center. Sevilla, who was only 15 years old, and an 18-year-old friend, Eric Garcia, were at the top of the escalator near Macy's Department Store and Abercrombie & Fitch when they saw four other teenagers they knew at the bottom of the escalator. Garcia ran down the escalator screaming and punched one of the other teenagers in the face. Sevilla pulled a handgun from his waistband, "took a shooter's stance," and fired 10 rounds of bullets and then 7 more at one of the victims after she got up and tried to run away.

The shots sent people into hiding or fleeing for the exits. Eight people, who ranged in age from 18 to 66 and included four innocent bystanders and four members of the two groups involved in the altercation, were hospitalized with wounds to their arms and legs. Wauwatosa police officers arrived within a minute—they had been responding to another, less serious situation elsewhere in the mall—and Wauwatosa Fire Department paramedics arrived shortly after. Fortunately, none of the victims was seriously hurt, and the Milwaukee region's primary trauma center is only three miles away at the Milwaukee Regional Medical Center.

When the police arrived, they were unaware that Sevilla had run out of the mall with other patrons. Surveillance video from the Best Buy store across Mayfair Road later showed the boy running from the mall and climbing into an orange SUV, which an Uber investigator learned had been called by a number associated with Sevilla's father. Police had only a vague description of the shooter and urged the public to stay away from the mall as the investigation continued.[20]

Immediately, I began receiving emails and telephone calls from CNN, the *New York Times*, the *Washington Post*, the *Wall Street Journal*, NHK Japan Broadcasting Corporation, and local TV stations, among other media outlets. I responded with information provided to me by the Wauwatosa Police Department. That night the Mayfair shooting was one of the lead stories on the *NBC Evening News*. "The mayor of Wauwatosa says 'the perpetrator is at large at this time. There are approximately 75 police officers on the scene,'" anchor Lester Holt reported.

Residents were frantic, calling and writing to ask me if they were safe. The next day I issued a statement to reassure the community: All eight people who were shot were recovering; the mall was secure but closed for the day; a preliminary investigation indicated that the shooting was not a random act; and WPD investigators, with the assistance of the Federal Bureau of Investigation, were interviewing victims and witnesses to identify and arrest the suspect. I asked that any information about the suspect's identity or location be shared with the WPD immediately and reassured people that they and Mayfair Mall were safe. I thanked the WPD and nearby police departments for protecting shoppers and employees, and the Wauwatosa Fire Department for attending to the victims' injuries and transporting them safely to the hospital. I closed by saying the WPD would provide additional information as it became available.

I also included this statement: "Guns have no place in shopping malls or other places in which crowds of people gather. Mayfair has a strict no-gun policy. If the shooter had complied with that policy, no one would have been hurt yesterday."[21]

Even though eight people had been shot while Christmas shopping and the shooter was a 15-year-old, I received emails and telephone calls from gun advocates around the country condemning me for my statement that "guns have no place in shopping malls." One email said, "I find it ridiculous to say that guns have no place in shopping malls or other places where large crowds gather. Even though you have a strict no-gun policy, when is the last time a criminal was concerned about our laws? Don't try and restrict the freedom of law-abiding citizens due to the horrific actions of a criminal. We need MORE responsible gun owners in Wisconsin. Please start blaming the criminal for their actions, not the gun." I ignored most of the messages but responded to a few. "Police are trained to use their weapons," I wrote. "There is no such training requirement for civilians in Wisconsin. Further, state law allows property owners to ban guns on their properties. Mayfair has banned guns. More guns would not have helped the situation. None of this excuses the criminals. I prefer to leave policing to the police."

On Saturday night, the WPD arrested Sevilla in a car on Milwaukee's South Side. In the car were several relatives along with a suitcase packed with his clothes, the handgun used in the shooting, and a list of telephone numbers.[22] The following day, the

WPD and I held a press conference to announce Sevilla's arrest. A postelection rally for President Trump had been held outside the closed mall on Saturday. Some rallygoers had carried guns. Reporters asked for comment. "That rally, as I understand it, was planned a week ahead of time," I said. "I think it was unfortunate they decided to come with what happened the day before. I don't think people should come to political rallies with guns. I respect the First Amendment rights of everybody for political rallies and protests. If it were up to me, I would have said, please do not come, do not bring guns, honor the fact that our community is suffering right now."

In a year in which The People's Revolution had protested in Wauwatosa week after week, some left-wing residents who supported those protests demanded that we not allow the pro-Trump rally to proceed. I reminded them that the ACLU's protest guidance correctly states, based on US Supreme Court cases, that a "permit cannot be denied because the event is controversial or will express unpopular views" and that the government must treat protesters and counterprotesters equally. In plainer English, lawyer and columnist David French has written, criticizing right-wing efforts to suppress speech, "No viable constitutional doctrine declares 'Free speech for me and not for thee.'"[23] The critics also objected to the MAGA rally because the protesters might be carrying guns, a remarkable complaint given that TPR members had carried guns at every protest that year and one had fired a shotgun at Officer Mensah at his home.

After several rounds of legal maneuvering, Sevilla was charged as an adult. Eventually, he pleaded guilty to five counts of first-degree reckless injury with a dangerous weapon. In April 2023, he was sentenced to 15 years in prison plus 5 years of extended supervision.[24]

In the meantime, Wauwatosa had experienced another traumatic shooting. On December 10, 2020, WPD officer Amanda Hodgson shot a 35-year-old Black woman, Tinesha Jarrett, who had attacked another woman with a driveway plow stick.[25] The victim, a student at the nearby Medical College of Wisconsin, had stopped to ask Jarrett, who had earlier checked herself out of the Milwaukee County Behavioral Health Complex and was behaving erratically, if she was all right. When Hodgson arrived, she saw Jarrett carrying the plow stick and a long wooden stake with a pointed end. Jarrett hit the squad car with the stake, ignored orders to stop, advanced, and repeatedly yelled at Hodgson to shoot her. When Jarrett swung the stake and struck the squad car door, which was between them, Hodgson fired three times, striking her in the torso. Despite her injuries, Jarrett continued to yell and approached the car again. Another officer deployed his Taser. This did not stop her, either; it took several officers to subdue her. She was taken to a nearby hospital.

As police taped off the scene, 15 to 25 protesters gathered, chanting and demanding information from officers. The group eventually departed at about 2:00 a.m. Fortunately, Jarrett survived. But the incident took another toll: in mid-2021, Hodgson, who had been on the force for only nine months when the shooting occurred, resigned her patrol officer position. Though the Milwaukee County district attorney determined that she would not be charged for shooting Jarrett because "Hodgson had an actual subjective belief that potentially deadly force was necessary under the circumstances,"[26] the fact that she had to shoot a mentally ill woman weighed heavily on her. Like many other police officers, especially during 2020, the stress she suffered caused her to reconsider her career plans. Across the country, the pressure of police work and ongoing criticism of police had caused many officers to take early retirement, find other less stressful law enforcement work, or leave law enforcement altogether.[27]

On March 16, 2021, four months after the mass shooting at Mayfair Mall, a worker at a grocery distribution center in Oconomowoc, Wisconsin, 35 miles west of Milwaukee, shot and killed two other employees. The shooter, who later shot and killed himself during the manhunt, was from Wauwatosa. The *Milwaukee Journal Sentinel* asked for comment. "Wauwatosa mourns with Oconomowoc and Roundy's employees over the senseless murder of two Roundy's workers last night," I said. "The fact that the suspect was from Wauwatosa only adds to our sorrow. We all must work together to ensure that all workers, and all Americans, are safe from violence."[28]

Wauwatosa was lucky not to have suffered deaths in our mass shooting. Yet it only seemed a matter of time before another occurred, not because our community is dangerous—the only fatal shooting in Wauwatosa in 2020–2024 was Officer Mensah's killing of Alvin Cole in February 2020—but because it is in America, the home of the free, the brave, and the mass shooter. In 2023, at the urging of our fire and police chiefs, the city purchased a $300,000 rescue vehicle in preparation for the next tragedy. The steel-armored SUV is fitted with an extendable arm to retrieve victims as well as life-saving equipment so paramedics can immediately treat injured people. Similar vehicles have saved many lives, including, for example, in mass shootings at a Planned Parenthood clinic in Colorado Springs in 2015 and at the Pulse nightclub in Orlando in 2016.[29] But year after year, America continues to suffer daily mass shootings.

Polls consistently show that most Americans favor stricter restrictions on guns.[30] That sentiment goes unheeded. Mass shootings continue unabated.[31] As the toll of injuries and deaths has climbed, our state and national leaders have failed to take sufficient steps to stop our never-ending gun violence. Every day, communities like Wauwatosa and Oconomowoc must cope with the consequences of that inaction, and families are left to mourn the innocent victims.

POLICE BLUES

AFTER GEORGE FLOYD WAS MURDERED by a Minneapolis police officer, many Americans agreed that policing needed to change. What was not clear was what that change should be.

Some progressives and Black Lives Matter advocates called for "defunding the police." Elected officials across the country responded to that call in various ways, some out of a sincere desire for reform, some out of panic, some out of political calculation, and some out of a combination of the three motives. But regardless of the course they took, they found themselves off balance.

In part, there was confusion about what *defunding* meant. Some people wanted to actually abolish police departments, as if good intentions could abolish crime. Others wanted to spend less on police and more on social services like mental health, substance abuse treatment, and job training. Still others wanted not to spend less but to change how police function.[1]

In June 2020, shortly after Floyd was killed, Mayor Bill de Blasio reallocated $1 billion of the New York Police Department's $6 billion budget to youth groups and social services through other city agencies.[2] That month, an activist group, Black Visions, led a protest at Minneapolis mayor Jacob Frey's home. When he refused to support their demand to abolish the police department, protesters shouted, "Shame! Shame! Shame!" At a rally the next day, 9 members of the 13-member City Council vowed to "end" the department and create "a new transformative model for cultivating safety in Minneapolis." But as the summer went on and crime and public opposition increased, council members backed off that pledge and took the path of reform instead.[3] A *Minneapolis Star-Tribune* poll in August found that although two-thirds of residents had an unfavorable opinion of the police department, a plurality, including 50 percent of Blacks, opposed decreasing the size of the police force. Black Visions denounced the reform effort as "weak" and stated, "It is the nature of white supremacy, capitalism, patriarchy or any of these other systems of oppression to want to do what is necessary to save themselves."[4]

Similar efforts and statements were made in other cities.[5] In 2020, the Portland City Council cut $11 million from the Police Bureau's $200 million budget, in part because of the pandemic-caused budget crisis, and shifted $15 million to other agencies to respond to nonviolent calls. In July 2020, the PPB also disbanded a unit focused on gun-related crime, even though the number of homicides had nearly doubled from 2019 to 2020. More than 120 officers of the 1,000-officer PPB departed in the nine months following the Floyd murder and the ensuing turmoil in that city. A May 2021 poll conducted by the *Oregonian* newspaper found that Portland-area residents did not want fewer police officers; 24 percent wanted the same number and 50 percent wanted more. In a stark turnaround, Mayor Ted Wheeler and the city council began discussing how to increase police funding.[6]

In his famous 1943 article "A Theory of Human Motivation," psychologist Abraham Maslow posited a five-tiered hierarchy of human needs. As described by Dr. Nicole Celestine, the first tier consists of "physiological needs [like air, water, food, sleep, health, clothes, and shelter that] . . . are fundamental to human wellbeing and will always take priority over other needs. Next in the hierarchy are safety needs. If a person does not feel safe in their environment, they are unlikely to guide attention toward trying to meet higher-order needs" like love and belonging, self-esteem, and self-actualization.[7]

The basic human desire for security, order, and stability suggests why support for the BLM movement declined and support for the police rose during 2020 as crime ticked up and protests in some cities became violent.[8] During a fractious presidential election year, defunding the police did not receive broad support from Democratic elected officials, who might have been expected to be allies of defunding advocates. Democratic candidates Joe Biden and Senator Bernie Sanders (I-VT) supported reform instead. This did not deter Donald Trump and his supporters from falsely claiming that Biden supported defunding the police.[9]

Even many Blacks, who are among the most frequent victims of crimes, resisted cuts to police departments. In New York, several Black city council members opposed the $1 billion cut from the NYPD budget, comparing defunding the police to "colonization" and "political gentrification."[10] Similarly, referring to the Minneapolis City Council members who pledged to abolish the police department, Cathy Spann, a Black community activist, told the *New York Times*, "They didn't engage Black and brown people, and something about that does not sit right with me. Something about saying to the community, 'We need to make change together,' but instead you leave this community and me unsafe."[11] Portland police chief Chuck Lovell seconded that thought. "What I know is that being chief, and being a Black chief in particular, this movement to really exclude police from some facets of enforcement or community interaction, it really bears the brunt on the African American community," he said. "These shootings have an outsized impact on people of color."[12] In his 2021 book *Last Best Hope: America in Crisis and Renewal*, George Packer observed that in many cities, the "defund the police" effort "was stopped by local Black citizens, who wanted better, not less, policing."[13]

In 2021, reported *Bloomberg CityLab*, the 50 largest US cities reduced their police budgets by 5.2 percent overall; but partly because of pandemic-related cuts to other agencies, police spending as a share of city expenditures rose slightly, and 26 of those cities increased their police budgets.[14] Generally, elected officials did not pay a penalty for such actions. In November 2020, Portland mayor Wheeler won reelection over a candidate far to his left politically.[15]

A year later, in November 2021, a *Washington Post* headline proclaimed, "In Mayoral Elections Nationwide, Voters Opt for Pragmatism over Ideology."[16] The Black mayor of Buffalo, Byron Brown, was reelected in a write-in campaign over a self-proclaimed socialist who had advocated reducing the police budget by $7.5 million.[17] Seattle's city council president, who had advocated cutting the police budget in half, lost the mayor's race by almost 18 percent.[18] Similarly, the Minneapolis mayoral election focused on police reform and defunding. Like other major US cities, Minneapolis had seen a rise in robbery, murder, and other crimes in 2020 and 2021. During his 2021 reelection campaign, Mayor Frey released a plan to address the violence, criticizing local officials who "fought to abolish or defund the police" and promising additional resources and officers.[19] Frey was reelected by 42.8–21.1 percent over his closest challenger in a four-way race. In ranked-choice voting, he received 56.2 percent of the vote over the second-place candidate. By a similar 56–44 percent margin, voters rejected a referendum to abolish the Minneapolis Police Department and replace it with a Department of Public Safety.[20] But Minneapolis had not abandoned its liberal politics; referendums on a limit on rent increases and on a charter amendment to permit the city to impose rent controls both passed by 53–47 percent.[21]

Also in November 2021, New York City elected its second Black mayor. Eric Adams had pushed for police reform when he served as an NYPD captain, but, noted the *New York Times*, "amid a spike in gun violence and jarring attacks on the subway that fueled public fears about crime, Mr. Adams emerged as one of [the Democratic] party's most unflinching advocates for the police maintaining a robust role in preserving public safety. He often clashed with those who sought to scale back law enforcement's power in favor of promoting greater investments in mental health and other social services."[22]

The same week as Adams's victory, Congressman James Clyburn (D-SC), as majority whip the highest-ranking African American member of the US House of Representatives, told the *Washington Post*, "What I try to do is demonstrate by precept and example how we are to proceed as a party. When I spoke out against sloganeering, like 'Burn, baby, burn' in the 1960s and 'defund the police,' which I think is cutting the throats of the [Democratic] party, I know exactly where my constituents are. They are against that, and I'm against that."[23]

Summing up the November 2021 elections, the *Post* commented, "In big-city elections from coast to coast, voters had the option to elect candidates advocating the sort of revolutionary change promoted in recent years by protesters on the streets and left-wing lawmakers in Congress. Instead, they largely opted for more consensus-minded candidates who may back progressive values and policies, but who have emphasized less divisive and dramatic tactics to get there." Aseem Prakash, a political science professor at the University of Washington at Seattle, told the *Post*, "The message for the political class is that voters want quality of life. They want politicians to solve problems. They don't want division. They don't want finger-pointing. And they have faith in reforming institutions, not abolishing them."[24]

Because I was a newly elected mayor, the referendum on my service had to wait until April 2024. In the meantime, like other cities, Wauwatosa focused on reform while maintaining the police budget. In addition to initiatives in our Health and Human Resources Departments, we made important changes to the

Wauwatosa Police Department. In 2020, the city purchased body cameras for WPD officers; provided implicit bias training for officers, other city employees, and elected officials; and hired the Center for Public Safety Management (CPSM) of Washington, DC, to review the WPD's operations. CPSM's study, presented in July 2021, addressed hiring strategies; reviewed data for service calls, including the type of staff (uniformed or not) best prepared for future calls; and analyzed the WPD's equity and training policies, focusing on best practices for use of force. Among other recommendations, CPSM urged the WPD to hire a "licensed professional counselor" to "provide ongoing training [to officers] in dealing with mentally ill persons and homeless persons, and review body camera video from all mental health calls for service to provide guidance to officers on how to enhance their handling of this type of call for service with the primary focus on safety and de-escalation techniques."[25] Based on this recommendation, the city hired a social worker to work with the police, fire, and health departments to focus on follow-up visits after crises. WPD officers, though already trained in crisis intervention, welcomed that hiring, which helps people struggling with mental health or substance use disorders to get care rather than be arrested or incarcerated.[26]

Perhaps the most consequential change began on February 1, 2021, when Chief Barry Weber announced his retirement effective June 1, and the Wauwatosa Police and Fire Commission began the process of hiring a new chief.[27] His retirement was the product of months of careful negotiations by the city administrator and me. We could not give him, or the public, any impression that he was being pushed out; he was under no obligation to retire and could have rescinded his retirement at any time. Under Wisconsin law, a police chief serves during times of good behavior and may be removed by a police and fire commission only for "just cause." Except in rare cases, this means that a chief serves as long as he wants.[28]

"I wrote to you during the start of our recent troubles and expressed my opinion that Wauwatosa was not the right place for Officer Mensah and that it was time for Chief Weber to retire," a resident said in an email to me. "You responded and stated that you were engaged in the problem, but cautioned that there was a process to follow and we had to let this play out. It seems that things have worked out pretty well." This sigh of relief was typical of residents who understood that after 31 years as chief, it was time for Weber to go. In his early years, he had restored public trust in the WPD and made it the city's most racially diverse department.[29] But during 2020, he divided the community by being defensive. A couple of times, he complained to me, "A few months ago, we were the most popular department in Wauwatosa. I don't know what happened." Each time, I replied, "Chief—George Floyd happened."

During his tenure, he also internally pitted officers against elected officials and the WPD against City Hall. This caused us problems with the Wauwatosa Peace Officers Association (WPOA). In many cities, police unions have contentious relationships with mayors and the public.[30] Regardless of what is happening in a city or whether officers conduct themselves appropriately, police unions expect unquestioning support because of the difficulty and danger of their work.[31] This problem is not unique to Wauwatosa. In Portland, police officers resisted District Attorney Mike Schmidt's decision to focus on cases of violence or vandalism and not to charge protesters who simply resisted arrest or refused to disperse after a police order. The officers, reported the *New York Times,* seemed to regard Schmidt as not being on "our team."[32] What was different in Wauwatosa was how events unfolded.

After Officer Mensah shot and killed Alvin Cole in February 2020, the third person of color he had killed in five years, there were few protests. That changed immediately after the Floyd murder, when almost-daily protests erupted. As noted earlier, on July 14, the Common Council passed a resolution, 14–1, directing Weber and the city administrator to negotiate Mensah's departure from city employment. The next day, the WPFC, acting on a complaint filed by the family of one of Mensah's victims, unanimously voted to suspend him and retained an attorney to conduct an investigation. Even though under Wisconsin law only the WPFC has authority to discipline a police officer, the WPOA alleged that the Common Council's resolution had "tainted" the WPFC.[33] I disagreed. "We didn't tell the Police and Fire Commission what to do; we don't have the authority to do that," I told a reporter. "What we suggested was that there might be alternative ways of resolving the situation. And we instructed the city administrator and the police chief, not the [WPFC], to explore those alternatives." I also rejected the WPOA's argument that we should not seek to resolve the matter outside the WPFC. "We are the elected officials," I said, "and the city, the mayor, and the Common Council have to respond to people across the political spectrum and deal with issues that are plaguing the city."[34]

In a letter, the president of the world's largest organization of law enforcement officers, the Fraternal Order of Police (FOP), headquartered in Nashville, Tennessee, denounced the Common Council, the WPFC, and me for "sullying" Mensah's reputation "to fuel the fires of anti-police sentiment."[35] Like the WPOA, the FOP failed to understand that the WPD, which was under considerable stress, would not see the end of protests until the Mensah situation was resolved.

The FOP's position was no surprise. As Adam Serwer reported in the *Atlantic*, "in 2016, the FOP demanded that Walmart cease selling Black Lives Matter T-shirts. It denounced Nike for its ad campaign involving [Black quarterback] Colin Kaepernick, who was purged from the [National Football League] for protesting police misconduct. If you go to the FOP's Twitter feed, you can find a steady stream of clips from conservative outlets such as Newsmax and Fox News showing FOP representatives attacking policies like bail reform, slamming Democratic elected officials, and blaming Black-rights activists for the recent rise in homicides. . . . What you won't find on the national FOP Twitter feed, however, are condemnations of the Capitol rioters who attacked police officers on January 6 [2021]. . . . You won't find any clips of FOP members on Fox News confronting its prime-time hosts for mocking the testimony of police officers who faced the mob that day."[36]

With emotions running high, lawyers and politicians stoking anger, and protesters carrying guns, the Common Council, city administrator, and I all believed Mensah's life would be in danger if an unstable person decided to engage in frontier justice, as when someone fired a shotgun at his house during the melee there on August 8, 2020.[37] Responding to emails, I noted that the city would be in a difficult situation morally, legally, and financially if Mensah shot and killed a fourth person, and his life would likely be in more danger even if the shooting was deemed justified. I concluded my responses with this statement: "Experts we have consulted tell us that Officer Mensah is unique, in that no other officer in America has shot and killed three people while on duty, and in such a short time span (five years). We cannot ignore this dangerous and difficult situation. That is why we are exploring alternatives while the [WPFC] investigates and decides the current citizen complaints filed against him."

Chief Weber shared that concern. Publicly, he defended Mensah and said he intended to restore him to duty. Privately, in meetings with Archambo and me, he said, "I know I can't put Mensah back on the street." It would have helped me, the council, and the community if he had made that statement in public. Instead, we later learned, he told his officers that City Hall was anti-Mensah.

The WPOA's leaders sent a letter to the council and me challenging my characterization of Mensah's situation as "unique."[38] They said other officers around the country had been involved in multiple shootings, too. But my statements were supported by experts. In a *Washington Post* op-ed, law professors John Rappaport of the University of Chicago and Ben Grunwald of Duke University wrote that "Mensah's record is extraordinary, statistically speaking; most officers have never fired their weapon at all."[39] Similarly, on October 7, 2020, when Milwaukee County district attorney John Chisholm announced his decision not to charge Mensah with a crime for his third killing, both he and the WPFC's independent investigator, Steven Biskupic, shared their concern about the possibility of another shooting.[40] Biskupic, a former US Attorney, recommended that the WPFC terminate Mensah's employment to avoid the "extraordinary, unwarranted and unnecessary risk" of a fourth shooting.[41] It seemed clear to everyone but the WPOA and FOP that Mensah could not remain employed by Wauwatosa.

But the WPOA's concern was understandable. All of us who dealt with the protests of 2020 suffer from some degree of post-traumatic stress, especially WPD officers. Their complaints, often expressed indirectly but also in person to me during a tense meeting with the union leadership in September 2020, revealed a fear that if any of them had to engage in controversial actions, much less shoot someone in the line of duty, they would lose their jobs.

But I did not suspend Mensah; the WPFC did. As time went on, the WPOA also blamed me for reaching out to protesters to try to bring peace to Wauwatosa; for holding a community listening session on July 21, 2020; for creating an ad hoc committee to address policing issues; and for allegedly encouraging protesters to engage in violence. It also released a survey that said that 100 percent of its members believed I did not support them.[42] None of this had merit—the Common Council sponsored the listening session and created the ad hoc committee, and I regularly denounced violence—but mayors are lightning rods for community frustrations. And I took an equal amount of flak from protesters and left-wing residents for being too supportive of the police.

Then the WPOA's campaign against me took a darker turn. On January 11, 2021, a reporter showed me a PowerPoint presentation he had obtained through an open-records request. The PowerPoint was created by a WPD detective during the investigation of the August 8, 2020, melee at Mensah's home. One slide displayed the letters "HVT" ("high value target") next to my photo and falsely alleged that I had "sanctioned violence against Mensah," "continually provide[d] outright lies and misleading information to the public," "permitted the People's Revolution to run the City of Wauwatosa meetings, [and] had discussions and Q&A sessions not outlined on meeting agendas, in violation of Open Meeting laws." It also said there was no probable cause to think that I had any "involvement in the [August 8th] shooting . . . yet."[43]

In a statement issued to the media on January 13, I noted that Chief Weber had assured me that he was not aware of the PowerPoint and that the WPD did not consider me a "high value target" or involved in the August 8 incident and had never sought evidence against me to substantiate any criminal allegation. He also told me that he had opened an investigation and that discipline of those responsible was likely. I added, "The PowerPoint must be viewed [as] a few disgruntled union members express[ing] their personal opinions in an inappropriate fashion while on duty. Regardless of the context, strong opinions do not justify inappropriate behavior. Public employees have a legal obligation to do their job without regard to their personal opinions, and certainly have an obligation to ensure that their statements are not untruthful or misleading. When the PowerPoint was created, the creators violated these obligations to the City and the public. Such actions can only drive a wedge between the WPD and the people it serves."[44]

The PowerPoint did sow more skepticism of the WPD. "Police became emotional and defensive in response to protests," a Milwaukee columnist wrote. "And the reaction of police suggests they took these protests personally. . . . And the Wauwatosa

Police declared that the city's mayor . . . was a 'target' because of how he responded to the protests and the department's handling of them."[45] For critics, the PowerPoint confirmed that the WPD and WPOA were serving their own interests, not the community's. Ultimately, the detective received a written reprimand. I strongly disagreed with that slap on the wrist, but because I did not want to cause Weber to rescind his pending retirement, I said I would agree to the minimal penalty if Weber issued a public statement reaffirming the principle of civilian control over the police.[46] He did.

After Weber announced his retirement on February 1, 2021, an impatient Wauwatosa progressive suggested that I ask the entire WPFC to resign and appoint new commissioners—"not because they have done anything wrong," he wrote in an email, "but just because the city and its police department need a fresh start, with fresh eyes, and a clean slate." I replied that I would be replacing one commissioner with a person of color[47] but that the WPFC members, who had served well under pressure in 2020, could ignore any request for resignation while serving out their terms.[48] I noted the many reforms enacted during my first nine months as mayor and told him that we were working on additional reforms and that a new chief would bring the WPD fresh leadership and vision. But I reminded him, reform takes time: proposals must be reviewed by staff, discussed in committee, and passed by the Common Council.

Alternatively, he urged me to abolish the WPD by contracting with another city or the Milwaukee County sheriff to provide law enforcement services, as Wisconsin law allows. That, I said, was unrealistic; there was no possibility the council would abolish the WPD. To illustrate that reform requires realism and political skill, I offered him an exchange—depicted in *Lincoln*, the 2012 movie directed by Steven Spielberg—between President Lincoln and impatient congressman Thaddeus Stevens, the leader of the Radical Republicans, with whom Lincoln was working to enact the Thirteenth Amendment to abolish slavery. "A compass, I learnt when I was surveying, it'll . . . point you True North from where you're standing, but it's got no advice about the swamps and deserts and chasms that you'll encounter along the way," Lincoln said. "If in pursuit of your destination, you plunge ahead, heedless of obstacles, and achieve nothing more than to sink in a swamp, what's the use of knowing True North?"[49]

I also addressed the resident's frustration that in Wisconsin only police and fire commissions, not elected officials, have authority to hire, fire, and discipline police chiefs and officers. I offered him the same idea that I shared with Senator Tammy Baldwin and others who expressed concern about the WPD's direction under Chief Weber: the legislature could limit police and fire chiefs to 10-year terms with the possibility of a single renewal by the Common Council. Such limits would match the 10-year terms for Wisconsin Supreme Court justices and the limit on the service of the director of the Federal Bureau of Investigation. Without such limits, it is difficult for mayors and common councils to truly control a chief's actions. I reminded him that at the city level, however, we are required to carry out the laws given to us by the legislature. Any statutory reform must be made by that body.[50]

Following Weber's retirement, I did replace two WPFC commissioners. One was the chair, who wearily resigned after 10 years of service, and the other was a commissioner whose term had expired, because she had expressed resentment about an email I sent to the WPFC in March 2021 opposing Weber's promotion of the detective who had labeled me a "high value target." In their places, I appointed an African American insurance executive whose father had served as a military police officer and a college dean who was Wisconsin's leading expert on policing. Before doing so, I had them promise to uphold the principle of civilian control over the police and to welcome opinions expressed to them by elected officials and members of the public about how their community's police department should function. They readily agreed.

In the end, almost everyone wants a safe community in which people are treated fairly, regardless of race, ethnicity, or socioeconomic status. This was underscored in a 2022 Public Policy Polling survey of Wisconsin's Democratic and Republican primary voters about immigration, race, policing, gender identity, and other issues. Public Policy Polling discovered common ground. For example, 71 percent of Democrats and 93 percent of Republicans agreed that "America is not perfect, but it is good to be patriotic and proud of the country," and 69 percent of Democrats and 91 percent of Republicans agreed that "police misconduct and brutality against people of any race is wrong, and we need to reform police conduct and recruitment. More and better policing is needed for public safety, and that cannot be provided by 'defunding the police.'"[51]

Without question, police officers have a tough job and often feel underappreciated. As one expert observed, we can work better together if we say, "How can we support you to do what you do best?" The stress of 2020 and uptick of crime in 2020 and 2021 created a nationwide shortage of officers.[52] In 2021, the Wauwatosa Common Council voted to offer bonuses and other incentives to help the WPD recruit new officers, and it renewed that program in 2024.[53] But as important as the police are, they are still only one department among many in a city government led by civilians elected by other civilians. At times elected officials must respond to community needs in ways that, to police, can seem uncomfortable or inefficient.[54] It is counterproductive, however, for police to attack officials who are trying to work with them to calm their cities.

My disagreement was never with patrol officers but with the WPOA's leaders.[55] Because they singled me out, I worried that officers would not protect my wife and me when protesters came to our home night after night. But the officers did their jobs. For that, I will always be grateful. Still, the old-school WPOA leaders, focused only on their own concerns, never accepted that the WPD does not make city policy or appreciated that a divided community was demanding that its mayor find solutions to community discord. In the years since, new, younger WPOA leaders have been more collaborative and more in tune with community needs.

We are all in this together. "I think other people are just understanding that this is a really challenging time to be a police officer," Portland mayor Wheeler told the *Washington Post* in 2021. "And we are finally putting racial disparity and institutional racism front and center in our society. This is an opportunity for us to be honest about its existence, to call it out for what it is and to change it. The legacy of George Floyd is that he gave us this opportunity to address these issues that have been with us for hundreds of years. What he gave us is the conversation, and we're not going to waste it here."[56]

ECHOES AND AFTERSHOCKS

"THE PAST IS NEVER DEAD. It's not even past."[1]

Never did William Faulkner's words seem more true than in the years following 2020. Though the pandemic ended, its impact lingered. Over time, the media, which first referred to the disease by its scientific designation of "COVID-19," began referring to it as "COVID" and then "Covid-19," "Covid," and finally "covid," reflecting, perhaps, the disease's diminishing impact. But doctors had not solved the mystery of "long COVID." Mental health suffered. Social behaviors evolved. Dress codes changed. Reckless driving increased. The commercial and residential real estate markets experienced upheavals. Young workers refused to return to the office. Skepticism of science continued and remained a political issue. The same presidential candidates who competed in 2020 competed again, for a while, in 2024.

Our racial problems remained with us, too. In the years following 2020, the Minneapolis police officers involved in George Floyd's murder went to prison,[2] but in 2021 the Kenosha County district attorney announced that he would not bring charges against the officer who shot Jacob Blake, and a Kenosha County jury found Kyle Rittenhouse, who had shot and killed two BLM protesters, not guilty of homicide, attempted homicide, and reckless endangerment after he testified that he had acted in self-defense.[3] The man who murdered a BLM protester in Austin was sentenced to 25 years in prison but was pardoned by the governor of Texas.[4] The Louisville police officer who killed Breonna Taylor was first acquitted of state charges of reckless behavior and then, in a second federal trial on charges of violating Taylor's civil rights after the first jury could not reach a verdict, was found guilty.[5] Lawsuits against Wauwatosa and Officer Mensah muddled on. Reforms enacted after the Floyd murder unraveled. The national reckoning on race and policing continued to play out.[6]

The changes engendered by the events of 2020 vexed mayors as they tried to return their communities to normal. But returning to pre-2020 life was impossible. Americans and their leaders searched for a new equilibrium.[7]

HEALTH EFFECTS

During the pandemic, hospitals and clinics postponed or deferred many elective surgeries, and many people, out of fear, did not get regular medical care.[8] That compounded COVID's impact on longevity, and life expectancy for Americans plunged before beginning to rebound, slowly.[9] Among those who survived COVID infections were millions of people, 6.4 percent of the American population, who suffered from various symptoms lumped together in the category of "long COVID"—chronic fatigue, brain fog, difficulty breathing, joint pain, and loss of taste and smell, among others—that persisted for years after the infections began. Medical researchers and practitioners could not find a cause or cure for this syndrome.[10]

Even among those otherwise unaffected by COVID, the pandemic had long-term impacts. In a report called "Stress in America 2023," the American Psychological Association stated that "our society is experiencing the psychological impacts of a collective trauma." The association's chief executive officer, Dr. Arthur C. Evans Jr., said, "The COVID-19 pandemic created a collective experience among Americans. While the early-pandemic lockdowns may seem like the distant past, the aftermath remains." But the report also highlighted the impact of "global conflicts, racism and racial injustice, inflation, and climate-related disasters" on our psyches.[11]

Others noted our trauma. "As of last year, four in 10 Americans knew at least one person who died from Covid," Ana Marie Cox observed in the *New Republic* in 2023. "This year, three in 10 Americans say they know someone who has been affected by an opioid addiction, and one in five knows someone who's died from a painkiller overdose. In 2022, more than three million adults were displaced by some form of natural disaster—that's more than three times as many displaced per year between 2008 and 2021. Last year, some cities saw a 50 percent increase in evictions over pre-pandemic levels. One in five knows someone who's died due to gun violence; one in six has witnessed a shooting; 21 percent have been personally threatened by a gun. Half of Americans know someone personally who has experienced at least one of those events."[12]

During the pandemic, America's schoolchildren were profoundly and negatively affected academically, socially, and mentally by being out of school as schools relied on virtual learning to keep students, teachers, and staff safe. "There's fairly good consensus that, in general, as a society, we probably kept kids out of school longer than we should have," Dr. Sean O'Leary, a pediatric infectious disease specialist, told the *New York Times* in 2024.[13]

A CDC survey found that more than 40 percent of students reported that they were so sad or hopeless in 2021 that they stopped their regular activities.[14] This was reflected in the fact that 72 percent of public schools reported an increase in chronic absenteeism during the 2021–22 school year, the first year following the turn to all-virtual classes during the pandemic. The American Enterprise Institute estimated that in the 2022–23 school year, 26 percent of public school students were chronically absent—missing at least 10 percent of the school year for any reason—compared with 15 percent before the pandemic. In Milwaukee, the problem was even worse: the city's public schools had a chronic absenteeism rate of 37 percent in 2019 but 50 percent in 2023. Everywhere, the increased absenteeism aggravated discipline problems.[15]

"The trends suggest that something fundamental has shifted in American childhood and the culture of school, in ways that may be long lasting," explained Sarah Mervosh and Francesca Paris of the *Times*. "What was once a deeply ingrained habit—wake up, catch the bus, report to class—is now something far more tenuous. 'Our relationship with school became optional,' said Katie Rosanbalm, a psychologist and associate research professor with the Center for Child and Family Policy at Duke University."[16] Of course, that change was not beneficial. Test scores in 2023 showed that students had not recovered academically from their losses during the pandemic and fell farther behind the longer they were limited to virtual learning.[17] The ongoing absenteeism only made it harder to catch up.[18]

Post-lockdown, student mental health became an ongoing concern for school districts nationwide.[19] Though Wisconsin cities and school districts are legally separate entities, the Wauwatosa Health Department hired two social workers to work with the city's public and private schools to address the pandemic's lingering impact on students. The social workers conduct mental health assessments, make referrals to mental health providers, and educate students, teachers, and families on mental health topics. Another social worker was hired to work with our police and fire departments to help individuals of all ages reduce repeated mental health episodes and minimize negative interactions that could have fatal consequences. As in many other cities, the new positions were funded by the federal American Rescue Plan Act.[20]

ZOOMING TO WORK

The pandemic also changed how people worked and interacted with others. When state and local governments ordered shutdowns in March 2020, 50 million Americans started working from home,[21] enabled by computer technology that was not available during the Spanish flu pandemic 100 years earlier. Across the country, many employers and employees did their work with the help of remote conferencing provided by Zoom, Microsoft Teams, and similar applications.

In a *New York Times* essay, Harvard University economist Edward Glaeser and Massachusetts Institute of Technology urban planning expert Carlo Ratti wrote, "In 1980 the futurist Alvin Toffler argued that information technology would make urban offices largely obsolete, with workers using residential 'electronic cottages' instead. For 40 years, he was wrong. Then, in an instant, it seemed that he was right. The office tower, like the port and the train station before it, had its relevance challenged by a competing technology: Zoom. In the early days of the Covid pandemic, remote work was expected to last only for a few weeks or months, but now it seems clear that some mix of in-person and fully remote work is here to stay. The office has its advantages, but many people are willing to give them up for the convenience and flexibility of working mostly from home."[22]

Over time, workers did begin returning to the office, but not in pre-pandemic numbers. In early 2020, 62 percent of "full-day paid work" was done at home. By July 2023, according to Stanford University economics professor Nicholas Bloom, that had been halved, to 31 percent. But, he found, office occupancy rates were only at 50 percent of February 2020 levels. He noted that though the pandemic accelerated the trend, it had been a trend in the making over decades as technology evolved. He saw many benefits:

> Hybrid work arrangements have killed the return-to-office hype. Employees equate a mix of working in the office and working from home to an 8 percent raise. They don't have to deal with the daily hassle and costs of a commute. In fact, the process of getting to work is more despised by employees than the need to actually work. And at the end of the day, despite all the noise some business executives made to the contrary, remote work saves companies money. It cuts overhead, boosts productivity and is profitable. And what is profitable in a capitalist economy sticks. Thankfully, remote work also has major benefits for society, including improving the climate by cutting billions of miles of weekly commuting and supporting families by liberating parents' time. We all should celebrate the resilience of our workers and the benefits of working from home.[23]

Mayors and building owners were not celebrating, however. As people stopped commuting, office space fell vacant—and became less valuable. A report revealed that under 50 percent of the space in 24 federal agency headquarters buildings in Washington, DC, was in use in December 2023.[24] A month later, New York City had 95 million square feet of empty office space, the equivalent of 30 Empire State Buildings. Chicago had 60 million square feet of empty space, Los Angeles 44 million, and San Francisco 18.4 million.[25] Across the country, building owners took a hit to their balance sheets. In mid-2024, the US office vacancy rate was 20 percent, an all-time high. Many owners began converting offices into apartments, trying to address the housing shortage that had plagued America since the beginning of the Great Recession in 2008.[26]

Downtown restaurants and retailers suffered from a lack of business from people who now worked at home. Big-city mayors begged workers to come back downtown, and the federal government pushed to have its employees return.[27] Ironically, in August 2023 Zoom told employees who lived within 50 miles of a Zoom office that they had to work in person at least twice a week.[28] But across America, workers rebelled.[29] A Gallup survey in October 2023 found that for "remote-capable employees," hybrid work had become the most common work style and that one-third of hybrid workers would quit if required to return to the office full-time.[30] Responding to return-to-the-office mandates, top tech talent left Apple, Microsoft, and SpaceX for employment elsewhere.[31]

Many workers fled expensive cities like New York, San Francisco, Boston, and Seattle and moved to areas where they could continue to work for the same employers, but remotely and less expensively. Houston lost 12,000 residents from 2020 to 2021 and New York City more than 300,000.[32] It was assumed that when the pandemic ended, workers would return to their offices. Some returned, some did not. In 2023, a record number of people fled America's big cities for smaller ones.[33] Unfortunately for big cities, many of those people were in families with young children. A July 2024 report by the Economic Innovation Group found that since April 2020, the under-five population had declined by 18 percent in New York City, 15 percent in Cook County, Illinois (which includes Chicago), and 14 percent in Los Angeles County. But the decline was not limited to big cities. The report noted that "the U.S. population is rapidly growing older as birthrates fall. . . . The nation now has 890,000 fewer young children than before the pandemic—a 4.6 percent decline. Most counties across the country are home to a declining number of young kids, with profound consequences for school systems and long-term population growth prospects. In 2023, 58 percent of all counties in the U.S. experienced declines in their under-five populations. Since April 2020, two-thirds of all counties' under-five populations have shrunk."[34]

Prominent futurist Richard Florida agreed with other experts that "the pandemic accelerated trends and changes that were already well underway. . . . But the biggest shift of all was one that few predicted: There has been a massive spike in housing prices and rents, a metastasizing problem of housing affordability that is plaguing communities of all shapes and sizes—big cities, small cities, established cities, upcoming cities, suburbs, and rural areas."[35] The problem is not enough housing, a problem made worse by rising interest rates. Since 2020, Wauwatosa, as Milwaukee's second downtown, has struggled along with bigger cities with dual issues of keeping its office buildings filled while meeting the strong housing demand. A *Forbes* magazine analysis in 2024 ranked metro Milwaukee as the nation's fifth-most competitive rental market, with some of the country's steepest rent increases, and Wauwatosa's apartments are among the region's priciest.[36] More housing is needed in Wauwatosa and elsewhere, but NIMBY (Not in My Back Yard) groups oppose efforts to bring more apartments to suburbs.[37]

Though the exodus to smaller cities and towns, away from the expensive metropolitan areas on the East and West Coasts, caused increases in rent and home prices in more affordable markets, it also provided an economic boost to some less populated areas. And economists surveyed by *New York Times* business reporter Emma Goldberg noted that remote work confers positive and negative impacts on working mothers; they generally benefit from the flexibility of being able to work remotely by being able to stay in the work force, but remote work also seems to penalize them when it comes to career advancement.[38]

Remote work did not help workers who could not work remotely, like hospital, construction, or transportation employees, many of whom were people of color.[39] Wealthier Americans benefited most from technology. For them, deliveries from Amazon and food vendors softened the blow of being confined to home. "What lockdown? went the viral tweet, describing it as rather 'the middle class hiding while working-class people bring them things,'" wrote Sigrid Nunez in *The Vulnerables*, her 2023 novel about navigating the pandemic. "Another version: white people hiding while Black and brown people bring them things."[40] For those paying attention, the varying impacts of the pandemic hammered home our country's inequities.

The pandemic changed how we behaved in other ways, too. Researchers found that in the years after the pandemic ended, Americans were walking less; drinking more alcohol; dressing more casually at work; eating more food from drive-throughs and less in sit-down restaurants; going less often to movies, the theater, museums, and church; saving less and spending more on "live in the moment" experiences; and wearing sweatpants during Zoom meetings. Remote work was allowing us to sleep longer, too.[41] In some ways, it seemed, our lives had improved; in other ways, not so much.

A 2023 study in *Scientific Reports* found that "Zoom fatigue" may take a toll on the brain and the heart.[42] And Glaeser and Ratti warned,

> Our research at M.I.T. shows that when we replace in-person interactions with Zoom rooms, our social lives become narrow and homogenous. Parallel research at Microsoft found that "firm-wide remote work caused the collaboration network of workers to become more static and siloed, with fewer bridges between disparate parts." We may have a few close friends online, but we cannot sustain a network of weak ties—the casual acquaintances we run into in the halls or on the bus. We are exposed to less diversity of background and thought, and ideas flow less freely. More permanent remote work could stunt innovation and economic growth as it shrinks our social fabric. If the office is not returning to its central position in our lives, then humanity, as a social species, must find new opportunities for mixing in physical space.[43]

Remote conferencing also changed how governments do business. Due to health concerns about social distancing during the pandemic, the Wauwatosa Common Council conducted its meetings completely on Zoom from July 2020 to January 2022. Since then, all council meetings have been conducted in hybrid fashion, with elected officials in person and many members of the public choosing to watch or participate via Zoom. They can watch videos of our meetings 24 hours a day on the city's website, too. And the mayor of Wauwatosa no longer spends all day at City Hall. I participate in Zoom meetings and send and respond to emails and telephone calls from the desk in my bedroom alcove—sometimes wearing shorts or sweatpants—and travel to City Hall as needed to sign documents, attend meetings, or confer with staff in person. At my outside meetings, almost no one wears a tie or dresses formally anymore.

Society had changed, but when Donald Trump returned to the White House for a second term in January 2025, one of his first actions was to issue an executive order requiring all federal civilian employees to return to the office full time or lose their jobs. The previous year, the US Office of Personnel Management told Congress that "54% of the 2.3 million civilians employed by the federal government work entirely in-person given the nature of their jobs. About 10%, or 228,000 employees, work entirely remotely." This meant that 36 percent worked in hybrid fashion. Trump's order ignored collective bargaining agreements that allowed employees in certain agencies to work remotely and was expected to affect the government's ability to retain and attract employees in the new world of work.[44] Like King Canute in the old English tale, it seemed unlikely that even an American president, however powerful, could turn back the tide.[45]

HELL ON WHEELS

As previously described, in 2020 the US experienced its biggest one-year increase in homicides ever, a spike that continued into 2021. That increase receded along with the pandemic. One type of crime did continue past the early surge, however—reckless driving, which has been called a nationwide "public health crisis" and "silent epidemic."[46]

Writing in the *New York Times Magazine,* Matthew Shaer reported that the number of car crashes in the United States rose

16 percent from 2020 to 2021 to more than six million (about 16,500 wrecks a day), and 42,939 Americans died in car crashes in 2021, the highest number in 15 years. He explored multiple theories for why America had been propelled into a reckless-driving hell. He began with the "collective trauma" identified in the American Psychological Association's "Stress in America 2023" report. "According to the report, . . . just 34 percent of American adults have confidence in the direction the country is going, while a third of respondents said they had too much anxiety in their lives to think about the future at all. Nearly a half wished they had someone—anyone—who could help them manage a daily barrage of stressors," Shaer wrote. "'All those emotions, they have to go somewhere,' says Ryan Martin, a psychologist at the University of Wisconsin and a specialist in the science of anger. More often than not, Martin contends, we find that outlet in a car."[47]

For some young people, reckless driving and car crashes were by-products of stealing cars for joy rides. Auto thefts soared in part because of social media videos publicizing how easy it was to steal Kia and Hyundai cars, some by a group of teenagers self-named the "Kia Boyz."[48] Milwaukee had only averaged 39 traffic deaths per year from 2008 to 2012, but in 2021, 65 people died from reckless driving there, followed by 77 in 2022 and 74 in 2023.[49] This was not just a big-city problem; reckless driving and its deadly consequences spilled over into suburbs and small towns, too. As in cities across the country, reckless driving became a daily issue in Wauwatosa and nearby communities.[50]

While intensifying enforcement at traffic hot spots, Wauwatosa and other cities have also implemented "road diets"—lowering speed limits; changing road design by creating protected sidewalks and bike lanes, speed bumps, and "bump-outs" to pinch and narrow streets; and reducing the number of traffic lanes to allow for more refuge islands, bike lanes, and parking. Narrow streets are safer streets, especially for pedestrians and bike riders, because they slow the flow of traffic.[51] Putting in speed and red-light cameras can make a difference, too, though they are sometimes challenged as violations of privacy or as too focused on Black and Latino neighborhoods.[52] Though these measures might seem simple to implement, retrofitting streets and roads is expensive.[53] New York City, for example, has 6,300 miles of roads and more than 39,000 intersections. But for the sake of pedestrians and drivers, America's streets must be reconfigured.[54]

PROTESTS REDUX

Wide-scale protests returned in 2024. For some, it was a reversion to 2020. For others, it harkened back to the Occupy Wall Street protests of 2011. For those of a certain age, it took us back even further to 1968, *The Strawberry Statement*, the occupation of Columbia University buildings, and the heartache of our country being ripped apart socially, politically, and physically during the Vietnam War and the civil rights movement.[55]

The protests of 2024 had their origin in a brutal attack on October 7, 2023. That day, members of a terrorist group, Hamas, entered Israel from the Gaza Strip and raped, captured, and killed Israelis. For months, Israel tried to eliminate the Hamas threat by repeatedly bombing Gaza, killing and injuring thousands of Palestinians, and leaving millions homeless in ghastly scenes shown nightly on American television. In 2024, protests over Israel's actions exploded on American college campuses, most prominently at Columbia, but more seemed to be at stake: the collective trauma felt by students who had been cut adrift emotionally in school lockdowns during the pandemic had found new expression in campus protests. For many, wrote Jeremy W. Peters in the *New York Times*, "the issues are closer to home, and at the same time, much bigger and broader. In their eyes, the Gaza conflict is a struggle for justice, linked to issues that seem far afield. They say they are motivated by policing, mistreatment of Indigenous people, discrimination toward Black Americans and the impact of global warming." For these students, the issues that drove the 2020 protests had not been resolved but had expanded.[56]

Perhaps inevitably in a spontaneous, leaderless, and unorganized mass movement, what began as sincere and peaceful protests did not always stay that way. Good-faith concern for the obvious plight of Palestinians sometimes tilted into antisemitism, in contrast to the civil rights and anti–Vietnam War protests of the 1960s, which demanded equality and respect for all people.[57] As in 2020, protests occasionally turned violent, such as when Columbia students and others smashed windows and occupied one of the same buildings, Hamilton Hall, that student protesters had occupied in 1968. As in 2020, when outside agitators caused much of the illegal activity in Kenosha, Wauwatosa, and other communities, it appeared that outsiders had infiltrated the protests at Columbia and other campuses and stoked some of the violence.[58]

Responding to the destruction at Columbia and other campuses, President Biden called for calm, saying, "Violent protest is not protected. Peaceful protest is. It's against the law when violence occurs. Destroying property is not a peaceful protest. It's against the law."[59] This was the same message that other mayors and I had conveyed repeatedly, without success, during the protests of 2020.

Though many people took sides, it was possible to support Israelis who were the victims of the Hamas attack while also condemning the Israeli government's destruction of Gaza and killing of innocent Palestinians.[60] But in 2024, as in 1968 and 2020, violence, destruction, and political rigidity cost protesters public support.[61] There was a better path, paved years earlier in Northern Ireland, which had been plagued by armed and deadly sectarian conflict for 30 years in the late twentieth century. The uneasy peace that has held there since 1998 began with reciprocal acknowledgement that both sides had legitimate grievances.[62] That lesson has been ignored in the Middle East. "It's time to take back the Israel-Palestine debate from the radicals on both sides," urged *Vox* senior correspondent Zack Beauchamp in the midst of the 2024 protests.[63] Doing so required melding the passion of the young with the hard-earned wisdom of their elders. It was apparent that time had not arrived.

COURTING CONTROVERSY

Also not ended was litigation against Wauwatosa and me. As previously described, in two lawsuits, *Knowlton v. City of Wauwatosa* and *Radke v. City of Wauwatosa*, federal courts rejected the claim that the emergency proclamation, curfew, and police actions of October 7–12, 2020, had violated the First and Fourth Amendments to the US Constitution.

This did not stop Kimberley Motley, the lawyer who lost *Knowlton*, from bringing two more federal cases in late 2023 making the same allegations on behalf of some of the same plaintiffs. In April 2024, US Magistrate Judge Nancy Joseph dismissed the new cases, calling the claims in *Rivera v. City of Wauwatosa* and *Cole v. City of Wauwatosa* "textbook examples of claim preclusion and/or improper claim-splitting." In layman's terms, this means that litigants don't get two kicks at the same cat—the same plaintiffs' claims had already been litigated, and failed, in *Knowlton*. Joseph held that Motley should have awaited the US Court of Appeals for the Seventh Circuit's ruling on the appeal in *Knowlton*.[64] The city gave Motley the opportunity to withdraw *Rivera* and *Cole* before filing a motion to sanction her for her improper actions, but she declined. For that reason, in June 2024 Joseph ordered Motley to pay the attorney's fees and costs incurred by the city in *Rivera* and *Cole*.[65] The bill totaled $14,305.

Meanwhile, in October 2023, three years after the curfew began, Kathryn Knowlton, a lawyer who was the lead plaintiff in the *Knowlton* case, had brought a Wisconsin state court lawsuit, *Fanning v. City of Wauwatosa*, on behalf of two previous *Knowlton* plaintiffs. They again alleged that the curfew and police actions in October 2020 had violated their rights, this time under the Wisconsin Constitution, and sought compensatory and punitive damages for the alleged violations.

In *Radke* and *Knowlton,* the plaintiffs argued (among other things) that their federal constitutional rights had been violated because my emergency proclamation was not validly enacted under state law. In *Radke,* US district judge Lynn Adelman held that "the question of whether the curfew was valid under state law is not relevant to the analysis of whether the challenged actions of the defendants violated the First Amendment [to the US Constitution]. That is so because the constitutionality of a time, place, and manner restriction is determined by federal constitutional standards rather than by state or municipal law."[66] Judge Joseph made a similar ruling in *Knowlton.*[67]

Picking up where *Radke* and *Knowlton* left off, the *Fanning* lawsuit was based primarily on Chapter 323 of the Wisconsin Statutes. Section 323.11 states, "The governing body of any local unit of government may declare, by ordinance or resolution, an emergency . . . whenever conditions arise by reason of a riot or civil commotion, a disaster, or an imminent threat of a disaster, that impairs transportation, food or fuel supplies, medical care, fire, health or police protection, or other critical systems of the local unit of government." Section 323.14(4)(b) states, "If, because of the emergency conditions, the governing body of the local unit of government is unable to meet promptly, the chief executive officer . . . of any local unit of government shall exercise by proclamation all of the powers conferred . . . under . . . s. 323.11 that appear necessary and expedient."

In their court complaint, the *Fanning* plaintiffs alleged that my emergency proclamation and curfew order violated Chapter 323 because nothing prevented the Wauwatosa Common Council from meeting to consider a possible curfew at any time before I issued the proclamation on October 7, 2020. As a result, they claimed, they were entitled to a judicial declaration that the proclamation, the curfew, and the tickets issued by police for curfew violations in October 2020 violated Chapter 323 and entitled to an injunction requiring the city to expunge any record of the proclamation and curfew order and prohibiting the city and me from disclosing the contents of any such record. Essentially, they wanted the court to say I had acted improperly, the curfew tickets should be rescinded, and any fines collected should be paid back.

In fact, the council did hold its regular weekly meeting on October 6, 2020, the day before I issued the proclamation. But this missed the point. At the council meeting on October 13, 2020, the day after the curfew ended, I explained that although Alvin Cole's family and attorney Motley had posted on Facebook that they would be meeting with District Attorney John Chisholm on October 7, which is why we prepared the proclamation in advance, we did not know when Chisholm would be making his determination on whether to charge Officer Mensah. He had not stated publicly, or privately to us, when he would do so, nor had he revealed what he would decide. We had expected him to announce his decision at an earlier meeting with the Cole family on June 11, 2020, but he changed his mind when he learned that an additional police video existed and needed to be reviewed. For all we knew, the same thing might happen again at his October 7 meeting with the Coles.

For these reasons, discussing the proclamation at the October 6 council meeting would have been premature. Depending on what Chisholm decided, we might not have had to issue the proclamation. Furthermore, as our city attorney explained to the council, the police strategy for protecting the community during possible unrest following Chisholm's announcement had to be kept confidential, and the Wisconsin Open Meetings Law would not allow the council to discuss that strategy in closed session. (We also feared that alderpersons might share confidential information with TPR leaders. We believed that one had already done so.)

At the October 13 meeting, I emphasized, as I had in the proclamation, that we were guided by what had happened in Kenosha a few weeks earlier, where two protesters were killed, scores were seriously injured, and $52 million of private property was destroyed. Though many Wauwatosa protesters had been peaceful, some had carried Molotov cocktails, smashed windows, and set fires, and many agitators came from out of state. "We could have done nothing to prepare and hoped for the best," I told the council, "but if injuries, deaths, and major property damage had occurred, we would have been correctly criticized for not preparing for the worst. . . . While I'm hearing from many people who oppose the measures we put in place, I'm also hearing from many people who are thanking us. The curfew is over. No one got killed. No one was seriously hurt. There was minimal property damage."[68] I also stressed that the people killed or injured in Kenosha were BLM protesters. We had tried to keep everyone safe.

Under Section 323.14(4)(b), the council could ratify, alter, modify, or repeal my proclamation, but no action taken would affect the prior validity of that order. Some alderpersons wanted to approve the proclamation. A few others objected to the curfew or grumbled about not being able to vote on the order in advance. Quickly, however, the council voted 10–4 to place the matter on file. The "no" votes were cast by alders who wanted to approve the order.[69]

Then, several years later, came the *Fanning* case. At a hearing in June 2024, Milwaukee County Circuit Court judge Glenn Yamahiro verbally granted the city's motion to dismiss the *Fanning* constitutional claims for the same reason that Judge Joseph had dismissed the *Rivera* and *Cole* cases two weeks earlier—the same claims by the same plaintiffs had failed in the *Knowlton* case. On the claim that my emergency proclamation violated Chapter 323 of the Wisconsin Statutes, Yamahiro—the judge who in 2021 had found probable cause to believe that Mensah had committed a crime when he killed Jay Anderson Jr., a finding later rejected by the special prosecutors he appointed—told the city's lawyers to draft an order putting his oral ruling into writing.[70]

The plaintiffs filed a motion for reconsideration, based in part on a supposed "good faith factual correction" that did not comply with the rules of evidence or procedure. On July 5, 2024, before the city could respond, Yamahiro reversed himself and entered a confusing order granting summary judgment for the plaintiffs on their Chapter 323 claim. That day, the city filed its own motion for reconsideration. Several months later, Yamahiro conceded that he had signed the wrong (plaintiffs') order and again dismissed the lawsuit.[71] After four years, the litigation against the city and me had finally come to an end.

The plaintiffs chose not to appeal. Either way, an appeals court decision would have had no practical impact. Though it would have provided guidance for the future, such a decision would have dealt with events that ended years before. Plaintiffs, judges, and historians enjoy the luxury of second-guessing; dealing with chaos and danger in real time in 2020, we did not.

For guidance throughout 2020, I fell back on decades of studying how leaders, especially Abraham Lincoln, handled other crises. I had no doubt that Mr. Lincoln would have issued the same curfew order I did. Early in the Civil War he suspended the constitutional privilege of the writ of habeas corpus—which allows prisoners to challenge their detention—because he believed that our country would fall apart if he did not do so. The suspension, which occurred while Congress was in recess and not able to take action itself, was controversial.

In his First Inaugural Address, delivered after seven states had seceded from the Union but a month before the attack on Fort Sumter, Lincoln reminded the rebels: "You have no oath registered in Heaven to destroy the government, while I shall have the most solemn one to preserve, protect, and defend it." Soon after the rebellion broke out, he gave the Union's commanding general the authority to suspend the writ of habeas corpus if the army believed that the release of prisoners, especially those in border states, would jeopardize the war effort.

Several months later, Lincoln delivered a message to Congress when it returned from its recess. He noted that Article I, Section 9, of the Constitution allows the writ to be suspended "when in cases of rebellion or invasion the public safety may require it." But a US court of appeals decision, *Ex parte Merryman*, held that only Congress had that authority.[72] Nonetheless, Lincoln asked Congress, "Are all the laws but one to go unexecuted, and the Government itself go to pieces lest that one be violated? Even in such a case, would not [my] official oath [to preserve and protect the Union] be broken if the Government should be overthrown when it was believed that disregarding the single law would tend to preserve it?" He continued: "Now it is insisted that Congress, and not the Executive, is vested with this power. But the Constitution itself, is silent as to which, or who, is to exercise the power; and as the provision was plainly made for a dangerous emergency, it cannot be believed the framers of the [Constitution] intended that . . . the danger should run its course, until Congress could be called together."[73] The detentions continued.

In the Wauwatosa lawsuits, the plaintiffs likewise insisted that only the Common Council, and not the mayor, had the authority to issue a curfew order. As a long-time lawyer and former law clerk to a US district judge, I was confident that my order complied with the US and Wisconsin Constitutions and that the Wisconsin Statutes gave me the power to declare an emergency if the Council could not meet. To paraphrase Lincoln, by enacting Chapter 323 the Wisconsin Legislature intended that if in the midst of a dangerous emergency the Common Council could not meet, the mayor had power to prevent calamity.

Though Wauwatosa's existential moment was not of the magnitude of a national civil war, it was no less real. As several federal courts held, our actions in October 2020, shortly after death and destruction occurred in nearby Kenosha, kept protesters and the community safe. Subsequently, that community indicated its approval: the Common Council did not oppose my curfew order, Wauwatosa residents reelected me by a large margin, and the court decisions in our favor stimulated little discussion. Though the protest plaintiffs had not moved on, Wauwatosa had.

In January 2022, the Common Council unanimously adopted an equity and inclusion statement: "The City of Wauwatosa is committed to creating a positive environment of equity and inclusion for all of its employees, those who live or work in Wauwatosa, and visitors to Wauwatosa. We believe that embracing the concept of equity and inclusion improves our community for everyone, and will assist us in ending disparities in quality of living that exist because of historic policies, practices, and systems in Wauwatosa." The council and I embedded those principles in the City's 2023–2027 strategic plan.[74]

In April 2022, African Americans ran for election to the council in three of Wauwatosa's eight aldermanic districts. Two of the three became the first Blacks elected to office in Wauwatosa; the other, who had a problematic history, was defeated.[75] A few months later, the Wauwatosa School Board selected an African American woman, from among seven candidates, to fill a vacancy left by a resignation.[76] In 2023, she was elected to the board along with another African American candidate, whom I had earlier appointed to the Police and Fire Commission. These elections and appointments to city commissions should lead to a local government ever more sensitive to an increasingly diverse population.

CIVICS LESSONS

While the collective trauma identified by psychologists caused a decline in civility and good behavior following 2020,[77] political polarization and declining confidence in public institutions post-pandemic only made the problem worse.[78] That current wave of polarization, which began in the 1990s,[79] accelerated with the elections of 2016 and 2020 and showed few signs of abating thereafter as Trump, Biden, and their loyalists did political battle.[80]

Post-2020, Trump continually claimed that he had never lost the election, though numerous analyses and scores of lawsuits had proved otherwise. He promised his supporters revenge for the hurt feelings that he and they felt from his loss. "I am your warrior, I am your justice," he told the Conservative Political Action Conference in March 2023. "And for those who have been wronged and betrayed, I am your retribution."[81] The controversy and suspicions he stoked with such words and with his dark warnings of an America overrun by immigrants, godless socialists, and other evil spirits, undermined public confidence in the American system. "This is the final battle," Trump warned, invoking Armageddon. "They know it, I know it, you know it, everybody knows it. This is it. Either they win or we win. And if they win, we no longer have a country."[82]

The desire for revenge and extreme polarization, between the political parties and even between members of a single party, threw sand in the gears of American government from the local level all the way up to Congress. In the 2023–25 term, the US House of Representatives barely functioned as the Republican majority's far-right-wing "Freedom Caucus" paralyzed the body with fights over ideological purity. For them, compromise and civility were dirty words.[83]

The dysfunction in our national and state capitals flowed down to the local level. Behavior at city council and school board meetings nationwide deteriorated as mobs disrupted proceedings over mask-wearing and vaccine requirements, police conduct, equity and inclusion efforts, sex education, and other hot-button issues. "Angry outbursts, hateful speech and unruly behavior not only disrupt governing board meetings," stated guidance from the Institute for Local Government, "but also increase polarization in the community and make serious discussion and problem-solving, including compromise, nearly impossible."[84] Princeton University's 2023 and 2024 surveys of US municipalities found that while Democratic local officials reported higher levels of insults, rates of severe hostility (such as harassment, threats, and attacks) did not differ substantially by party.[85]

Not surprisingly, extreme partisanship, physical threats, and bad civic behavior make people less likely to run for office.[86] In an analysis of 11,945 elections at all levels of government in 40 states during the first four months of 2024, Ballotpedia found that 8,802 (74 percent) were uncontested.[87] Commenting on Ballotpedia's similar analysis of 200 rural races in Wisconsin the previous year, a University of Wisconsin–Green Bay professor, David Helpap, told the *Appleton* (WI) *Post-Crescent*, "People may have interest in making sure the school board budget is balanced or that the parks are a good quality, but they don't necessarily want to deal with the national issues that have moved into these local governments." Professor Barry Burden, director of the University of Wisconsin–Madison's Elections Research Center, added, "The positions often entail significant time commitments, do not provide much if any monetary compensation, and subject people to complaints, criticism, and even harassment."[88]

As much as Americans understand the value of serving their community, for many the personal price had become too high.[89] "Politics is a contact sport," wrote Oregon political observer Steve Forrester in 2023, "but death threats are a new thing."[90] Democracy is the certain loser when fear, disgust, and polarization cause citizens to disengage from politics.

THE SECOND PANDEMIC ELECTION

Some voters and political observers wondered how Donald Trump won the 2024 presidential election despite a long list of statements, behaviors, and events that would have doomed any other candidate, including (but not limited to) conviction on 34 felony counts of falsifying business records, a civil judgment for sexual assault, threats to prosecute and execute political enemies, and criminal indictments for actions related to the insurrection at the US Capitol on January 6, 2021. Among the many reasons for his triumph, however, one loomed the largest: the lingering effects of inflation.[91]

The *Atlantic*'s Derek Thompson termed 2024 "the second COVID election." Jess Bidgood of the *New York Times* reached the same conclusion, in virtually the same words, calling it "the second pandemic election." They observed that the pandemic's impact was still being felt in our nation's economy, politics, and psyche. "Trump's victory is a reverberation of trends set in motion in 2020," Thompson explained. "In politics, as in nature, the largest tsunami generated by an earthquake is often not the first wave but the next one."[92] Bidgood agreed. "When President Biden came into office and vaccines made Covid less lethal, much of the public was eager to forget what had happened," she wrote. "But whether people talked about it, the pandemic had already set into motion some of the forces that would make President Biden's term in office rocky. It spurred global supply chain shocks that sent inflation soaring. In the years that followed, the public's faith in institutions eroded, and Trump and his allies sought to weaponize that distrust. Communities had fierce battles over school closures and curriculums. People worried about political violence and their economic future. There was also a political backlash against the racial justice protests that had unfolded during the pandemic's first year."

Bidgood reported a warning for Democrats from strategist Doug Sosnik: "Covid, in many ways, walked into this country's tribal politics, and really put it on steroids," he said, and added that the 2024 results might signal America's biggest shift to the right since Ronald Reagan was elected president in 1980.[93]

New York Yankees philosopher Yogi Berra reminded us that "it's tough to make predictions, especially about the future."[94] But it seems certain that as long as the pandemic's effects ripple through the global economy, America and the world will struggle to reach a new political equilibrium.

—ɯ—

THE SECOND-HARDEST JOB IN GOVERNMENT

AT ORIENTATION IN 1977, DEAN Donald Stokes welcomed graduate students to Princeton University's School of Public and International Affairs. "The most important attribute of a successful public servant is endurance," he told us. "You will go through times of struggle, and you will need endurance to carry you through. Our campus is full of exercise facilities and walking and running trails. I urge you to take advantage of them and develop your endurance to the fullest." Despite being a marathon runner, I did not fully appreciate his message until 2020.

The challenges of that year were "unlike anything I've ever seen," former Columbus, Ohio, mayor Michael B. Coleman told *Politico* in 2021. "The mayor's job is already the most difficult job in government, except for maybe the president of the United States. And life as a mayor is more challenging now than it has ever been."[1]

A city's fundamental mission is to provide basic services to residents—water, roads, garbage collection, snow plowing, traffic regulation, public health services, and police and fire protection.[2] That task, complicated by the need to find money to pay for those services, is daunting in the best of times. But 2020 added new levels of stress. "2020 unquestionably took a toll on mayors nationwide," the *New York Times* reported. "It was one of the most tumultuous years for American cities since the 1960s, with the social and economic disruptions of the coronavirus pandemic as well as racial justice protests that sometimes turned destructive."[3] Mayors surveyed by Boston University's Initiative on Cities that year expressed anxiety about the effects of lost tax revenue on their budgets while they dealt with the pandemic and resulting economic downturn. The initiative's executive director, Katharine Lusk, said that mayors "will tell you it's the most personal job in politics."[4] They fretted about the toll that the events of 2020 and 2021 took on the mental health of their constituents.[5]

But those events were hard on mayors' psyches, too. As *USA Today* reported in 2020, "Mayors face some of the same struggles as their constituents—a spouse sick with COVID-19 or children learning from home—as they tackle what some say is one of their most important jobs: helping their community cope mentally with the incredible uncertainty and projecting confidence they'll get through it."[6] Commenting on the stresses on elected officials, British psychologists recounted the periodic depression suffered even by esteemed leaders like Winston Churchill and Abraham Lincoln and noted, "Politics . . . requires resilience and an ability to thrive under pressure. In that respect, it's a lot like elite sports, albeit with a fraction of the reward and adulation. Inevitably such a profession brings with it mental health risks."[7]

During my BBC interview in 2020, I was asked how I was dealing with the crises in Wauwatosa. In part, I offered Robert Louis Stevenson's admonition to "keep your fears to yourself, but share your courage with others." In another interview, a journalist asked what I would recommend to other mayors faced with emotionally-charged protests. "We must stay centered and measured, be true to the law and our oaths of office, and play the long game," I replied. "The tortoise wins the race, not the hare."

In cities big or small, being mayor is a 24/7 job. Everywhere you go, people recognize you and raise their concerns—often,

I've learned, in a grocery store or while I'm standing in a locker room wrapped in a towel. You never know if you will be awakened in the middle of the night or pulled away on a weekend by an emergency call from the police or fire chief. Serving in elective office also requires thick skin—resilience—to withstand daily criticisms about a city's problems, and thicker yet during pandemics and months of protests. Being called a "fascist" or a "racist" for enforcing the law or preventing looting or burning of neighborhoods, while conversely being accused of not supporting the police, takes an enormous emotional toll. The toll is also great on mayors' families, who must endure protests and name-calling and provide emotional support to their loved ones while dealing with their own needs.

Under these stresses, mayors in Atlanta, St. Louis, Seattle, and other cities chose not to seek reelection.[8] The irony was that many were liberal Democrats who had taken flak from left-wing constituents for enforcing the law during violent protests.[9] Mayors who did stand for reelection in 2020 and 2021 faced stiff challenges, but, as described earlier, mayors in Portland, Buffalo, Minneapolis, New York, and elsewhere who supported enforcing the law, while seeking change, were reelected.[10] In 2023, a Democratic state senator, John Whitmire, defeated a liberal icon, Congresswoman Sheila Jackson Lee, for mayor of Houston with a tough-on-crime campaign, even though Lee had been endorsed by the outgoing mayor and Democratic luminaries like Bill and Hillary Clinton and former Speaker of the House Nancy Pelosi.[11]

During the demonstrations at my home in 2020, protesters demanded that I resign, even though I had just been elected to a four-year term. That October, when Governor Evers sent the National Guard to Wauwatosa and I declared a five-night curfew, I knew that our actions might be an impediment to reelection. But I had to focus on the city's needs, not on political preservation. Predictably, some people were unhappy. Several times as I worked in my yard, a man drove by, honked, yelled, and saluted me with his middle finger. Others condemned my actions a bit more politely by email. But almost every day for months after the curfew ended, people stopped me at stores, on the street, and elsewhere and thanked me for keeping the community safe. Marathon runners are not quitters, and for their sake I was not going to quit.

In 2024, I ran for reelection. Some residents were surprised I wanted to continue, given what I had endured and that the mayor is Wauwatosa's lowest-paid employee at $30,000 a year. (Milwaukee suburbs with similar populations pay their mayors between $85,000 and $110,000.) As a federal pensioner, however, I did not need the money; I wanted to serve my hometown. I also wanted a referendum on what had occurred in Wauwatosa in 2020.

As my campaign began in earnest in early 2024, those events were not ignored. During an interview for a possible endorsement by the Milwaukee Area Labor Council, a union representative asked me, "Have you reconsidered any of the actions you took in 2020?" My answer, quick, direct, and unapologetic, was one I had given before: "Every day since the curfew ended, I've searched my conscience about whether I acted appropriately. Every day, I've reached the same conclusion: I am comfortable with the decisions I made. If, only five weeks after eight blocks of Kenosha burned down and a creepy 17-year-old kid from Illinois killed two Black Lives Matter protesters there, I had done nothing to prepare for the worst, my hometown had burned down, and someone had gotten killed, that would been on my conscience until the day I died. That would have been on me."

I received the Labor Council's endorsement as well as endorsements from the (African American) Milwaukee County Executive, two former Wauwatosa mayors, and almost every member of the Wauwatosa Common Council (including our two Black alderpersons), among many others.[12] But some "progressive" residents had never forgiven me for the curfew and for the National

Guard coming to town. It was no secret they were searching for someone to run against me.

My opponents tried to label me as "conservative." I had not outgrown progressivism, however.[13] Though I was 70 years old, my politics had not changed since my upbringing in the 1960s: I still believed in racial equality, a clean environment, public education, and other causes embraced by the left. But as the son of two hardheaded newspaper reporters, one of whom served as vice chair of the Wisconsin Democratic Party during the Kennedy administration, I was also committed to getting things done rather than merely engaging in performative gestures,[14] and I rejected the notion that violence and destruction are a path to progress. My reelection campaign would test whether my politics and Wauwatosa's were still a match.

In Wisconsin, unlike many parts of the country, local officials are elected on a nonpartisan basis.[15] This is a blessing; echoing former New York City mayor Fiorello LaGuardia, I often remind residents and alderpersons that "there's no Democratic way to collect the garbage and no Republican way to plow the snow."[16] Nevertheless, because Wauwatosa had become solidly liberal, the election took on the flavor of a Democratic primary. My opponent, a young first-term alderman from Chicago, fronted the faction of Indivisible Tosa, Tosa Moms Tackling Racism, and The People's Revolution as well as NIMBY residents who opposed apartment developments despite our community's severe housing shortage. But I had broad support from liberals, moderates, and, as the less objectionable alternative, from the city's dwindling group of conservatives, though some refused to vote for me because they believed I had not supported the police in 2020. On April 2, 2024, Wauwatosa's voters elected me to a second four-year term. I won every aldermanic district and received 58.5 percent of the vote, about two points less than in 2020. Voters also reelected alderpersons who, like me, were center-left and pro-development, and rejected more extreme candidates. After four years of being second-guessed, I felt vindicated and liberated.

Finally, it seemed, 2020 was behind us, though the *Milwaukee Journal Sentinel*'s election report noted, "The COVID-19 pandemic and 2020 protests against former Wauwatosa Police Officer Joseph Mensah's shooting of 17-year-old Alvin Cole marked the start of McBride's first term as mayor."[17] Years from now, my obituary will surely include a similar statement.

The fissures exposed in 2020 remained, everywhere. The election of America's first Black president 12 years earlier had not marked the end of our country's racism and divisions; rather, it seemed to have reawakened them. Barack Obama's inaugural address was hopeful but not prescient. "Because we have tasted the bitter swill of civil war and segregation, and emerged from that dark chapter stronger and more united," he said in January 2009, "we cannot help but believe that the old hatreds shall someday pass; that the lines of tribe shall soon dissolve; that, as the world grows smaller, our common humanity shall reveal itself."[18]

In 2020, our humanity did reveal itself. It was not pretty. America has never been good about admitting the truth to itself, and in 2020 that failure led to Americans telling lies about race, COVID, vaccines, the economy, mass shootings, and the outcome of the presidential election.[19] The years after 2020 only deepened the divide. We seemed farther apart than ever on the role of science in our society and our lives, we lost our consensus on public education, and a substantial portion of our population denied climate change. Driven by (and spreading) false information on social media, conspiracy theorists created a dark Alice-in-Wonderland environment in which truth was fiction, consensus was impossible, and extremists called for their political opponents to be executed.[20]

Political polarization made it impossible to reach agreement on how to deal with the root causes of the reckoning touched off by the murder of George Floyd. One of our major parties, which calls itself "the party of Lincoln," abandoned its commitment to our republic's founding principle, the "self-evident" truth that "all men are created equal."[21] The Republican Party waged a campaign on the state and federal levels to prohibit slavery or "critical race theory" from being discussed in schools from K-12 through college and to eliminate "diversity, equity, and inclusion" (DEI) initiatives in education and employment.[22] In June 2023, in *Students for Fair Admissions, Inc. v. Harvard College*, the GOP-sponsored "originalist" justices on the US Supreme Court declared affirmative action in higher education a violation of the US Constitution.[23] In Virginia in 2024, the Shenandoah County School Board voted 5–1 to restore the names of Stonewall Jackson High School and Ashby-Lee Elementary School, honoring Confederate heroes—traitors and enslavers—whose names had been removed from those schools in 2020.[24] And immediately after taking office for a second term in 2025, President Trump decreed the elimination of DEI initiatives in the federal government.[25] The GOP's purported "color blindness" enabled it to ignore that full racial equality remains a goal, not an achievement.

In all these ways, so-called conservatives declared war on fact. But the far left does not get a free pass, either. A survey of 7,258 Americans by Emory University researcher Thomas H. Costello and five colleagues published in the *Journal of Personality and Social Psychology* in August 2021 revealed that antidemocratic attitudes exist on both ends of the electorate. The researchers found common traits between left-wing and right-wing authoritarians, including a "preference for social uniformity, prejudice towards different others, willingness to wield group authority to coerce behavior, cognitive rigidity, aggression and punitiveness towards perceived enemies, outsized concern for hierarchy, and moral absolutism." To measure left-wing authoritarianism, Costello and his colleagues asked subjects to score, on a scale of 1 to 7, sentiments such as "We need to replace the established order by any means necessary" and "I should have the right not to be exposed to offensive views." As Sally Satel observed in the *Atlantic*, "By agreeing with statements such as 'Getting rid of inequality is more important than protecting the so-called "right" to free speech,' [the left-wing subjects] showed an attitude called 'top-down censorship.'"[26] Equally troubling, a survey conducted in late 2023 by the University of Virginia's Center for Politics found that many Americans, on both left and right, are willing to give up constitutional rights like freedom of speech to help their political parties.[27]

That's not the American way, and it's not America. Though extremists believe that everyone thinks as they do, or should, most Americans remain in the political center. Moving forward, getting things done, requires appealing to the middle, not just true believers.[28] In a 2024 Gallup survey, 27 percent of voters identified as Republicans, 25 percent as Democrats, and 45 percent as independents. These findings were similar to those in previous polls.[29]

Post-2020, it has been easy to be pessimistic about working within our political system. Yet we have endured existential crises before: in the 1860s, our country survived a civil war fought over slavery; in the 1930s, gripped by despair during an economic depression, we overcame movements to abandon democracy and human rights;[30] and in the 1960s and 1970s, we healed a country divided by assassinations, an unpopular war, and the Watergate scandal. As impatient as we might be for progress or change, we sometimes forget that the wheels of politics and government turn slowly. "Government is hard," political pundit Fareed Zakaria has written. "American government is harder still. It's a political system designed to prevent tyranny, not facilitate speedy action. Power is checked, divided, and shared. Making it work takes energy, ingenuity, and, above all, a belief in government."[31]

Wauwatosa's evolution offers hope. Once a rigidly segregated community that excluded people of color, we have slowly returned to our abolitionist roots. Bucking national trends, we have embraced a considerable amount of positive change in the short time since George Floyd's death. But we still have miles to go.

For me, the most encouraging words came in an email from an official of a union that supported my reelection. "Please let us know how we can work together during your term in office," she wrote. "We want this relationship to be one of mutual respect and trust regardless of whether we always agree on every issue. We value our relationship with pro-labor elected leaders and know that we are all stronger together. . . . We look forward to working with you to make our community the best it can be for our members and your constituents."

We won't always agree on every issue, but to move forward we have no choice but to work together. In 1892, a Massachusetts editor wrote a pledge that is now recited almost every day by schoolchildren, mayors, city council members, and other Americans. His vow of loyalty to our country's flag was really to "the Republic for which it stands," an "indivisible" nation of diverse states and people. Francis Bellamy's Pledge of Allegiance, reflecting the sentiments of the Declaration of Independence and the Gettysburg Address, concludes with our national commitment to "liberty and justice for all."[32] That has always been worth striving for.

As Benjamin Franklin left Independence Hall after the Constitutional Convention completed its work in 1787, a prominent Philadelphian asked him what sort of government we had. "A republic," Franklin replied, "if you can keep it."[33]

As ever, our society is a work in progress. For all citizens, that requires not just a pledge but fidelity to our indivisible republic, a belief in representative government and the rule of law, and dedication to liberty and justice for all. It also requires a willingness to perform our civic duties.[34] Elected officials cannot do that work alone.

ACKNOWLEDGMENTS

THIS BOOK WOULD NOT HAVE been possible without the patience, support, and courage of my wife, Karen Barry, who has stood by me for 30 years, never more bravely or steadfastly than during the dark days of 2020, even though she never wanted me to be an elected official.

As always, I have been fortified by the support of my children, Meredith, Gillian, and Donovan McBride, and my sons-in-law, Matthew Meltzer and Eric Zidarich. Their encouragement kept my spirits strong through the months and years, and stops and starts, it took to write this book.

I am grateful to my brother Joseph McBride, an author published and lauded many times over, and my twin brother, Dr. Patrick McBride, both of whom encouraged me to write this book. They offered important early critiques, as did Wauwatosa city administrator Jim Archambo and my friends Jeffrey Roznowski and Mark Goldstein. I also am grateful to Dan Crissman, who as Editorial Director of the Indiana University Press showed enthusiasm for my book from the beginning; to the current Director of IU Press, Gary Dunham, who maintained that support; and to IU Press assistant acquisitions editor Anna Francis, who kept the book moving through the production process.

My thanks go as well to my friend Daniel Andera for his photographs and to GIS wizard Paul Vepraskas for his patience and his work on the maps that appear in this book.

Finally, I will always be grateful to my friends and neighbors, who showed faith in me by twice electing me as the mayor of my hometown.

NOTES

PREFACE

1. "Edge City," Wikipedia, last modified May 20, 2024, https://en.wikipedia.org/wiki/Edge_city; "List of Edge Cities," Wikipedia, 2000–2024, accessed May 27, 2024, https://en-academic.com/dic.nsf/enwiki/5389748; "Wauwatosa, Wisconsin—a Brief History," Wisconsin Historical Society, 2009, https://www.wisconsinhistory.org/Records/Article/CS2402.

2. Joel Garreau, *Edge City: Life on the New Frontier* (New York: Doubleday Books, 1991).

3. Kent Sepkowitz, "Opinion: Were Covid-19 Lockdowns a Mistake?," CNN, November 10, 2023, https://www.cnn.com/2023/11/10/opinions/covid-19-pandemic-lockdowns-sepkowitz.

MICROCOSM

1. Radley Balko, "Opinion: Don't Read Too Much into the Outcome of Derek Chauvin's Trial," *Washington Post*, April 1, 2021, https://www.washingtonpost.com/opinions/2021/04/01/dont-read-too-much-into-outcome-derek-chauvins-trial/; "Reimagine Safety: A Project of the Editorial Board, in Conversation with Outside Voices," *Washington Post*, March 16, 2021, https://www.washingtonpost.com/opinions/interactive/2021/reimagine-safety/.

2. Marco della Cava and Mike Stucka, "Mass Shootings Surge in Wisconsin as Nation Faces Record High," *USA Today*, March 5, 2021, https://

www.jsonline.com/story/news/2021/03/05/gda-mass-shootings-rise-in-2020-wi-pmjs/4344219/; Tom Jackman, "Homicides Rose 30 Percent in 2020, Survey of 34 U.S. Cities Finds: Robbery and Burglary Fell, Likely Related to the Pandemic, Expert Says," *Washington Post*, February 3, 2021, https://www.washingtonpost.com/crime-law/2021/02/03/homicides-rose-2020/; Elliot Hughes, "As Milwaukee Closes Book on Historic Year of Violence, There's Some Optimism for 2021. But Just Some," *Milwaukee Journal Sentinel*, January 1, 2021, https://www.jsonline.com/story/news/2021/01/01/cascade-factors-led-2020-milwaukee-violence-they-change/4073573001/; Derek Thompson, "Why America's Great Crime Decline Is Over: Even Before the Recent Mass Shootings, Violent Crime Was Surging to Its Highest Rate in 30 Years. Patrick Sharkey Illuminates What's Happening," *Atlantic*, March 24, 2021, https://www.theatlantic.com/ideas/archive/2021/03/is-americas-great-crime-decline-over/618381/.

3. John McWhorter, "Opinion: Our Racial Reckoning Could Have Come Sooner. What Made 2020 Different?," *New York Times*, June 10, 2022, https://www.nytimes.com/2022/06/10/opinion/pandemic-police-race.html; Emma Tucker and Peter Nickeas, "The US Saw Significant Crime Rise across Major Cities in 2020. And It's Not Letting Up," CNN, April 3, 2021, https://www.cnn.com/2021/04/03/us/us-crime-rate-rise-2020/index.html; Brenda Gayle Plummer, "Civil Rights Has Always Been a Global Movement," *Foreign Affairs*, June 19, 2020, https://www.foreignaffairs.com/articles/united-states/2020-06-19/civil-rights-has-always-been-global-movement.

4. Stephen Collinson, "Why Voters Don't Want Biden or Trump but Might Get Them Anyway in 2024," CNN, December 15, 2022, https://www.cnn.com/2022/12/15/politics/biden-trump-2024-analysis/index.html.

5. "U.S. Civil Unrest," Center for Disaster Philanthropy, last modified September 21, 2021, https://disasterphilanthropy.org/disasters/u-s-civil-unrest/.

6. Jonathan Coleman, *Long Way to Go: Black and White in America* (New York: Atlantic Monthly, 1997), 6.

PANDEMIC

1. Michelle Holshue et al., "First Case of 2019 Novel Coronavirus in the United States," *New England Journal of Medicine* 382, no. 10 (2020): 929–936, https://www.ncbi.nlm.nih.gov/pmc/articles/PMC7092802/;

Allison Aubrey, "Trump Declares Coronavirus a Public Health Emergency and Restricts Travel from China," National Public Radio, January 31, 2020, https://www.npr.org/sections/health-shots/2020/01/31/801686524/trump-declares-coronavirus-a-public-health-emergency-and-restricts-travel-from-c.

2. "Covid Origin: Why the Wuhan Lab-Leak Theory Is So Disputed," BBC News, March 1, 2023, https://www.bbc.com/news/world-asia-china-57268111.

3. "About COVID-19: What Is COVID-19?," US Centers for Disease Control and Prevention, updated April 9, 2024, https://www.cdc.gov/coronavirus/2019-ncov/your-health/about-covid-19.html; "Symptoms of COVID-19," US Centers for Disease Control and Prevention, updated March 15, 2024, https://www.cdc.gov/coronavirus/2019-ncov/symptoms-testing/symptoms.html.

4. "Trump Approves $8.3 Billion to Fight Coronavirus, Cancels Visit to CDC," Reuters, March 6, 2020, https://www.reuters.com/article/health-coronavirus-usa/trump-approves-8-3-billion-to-fight-coronavirus-cancels-visit-to-cdc-idUSL1N2AZ0Q1.

5. Heath Kelly, "The Classical Definition of a Pandemic Is Not Elusive," *Bulletin of the World Health Organization* 89 (2011): 540–541, https://www.ncbi.nlm.nih.gov/pmc/articles/PMC3127276/.

6. Sara M. Moniuszko, "Elvis Biopic, Which Shut Down after Tom Hanks Got COVID-19, Resuming Production in Australia," *USA Today*, September 10, 2020, https://www.usatoday.com/story/entertainment/movies/2020/09/10/tom-hanks-elvis-movie-halted-due-covid-19-resumes-production/5767551002/.

7. Kathryn Watson, "Trump Invokes Defense Production Act to Require GM to Produce Ventilators," CBS News, March 27, 2020, https://www.cbsnews.com/news/trump-invokes-defense-production-act-to-require-gm-to-produce-ventilators-2020-03-27/.

8. Lea Hamner et al., "High SARS-CoV-2 Attack Rate Following Exposure at a Choir Practice—Skagit County, Washington, March 2020," US Centers for Disease Control and Prevention, May 15, 2020, https://www.cdc.gov/mmwr/volumes/69/wr/mm6919e6.htm?s_cid=mm6919e6_w; Mike Baker, "Nursing Home Linked to 37 Coronavirus Deaths Faces Fine of $600,000," *New York Times*, April 2, 2020, https://www.nytimes.com/2020/04/02/us/virus-kirkland-life-care-nursing-home.html.

9. Joseph Goldstein and Jesse McKinley, "Coronavirus in N.Y.: Manhattan Woman Is First Confirmed Case in State," *New York Times*, March 1, 2020, https://www.nytimes.com/2020/03/01/nyregion/new

-york-coronvirus-confirmed.html; Jennifer Millman, “Midtown Lawyer Positive for Coronavirus Is NY’s 1st Case of Person-to-Person Spread,” WNBC-TV (New York), March 3, 2020, https://www.nbcnewyork.com/news/local/westchester-county-man-tests-positive-for-coronavirus-in-nys-1st-possible-community-spread-case-gov-cuomo/2310134/; “City Officials: 21 Positive Coronavirus Cases in New York City,” *Spectrum News* (New York), March 9, 2020, https://ny1.com/nyc/all-boroughs/news/2020/03/09/new-york-city-coronavirus-case-numbers-health-update; Mike Pearlstein, “New Orleans Is Second Only to Seattle in COVID-19 Cases per Capita,” WWL-TV (New Orleans), March 16, 2020, https://www.wwltv.com/article/news/health/coronavirus/perl-stats-story/289-f2e70da4-3e5b-48b5-8684-a0dd5dc0361d.

10. John Bacon and Lorenzo Reyes, “Coronavirus Live Updates: USNS Comfort Arrives in New York City; Anthony Fauci Defends Social Distancing; US Death Toll Tops 3,100,” *USA Today*, March 31, 2020, https://news.yahoo.com/coronavirus-live-updates-us-death-093743203.html.

11. Tanay Warerkar and Erika Adams, “NYC Officially Opens for Outdoor Dining on Monday,” *Eater New York*, June 18, 2020, https://ny.eater.com/2020/6/18/21295515/nyc-restaurants-outdoor-dining-sidewalk-seating; “COVID-19 Pandemic in New York City,” Wikipedia, last modified May 9, 2024, https://en.wikipedia.org/wiki/COVID-19_pandemic_in_New_York_City.

12. “21 Positive Coronavirus Cases”; Pearlstein, “New Orleans”; Meghann Myers, “The Army Corps of Engineers Has Two or Three Weeks to Get Thousands of New Hospital Beds Up and Running,” *Military Times*, March 27, 2020, https://www.militarytimes.com/news/your-military/2020/03/27/the-army-corps-of-engineers-has-two-or-three-weeks-to-get-thousands-of-new-hospital-beds-up-and-running/; “One in Three Americans Already Had COVID-19 by the End of 2020,” Mailman School of Public Health, Columbia University, August 26, 2021, https://www.publichealth.columbia.edu/news/one-three-americans-already-had-covid-19-end-2020.

13. Bacon and Reyes, “Coronavirus Live Updates”; Myers, “Army Corps of Engineers.”

14. “History of 1918 Flu Pandemic,” US Centers for Disease Control and Prevention, archived August 30, 2023, https://archive.cdc.gov/#/details?url=https://www.cdc.gov/flu/pandemic-resources/1918-commemoration/1918-pandemic-history.htm.

15. David Wallace-Wells, “Opinion: The Myth of Early Pandemic Polarization,” *New York Times*, June 28, 2023, https://www.nytimes.com

/2023/06/28/opinion/covid-pandemic-2020-or-covid-pandemic-politics.html.

16. "Gov. Tony Evers Mandates Closure of All K-12 Schools," Wisconsin Public Radio, March 13, 2020, https://www.wpr.org/gov-tony-evers-mandates-closure-all-k-12-schools; "City of Wauwatosa Proclamation," City of Wauwatosa, March 16, 2020, https://www.wauwatosa.net/home/showdocument?id=2677.

17. For example, see "Order #1: COVID-19 Public Health Plan for Suburban Milwaukee County," City of Wauwatosa, May 13, 2020, https://www.wauwatosa.net/home/showdocument?id=2741.

18. Trevor Hughes, "'It's Horrible': Hospitals Cancel Surgeries because of Coronavirus, Leaving Americans in Pain," *USA Today*, April 1, 2020, https://www.usatoday.com/story/news/nation/2020/04/01/coronavirus-surgery-cancellations-leave-thousands-pain-over-delays/5094469002/; J. R. Radcliffe and Erin Caughey, "A Timeline of How the COVID-19 Pandemic Has Played Out in Wisconsin," *Milwaukee Journal Sentinel*, March 11, 2021, https://www.jsonline.com/in-depth/news/local/milwaukee/2021/03/11/timeline-how-covid-19-has-played-out-wisconsin/4522813001/.

19. "Four Months After First Case, U.S. Death Toll Passes 100,000," *New York Times*, May 27, 2020, https://www.nytimes.com/2020/05/27/us/coronavirus-live-news-updates.html; Lisa Shumaker, "U.S. Coronavirus Deaths Top 20,000, Highest in World Exceeding Italy: Reuters Tally," Reuters, April 11, 2020, https://www.reuters.com/article/us-health-coronavirus-usa-casualties-idUSKCN21T0NA; Andrew Joseph, "Actual Covid-19 Case Count Could Be 6 to 24 Times Higher Than Official Estimates, CDC Study Shows," *Stat*, July 21, 2020, https://www.statnews.com/2020/07/21/cdc-study-actual-covid-19-cases/; "21 Positive Coronavirus Cases"; Pearlstein, "New Orleans."

20. "Wauwatosa Health Department Announces Changes to Contact Tracing Process," City of Wauwatosa, October 20, 2020, https://www.wauwatosa.net/Home/Components/News/News/2266/; Bacon and Reyes, "Coronavirus Live Updates"; Eric Levenson, "Wisconsin Is Setting Up a Field Hospital for Covid-19 Patients as a Surge in Cases Overwhelms Hospitals," CNN, October 8, 2020, https://www.cnn.com/2020/10/08/us/wisconsin-covid-outbreak/index.html.

21. John Bacon, Elinor Aspegren, and Grace Hauck, "Coronavirus Updates: Joe Biden Pledges to Deliver 100M Doses in 100 Days; US Reaches 15M Infections; Ohio State-Michigan Football Game Off," *USA Today*, December 8, 2020, https://www.usatoday.com/story/news/health/2020/12/08/covid-news-britain-vaccine-wyoming-california-donald-trump/6481339002/;

Holly Yan, "Covid-19 Now Kills More Than 1 American Every Minute. And the Rate Keeps Accelerating as the Death Toll Tops 300,000," CNN, December 14, 2020, https://www.cnn.com/2020/12/14/health/us-covid-deaths-300k/index.html.

22. Will Stone, "As Death Rate Accelerates, U.S. Records 400,000 Lives Lost to the Coronavirus," National Public Radio, January 19, 2021, https://www.npr.org/sections/health-shots/2021/01/19/957488613/as-death-rate-accelerates-u-s-records-400-000-lives-lost-to-the-coronavirus; Pien Huang, "'A Loss to the Whole Society': U.S. COVID-19 Death Toll Reaches 500,000," National Public Radio, February 22, 2021, https://www.npr.org/sections/health-shots/2021/02/22/969494791/a-loss-to-the-whole-society-u-s-covid-19-death-toll-reaches-500-000.

23. Michelle R. Smith and Andrew Meldrum, "A Year into the Coronavirus Pandemic, the Changed World Looks Back and Forward," Associated Press, reprinted in *Patriot-News*, March 11, 2021, https://www.pennlive.com/coronavirus/2021/03/a-year-into-the-coronavirus-pandemic-the-changed-world-looks-back-and-forward.html; "Virus Deaths Are Probably Two to Three Times More Than Official Records, the W.H.O. Says," *New York Times*, updated June 22, 2021, https://www.nytimes.com/live/2021/05/21/world/covid-vaccine-coronavirus-mask.

24. Lenny Bernstein, "U.S. Life Expectancy Continued to Fall in 2021 as Covid, Drug Deaths Surged," *Washington Post*, December 22, 2022, https://www.washingtonpost.com/health/2022/12/22/us-life-expectancy-decline-2021-covid-fentanyl/; Editorial Board, "Opinion: How the United States Can Solve Its Life Expectancy Problem," *Washington Post*, October 4, 2023, https://www.washingtonpost.com/opinions/2023/10/04/life-expectancy-solutions-united-states/; Joshua M. Sharfstein, "Here's How to Reverse the Drop in US Life Expectancy," Bloomberg News, December 6, 2022, https://www.bloomberg.com/news/articles/2022-12-06/here-s-how-to-reverse-the-drop-in-us-life-expectancy?cmpid=BBD120622_CITYLAB.

25. Julie Bosman, Sophie Kasakove, and Daniel Victor, "U.S. Life Expectancy Plunged in 2020, Especially for Black and Hispanic Americans," *New York Times*, July 21, 2021, https://www.nytimes.com/2021/07/21/us/american-life-expectancy-report.html; "COVID-19 Pandemic in the United States," Wikipedia, last modified April 24, 2024, https://en.wikipedia.org/wiki/COVID-19_pandemic_in_the_United_States.

26. "WHO Coronavirus (COVID-19) Dashboard," World Health Organization, as of 2:09 p.m. CST, October 12, 2023, https://covid19.who.int/; "14.9 Million Excess Deaths Associated with the COVID-19 Pandemic in

2020 and 2021," United Nations Department of Economic and Social Affairs, accessed October 13, 2023, https://www.un.org/en/desa/149-million-excess-deaths-associated-covid-19-pandemic-2020-and-2021; Gina Kolata, "Skeletons of 1918 Flu Victims Reveal Clues about Who Was Likely to Die," *New York Times*, October 9, 2023, https://www.nytimes.com/2023/10/09/health/1918-flu-skeletons.html.

27. "Candace Owens," Wikipedia, last modified May 24, 2024, https://en.wikipedia.org/wiki/Candace_Owens; Candace Owens, "One day, we will look back," Twitter, March 10, 2020, https://twitter.com/RealCandaceO/status/1237517974879133696?s=20.

28. David Ovalle, "Vaccine politics may be to blame for excess GOP deaths, study finds," *Washington Post*, July 24, 2023, https://www.washingtonpost.com/health/2023/07/24/covid-vaccines-republicans-deaths/.

29. "History of 1918 Flu Pandemic," US Centers for Disease Control and Prevention; Kolata, "Skeletons of 1918 Flu Victims."

30. Carol R. Byerly, "The U.S. Military and Influenza Pandemic of 1918–1919," *Public Health Reports* 125 (2010): 82–91, https://www.ncbi.nlm.nih.gov/pmc/articles/PMC2862337.

31. Nancy Tomes, "'Destroyer and Teacher': Managing the Masses during the 1918–1919 Influenza Pandemic," *Public Health Reports* 125 (2010): 48–62, https://www.ncbi.nlm.nih.gov/pmc/articles/PMC2862334/; ibid., 49.

32. Ibid., 52, 54–55, 56, 59.

33. J. Alexander Navarro, "Mask Resistance during a Pandemic Isn't New—in 1918, Many Americans Were Slackers," *Conversation*, October 29, 2020, https://theconversation.com/mask-resistance-during-a-pandemic-isnt-new-in-1918-many-americans-were-slackers-141687.

34. Tomes, "Destroyer and Teacher," 52, 54–55, 56, 59.

35. Amy Sherman, "What the 1918 Flu Pandemic Shows Us about Social Distancing," PolitiFact, April 17, 2020, https://www.politifact.com/factchecks/2020/apr/17/gretchen-whitmer/what-1918-flu-pandemic-shows-us-about-social-dista/; Jim Malewitz, "The State's 1918 Pandemic Shutdown Worked," *Urban Milwaukee*, May 1, 2020, https://urbanmilwaukee.com/2020/05/01/the-states-1918-pandemic-shutdown-worked/; Kenneth C. Davis, "Philadelphia Threw a WWI Parade That Gave Thousands of Onlookers the Flu," *Smithsonian Magazine*, September 21, 2018, https://www.smithsonianmag.com/history/philadelphia-threw-wwi-parade-gave-thousands-onlookers-flu-180970372/; J. Alexander Navarro and Howard Markel, "To Save Lives, Social Distancing Must Continue Longer Than We Expect," *Washington Post*, April 8, 2020,

https://www.washingtonpost.com/outlook/2020/04/08/save-lives-social-distancing-must-continue-longer-than-we-expect/.

36. Navarro and Markel, "To Save Lives"; Sherman, "What the 1918 Flu Pandemic Shows"; Angel N. Desai and Maimuna S. Majumber, "What Is Herd Immunity?," *JAMA* 324, no. 20 (2020): 2113, https://jamanetwork.com/journals/jama/fullarticle/2772168; Christine Wu, "What Is Herd Immunity?," WebMD, January 3, 2023, https://www.webmd.com/covid/what-is-herd-immunity.

37. Jason Willick, "Opinion: The Two Crises That Have Driven Republican Populism in the 2020s," *Washington Post*, August 25, 2023, https://www.washingtonpost.com/opinions/2023/08/25/two-crises-stoked-american-populism/; Ashley Kirzinger, Audrey Kearney, Liz Hamel, and Mollyann Brodie, "KFF Health Tracking Poll—Early April 2020: The Impact of Coronavirus on Life in America," KFF Health News, April 2, 2020, https://www.kff.org/coronavirus-covid-19/report/kff-health-tracking-poll-early-april-2020/.

38. "Chart Book: Tracking the Recovery from the Pandemic Recession," Center on Budget and Policy Priorities, November 16, 2023, https://www.cbpp.org/research/economy/tracking-the-recovery-from-the-pandemic-recession.

39. "COVID-19 Protests in the United States," Wikipedia, last modified April 20, 2024, https://en.wikipedia.org/wiki/COVID-19_protests_in_the_United_States#cite_note-75.

40. Paul Egan and Kathleen Gray, "Gov. Gretchen Whitmer Issues 'Stay at Home' Order for Michigan, Effective at Midnight," *Detroit Free Press*, March 23, 2020, https://www.freep.com/story/news/local/michigan/2020/03/23/michigan-shelter-in-place-order-coronavirus/2887578001/.

41. Derick Hutchinson and Ken Haddad, "Michigan Coronavirus (COVID-19) Cases up to 28,059; Death Toll Now at 1,921," ClickOn Detroit (WDIV-TV), April 15, 2020, https://www.clickondetroit.com/health/2020/04/15/michigan-coronavirus-covid-19-cases-up-to-28059-death-toll-now-at-1921/.

42. Paul Egan and Kara Berg, "Thousands Converge to Protest Michigan Governor's Stay-Home Order in 'Operation Gridlock,'" *USA Today*, April 15, 2020, https://www.usatoday.com/story/news/nation/2020/04/15/lansing-capitol-protest-michigan-stay-home-order/5139472002/; "COVID-19 Protests in the United States," Wikipedia.

43. Dartunorro Clark, "Hundreds of Protesters, Some Carrying Guns in the State Capitol, Demonstrate against Michigan's Emergency Measures," NBC News, April 30, 2020, https://www.nbcnews.com/politics

/politics-news/hundreds-protest-michigan-lawmakers-consider-extending-governors-emergency-powers-n1196886.

44. Abigail Censky, "Heavily Armed Protesters Gather Again at Michigan Capitol to Decry Stay-at-Home Order," National Public Radio, May 14, 2020, https://www.npr.org/2020/05/14/855918852/heavily-armed-protesters-gather-again-at-michigans-capitol-denouncing-home-order.

45. Veronica Stracqualursi, "Michigan Closes State Capitol as Protesters Gather against Stay-at-Home Order," CNN, May 14, 2020, https://www.cnn.com/2020/05/14/politics/michigan-state-capitol-protests/index.html; Lindsay Moore and Roberto Acosta, "Gov. Whitmer Says Protest 'Depicted Some of the Worst Racism' and Doesn't Represent Michigan," Michigan Live, May 4, 2020, https://www.mlive.com/coronavirus/2020/05/gov-whitmer-says-protest-depicted-some-of-the-worst-racism-and-doesnt-represent-michigan.html.

46. Michael Martina and Ben Klayman, "Republicans Take Aim at Michigan Governor over Virus Response," Reuters, April 14, 2020, https://www.reuters.com/article/us-health-coronavirus-michigan-governor/republicans-take-aim-at-michigan-governor-over-virus-response-idUSKCN21W2ZE/.

47. Stracqualursi, "Michigan Closes State Capitol"; Jon King, "Final Two Sentences Handed Down in Plot to Kidnap and Kill Whitmer," *Michigan Advance*, December 8, 2023, https://michiganadvance.com/briefs/final-two-sentences-handed-down-in-plot-to-kidnap-and-kill-whitmer/.

48. Reid J. Epstein and Kay Nolan, "A Few Thousand Protest Stay-at-Home Order at Wisconsin State Capitol," *New York Times*, April 24, 2020, https://www.nytimes.com/2020/04/24/us/politics/coronavirus-protests-madison-wisconsin.html.

49. Joseph Stiglitz, "Opinion: Time Is Up for Neoliberals," *Washington Post*, May 13, 2024, https://www.washingtonpost.com/opinions/2024/05/13/stiglitz-captialism-economics-democracy-book/.

50. "More Businesses and Organizations Take Advantage of Tosa Restarts Program," City of Wauwatosa, July 8, 2020, https://www.wauwatosa.net/Home/Components/News/News/2080/; "Wauwatosa Small Business Forgivable Loan Program," City of Wauwatosa, Spring 2021, https://www.wauwatosa.net/home/showpublisheddocument/3884/637607232289970000; "COVID-19 Information for Businesses," City of Wauwatosa, accessed May 25, 2021, https://www.wauwatosa.net/government/departments/development/economic-development/covid-19-information-for-businesses; "Wauwatosa Small Business Emergency

Relief Program," City of Wauwatosa, January 14, 2022, https://www.wauwatosa.net/Home/Components/News/News/2703/17.

51. Daniel Victor, Lew Serviss, and Azi Paybarah, "In His Own Words: Trump on the Coronavirus and Masks," *New York Times*, October 2, 2020, https://www.nytimes.com/2020/10/02/us/politics/donald-trump-masks.html.

52. German Lopez, "Why Trump's Goal to End Social Distancing by Easter Is So Dangerous," Vox, March 24, 2020, https://www.vox.com/policy-and-politics/2020/3/24/21193165/coronavirus-trump-press-briefing-social-distancing-experts.

53. Lauren Neergaard and Julie Pace, "Fauci: 'We're Not There Yet' on Key Steps to Reopen Economy," Associated Press, April 14, 2020, https://apnews.com/article/virus-outbreak-donald-trump-ap-top-news-infectious-diseases-politics-46ee40035d500c4190489aea0adb126b; Lopez, "Trump's Goal to End Social Distancing"; Sherman, "What the 1918 Flu Pandemic Shows"; Nicole Narea, "6 Reasons to Be Skeptical of Trump's Calls to Reopen the Economy," Vox, March 24, 2020, https://www.vox.com/2020/3/24/21191557/trump-coronavirus-economy-reopen-social-distance.

54. Willick, "Two Crises"; Kirzinger et al., "KFF Health Tracking Poll."

55. Rachel Weiner, "Republican House Members' Challenge to Mask Mandate Rejected by Court," *Washington Post*, July 1, 2023, https://www.washingtonpost.com/dc-md-va/2023/06/30/covid-mask-mandates-republicans-house/.

56. "Lawsuits about State Actions and Policies in Response to the Coronavirus (COVID-19) Pandemic," Ballotpedia, accessed May 27, 2024, https://ballotpedia.org/Lawsuits_about_state_actions_and_policies_in_response_to_the_coronavirus_(COVID-19)_pandemic.

57. Veronica Stracqualursi, "Republican-Led Wisconsin Legislature Sues to Reopen State from Stay-at-Home Order," CNN, April 22, 2020, https://www.cnn.com/2020/04/22/politics/wisconsin-legislature-sues-to-reopen-state-coronavirus/index.html; "Wisconsin Supreme Court Blocks Evers' Stay-Home Extension," *PBS News Hour*, May 13, 2020, https://www.pbs.org/newshour/politics/wisconsin-supreme-court-blocks-evers-stay-home-extension.

58. Will Cushman, "Wisconsin Supreme Court Confirms Time Limit on Governor's Emergency Powers," PBS Wisconsin, March 31, 2021, https://pbswisconsin.org/news-item/wisconsin-supreme-court-confirms-time-limit-on-governors-emergency-powers/; Edward A. Fallone,

"Wisconsin Supreme Court Misinterprets Emergency Powers," *Marquette University Law School Faculty Blog*, April 21, 2020, https://law.marquette.edu/facultyblog/2020/04/the-wisconsin-supreme-court-misinterprets-emergency-powers/.

59. Tina Nguyen, "Anthony Fauci Becomes a Fringe MAGA Target," *Politico*, March 24, 2020, https://www.politico.com/news/2020/03/24/anthony-fauci-fringe-maga-target-147401; Isaac Stanley-Becker, Yasmeen Abutaleb, and Devlin Barrett, "Anthony Fauci's Security Is Stepped Up as Doctor and Face of U.S. Coronavirus Response Receives Threats," *Washington Post*, April 1, 2020, https://www.washingtonpost.com/politics/anthony-faucis-security-is-stepped-up-as-doctor-and-face-of-us-coronavirus-response-receives-threats/2020/04/01/ff861a16-744d-11ea-85cb-8670579b863d_story.html; Mike Freeman, "Anti-Vaxxer Aaron Rodgers Makes a Fool of Himself Mocking Travis Kelce as 'Mr. Pfizer,'" *USA Today*, October 6, 2023, https://www.jsonline.com/story/sports/columnist/mike-freeman/2023/10/06/aaron-rogers-travis-kelce-mr-pfizer-covid/71057922007/; Christopher Kuhagen, "Aaron Rodgers Wants to Team with RFK Jr. to Debate the COVID Vaccine against 'Mr. Pfizer' Travis Kelce and Dr. Anthony Fauci," *Milwaukee Journal Sentinel*, October 11, 2023, https://www.jsonline.com/story/sports/nfl/packers/2023/10/10/aaron-rodgers-wants-rfk-jr-to-debate-vaccine-against-mr-pfizer-travis-kelce-dr-anthony-fauci/71135871007/; Weiner, "Republican House Members' Challenge."

60. Yingying Chen, Jacob Long, Jungmi Jun, Sei-Hill Kim, Ali Zain, and Colin Piacentine, "Anti-intellectualism amid the COVID-19 Pandemic: The Discursive Elements and Sources of Anti-Fauci Tweets," *Public Understanding of Science* 32, no. 5 (2023): 641–657, https://www.ncbi.nlm.nih.gov/pmc/articles/PMC9892881/.

61. Rachel Treisman, "How Is Each State Responding to COVID-19?," National Public Radio, December 4, 2020, https://www.npr.org/2020/03/12/815200313/what-governors-are-doing-to-tackle-spreading-coronavirus; "See Reopening Plans and Mask Mandates for All 50 States," *New York Times*, July 1, 2021, https://www.nytimes.com/interactive/2020/us/states-reopen-map-coronavirus.html.

62. Desai and Majumber, "What Is Herd Immunity?"; Donald G. McNeil Jr, "How Much Herd Immunity Is Enough?," *New York Times*, December 24, 2020, https://www.nytimes.com/2020/12/24/health/herd-immunity-covid-coronavirus.html; Wu, "What Is Herd Immunity?"

63. Bill Glauber and Mary Spicuzza, "Milwaukee Wins Tight Race to Host the 2020 Democratic Convention," *Milwaukee Journal Sentinel*,

March 11, 2019, https://www.jsonline.com/story/news/politics/2019/03/11/dnc-milwaukee-picked-host-2020-democratic-national-convention/2836684002/; "2020 Democratic National Convention to Be Held in Milwaukee," CBS News, March 11, 2019, https://www.cbsnews.com/news/2020-democratic-national-convention-to-be-held-in-milwaukee/; Chris Foran, "Beer, Floor Fights and 'the America of Tomorrow': Milwaukee's First National Political Convention," *Milwaukee Journal Sentinel*, August 17, 2020, https://www.jsonline.com/story/life/green-sheet/2019/02/19/milwaukees-first-national-political-convention-floor-fights-reined/2880764002/.

64. Jennifer Jacobs and Drew Armstrong, "Trump's 'Operation Warp Speed' Aims to Rush Coronavirus Vaccine," Bloomberg News, April 29, 2020, https://www.bloomberg.com/news/articles/2020-04-29/trump-s-operation-warp-speed-aims-to-rush-coronavirus-vaccine?embedded-checkout=true; "COVID-19 Vaccines," U.S. Department of Health and Human Services, September 13, 2023, https://www.hhs.gov/coronavirus/covid-19-vaccines/index.html.

65. "Project Lightspeed," BioNTech, accessed October 28, 2023, C:/Users/Owner/Downloads/BioNTech_Factsheet_Project_Lightspeed_mRNA_Technology.pdf; "U.S. Government Engages Pfizer to Produce Millions of Doses of COVID-19 Vaccine," US Department of Health and Human Services, July 22, 2020, https://web.archive.org/web/20201217220648/https://www.hhs.gov/about/news/2020/07/22/us-government-engages-pfizer-produce-millions-doses-covid-19-vaccine.html.

66. Rachel Elbaum and Alexander Smith, "U.K. Becomes First Country to Approve Pfizer-BioNTech Covid-19 Vaccine," NBC News, December 2, 2020, https://www.nbcnews.com/news/world/u-k-becomes-first-country-approve-pfizer-biontech-covid-19-n1249651; Dakin Andone and Christina Maxouris, "US Covid-19 Hospitalizations Hit Record High for 7th Straight Day," CNN, December 12, 2020, https://www.cnn.com/2020/12/12/health/us-coronavirus-saturday/index.html; Berkeley Lovelace Jr., "FDA Approves Second Covid Vaccine for Emergency Use as It Clears Moderna's for U.S. Distribution," CNBC, December 18, 2020, https://www.cnbc.com/2020/12/18/moderna-covid-vaccine-approved-fda-for-emergency-use.html.

67. "One in Three Americans Already Had COVID-19 by the End of 2020," Mailman School of Public Health, Columbia University, August 26, 2021, https://www.publichealth.columbia.edu/news/one-three-americans-already-had-covid-19-end-2020.

68. Luis Ferré-Sadurni and Joseph Goldstein, "1st Vaccination in U.S. Is Given in New York, Hard Hit in Outbreak's First Days," *New York Times*, December 14, 2020, https://www.nytimes.com/2020/12/14/nyregion/coronavirus-vaccine-new-york.html.

69. Sharon LaFraniere and Zach Montague, "Pfizer Seals Deal with U.S. for 100 Million More Vaccine Doses," *New York Times*, December 23, 2020, https://www.nytimes.com/2020/12/23/us/politics/pfizer-vaccine-doses-virus.html.

70. Melissa Repko, "CVS Health, Walgreens Start to Provide Covid Vaccines at Thousands of Hard-Hit Nursing Homes," CNBC, December 18, 2020, https://www.cnbc.com/2020/12/18/cvs-health-walgreens-start-providing-covid-vaccines-at-thousands-of-hard-hit-nursing-homes-.html.

71. Christina Maxouris, "Covid-19 Vaccine Demand Is Slowing in Parts of the US. Now an Uphill Battle Starts to Get More Shots into Arms," CNN, April 18, 2021, https://www.cnn.com/2021/04/18/us/covid-vaccine-slowing-us-demand/index.html; Joshua Berlinger et al., "April 29 Coronavirus News," CNN, April 29, 2021, https://www.cnn.com/world/live-news/coronavirus-pandemic-vaccine-updates-04-29-21/h_40d99e1d1aab9c3a21ec4aab66071f86.

72. Alec Tyson, Courtney Johnson, and Cary Funk, "U.S. Public Now Divided over Whether to Get COVID-19 Vaccine," Pew Research Center, September 17, 2020, https://www.pewresearch.org/science/2020/09/17/u-s-public-now-divided-over-whether-to-get-covid-19-vaccine/; Tara Law, "More Than Half of Americans Worry That White House Pressure Will Lead to a Rushed Coronavirus Vaccine," *Time*, September 11, 2020, https://time.com/5887777/rushed-vaccine-democrats-republicans/.

73. Lisa Maragakis and Gabor David Kelen, "Is the COVID-19 Vaccine Safe?," Johns Hopkins School of Medicine, January 4, 2022, https://www.hopkinsmedicine.org/health/conditions-and-diseases/coronavirus/is-the-covid19-vaccine-safe#.

74. Yasmeen Abutaleb, Laurie McGinley, and Carolyn Y. Johnson, "How the 'Deep State' Scientists Vilified by Trump Helped Him Deliver an Unprecedented Achievement," *Washington Post*, December 14, 2020, https://www.washingtonpost.com/health/2020/12/14/trump-operation-warp-speed-vaccine/.

75. Sara M. Constantino, Alicia D. Cooperman, Robert O. Keohane, and Elke U. Weber, "Personal Hardship Narrows the Partisan Gap in COVID-19 and Climate Change Responses," *Proceedings of the National*

Academy of Sciences 119, no. 46 (2022): e2120653119, https://www.pnas.org/doi/10.1073/pnas.2120653119.

76. Toby Bolsen and Risa Palm, "Politicization and COVID-19 Vaccine Resistance in the U.S.," *Progress in Molecular Biology and Translational Science* 188 (2021): 81–100, https://www.ncbi.nlm.nih.gov/pmc/articles/PMC8577882/; "Is Hydroxychloroquine a Treatment for COVID-19?," Mayo Clinic, September 26, 2023, https://www.mayoclinic.org/diseases-conditions/coronavirus/in-depth/hydroxychloroquine-treatment-covid-19/art-20555331; Toluse Olorunnipa, "Trump Uses Republican Convention to Try to Rewrite Coronavirus History, Casting Himself as Lifesaving Hero," *Washington Post,* August 26, 2020, https://www.washingtonpost.com/politics/trump-coronavirus-convention/2020/08/25/e3741c40-e6e1-11ea-970a-64c73a1c2392_story.html; Allyson Chu, Katie Shepherd, Brittany Shammas, and Colby Itkowitz, "Trump Claims Controversial Comment about Injecting Disinfectants Was 'Sarcastic,'" *Washington Post,* April 24, 2020, https://www.washingtonpost.com/nation/2020/04/24/disinfectant-injection-coronavirus-trump/; Victor et al., "In His Own Words."

77. Wallace-Wells, "Myth of Early Pandemic Polarization."

78. Kuhagen, "Aaron Rodgers"; Katie Roiphe, "A 'Mirror World' Where Leftist Disdain Feeds Right-Wing Paranoia," *New York Times,* September 7, 2023, https://www.nytimes.com/2023/09/07/books/review/doppelganger-naomi-klein.html.

79. "Anti-vaccine Mandate Rally: LA City Employees Say They're Ready to Lose Their Jobs over Requirement," KABC-TV (Los Angeles), November 8, 2021, https://abc7.com/protest-mandate-vaccine-grand-park/11212579/; Weiner, "Republican House Members' Challenge"; Vera Bergengruen, "How the Anti-vax Movement Is Taking over the Right," *Time,* January 26, 2022, https://time.com/6141699/anti-vaccine-mandate-movement-rally/.

80. Darius Tahir, "How the Mixed Messaging of Vaccine Skeptics Sows Seeds of Doubt," KFF Health News, June 8, 2023, https://kffhealthnews.org/news/article/how-the-mixed-messaging-of-vaccine-skeptics-sows-seeds-of-doubt/; *Arizona v. Mayorkas,* 143 S. Ct. 478, slip op. at 4 (2023), https://www.supremecourt.gov/opinions/22pdf/22-592_5hd5.pdf.

81. Ovalle, "Vaccine Politics."

82. Hannah Knowles and Fenit Nirappil, "Bashing Covid Boosters, DeSantis Contrasts with Trump and Worries Experts," *Washington Post,*

September 16, 2023, https://www.washingtonpost.com/politics/2023/09/16/desantis-booster-shots-covid-trump/; Dan Merica, "Trump Met with Boos after Revealing He Received Covid-19 Booster," CNN, December 21, 2021, https://www.cnn.com/2021/12/20/politics/donald-trump-booster-shot-boos/index.html.

83. Frances Robles, Neil MacFarquhar, and Miriam Jordan, "Nursing Homes, Ravaged by Covid-19, Start Vaccinating the Most Vulnerable," *New York Times*, December 17, 2020, https://www.nytimes.com/2020/12/17/us/coronavirus-vaccines-nursing-homes.html; Ovalle, "Vaccine Politics."

84. "Governor Ron DeSantis Signs Legislation to Protect Florida Jobs," State of Florida, November 18, 2022, https://www.flgov.com/2021/11/18/governor-ron-desantis-signs-legislation-to-protect-florida-jobs/; Ovalle, "Vaccine Politics."

85. Amy Maxmen, "How Lawmakers in Texas and Florida Undermine Covid Vaccination Efforts," CNN, November 10, 2023, https://www.cnn.com/2023/11/10/health/some-states-curtail-covid-vaccination-efforts.

86. Akilah Johnson, "Can Politics Kill You? Research Says the Answer Increasingly Is Yes," *Washington Post*, December 16, 2022, https://www.washingtonpost.com/health/2022/12/16/politics-health-relationship/; Wallace-Wells, "Myth of Early Pandemic Polarization."

87. Ovalle, "Vaccine Politics"; "The Deadly Price of Pandemic Politics," University of Maryland School of Public Health, June 3, 2022, https://sph.umd.edu/news/deadly-price-pandemic-politics.

88. Johnson, "Can Politics Kill You?"; Nancy Krieger, Christian Testa, Jarvis T. Chen, William P. Hanage, and Alecia J. McGregor, "Relationship of Political Ideology of US Federal and State Elected Officials and Key COVID Pandemic Outcomes Following Vaccine Rollout to Adults: April 2021–March 2022," *Lancet Regional Health—Americas* 16 (2022): 100384, https://www.sciencedirect.com/science/article/pii/S2667193X22002010.

89. Ovalle, "Vaccine Politics."

90. "Interim Public Health Recommendations for Fully Vaccinated People," Centers for Disease Control and Prevention, May 13, 2021, https://www.cdc.gov/coronavirus/2019-ncov/vaccines/fully-vaccinated-guidance.html; Roni Caryn Rabin, Apoorva Mandivilli, and Noah Weiland, "Vaccinated Americans May Go without Masks in Most Places, Federal Officials Say," *New York Times*, May 13, 2021, https://www.nytimes.com/2021/05/13/health/coronavirus-masks-cdc.html.

91. "Vaccine Acceptance and Accessibility in Wauwatosa," City of Wauwatosa, May 4, 2021, https://www.wauwatosa.net/Home/Components/News/News/2485/17.

92. Evan Casey, "Wauwatosa's Mayor Wants to Give $50 or $100 Gift Cards for Those Who Get the COVID Vaccine," *Milwaukee Journal Sentinel*, May 25, 2021, https://www.jsonline.com/story/communities/west/news/wauwatosa/2021/05/25/wauwatosa-mayor-dennis-mcbride-wants-give-gift-cards-vaccines/7418809002/; Rose Schmidt, "Wauwatosa Mayor Proposes Financial Incentive for People Who Are Fully Vaccinated," WDJT-TV (Milwaukee), May 21, 2021, https://cbs58.com/news/wauwatosa-mayor-proposes-financial-incentive-for-people-who-are-fully-vaccinated.

93. Casey, "Wauwatosa's Mayor."

94. Tommy Thompson and Jim Langdon, "Opinion: Pandemic Politics Made Battling COVID at UW Tougher. Masks and Vaccines Made a Difference," *Milwaukee Journal Sentinel*, October 20, 2023, https://www.jsonline.com/story/opinion/2023/10/20/covid-uw-madison-vaccines-mask-mandates-students-health/71062085007/.

95. "Wauwatosa Vaccine Prize Drawing: Get Vaccinated and Enter for a Chance to Win a Prize," City of Wauwatosa, July 7, 2021, https://www.wauwatosa.net/Home/Components/News/News/2556/17; "Wauwatosa Launches New COVID-19 Vaccine Campaign," City of Wauwatosa, February 9, 2022, https://www.wauwatosa.net/Home/Components/News/News/2715/17.

96. Dennis McBride, "A Message from the Mayor," *Tosa Connection*, Fall 2021, 6.

97. "Milwaukee County COVID-19 Surveillance Dashboard," Milwaukee County, accessed December 7, 2022, https://www.arcgis.com/apps/dashboards/018eedbe075046779b8062b5fe1055bf; Yasmin Tayag, "It's Beginning to Look a Lot Like Another COVID Surge," *Atlantic*, December 9, 2022, https://www.theatlantic.com/health/archive/2022/12/covid-us-new-cases-winter-surge/672415/; Katherine J. Wu, "Is COVID a Common Cold Yet?," *Atlantic*, December 15, 2022, https://www.theatlantic.com/health/archive/2022/12/covid-common-cold-status-differentiation/672472/.

98. Nick Tate, "Haven't Had COVID Yet? Wanna Bet?," WebMD, August 2, 2022, https://www.webmd.com/lung/news/20220802/havent-had-covid-yet-wanna-bet.

99. Rob Stein, "In Wave after Deadly Wave, COVID Has Claimed 1 Million Lives in the U.S.," National Public Radio, May 17, 2022, https://

www.npr.org/sections/health-shots/2022/05/17/1093651037/us-one-million-deaths.

100. John Gramlich, "Two Years into the Pandemic, Americans Inch Closer to a New Normal," Pew Research Center, March 3, 2022, https://www.pewresearch.org/2022/03/03/two-years-into-the-pandemic-americans-inch-closer-to-a-new-normal/; "Americans Are Moving On from COVID-19 Despite Acknowledged Risks," Ipsos, September 13, 2022, https://www.ipsos.com/en-us/news-polls/axios-ipsos-coronavirus-index; Tayag, "Another COVID Surge"; Wu, "Is COVID a Common Cold Yet?"

101. Gramlich, "Two Years into the Pandemic"; "Americans Are Moving On," Ipsos; Wu, "Is COVID a Common Cold Yet?"

102. Kate Sullivan, Jamie Gumbrecht, Allie Malloy, and Kevin Liptak, "Biden: 'The Pandemic Is Over,'" CNN, September 18, 2022, https://www.cnn.com/2022/09/18/politics/biden-pandemic-60-minutes/index.html; Eric Berger, "Biden's Claim That Covid Pandemic Is Over Sparks Debate Over Future," *Guardian*, September 24, 2022, https://www.theguardian.com/world/2022/sep/24/covid-not-over-biden-remarks-cbs-60-minutes.

103. David Leonhardt, "A Positive Covid Milestone," *New York Times*, July 17, 2023, https://www.nytimes.com/2023/07/17/briefing/covid.html; "End of the Federal COVID-19 Public Health Emergency (PHE) Declaration," Centers for Disease Control and Prevention, September 12, 2023, https://www.cdc.gov/coronavirus/2019-ncov/your-health/end-of-phe.html.

104. Leonhardt, "Positive Covid Milestone" ; Ovalle, "Vaccine Politics."

105. Benjamin Mueller and Gina Kolata, "Nobel Prize Awarded to Covid Vaccine Pioneers," *New York Times*, October 2, 2023, https://www.nytimes.com/2023/10/02/health/nobel-prize-medicine.html.

106. Covid Crisis Group, *Lessons from the Covid War: An Investigative Report* (New York: Public Affairs, 2023).

107. Ibid.; Wallace-Wells, "Myth of Early Pandemic Polarization."

108. Ibid.

109. Erika Edwards, "Childhood Vaccinations in the U.S. Fall Again, Leaving Kids at Risk for Preventable Disease," NBC News, January 12, 2023, https://www.nbcnews.com/health/health-news/childhood-vaccinations-us-fall-leaving-kids-risk-preventable-disease-rcna65493; Elizabeth Williams, Robin Rudowitz, and Sophia Moreno, "Headed Back to School in 2023: A Look at Children's Routine Vaccination Trends," KFF Health News, July 31, 2023, https://www.kff.org/coronavirus-covid-19/issue-brief/headed-back-to-school-in-2023-a-look-at-childrens-routine

-vaccination-trends/; Sarah Volpenhein, "1 in 10 Schoolchildren Are Not Up-to-Date on Vaccines in Wisconsin, amid Drop in Childhood Immunization Rates," *Milwaukee Journal Sentinel*, August 18, 2023, https://www.jsonline.com/story/news/health/2023/08/18/1-in-10-wisconsin-schoolchildren-not-up-to-date-on-vaccines/70606328007/; Sheryl Gay Stolberg, "'Medical Freedom' Activists Take Aim at New Target: Childhood Vaccine Mandates," *New York Times*, December 3, 2023, https://www.nytimes.com/2023/12/03/us/politics/mississippi-childhood-vaccine-mandates.html.

110. Carma Hassan, "Health Misinformation and Lack of Confidence in Vaccines Continue to Grow, Years after the Covid-19 Pandemic, Survey Shows," CNN, November 1, 2023, https://www.cnn.com/2023/11/01/health/vaccine-misinformation-survey.

111. Editorial Board, "Opinion: Measles Is More Contagious Than the Coronavirus. And It's Back," *Washington Post*, April 14, 2024, https://www.washingtonpost.com/opinions/2024/04/14/measles-cases-rise-danger-vaccine/; Lena H. Sun and Lauren Weber, "Florida Surgeon General Defies Science amid Measles Outbreak," *Washington Post*, February 22, 2024, https://www.washingtonpost.com/health/2024/02/22/florida-measles-outbreak-ladapo/.

112. Christina Jewett, "Kennedy Sought to Stop Covid Vaccinations 6 Months After Rollout," *New York Times*, January 17, 2025, https://www.nytimes.com/2025/01/17/health/rfk-jr-covid-vaccines.html.

113. Christian Edwards, "What Is the World Health Organization and Why Does Trump Want to Leave It?," CNN, January 21, 2025, https://www.cnn.com/2025/01/21/world/world-health-organization-trump-withdraw-explainer-intl/index.html.

A LONG, HOT SUMMER

1. Freda Moon, "36 Hours in Portland, Ore.," *New York Times*, August 25, 2011, https://www.nytimes.com/2011/08/28/travel/36-hours-in-portland-ore.html.

2. Steve Karnowski and Amy Forliti, "Witnesses: Onlooker Anger Increased as Floyd Stopped Moving," Associated Press / Oregon Public Broadcasting, March 30, 2021, https://www.opb.org/article/2021/03/31/george-floyd-derek-chauvin-trial-minnesota/; Nicholas Bogel-Burroughs, "Prosecutors Say Derek Chauvin Knelt on George Floyd for Nine Minutes and 29 Seconds, Longer Than Initially Reported," *New York Times*, March

30, 2021, https://www.nytimes.com/2021/03/30/us/derek-chauvin-george-floyd-kneel-9-minutes-29-seconds.html; Audra D. S. Burch, Amy Harmon, Sabrina Tavernise, and Emily Badger, "The Death of George Floyd Reignited a Movement. What Happens Now?," *New York Times,* April 20, 2021, https://www.nytimes.com/2021/04/20/us/george-floyd-protests-police-reform.html.

3. Burch et al., "Death of George Floyd"; Larry Buchanan, Quoctrung Bui, and Jugal K. Patel, "Black Lives Matter May Be the Largest Movement in U.S. History," *New York Times,* July 3, 2020, https://www.nytimes.com/interactive/2020/07/03/us/george-floyd-protests-crowd-size.html.

4. "U.S. Civil Unrest," Center for Disaster Philanthropy, accessed July 26, 2023, https://disasterphilanthropy.org/disasters/u-s-civil-unrest/; Jason Silverstein, "The Global Impact of George Floyd: How Black Lives Matter Protests Shaped Movements Around the World," CBS News, June 4, 2021, https://www.cbsnews.com/news/george-floyd-black-lives-matter-impact/.

5. Aaliyah Harris and Shama Nasinde, "How UK Protesters Are Taking the Spark of Black Lives Matter Back to Their Hometowns," CNN, December 4, 2020, https://edition.cnn.com/2020/12/04/uk/uk-hometowns-black-lives-matter-intl/index.html; "United States Racial Unrest (2020-Present)," Wikipedia, last modified May 21, 2024, https://en.wikipedia.org/wiki/2020-2023_United_States_racial_unrest.

6. Khalil Gibran Muhammad, "How Hubert Humphrey Tried to Make Minneapolis, and America, Less Racist," *New York Times,* August 27, 2023, https://www.nytimes.com/2023/07/13/books/review/into-the-bright-sunshine-samuel-g-freedman.html.

7. Ibid.; Ernesto Londoño, Glenn Thrush, Mitch Smith, and Dan Simmons, "Minneapolis Police Used Illegal, Abusive Tactics for Years, Justice Department Finds," *New York Times,* June 16, 2023, https://www.nytimes.com/2023/06/16/us/doj-report-minneapolis-police.html.

8. Muhammad, "How Hubert Humphrey Tried."

9. Anjuli Sastry Krbechek and Karen Grigsby Bates, "When LA Erupted in Anger: A Look Back at the Rodney King Riots," National Public Radio, April 26, 2017, https://www.npr.org/2017/04/26/524744989/when-la-erupted-in-anger-a-look-back-at-the-rodney-king-riots; Katie Benner, "Eric Garner's Death Will Not Lead to Federal Charges for N.Y.P.D. Officer," *New York Times,* July 16, 2019, https://www.nytimes.com/2019/07/16/nyregion/eric-garner-daniel-pantaleo.html; Eugene Robinson, "Opinion: Black People Are Being Killed for Being Black.

Again," *Washington Post*, August 28, 2023, https://www.washingtonpost.com/opinions/2023/08/28/jacksonville-shootings-racism-discrimination-opinion/; "United States Racial Unrest," Wikipedia.

10. Benner, "Eric Garner's Death"; David Montgomery, "The Death of Sandra Bland," *New York Times*, May 8, 2019, https://www.nytimes.com/2019/05/08/us/sandra-bland-texas-death.html; Elizabeth Chuck, "Jamar Clark: Tension Rises after Killing of Unarmed Minneapolis Man," NBC News, November 18, 2015, https://www.nbcnews.com/news/nbcblk/jamar-clark-tension-rises-between-after-killing-unarmed-minneapolis-man-n466241; Mitch Smith, "Philando Castile Family Reaches $3 Million Settlement," *New York Times*, June 16, 2017, https://www.nytimes.com/2017/06/26/us/philando-castile-family-settlement.html; Robinson, "Opinion"; "United States Racial Unrest," Wikipedia.

11. Richard Fausset, "What We Know about the Shooting Death of Ahmaud Arbery," *New York Times*, August 8, 2022, https://www.nytimes.com/article/ahmaud-arbery-shooting-georgia.html; Richard A. Oppel Jr., Derrick Bryson Taylor, and Nicholas Boegl-Burroughs, "What to Know about Breonna Taylor's Death," *New York Times*, March 9, 2023, https://www.nytimes.com/article/breonna-taylor-police.html; Aimee Ortiz, "What to Know about the Death of Rayshard Brooks," *New York Times*, November 21, 2022, https://www.nytimes.com/article/rayshard-brooks-what-we-know.html; Christina Morales, "What We Know about the Shooting of Jacob Blake," *New York Times*, November 16, 2021, https://www.nytimes.com/article/jacob-blake-shooting-kenosha.html; Robinson, "Opinion"; Radley Balko, "Opinion: Don't Read Too Much into the Outcome of Derek Chauvin's Trial," *Washington Post*, April 1, 2021, https://www.washingtonpost.com/opinions/2021/04/01/dont-read-too-much-into-outcome-derek-chauvins-trial/.

12. Cheryl Corley, "1 Year Later, the Video of George Floyd's Death Has Lasting Impacts," National Public Radio, May 7, 2021, https://www.npr.org/2021/05/07/994539600/1-year-later-the-video-of-george-floyds-death-has-lasting-impacts.

13. "United States Racial Unrest," Wikipedia.

14. John McWhorter, "Opinion: Our Racial Reckoning Could Have Come Sooner. What Made 2020 Different?," *New York Times*, June 10, 2022, https://www.nytimes.com/2022/06/10/opinion/pandemic-police-race.html.

15. "U.S. Civil Unrest," Center for Disaster Philanthropy; Emma Tucker and Peter Nickeas, "The US Saw Significant Crime Rise across

Major Cities in 2020. And It's Not Letting Up," CNN, April 3, 2021, https://www.cnn.com/2021/04/03/us/us-crime-rate-rise-2020/index.html.

16. C. P. Jones, C. M. Bright, and C. T. Laurencin, eds., *The Impacts of Racism and Bias on Black People Pursuing Careers in Science, Engineering, and Medicine: Proceedings of a Workshop* (Washington, DC: National Academies Press, 2020), ch. 4, "Segregation in Housing and Education," https://www.ncbi.nlm.nih.gov/books/NBK565026/.

17. Grace Hauck, Trevor Hughes, Omar Abdel-Baqui, Ricardo Torres, and Hayes Gardner, "'A Fanciful Reality': Trump Claims Black Lives Matter Protests Are Violent, but the Majority Are Peaceful," *USA Today*, October 24, 2020, https://www.usatoday.com/in-depth/news/nation/2020/10/24/trump-claims-blm-protests-violent-but-majority-peaceful/3640564001/; Erica Chenoweth and Jeremy Pressman, "This Summer's Black Lives Matter Protesters Were Overwhelmingly Peaceful, Our Research Finds," *Washington Post*, October 16, 2020, https://www.washingtonpost.com/politics/2020/10/16/this-summers-black-lives-matter-protesters-were-overwhelming-peaceful-our-research-finds/; "United States Racial Unrest," Wikipedia.

18. Rilyn Eischens, "From Building Damage to Police Payouts, the Costs of Floyd's Killing Are Piling Up," *Minnesota Reformer*, November 30, 2020, https://minnesotareformer.com/2020/11/30/from-building-damage-to-police-payouts-the-costs-of-floyds-killing-are-piling-up/; "George Floyd Protests in Minneapolis-St. Paul," Wikipedia, last modified February 18, 2024, https://en.wikipedia.org/wiki/George_Floyd_protests_in_Minneapoli-Saint_Paul.

19. Josh Penrod and C. J. Sinner, "Buildings Damaged in Minneapolis, St. Paul after Riots," *Minneapolis Star Tribune*, July 13, 2020, https://www.startribune.com/a-deeper-look-at-areas-most-damaged-by-rioting-looting-in-minneapolis-st-paul/569930671/; "United States Racial Unrest," Wikipedia.

20. Maggie Haberman and Alexander Burns, "Trump's Looting and 'Shooting' Remarks Escalate Crisis in Minneapolis," *New York Times*, May 29, 2020, https://www.nytimes.com/2020/05/29/us/politics/trump-looting-shooting.html; Derrick Bryson Taylor, "George Floyd Protests: A Timeline," *New York Times*, November 5, 2021, https://www.nytimes.com/article/george-floyd-protests-timeline.html.

21. Dave Orrick, "Curfew Ordered in St. Paul, Minneapolis, Other Communities," *Twin Cities Pioneer Press*, May 29, 2020, https://www

.twincities.com/2020/05/29/curfew-friday-saturday-minneapolis-st-paul-george-floyd-protests/.

22. Mayor Jacob Frey, "What started as largely peaceful protests," X (Twitter), May 30, 2020, https://twitter.com/MayorFrey/status/1266778552072056833; Tess Owen, "Far-Right Extremists Are Hoping to Turn the George Floyd Protests into a New Civil War," Vice News, May 29, 2020, https://www.vice.com/en/article/pkyb9b/far-right-extremists-are-hoping-to-turn-the-george-floyd-protests-into-a-new-civil-war; Haberman and Burns, "Trump's Looting and 'Shooting' Remarks."

23. Alexander Mallin, "'Boogaloo Bois' Member Charged in Attack on Minneapolis Police Precinct during George Floyd Protests," ABC News, October 23, 2020, https://abcnews.go.com/Politics/boogaloo-bois-member-charged-attack-minneapolis-police-building/story?id=73789955&s=03.

24. Taylor, "George Floyd Protests."

25. Katie Warren and Joey Hadden, "How All 50 States Are Responding to the George Floyd Protests, from Imposing Curfews to Calling in the National Guard," *Business Insider*, June 4, 2020, https://www.businessinsider.com/us-states-response-george-floyd-protests-curfews-national-guard-2020-6; "United States Racial Unrest," Wikipedia.

26. Kaelan Deese, "Vandalism, Looting Following Floyd Death Sparks at Least $1B in Damages Nationwide: Report," *Hill*, June 4, 2020, https://thehill.com/homenews/news/516742-vandalism-looting-after-floyd-death-sparks-at-least-1-billion-in-damages-report/; "United States Racial Unrest," Wikipedia.

27. Emily Olson, "Antifa, Boogaloo Boys, White Nationalists: Which Extremists Showed Up to the US Black Lives Matter Protests?," Australian Broadcasting Corporation, June 27, 2020, https://www.abc.net.au/news/2020-06-28/antifa-boogaloo-extremists-at-us-floyd-protests/12388260; Meg Kelly and Elyse Samuels, "Who Caused the Violence at Protests? It Wasn't Antifa," *Washington Post*, June 22, 2020, https://www.washingtonpost.com/politics/2020/06/22/who-caused-violence-protests-its-not-antifa/; "United States Racial Unrest," Wikipedia.

28. Liam Dillon and Jaclyn Cosgrove, "'I Guess America Is Finally Listening': Why George Floyd Protests Have Spread to Affluent Suburbs," *Los Angeles Times*, June 6, 2020, https://www.latimes.com/california/story/2020-06-06/george-floyd-protests-suburbs.

29. Sam Kelly, "Several Suburbs Set Curfew as Officials Brace for Unrest," *Chicago Sun-Times*, May 31, 2020, https://chicago.suntimes

.com/2020/5/31/21276405/chicago-suburbs-curfews-protests-looting-george-floyd.

30. "City of Wauwatosa Announces 9 pm Curfew," City of Wauwatosa, May 30, 2020, https://www.wauwatosa.net/Home/Components/News/News/2016/; "Statement from Mayor Dennis McBride (May 31, 12:30 pm)," City of Wauwatosa, May 31, 2020, https://www.wauwatosa.net/Home/Components/News/News/2016/.

31. *Tinius v. Choi et al.*, 77 F.4th 691, 701 (D.C. Cir. 2023), citing *Menotti v. City of Seattle*, 409 F.3d 1113, 1117, 1118, 1120, 1122, 1123, 1132 (9th Cir. 2005); "1999 Seattle WTO Protests," Wikipedia, last modified February 11, 2024, https://en.wikipedia.org/wiki/1999_Seattle_WTO_protests.

32. Mike Carter, Daniel Beekman, Heidi Groover, and Paul Roberts, "How a Year of Protests Changed Seattle," *Seattle Times*, December 29, 2020, https://www.seattletimes.com/seattle-news/how-a-year-of-protests-changed-seattle/.

33. Kevin Flower, Artemis Moshtaghian, Elle Reeve, and Susannah Cullinane, "Shooting in Seattle Protest Zone Leaves One Dead. Police Say 'Violent Crowd' Denied Them Entry," CNN, June 21, 2020, https://www.cnn.com/2020/06/20/us/seattle-capitol-hill-chop-chaz-shooting/index.html; Lia Eustachewich, "How the Seattle CHOP Zone Went from Socialist Summer Camp to Deadly Disaster," *New York Post*, July 1, 2020, https://nypost.com/2020/07/01/how-seattle-chop-went-from-socialist-summer-camp-to-deadly-disaster/.

34. Alex Hardgrave, "Police Clear Protesters, Makeshift Barriers in Pearl District as Sun Rises," *Oregonian* / Oregon Live, June 18, 2020, https://www.oregonlive.com/news/2020/06/police-clear-protesters-makeshift-barriers-in-pearl-district-as-sun-rises.html; Jamie Hale and Beth Nakamura, "March to Portland Mayor Ted Wheeler's Home Declared Riot Monday as Burning Debris Thrown into Building: Key Takeaways," *Oregonian*, August 31, 2020, https://www.oregonlive.com/portland/2020/09/protesters-march-to-portland-mayor-ted-wheelers-residence-monday-throw-birthday-party-demand-resignation-live-updates.html.

35. Conrad Wilson, "Investigators Complete Review of Federal Police Shooting That Killed Wanted Portland Activist," Oregon Public Broadcasting, March 31, 2021, https://www.opb.org/article/2021/03/31/investigation-federal-police-shooting-wanted-portland-activist/; Hale and Nakamura, "March to Wheeler's Home."

36. Hale and Nakamura, "March to Wheeler's Home."

37. Everton Bailey Jr., "Portland Bans Police from Working with Federal Law Enforcement, Targeting Journalists and Legal Observers during Protests," *Oregonian* / Oregon Live, July 22, 2020, https://www.oregonlive.com/portland/2020/07/portland-bans-police-from-working-with-federal-law-enforcement-targeting-journalists-and-legal-observers-during-protests.html; "Index Newspapers LLC v. City of Portland," ACLU Oregon, July 22, 2020, https://www.aclu-or.org/en/cases/index-newspapers-llc-v-city-portland#; Conrad Wilson, "DHS Sent More Than 750 Federal Officers, Spent Millions Responding to Portland Protests," Oregon Public Broadcasting, April 21, 2021, https://www.opb.org/article/2021/04/21/dhsreport-says-750-federal-officers-sent-to-2020-protests-in-portland/; Lawrence Hurley, "Portland Protesters Were Beaten, Shot At and Snatched. Years Later, They Are Frustrated by Legal Blockades to Accountability," NBC News, December 12, 2023, https://www.nbcnews.com/politics/supreme-court/portland-protesters-bivens-rcna128596; "DHS Had Authority to Deploy Federal Law Enforcement Officers to Protect Federal Facilities in Portland, Oregon, but Should Ensure Better Planning and Execution in Future Cross-Component Activities," Office of Inspector General, US Department of Homeland Security, April 16, 2021, https://www.oig.dhs.gov/reports/2021/dhs-had-authority-deploy-federal-law-enforcement-officers-protect-federal-facilities-portland-oregon-should-ensure-better-planning-and.

38. Hannah Ray Lambert, "Portland Protests: What Happened in 2020, What's Next in 2021," KOIN-TV (Portland), December 31, 2020, https://www.koin.com/news/protests/portland-protests-what-happened-in-2020-whats-next-in-2021/; Kirk Johnson and Sergio Olmos, "After a Year of Protests, Portland Is Ready to Move On. But Where?," *New York Times*, June 9, 2021, https://www.nytimes.com/2021/06/09/us/portland-protests.html.

39. Dirk VanderHart, "Everybody Hates Portland: The City's Compounding Crises Are an X-factor This Year," Oregon Public Broadcasting, May 13, 2022, https://www.opb.org/article/2022/05/13/portland-oregon-crime-homelessness-gloom-election-politics/; Alicia Victoria Lozano, "Progressive California and Oregon Revive the War on Drugs amid Fentanyl Crisis," NBC News, March 20, 2024, https://www.nbcnews.com/news/us-news/california-oregon-reviving-war-drugs-fentanyl-crisis-rcna142387.

40. Bill Kacaraba, "Seattle Voters Continue to Feel Pessimistic about Direction of City," MyNorthwest, June 9, 2023, https://mynorthwest.com/3898830/seattle-voters-continue-to-feel-pessimistic-about-direction

-of-city/; "Survey of Likely November 2023 Voters, City of Seattle," EMC Research, May 2023, https://downtownseattle.org/app/uploads/2023/06/DSA-Downtown-Recovery-Report-EMC-May-2023.pdf.

41. "2 Officers Shot in Louisville Protests over Breonna Taylor Charging Decision," *New York Times*, September 23, 2020, https://www.nytimes.com/2020/09/23/us/breonna-taylor-decision-verdict.html; Madeline Holcomb, Steve Almasy, and Dakin Andone, "Police Declare Unlawful Assembly after Windows Shattered during Breonna Taylor Protests," CNN, September 24, 2020, https://www.cnn.com/2020/09/24/us/louisville-breonna-taylor-officers-indictment-protests/index.html.

42. "Homicide Suspect Who Shot Self on Nicollet Mall Identified," WCCO-TV (Minneapolis), August 28, 2020, https://www.cbsnews.com/minnesota/news/homicide-suspect-who-shot-self-on-nicollet-mall-identified/; "Unrest Grows in Downtown Minneapolis after Police Say Murder Suspect Killed Himself on Nicollet Mall," WCCO-TV (Minneapolis), August 28, 2020, https://www.cbsnews.com/minnesota/news/homicide-reported-at-garage-in-downtown-minneapolis/.

43. "Minneapolis under Curfew Again after Businesses Looted, Vandalized," Minnesota Public Radio, August 27, 2020, https://www.mprnews.org/story/2020/08/27/national-guard-activated-to-quell-unrest-in-minneapolis; Corrine Hess, "Wauwatosa Mayor Stands by His Handling of Black Lives Matter Protests: McBride Says He Didn't Want His City to Become Another Kenosha," Wisconsin Public Radio, October 27, 2021, https://www.wpr.org/wauwatosa-mayor-stands-his-handling-black-lives-matter-protests; Connor Perrett, "Curfews Can Be Effective in Preventing Looting and Violence amid Social Unrest but Opponents Say They Give Police Too Much Power," *Insider*, June 3, 2020, https://www.insider.com/experts-say-curfew-orders-can-be-effective-in-stopping-violence-2020-6.

44. "Diner Owners Sue City over Property Damage in Floyd Protests," Associated Press, February 9, 2021, https://apnews.com/article/lawsuits-minnesota-minneapolis-racial-injustice-a2742fb5427279ce5d2cb86bbe1f59ee; "Legal Settlement: *Kacey White, Charles Stotts, d/b/a Town Talk Diner v. City of Minneapolis, et al.* (RCA-2022-01206)," City of Minneapolis, January 9, 2023, https://lims.minneapolismn.gov/RCA/10271; Anthony Gockowski, "Insurance Company Sues Minneapolis for 'Negligence' during George Floyd Riots," Alpha News, January 25, 2024, https://alphanews.org/insurance-company-sues-minneapolis-for-negligence-during-george-floyd-riots/.

45. Richard Saunders, "Milwaukee and Chicago: One City or Two?," *Midwesterner*, June 14, 2012, https://globalmidwest.typepad.com/global-midwest/2012/06/milwaukee-and-chicago-one-city-or-two.html#; Julie Bosman and Sarah Mervosh, "Wisconsin Reels after Police Shooting and Second Night of Protests," *New York Times*, August 24, 2020, https://www.nytimes.com/2020/08/24/us/kenosha-police-shooting.html; Isabel Wilkerson, *The Warmth of Other Suns: The Epic Story of America's Great Migration* (New York: Random House, 2010), 242–246, 267, 398, 416.

46. Michael Shields and Andrew Stettner, "Promises Unfulfilled: Manufacturing in the Midwest," Policy Matters Ohio, September 28, 2020, https://www.policymattersohio.org/research-policy/fair-economy/work-wages/trade/promises-unfulfilled-manufacturing-in-the-midwest; Jonathan Coleman, *Long Way to Go: Black and White in America* (New York: Atlantic Monthly Press, 1997), 6 and generally.

47. Morales, "Shooting of Jacob Blake"; Liz Snyder, "The Jacob Blake Shooting and Its Aftermath: A Timeline of Events," *Kenosha News*, August 21, 2022, https://kenoshanews.com/the-jacob-blake-shooting-and-its-aftermath-a-timeline-of-events/article_f43d94c2-1f3b-11ed-9f17-1f6637bbb0cb.html.

48. "Timeline: The Jacob Blake Shooting and the Unrest That Followed," NBC5 Chicago, August 28, 2020, https://www.nbcchicago.com/news/local/timeline-the-jacob-blake-shooting-and-the-unrest-that-followed/2329811/; Drew Dawson, "Kenosha Man Sentenced for Injuring Officer during 2020 Jacob Blake Protests," *Milwaukee Journal Sentinel*, January 7, 2023, https://www.jsonline.com/story/news/crime/2023/01/07/kenosha-man-sentenced-for-injuring-officer-during-2020-jacob-blake-protests/69787613007/.

49. Bruce Vielmetti, "Man Seen with Kyle Rittenhouse Victim Charged with Arson in Kenosha," *Milwaukee Journal Sentinel*, January 26, 2021, https://www.jsonline.com/story/news/crime/2021/01/26/man-kyle-rittenhouse-victim-charged-arson-kenosha/4265464001/; "Kenosha Unrest Shooting," Wikipedia, last modified April 17, 2024, https://en.wikipedia.org/wiki/Kenosha_unrest_shooting.

50. Charles Homans, "Kyle Rittenhouse and the New Era of Political Violence: What Brought the Teenager and So Many Others to the Streets of Kenosha, Wis., Equipped for War?," *New York Times*, October 26, 2021, https://www.nytimes.com/2021/10/26/magazine/kyle-rittenhouse-kenosha-wisconsin.html.

51. J. David Goodman, "Texas Governor Pardons Man in Fatal Shooting of Protester in 2020," *New York Times*, May 16, 2024, https://

www.nytimes.com/2024/05/16/us/texas-abbott-pardon-daniel-perry .html.

52. Jaclyn Peiser, Mark Guarino, and Mark Berman, "Kenosha Peaceful on Fourth Night of Protests as Armed Militias Stay Away after Deadly Shooting," *Washington Post*, August 27, 2020, https://www.washington post.com/nation/2020/08/27/kenosha-protest-militias-blake-shooting/.

53. Steve Gardner, "Bucks Players Explain Their Decision Not to Play: 'Our Focus Today Cannot Be on Basketball,'" *USA Today*, August 26, 2020, https://www.usatoday.com/story/sports/nba/bucks/2020/08/26 /bucks-players-explain-decision-boycott-after-jacob-blake-shooting /5639896002/; Natasha Korecki, "'It's Playing into Trump's Hands': Dems Fear Swing-State Damage from Kenosha Unrest: Some Wisconsin Democrats Worry That the Images of Violence and Destruction Will Turn Suburban Voters against the Party," *Politico*, August 27, 2020, https://www .politico.com/news/2020/08/27/its-playing-into-trumps-hands-dems-fear -swing-state-backlash-after-kenosha-carnage-402953; Morales, "Shooting of Jacob Blake."

54. Erin Myers, "Jacob Blake's Mom Calls for Peaceful Protests, Says He Would Not Be Pleased with 'the Violence and the Destruction,'" KTLA-TV (Los Angeles), August 26, 2020, https://ktla.com/news/nationworld /jacob-blakes-mom-calls-for-peaceful-protests-says-he-would-not-be -pleased-with-the-violence-and-the-destruction/.

55. "Kenosha Unrest," Wikipedia, last modified August 21, 2023, https://en.wikipedia.org/wiki/Kenosha_unrest; "Kenosha Update Recap: Aug. 25 Jacob Blake Shooting Coverage," *Milwaukee Journal Sentinel*, August 25, 2020, https://www.jsonline.com/story/news/local/wisconsin /2020/08/25/wisconsin-police-shooting-jacob-blake-live-updates -kenosha/5632468002/; "2 Dead, 1 Injured in Overnight Protests in Wisconsin Over Jacob Blake Shooting," Spectrum News 1 (Madison), August 26, 2020, https://spectrumnews1.com/wi/madison/news/2020/08/25 /kenosha-live-updates--the-latest-on-protests-in-wisconsin-for-tuesday --august-25; "Atlanta Protests Over Jacob Blake Take Destructive Turn in Downtown; 8 Arrested," WSB-TV (Atlanta), August 26, 2020, https:// www.wsbtv.com/news/local/atlanta/atlanta-protests-over-jacob-blake -take-destructive-turn-downtown/A5RTHYXMKNF6HLS3JW7BHEA QHY/; Paul Walsh, "11 Protesting Kenosha Police Shooting Arrested After Jail Damaged in Minneapolis," *Minneapolis Star Tribune*, August 25, 2020, https://www.startribune.com/11-protesting-kenosha-police-shooting -arrested-after-jail-damaged-in-mpls/572214592/; Kerry Burke, "It Keeps Happening: Hundreds of Protesters Fill Manhattan Streets to Condemn

Shooting of Wisconsin Black Man in Front of His Children," *New York Daily News*, August 24, 2020, https://www.nydailynews.com/new-york/ny-protest-blm-jacob-blake-20200825-vwkinxjg7jew5kssjexy2eevd4-story.html; "Large Protest Held in Manhattan Following Weekend Police Shooting of Jacob Blake in Wisconsin," CBS New York, August 24, 2020, https://www.cbsnews.com/newyork/news/jacob-blake-shooting-wisconsin-protest-march-manhattan-new-york-city/; Bob Brooks, "Protest Held in Philadelphia for Jacob Blake Who Was Shot by Police in Wisconsin," WPVI-TV (Philadelphia), August 27, 2020, https://6abc.com/jacob-blake-shooting-philadelphia-protest-philly-bideo/6390453; Leila Miller and Luke Money, "Hundreds of Protesters Take to Streets of Downtown L.A. to Decry Police Shootings," *Los Angeles Times*, August 25, 2020, https://www.latimes.com/california/story/2020-08-25/protesters-marching-in-downtown-l-a-monday-night-decry-police-shootings; Leila Miller, "Protesters March in Downtown L.A. Over Jacob Blake Shooting," *Los Angeles Times*, August 27, 2020, https://www.latimes.com/california/story/2020-08-26/downtown-los-angeles-jacob-blake-protest; "More Than a Dozen Arrested in Oakland Protests, Police Say," KGO-TV (San Francisco), August 29, 2020, https://abc7news.com/oakland-protests-arrests-jacob-blake-demonstration/6394911/; Molly Sullivan, Dale Kassler, Tony Bizjak, and Theresa Clift, "Sacramento Protests Over Kenosha Shooting; Damage at City Hall and Sheriff's, DA's Offices," *Sacramento Bee*, August 27, 2020, https://www.sacbee.com/news/local/crime/article245309185.html; Mark Saunders, "Multiple People Arrested During Protest in Downtown San Diego Over Shooting of Jacob Blake," ABC10 News (San Diego), August 28, 2020, https://www.10news.com/news/local-news/demonstrators-gather-in-downtown-san-diego-to-protest-wisconsin-shooting-of-jacob-blake; Amanda del Castillo, "San Jose Mayor's Home Vandalized as Hundreds Protest Downtown Against Police Brutality, Jacob Blake Shooting," KGO-TV (San Francisco), August 29, 2020, https://abc7news.com/san-jose-protest-jacob-blake-mayor-sam-liccardo-home-vandalized-downtown-sj/6394638/; Joel Moreno, "Protesters Dig In Outside Seattle Fire Station; Jacob Blake's Aunt Speaks Out," KOMO-TV (Seattle), August 27, 2020, https://komonews.com/news/local/protesters-dig-in-outside-seattle-fire-station-jacob-blakes-aunt-speaks-out; Richie Ramos, "At Least 2 Arrested as Third Round of Protests Unfolds in Downtown Sacramento," CBS Sacramento, August 29, 2020, https://www.cbsnews.com/sacramento/news/arrests-made-third-round-of-protests-planned-for-downtown-sacramento-saturday/; George Kelly, "Oakland: 'Agitators' Vandalize Courthouse Following Mostly

Peaceful Jacob Blake Protest," *East Bay Times*, August 26, 2020, https://www.eastbaytimes.com/2020/08/26/oakland-jacob-blake-protesters-prepare-to-gather-downtown/.

56. G. Kelly, "Oakland"; Sullivan et al., "Sacramento Protests"; Moreno, "Protesters Dig In"; M. Saunders, "Multiple People Arrested"; "More Than a Dozen Arrested," KGO-TV (San Francisco); Del Castillo, "San Jose Mayor's Home"; Ramos, "At Least 2 Arrested."

57. Dylan Brogan, "'No Bad Protesters. No Good Cops,'" *Isthmus*, August 25, 2020, https://isthmus.com/news/news/no-bad-protesters-no-good-cops/; "Kenosha, Madison See Continued Unrest in Wake of Officer-Involved Shooting," WisPolitics, August 25, 2020, https://www.wispolitics.com/2020/kenosha-madison-see-continued-unrest-in-wake-of-officer-involved-shooting/; Maddie Burakoff, "In Madison, Another Night of Unrest after Jacob Blake Shooting," Spectrum News, August 25, 2020, https://spectrumnews1.com/wi/milwaukee/news/2020/08/25/in-madison--another-night-of-unrest-after-jacob-blake-shooting; "Two Charged with Arson in Madison during Unrest Following Jacob Blake Shooting," WKOW-TV (Madison), September 23, 2020, https://www.wkow.com/archive/two-charged-with-arson-in-madison-during-unrest-following-jacob-blake-shooting/article_7509f52a-8e70-5548-b046-c5be9eee43be.html.

58. "Media Release," Kenosha Police Department, August 27, 2020, https://www.facebook.com/Kenoshapolice/photos/a.10151999394132207/10158499263417207/.

59. J. R. Radcliffe, "Kenosha Update Recap: Coverage from Aug. 27," *Milwaukee Journal Sentinel*, August 27, 2020, https://www.jsonline.com/story/news/2020/08/27/wisconsin-police-shooting-jacob-blake-live-updates-kenosha/5642326002/.

60. J. R. Radcliffe, "Kenosha Update Recap: Aug. 28 Jacob Blake, Protest Shooting Coverage," *Milwaukee Journal Sentinel*, August 29, 2020, https://www.jsonline.com/story/news/2020/08/28/wisconsin-police-shooting-jacob-blake-live-updates-kenosha/5654147002/; Madison Goldbeck, "Kenosha County Ends State of Emergency Curfew," WDJT-TV (Milwaukee), September 2, 2020, https://www.cbs58.com/news/kenosha-county-ends-state-of-emergency-curfew.

61. Bill Glauber, "'We're Blessed': Spring Brings a Sense of Renewal to Kenosha as It Emerges from the Violent Protests of Last Summer," *Milwaukee Journal Sentinel*, April 20, 2021, https://www.jsonline.com/story/news/2021/04/20/grit-resilience-kenosha-business-leaders-trying-move-forward/7156905002/; Bruce Vielmetti, "Pair Charged in Kenosha

Looting during Jacob Blake Protests," *Milwaukee Journal Sentinel*, February 22, 2021, https://www.jsonline.com/story/news/crime/2021/02/22/pair-charged-kenosha-looting-during-jacob-blake-protests-august/4539196001/; "Kenosha Unrest," Wikipedia, last modified February 18, 2021, https://en.wikipedia.org/wiki/Kenosha_unrest.

62. Drake Bentley, "Four Men, Three of Which from Minnesota, Have Been Indicted on Charges Relating to Kenosha Unrest," *Milwaukee Journal Sentinel*, July 13, 2021, https://www.jsonline.com/story/news/local/wisconsin/2021/07/13/four-men-have-been-indicted-actions-related-kenosha-unrest/7960328002/.

63. Glauber, "We're Blessed."

OUR TOWN

1. Richard Schickel, *Good Morning, Mr. Zip Zip Zip* (Chicago: Ivan R. Dee, 2003), 3; Sam Roberts, "Richard Schickel, Movie Critic, Author and Filmmaker Dies at 84," *New York Times*, February 20, 2017, https://www.nytimes.com/2017/02/20/movies/richard-schickel-dead-time-film-critic.html. The Wisconsin Historical Society says that "Wauwatosa" might refer to an Indian chief known as "the great walker" or "dim of memory" from a Native American word, *wawatosi*. It also might be a combination of two similar Menomonee and Potawatomi words meaning "firefly" and "the lost brave." Locals prefer "firefly" or "Land of the Firefly" after Potawatomi Chief Wauwataesie. (See "Wauwatosa [origin of place name]," Wisconsin Historical Society, accessed August 29, 2022, https://www.wisconsinhistory.org/Records/Article/CS14186; Bob Dohr, "What's in a Name? The Story behind How Milwaukee's Suburbs like West Allis, New Berlin, and Wauwatosa Got Their Names," *Milwaukee Journal Sentinel*, August 29, 2022, https://www.jsonline.com/story/communities/southwest/news/2022/08/29/story-behind-how-some-milwaukee-suburbs-got-their-names-west-allis-greenfield-new-berlin-wauwatosa/10007488002/.)

2. Marie Rohde, "Wauwatosa: No One Picture Captures City's Different Faces," *Milwaukee Journal*, circa November 1984.

3. Evan Casey, "Joseph Mensah, The Former Wauwatosa Police Officer Who Killed Three People, Has Been Hired as a Waukesha County Deputy," *Milwaukee Journal Sentinel*, January 26, 2021, https://www.jsonline.com/story/communities/west/news/2021/01/26/ex-wauwatosa

-police-officer-joseph-mensah-hired-as-waukesha-county-deputy/4259934001/.

4. "City of Wauwatosa Demographic Overview," City of Wauwatosa, accessed May 27, 2024, https://www.wauwatosa.net/home/showdocument?id=3988.

5. Bill Glauber, "Mayfair a Cultural Crossroads," *Milwaukee Journal Sentinel*, January 8, 2011, https://archive.jsonline.com/news/milwaukee/113147564.html/; Dennis McBride, "Our Enduring Racism Is the Problem, Not a Mall," *Milwaukee Journal Sentinel*, February 24, 2007, http://www.jsonline.com/story/index.aspx?id=569676.

6. Julius Ruff, "Adapted from the Sesquicentennial History," First Congregational Church of Wauwatosa website, accessed December 15, 2022, https://www.firstchurchtosa.org/about-us/history/; "Our History," Underwood Memorial Baptist Church, accessed May 27, 2024, https://underwoodchurch.org/history/.

7. Schickel, *Good Morning*, 8–9; Will Gosner, "Sundown Town," *Encyclopedia Britannica*, accessed September 25, 2023, https://www.britannica.com/place/sundown-town.

8. Dennis McBride, "History in Color: Race Matters in Wauwatosa," *Historic Wauwatosa* (Wauwatosa Historical Society newsletter), April 2006, 1, 2; Evan Casey, "Her Black Uncle Faced Racism after Trying to Build a Home in Wauwatosa in the 1950s. She Wrote an Award-Winning Essay About His Struggle," *Milwaukee Journal Sentinel*, July 27, 2021, https://www.jsonline.com/story/communities/west/news/wauwatosa/2021/07/27/lora-hyler-wins-wisconsin-writers-association-award-uncle-zeddies-story-facing-racism-in-wauwatosa/8034640002/.

9. John Schmid, "Milwaukee's Trauma Care Initiatives Are Meant to Heal. Now They Are at the Heart of the City's Racial Divide," *Milwaukee Journal Sentinel*, June 18, 2019, https://www.jsonline.com/story/news/solutions/2019/06/18/centuries-old-racism-haunts-efforts-treat-milwaukee-trauma-epidemic/2580146002/.

10. "Read the Award-Winning Essay About Wauwatosa's Pioneering Black Homeowner: Zeddie Q. Hyler Fought Discrimination, Intimidation and Racial Covenants to Build 'The Ponderosa' in 1955—with Some Key Allies," *Milwaukee Magazine*, September 12, 2021, https://www.milwaukeemag.com/zeddie-hyler-essay/.

11. McBride, "History in Color," 1, 2; John Gurda, *The Making of Milwaukee* (Milwaukee: Milwaukee County Historical Society, 1999), 369–370; Barbara J. Miner, *Lessons from the Heartland: A Turbulent Half-Century of Public Education in an Iconic American City* (New York: New

Press, 2013), 59–60; "50-Year Ache: How Far Has Milwaukee Come Since the 1967 Civil Rights Marches?," *Milwaukee Journal Sentinel*, accessed February 19, 2021, https://projects.jsonline.com/topics/50-year-ache/.

12. McBride, "History in Color," 1, 3; Robert W. Coakley, Paul J. Schelps, and Vincent H. Demma, *Use of Troops in Civil Disturbances Since World War II, 1945–1965*, OCMH Study 83, rev. ed. (Washington, DC: Office of the Chief of Military History, 1971), 75–81, accessed August 19, 2021, https://books.google.com/books?id=-xQUMBseEIQC&pg=RA1-PA75&lpg=RA1-PA75&dq=august+1966+wauwatosa+cannon+groppi&source=bl&ots=kCdKDJJa_n&sig=ACfU3U2x-xpP_yFGHq22fSbYLTTv_h8mNg&hl=en&sa=X&ved=2ahUKEwijxryK77_yAhUHWsoKHcPtBaYQ6AF6BAgaEAM#v=onepage&q=august%201966%20wauwatosa%20cannon%20groppi&f=false; Matthew J. Prigge, "Wauwatosa's Civil Rights Struggle Honored in Special Exhibit," *Shepherd Express*, June 26, 2017, https://shepherdexpress.com/news/happening-now/wauwatosa-s-civil-rights-struggle-honored-special-exhibit/#/questions.

13. Reggie Jackson, "A White Utopia: How a Segregated Milwaukee Created the Arrogance of Suburbia," *Milwaukee Independent*, December 16, 2020, http://www.milwaukeeindependent.com/featured/white-utopia-segregated-milwaukee-created-arrogance-suburbia/; Mike Gousha and John D. Johnson, "Census Shows the Milwaukee Area Is More Diverse, but Overall Growth Remains Sluggish," *Milwaukee Journal Sentinel*, September 23, 2021, https://www.jsonline.com/story/news/solutions/2021/09/23/census-milwaukee-area-more-diverse-but-overall-growth-sluggish/5786829001/; Isabel Wilkerson, *The Warmth of Other Suns: The Epic Story of America's Great Migration* (New York: Random House, 2010), 398; "Housing Segregation Still Sidelining People of Color from Dream Homes," *Nightline* (ABC News), February 9, 2022, https://abcnews.go.com/Nightline/video/housing-segregation-sidelining-people-color-ream-homes-82794840.

14. Michael Rosen and Charlie Dee, "Opinion: RNC Bust Shows That Tourism and Entertainment Alone Won't Transform Milwaukee's Economy," *Milwaukee Journal Sentinel*, August 5, 2024, https://www.jsonline.com/story/opinion/2024/08/05/rnc-milwaukee-bucks-down town-third-ward/74592620007/; Patrick D. Jones, *The Selma of the North: Civil Rights Insurgency in Milwaukee* (Cambridge, MA: Harvard University Press, 2010); Schmid, "Milwaukee's Trauma Care Initiatives."

15. Alex Growth, "Are You Making Enough to Live Comfortably in Milwaukee? Here's How Much You Need," *Milwaukee Journal Sentinel*, May 15, 2024, https://www.jsonline.com/story/news/local/2024/05/15

/how-much-do-you-need-to-make-to-live-comfortably-in-milwaukee/73682954007/.

16. "Blog Recap: Coverage of Milwaukee's Protest on Friday, May 29, 2020," *Milwaukee Journal Sentinel*, May 29, 2020, https://www.jsonline.com/story/news/2020/05/29/milwaukee-protest-george-floyd-killing-live-27th-and-center/5284428002/; Emily Files, Marti Mikkelson, Lauren Sigfusson, and Chuck Quirmbach, "May 30: Tear Gas Deployed, Some Stores Vandalized After Peaceful Protests in Milwaukee," WUWM Radio (89.7 FM), May 30, 2020, https://www.wuwm.com/news/2020-05-30/may-30-tear-gas-deployed-some-stores-vandalized-after-peaceful-protests-in-milwaukee.

17. Molly Beck, Lawrence Andrea, and Patrick Marley, "After Peaceful Afternoon Protests, Madison Erupts into Looting, Destruction," *Milwaukee Journal Sentinel*, May 30, 2020, https://www.jsonline.com/story/news/politics/2020/05/30/george-floyd-protests-madison-demonstrators-recall-tony-robinson/5293284002/; Laura Schulte, "'It's Going to Be Tough': Downtown Madison Businesses Grappling with Effects of Protests, COVID-19," *Milwaukee Journal Sentinel*, January 22, 2021, https://www.jsonline.com/story/news/2021/01/22/its-going-tough-downtown-madison-businesses-grappling-effects-protests-covid-19/4205422001/.

18. "City of Wauwatosa Announces 9 pm Curfew," City of Wauwatosa, May 30, 2020, https://www.wauwatosa.net/Home/Components/News/News/2016/; "Statement from Mayor Dennis McBride (May 31, 12:30 pm)," City of Wauwatosa, May 31, 2020, https://www.wauwatosa.net/Home/Components/News/News/2016/.

19. Evan Casey, "'This Is Unity at Its Best': Hundreds Protest in Wauwatosa to Call for Peace, Change in Wake of George Floyd's Death," *Milwaukee Journal Sentinel*, June 3, 2020, https://www.jsonline.com/story/communities/west/news/wauwatosa/2020/06/03/george-floyd-protest-hundreds-gather-wauwatosa-peaceful-event/3139725001/.

20. "Mayor's Statement on Racial Justice and Equity," City of Wauwatosa, June 5, 2020, https://www.wauwatosa.net/Home/Components/News/News/2024/17.

21. Minutes from June 10, 2020, special meeting of City of Wauwatosa Common Council, City of Wauwatosa, http://wauwatosacitywi.iqm2.com/Citizens/FileOpen.aspx?Type=15&ID=2742&Inline=True.

22. Evan Casey, "The Prohibition of Carotid and Neck Restraints in Wauwatosa Is a 'Civil Rights Victory,' Chairperson Says," *Milwaukee Journal Sentinel*, August 6, 2020, https://www.jsonline.com/story

/communities/west/news/wauwatosa/2020/08/06/wauwatosa-bans-use-carotid-neck-restraints-official-calls-civil-rights-victory/3300322001/; "Making Wauwatosa More Inclusive," City of Wauwatosa, https://www.wauwatosa.net/government/open-government/making-wauwatosa-more-inclusive.

23. "Milwaukee Co. DA Has New Evidence on Alvin Cole's Death," *Spectrum News* (Milwaukee), June 12, 2020, https://spectrumnews1.com/wi/milwaukee/news/2020/06/12/milwaukee-co--da-has-new-evidence-on-alvin-cole-s-death.

24. Kim Shine, "Family Files Complaint Against Wauwatosa police Officer Involved in Three Deadly Shootings," WDJT-TV (Milwaukee), June 18, 2020, https://www.cbs58.com/news/family-files-complaint-against-wauwatosa-police-officer-involved-in-three-deadly-shootings.

25. Wisconsin Statutes § 62.13(5).

26. J. R. Ross, "Trump Claims He Saved Kenosha. Wisconsin Voters Aren't Buying It," *Politico*, September 1, 2020, politico.com/news/magazine/2020/09/01/donald-trump-kenosha-wisconsin-2020-406865; Clara Neupert, "Another Way: A Former Chief Says Police Should Ditch Riot Gear, Tear Gas at Protests," *Wisconsin Watch*, December 9, 2020, https://madison.com/ct/news/local/another-way-a-former-chief-says-police-should-ditch-riot-gear-tear-gas-at-protests/article_2258ca26-7da7-5421-a6be-b9df28cad1e3.html; Schulte, "It's Going to Be Tough"; "Protester Involved in Pulling Down Abolitionist's Statue Outside Wisconsin State Capitol Gets 6 Months in Jail," *Milwaukee Journal Sentinel*, May 26, 2023, https://www.jsonline.com/story/news/crime/2023/05/26/protester-involved-in-pulling-down-statue-in-madison-gets-jail-term/70262951007/.

27. "50-Year Ache: How Far Has Milwaukee Come Since the 1967 Civil Rights Marches?," *Milwaukee Journal Sentinel*, accessed February 19, 2021, https://projects.jsonline.com/topics/50-year-ache/; Bobby Tanzilo, "Construction Begins to Convert Old Gimbels-Schusters to Thrive On HQ," *OnMilwaukee*, June 7, 2022, https://onmilwaukee.com/articles/thrive-on-construction; "Blog Recap: Coverage of Milwaukee's Protest on Friday, May 29, 2020," *Milwaukee Journal Sentinel*; Files, et al., "May 30."

28. Doug Erickson, "When Bomb Tore through Sterling Hall 50 Years Ago, He Was Inside: 'I Still Have Flashbacks,'" University of Wisconsin-Madison News, August 18, 2020, https://news.wisc.edu/when-bomb-tore-through-sterling-hall-he-was-inside-i-still-have-flashbacks/.

29. "50-Year Ache"; Tanzilo, "Construction Begins to Convert Old Gimbels-Schusters."

30. Marc Fisher, "Opinion: Larry Noodged Me for Four Decades. I'm Glad He Did," *Washington Post*, July 24, 2024, https://www.washingtonpost.com/opinions/2024/07/24/larry-rosen-dc-riots/.

31. "Common Council Creates Ad Hoc Committee to Address Policing and Systemic Inequities," City of Wauwatosa, July 24, 2020, https://www.wauwatosa.net/Home/Components/News/News/2114/17; Isiah Holmes, "Chair Reacts to Wauwatosa Police Union's Call to Disband Social Justice Committee," *Wisconsin Examiner*, September 17, 2020, https://wisconsinexaminer.com/2020/09/17/chair-reacts-to-wauwatosa-police-unions-call-to-disband-the-racial-justice-committee/.

32. In 2002, I filed a federal lawsuit against Target Corporation in the US District Court for the Eastern District of Wisconsin, alleging that Target had violated Title VII of the Civil Rights Act of 1964 by not hiring African Americans as assistant managers in its District 110 (headquartered in Wauwatosa) based on their race. In 2007, Target agreed to pay $510,000 to four African Americans who were denied jobs. The settlement followed a decision, *EEOC v. Target Corporation*, 460 F.3d 946 (7th Cir. 2006), by the US Court of Appeals for the Seventh Circuit rejecting Target's attempt to dismiss the case. The decision established that the trial court could admit expert testimony to the effect that Target may have identified the applicants as Black, and discriminated without meeting them, based on their names (in résumés) or accents (heard during telephone conversations). This was the first federal court to make such a ruling in a Title VII case. Though I was the lawyer who brought this case and litigated it at the district court level, it is EEOC policy that appeals from district court decisions are handled by the agency's Appellate Division at EEOC headquarters. Nevertheless, I did work with, and advise, the EEOC lawyer, James M. Tucker, who successfully argued the appeal.

33. "Judgment in a Civil Case" and "Consent Decree," *EEOC v. Austin J. Decoster d/b/a Decoster Farms of Iowa and Iowa Ag L.L.C.*, Civil Action No. CO2-3077 MWB (N.D. Iowa), October 3, 2002, https://ecommons.cornell.edu/bitstream/handle/1813/80012/EEOC_v__Austin_J__Decoster_SCANNED.pdf?sequence=1&isAllowed=y.

34. "Rape in the Fields," *PBS Frontline*, June 25, 2013, https://www.pbs.org/video/frontline-rape-fields-show/.

35. Michael Levenson, "For Mayor Jacob Frey of Minneapolis, a Stinging Rebuke," *New York Times*, June 7, 2020, https://www.nytimes.com/2020/06/07/us/minneapolis-mayor-jacob-frey-walk-of-shame.html.

36. Jessica Donati, "Outside Milwaukee, Protests Over One Officer's Three Killings: Alvin Cole, 17, Was Shot Five Times by Officer While

Fleeing Police in February," *Wall Street Journal*, June 24, 2020, https://www.wsj.com/articles/outside-milwaukee-protests-over-one-officers-three-killings-11593008818.

37. Evan Casey, "'We Shut Down Mayfair': Protesters March Throughout the Mall before Making Way to Police Department," *Milwaukee Journal Sentinel*, June 24, 2020, https://www.jsonline.com/story/communities/west/news/wauwatosa/2020/06/24/protesters-shut-down-mayfair-mall-call-justice-alvin-cole-joseph-mensah-wauwatosa-wisconsin/3255060001/; Evan Casey, "15 Seconds. 15 Shots. Here's a Timeline on How a Fatal Shooting in February Set Off a Summer of Protests and Unrest in Wauwatosa," *Milwaukee Journal Sentinel*, October 7, 2020, https://www.jsonline.com/story/communities/west/news/wauwatosa/2020/08/18/timeline-after-officer-joseph-mensah-killed-alvin-cole-mayfair-mall-wauwatosa/3343685001/.

38. Evan Casey and Christopher Kuhagen, "Jay-Z's Social Justice Group Calls for Prosecution of a Wauwatosa Officer Who Has Shot and Killed Three People. Here's What We Know," *Milwaukee Journal Sentinel*, July 2, 2020, https://www.jsonline.com/story/communities/west/news/wauwatosa/2020/07/02/wauwatosa-police-officer-mensah-has-killed-three-people-five-years/5356213002/.

39. Jonas Brothers, "To: John Chisholm, Milwaukee County District Attorney," *X (Twitter)*, July 2, 2020, https://twitter.com/jonasbrothers/status/1278754538833375232; Jonas Brothers, "To: John Chisholm, Milwaukee County District Attorney," *Instagram*, July 2, 2020, https://www.instagram.com/p/CCJj7jUHlui/?hl=en.

40. Isiah Holmes, "Pressure Mounts on Tosa PD, Including from Jay-Z," *Wisconsin Examiner*, July 9, 2020, https://wisconsinexaminer.com/2020/07/09/pressure-mounts-on-tosa-pd-including-from-jay-z/.

41. *Jacobs v. Major*, 139 Wis.2d 492, 407 N.W.2d (1987) (under the Wisconsin Constitution, shopping centers are not governmental forums and may exclude members of the public from engaging in protests on their premises).

42. Jim Piwowarczyk, "Inside The Peoples Revolution: Gang Ties, Felonies, a State Rep & Congressional Staffer," Wisconsin Right Now, January 30, 2021, https://www.wisconsinrightnow.com/2021/01/30/the-peoples-revolution/; "How The 'People's Revolution' Led a Textbook Insurgency In Wauwatosa And Escaped Justice," MacIver News, November 1, 2022, https://www.maciverinstitute.com/2022/11/how-the-peoples-revolution-led-a-textbook-insurgency-in-wauwatosa-and-escaped

-justice/; Ricardo Torres, "Milwaukee Activist Khalil Coleman and Two Others Arrested in Kentucky and Charged with Robbery," *Milwaukee Journal Sentinel*, February 17, 2021, https://www.jsonline.com/story/news/local/milwaukee/2021/02/17/milwaukee-activist-khalil-coleman-and-two-others-arrested-kentucky/6783778002/; Jordyn Noennig, "Prominent Milwaukee Activist Khalil Coleman Has Been Found Guilty of Robbery in Kentucky," *Milwaukee Journal Sentinel*, April 9, 2022, https://www.jsonline.com/story/news/2022/04/09/milwaukee-activist-khalil-coleman-found-guilty-robbery-kentucky-kenton-county-court/9524426002/; Brian Planalp, "Man Drove 7 Hours, Picked Wrong NKY House in 'Mind-Boggling' Robbery Scheme," WXIX-TV (Cincinnati), August 3, 2022, https://www.fox19.com/2022/08/03/wisconsin-man-drove-7-hours-picked-wrong-nky-house-mind-boggling-crime-gone-wrong/; Emma Colton, "Milwaukee BLM 'Militant' Says Waukesha Christmas Parade Attack May Be Start of 'Revolution': Activist Vaun Mayes Said, 'It Sounds Possible That the Revolution Has Started in Wisconsin,'" WITI-TV (Milwaukee), November 23, 2021, https://www.foxnews.com/us/milwaukee-blm-activist-christmas-parade-attack-revolution-waukesha.

43. Holmes, "Pressure Mounts on Tosa PD"; Samantha Hendrickson, "'You Are Not Listening to Us': Protesters Arrested at Mayfair Mall, Clash with Wauwatosa Common Council," *Milwaukee Journal Sentinel*, July 8, 2020, https://www.jsonline.com/story/communities/west/news/wauwatosa/2020/07/08/protesters-arrested-mayfair-clash-wauwatosa-common-council/5398294002/; "Protesters Gather in Wauwatosa, Interrupt Common Council Meeting Demanding Accountability," WDJT-TV (Milwaukee), July 7, 2020, https://www.cbs58.com/news/protesters-gather-in-wauwatosa-interrupt-common-council-meeting-demanding-accountability.

44. "One Year Since the Jan. 6 Attack on the Capitol," United States Attorney's Office for the District of Columbia, January 6, 2022, https://www.justice.gov/usao-dc/one-year-jan-6-attack-capitol.

45. Jim Piwowarczyk, "Wauwatosa Protest Group Organizer Is a Felon Serial Burglar," Wisconsin Right Now, September 17, 2020, https://www.wisconsinrightnow.com/2020/09/17/brian-thomas-anderson/.

46. Isiah Holmes, "Tosa PD Protesters Issue List of Demands," *Wisconsin Examiner*, July 10, 2020, https://urbanmilwaukee.com/2020/07/10/wauwatosa-pd-protesters-issue-list-of-demands/.

47. "Know Your Rights: Protesters' Rights," American Civil Liberties Union, accessed December 26, 2021, https://www.aclu.org/know-your-rights/protesters-rights/.

48. "Wauwatosa Common Council Orders City to Address Officer Mensah's Employment: The Common Council and the Police Chief to Effectuate Such a Change as Quickly as Possible," City of Wauwatosa, July 15, 2020, https://www.wauwatosa.net/Home/Components/News/News/2096/17.

49. Evan Casey, "The Wauwatosa Police Officer Who Has Shot and Killed Three People in the Last Five Years Has Been Suspended, Commission Rules," *Milwaukee Journal Sentinel*, July 15, 2020, https://www.jsonline.com/story/communities/west/news/wauwatosa/2020/07/15/officer-joseph-mensah-suspended-wauwatosa-police-and-fire-commission/5446849002/; Isiah Holmes, "Tosa Officer's Suspension Is Just One Chapter in an Ongoing Saga," *Wisconsin Examiner*, July 17, 2020, https://wisconsinexaminer.com/2020/07/17/tosa-officers-suspension-is-just-one-chapter-in-an-ongoing-saga/.

50. "Public Listening Session: You Asked, We Answered," City of Wauwatosa, August 21, 2020, https://www.wauwatosa.net/Home/Components/News/News/2168/17; Isiah Holmes, "Listening Session on Race and Equity in Tosa Is Mass Catharsis for Residents," *Wisconsin Examiner*, July 23, 2020, https://wisconsinexaminer.com/2020/07/23/listening-session-on-race-and-equity-in-tosa-is-mass-catharsis-for-residents/; "Veiled Threats and BLM Demands at Wauwatosa Listening Session," MacIver News Service, July 23, 2020, https://www.maciverinstitute.com/2020/07/veiled-threats-at-wauwatosa-listening-session/.

51. Shaun Gallagher, "Protesters Arrived at Wauwatosa Mayor's Home in Defiance of City Ordinance, Mayor Says," WTMJ-TV (Milwaukee), August 14, 2020, https://www.tmj4.com/news/local-news/protesters-arrived-at-wauwatosa-mayors-home-in-defiance-of-city-ordinance-mayor-says; Isiah Holmes, "Tosa PD Escalates Tactics Against Protesters Following Incident at Officer's Home," *Wisconsin Examiner*, August 17, 2020, https://wisconsinexaminer.com/2020/08/17/tosa-pd-escalates-tactics-against-protesters-following-incident-at-officers-home/; Jim Piwowarczyk, "Inside The Peoples Revolution."

52. Evan Casey, "Officer Joseph Mensah Was Physically Assaulted by Protesters and a Gunshot Was Fired into His Home, Wauwatosa Police Say," *Milwaukee Journal Sentinel*, August 9, 2020, https://www.jsonline.com/story/communities/west/news/wauwatosa/2020/08/09/wauwatosa-police-officer-joseph-mensah-physically-assaulted/3330610001/; "Wauwatosa Officer Joseph Mensah Physically Assaulted, Shot At during Protest, Police Say," WTMJ-TV (Milwaukee), August 9, 2020, https://www.tmj4.com/news/local-news/wauwatosa-officer-joseph-mensah-physically

-assaulted-shot-at-during-protests; "Wauwatosa Police: Officer Mensah Physically Assaulted, Shot At by Protesters at His Home," WDJT-TV (Milwaukee), August 9, 2020, https://www.cbs58.com/news/wauwatosa-officer-mensah-physically-assaulted-shot-at-by-protesters.

53. Casey, "Joseph Mensah"; Casey, "Officer Joseph Mensah Physically Assaulted"; Katie DeLong, "Wauwatosa Mayor Warns Protesters Could Be Arrested, Fined on Private Property, for Blocking Traffic," WITI-TV (Milwaukee), August 13, 2020, https://www.fox6now.com/news/wauwatosa-mayor-warns-protesters-could-be-arrested-fined-on-private-property-for-blocking-traffic; "People's Revolution Led a Textbook Insurgency," MacIver News Service.

54. Casey, "Joseph Mensah."

55. Wauwatosa Police Department Incident Report No. 20-014889, August 2020.

56. Evan Casey, "Rep. Jim Sensenbrenner Says He's Ready to Send Federal Agents to Wauwatosa in Aftermath of Protest at Officer Mensah's Home," *Milwaukee Journal Sentinel*, August 11, 2020, https://www.jsonline.com/story/communities/west/news/wauwatosa/2020/08/11/federal-agents-would-bring-peace-wauwatosa-after-protest-at-joseph-mensah-home-jim-sensenbrenner/3347209001/; Everton Bailey Jr., "Portland Bans Police from Working with federal Law Enforcement, Targeting Journalists and Legal Observers during Protests," *Oregonian/Oregon Live*, July 22, 2020, https://www.oregonlive.com/portland/2020/07/portland-bans-police-from-working-with-federal-law-enforcement-targeting-journalists-and-legal-observers-during-protests.html.

57. M. D. Kittle, "Wauwatosa Protests Turn Destructive After Mensah Decision," Empower Wisconsin, October 8, 2020, https://empowerwisconsin.org/wauwatosa-protests-turn-destructive-after-mensah-decision/; "People's Revolution Led a Textbook Insurgency," MacIver News Service.

58. U.S. Rep. Jim Sensenbrenner, "PRESS RELEASE: Letter to Wauwatosa Mayor Dennis McBride Regarding Restoring Law and Order in the City," reprinted by *Urban Milwaukee*, August 11, 2020, https://urbanmilwaukee.com/pressrelease/letter-to-wauwatosa-mayor-dennis-mcbride-regarding-restoring-law-and-order-in-the-city/; Casey, "Rep. Jim Sensenbrenner"; Evan Casey and Christopher Kuhagan, "Wisconsin Police Officer Who Fatally Shot Three People in the Last Five Years Is Resigning," *Milwaukee Journal Sentinel*, November 18, 2020, https://www.usatoday.com/story/news/nation/2020/11/18/wisconsin-cop-who-killed-three-people-last-five-years-resigning/6337904002/; Kittle, "Wauwatosa

Protests Turn Destructive"; "People's Revolution Led a Textbook Insurgency," MacIver News Service; Jim Piwowarczyk, "Wisconsin Right Now Wall of Shame: The Top 30 LOSERS of 2020," Wisconsin Right Now, January 1, 2021, https://www.wisconsinrightnow.com/2021/01/01/2020-wisconsin-losers/.

59. "Mayor's Statement on Need for Peaceful Protests," City of Wauwatosa, August 13, 2020, https://www.wauwatosa.net/government/open-government/making-wauwatosa-more-inclusive/-item-2149/; "Wauwatosa Mayor Creates Stricter Rules for Protests," WTMJ-TV (Milwaukee), August 14, 2020, https://wtmj.com/news/politics/2020/08/13/wauwatosa-mayor-creates-stricter-rules-for-protests/; Angelica Sanchez, "Wauwatosa Mayor Calls for Peaceful Protests, Says Firing Officer Mensah, Police Chief 'Very Difficult to Do,'" WITI-TV (Milwaukee), August 14, 2020, https://www.fox6now.com/news/wauwatosa-mayor-calls-for-peaceful-protests-says-firing-officer-mensah-police-chief-very-difficult-to-do; Derrick Rose, "Wauwatosa Police Tackle Protester while Blocking Mayor's House," WISN-TV (Milwaukee), August 14, 2020, https://www.wisn.com/article/wauwatosa-police-tackle-protester-while-blocking-mayors-house/33610322; Isiah Holmes, "Tosa Police Issue Gets More Heated: Other Suburb's Police Massing Against Protesters. Sensenbrenner, Police Chief, Talk Radio Condemn Protests," *Wisconsin Examiner,* August 17, 2020, https://urbanmilwaukee.com/2020/08/17/tosa-police-issue-gets-more-heated/.

60. Wauwatosa Police Department Incident Report No. 20-015259, August 2020; Rose, "Wauwatosa Police Tackle Protester"; Holmes, "Tosa Police Issue"; Jim Piwowarczyk, "Wauwatosa Policing Committee Chair Threatened to Knock Out Police Officer [VIDEO]," Wisconsin Right Now, September 25, 2020, https://www.wisconsinrightnow.com/2020/09/25/wauwatosa-police-inequities-committee-john-larry/; Defend the Heroes, "Wauwatosa: Hypocrisy, John Larry & Heather Kuhl (aka Vanilla Vixen)," YouTube, September 2020, https://www.youtube.com/watch?v=b8ofYQJDwSw.

61. Evan Casey, "Four Neighbors Received a Letter That Said Wauwatosa Should Be Kept Free from Blacks," *Milwaukee Journal Sentinel,* September 1, 2020, https://www.jsonline.com/story/communities/west/news/wauwatosa/2020/09/01/wauwatosa-neighbors-received-racist-letters/3454692001/; Evan Casey, "I Am Appalled: Wauwatosa's Mayor and Other Community Leaders Denounce Racist Letters Sent to Residents," *Milwaukee Journal Sentinel,* September 3, 2020, https://www

.jsonline.com/story/communities/west/news/wauwatosa/2020/09/03/wauwatosa-mayor-dennis-mcbride-denounces-racist-letter/5708022002/; Hillary Mintz, "Tosa Residents Receive 'Keep Wauwatosa White' Letter: 'Racism Is Immoral. It's Unjust. It's Unconstitutional. It's Despicable,' Wauwatosa Mayor Dennis McBride Says," WISN-TV (Milwaukee), September 3, 2020, https://www.wisn.com/article/tosa-residents-receive-keep-wauwatosa-white-letter/33918300#.

62. "Dotun Adebayo," Wikipedia, last modified on May 12, 2024, https://en.wikipedia.org/wiki/Dotun_Adebayo.

63. Aaron Maybin and Kasey Chronis, "'We Expect Unrest': Wauwatosa Awaits Decision in Alvin Cole Shooting," WITI-TV (Milwaukee), October 8, 2020, https://www.fox6now.com/news/we-expect-unrest-wauwatosa-awaits-decision-in-alvin-cole-shooting.

64. Letter from State Senator Dale Kooyenga and State Representative Rob Hutton to Wauwatosa Mayor Dennis R. McBride, *Wheeler Report*, September 23, 2020, http://www.thewheelerreport.com/wheeler_docs/files/092320lettertomayor.pdf.

65. "Charging Decision Expected in Fatal Police Shooting of Teen," Associated Press, October 6, 2020, https://www.usnews.com/news/us/articles/2020-10-06/charging-decision-expected-in-fatal-police-shooting-of-teen.

66. "Proclamation of Emergency," City of Wauwatosa, September 30, 2020, https://www.wauwatosa.net/home/showpublisheddocument?id=3145.

67. Dana Thiede, "Restaurant Owners Sue City of Minneapolis, Mayor Frey over Response to Unrest," KARE-11 (Minneapolis), February 10, 2021, https://www.kare11.com/article/news/local/restaurant-owners-sue-city-of-minneapolis-mayor-over-response-to-unrest/89-b4d92913-88a2-4f41-bd4c-788899d68b59.

68. "Fires Set, Businesses Looted during 3rd Night of Unrest in Milwaukee," WITI-TV (Milwaukee), June 1, 2020, https://www.fox6now.com/news/fires-set-businesses-looted-during-3rd-night-of-protests-in-milwaukee.

69. Karen Pilarski, "Wauwatosa Woman Charged with Arson after Starting Three Fires at Her Apartment Complex, Complaint Says," *Milwaukee Journal Sentinel*, June 18, 2019, https://www.jsonline.com/story/communities/west/news/wauwatosa/2019/06/18/police-tosa-mom-charged-arson-apartment-building-fires/1486795001/; Scott Anderson, "Wauwatosa Arson Suspect Had Cell Phone Data Trail: Report,"

Wauwatosa Patch, June 18, 2019, https://patch.com/wisconsin/wauwatosa/wauwatosa-arson-suspect-had-cell-phone-data-trail-report.

70. Bruce Vielmetti, "Witness Intimidation Charge Added to Firebomb Plot Case Against Community Activist," *Milwaukee Journal Sentinel*, October 21, 2019, https://www.jsonline.com/story/news/crime/2019/10/21/activist-vaun-mayes-charged-witness-intimidation-firebomb-plot-case/4027038002/; Julie Bosman, "Wisconsin Man Found Guilty of Killing 6 in Christmas Parade Attack," *New York Times*, October 26, 2022, https://www.nytimes.com/2022/10/26/us/darrell-brooks-wisconsin-parade-verdict.html; Colton, "Milwaukee BLM 'militant'"; Zoie Henry, "Milwaukee Activist Vaun Mayes Enters Guilty Plea in Riot Case," WISN-TV (Milwaukee), October 16, 2024, https://www.wisn.com/article/milwaukee-activist-vaun-mayes-enters-guilty-plea-in-riot-case/62628609.

71. Wisconsin Statutes §§ 323.11 and 323.14(4)(b).

72. Letter from Milwaukee County district attorney John Chisholm to Chief Barry Weber, City of Wauwatosa Police Department, re: "February 2nd 2020 Critical Incident Involving Officer Joseph Mensah and Alvin Cole at Mayfair Mall," October 7, 2020, 14, https://www.documentcloud.org/documents/7224668-Milwaukee-County-District-Attorney-John-Chisholm.html; Sara Sidner, Raja Razek, and Nicole Chavez, "Wauwatosa Police Officer Won't Face Charges in Deadly Shooting of 17-Year-Old Alvin Cole," CNN, October 8, 2020, https://www.cnn.com/2020/10/07/us/wauwatosa-wisconsin-police-shooting-alvin-cole/index.html; Evan Casey and Eddie Morales, "Milwaukee County District Attorney Will Not Charge Police Officer Joseph Mensah in Shooting Death of Alvin Cole," *Milwaukee Journal Sentinel*, October 7, 2020, https://www.jsonline.com/story/communities/west/news/wauwatosa/2020/10/07/wauwatosa-police-officer-joseph-mensah-da-decision-coming/3446512001/; "Report of Independent Investigator Steven M. Biskupic to the Wauwatosa Police and Fire Commission Regarding the Conduct of Wauwatosa Police Officer Joseph Mensah," Wauwatosa Police & Fire Commission, October 7, 2020, 1, 30, http://fox11digital.com/news/PDFs/Report%20of%20Independent%20Investigator_Part1.pdf; Ashley Luthern, "Outside Investigator: Tosa Officer Should Be Fired, Citing 'Extraordinary' Risk of a Fourth Fatal Shooting," *Milwaukee Journal Sentinel*, October 7, 2020, https://www.jsonline.com/story/news/crime/2020/10/07/wauwatosa-police-officer-joseph-mensah-should-fired-shootings-report-says/5909137002/; "Investigative Synopsis of the Officer Involved Death (OID) of Alvin T. Cole," Milwaukee Police Department, February 2020, https://city.mil

waukee.gov/ImageLibrary/Groups/mpdAuthors/PDFs/Wauwatosa-Alvin-Cole-Investigative-Synopsis.

73. "Press Release: Statement from Mayor Dennis McBride," *Urban Milwaukee*, October 7, 2020, https://urbanmilwaukee.com/pressrelease/statement-from-mayor-dennis-mcbride/.

74. Maybin and Chronis, "We Expect Unrest"; Casey, "Joseph Mensah."

75. Casey and Morales, "Milwaukee County District Attorney."

76. "Statement from Mayor Dennis McBride," City of Wauwatosa, October 7, 2020, https://www.wauwatosa.net/home/showpublisheddocument/3149/637376769309370000.

77. Casey and Morales, "Milwaukee County District Attorney."

78. "Summary of Events; October 7-11 Civil Unrest Operations" memorandum from Wauwatosa Police Department Captain Luke Vetter to City Administrator James Archambo, City of Wauwatosa, November 16, 2020, at 2.

79. Allison Dirr and Mary Spicuzza, "Highland Park Shooting Suspect Contemplated Attack in Madison, Authorities Say," *Milwaukee Journal Sentinel*, July 6, 2022, https://www.jsonline.com/story/news/crime/2022/07/06/highland-park-shooting-suspect-contemplated-shooting-madison/7821306001/.

80. "Summary of Events," Vetter to Archambo, 4.

81. Casey, "Joseph Mensah."

82. "Summary of Events," Vetter to Archambo.

83. "28 Arrested in Wisconsin Protests Over Police Slaying of Teen," *Taiwan News*, October 11, 2020, https://www.taiwannews.com.tw/en/news/4027556; "28 Arrested, Tear Gas Used in Wisconsin Protests," *Indian Express*, October 11, 2020, https://indianexpress.com/article/world/28-arrested-tear-gas-used-in-wisconsin-protests-6720394/; "28 Arrested in Wisconsin Protests Over Police Slaying of Teen," *Chicago Tribune*, October 10, 2020, https://www.chicagotribune.com/nation-world/ct-nw-wisconsin-protests-police-shooting-teen-alvin-cole-20201010-5i5063xijfhkvbslbvn7xa5xma-story.html; Katie Shepherd, "'Y'all Killed My Son': Mother of Black Teen Killed by Wisconsin Police Hospitalized After Arrest at Protest," *Washington Post*, October 9, 2020, https://www.washingtonpost.com/nation/2020/10/09/wisconsin-protest-alvin-cole-arrest/; "Protests Follow after Officer Is Cleared in Killing of Black Teen Outside Milwaukee," *Los Angeles Times*, October 8, 2020, https://www.latimes.com/world-nation/story/2020-10-08/protests-officer-cleared-killing-black

-teen-milwaukee; Maria Cramer, "Decision Not to Charge Wisconsin Officer In Fatal Shooting Draws Protests," *New York Times*, October 8, 2020, https://www.nytimes.com/2020/10/08/us/joseph-mensah-alvin-cole-milwaukee.html; Barbara Campbell, "Protesters March Against Decision Not to Charge Officer in Wauwatosa, Wis., Death," National Public Radio, October 8, 2020, https://www.npr.org/2020/10/08/921444774/protesters-march-against-decision-not-to-charge-officer-in-wauwatosa-wis-death.

84. Evan Casey and Eddie Morales, "'It's a Shame': Businesses Vandalized in Wauwatosa After the Announcement of the Decision Not to Charge Officer Mensah," *Milwaukee Journal Sentinel*, October 8, 2020, https://www.jsonline.com/story/communities/west/news/wauwatosa/2020/10/08/wauwatosa-police-officer-joseph-mensah-decision-protests-turn-violent/5924160002/.

85. Ibid.; Madison Dibble, "Wisconsin City Rattled by Riots Following Decision Not to Charge Officer Involved in Shooting of 17-Year-Old," *Washington Examiner*, October 8, 2020, https://www.washingtonexaminer.com/news/wisconsin-city-rattled-by-riots-following-decision-not-to-charge-officer-involved-in-shooting-of-17-year-old; Lee Brown, "BLM Mobs Smash Windows in Residential Homes During Wisconsin Protests," *New York Post*, October 8, 2020, https://nypost.com/2020/10/08/blm-mobs-smash-windows-in-residential-homes-during-wisconsin-protests/; Sidner, et al., "Wauwatosa Police Officer"; Todd Richmond, "Protests Spark in Wisconsin after Police Officer Not Charged for Death of Black Man," Associated Press, October 8, 2020, https://globalnews.ca/news/7385485/wisconsin-alvin-cole-shooting-police-protests/.

86. Evan Casey and Elliot Hughes, "Here's What We Know About the Protest-Related Arrests Made in Wauwatosa on Thursday Night," *Milwaukee Journal Sentinel*, October 9, 2020, https://www.jsonline.com/story/communities/west/news/wauwatosa/2020/10/09/wauwatosa-mensah-protests-cole-family-arrested-mom-out-hospital/5936276002/.

87. "Summary of Events," Vetter to Archambo, 3–4; Sidner, et al., "Wauwatosa Police Officer"; Casey and Morales, "It's a Shame"; Casey and Kuhagan, "Wisconsin Police Officer."

88. "Decision and Order" in *Paige Radke v. City of Wauwatosa, et al.*, Case No. 21-C-0247 (E.D. Wis.) (Adelman, J.), August 24, 2022, at 13–14.

89. "Decision and Order" in *Radke*, at 8–9; "Decision and Order on Plaintiffs' Motion for Partial Summary Judgment, Defendants' Motion for Summary Judgment, The Parties' Motions to Strike, and Plaintiffs' Motions for Sanctions" in *Knowlton, et al. v. City of Wauwatosa, et al.*, Case No. 20-CV-1660 (E.D. Wis.) (Joseph, Mag. J.), March 13, 2023, at 16.

90. Casey and Hughes, "Here's What We Know"; Justin Bey, "Jay-Z and Team Roc Post Bond and Pay Fines for Alvin Cole's Mother and Others Arrested at Wisconsin Protests," CBS News, October 9, 2020, https://www.cnn.com/2020/10/07/us/wauwatosa-wisconsin-police-shooting-alvin-cole/index.html.

91. "Summary of Events," Vetter to Archambo, 4.

92. Casey and Kuhagan, "Wisconsin Police Officer"; Doha Madani and the Associated Press, "Wisconsin Police Chief Says He Has No Reason to Fire Officer Who Fatally Shot Alvin Cole," NBC News, October 12, 2020, https://www.nbcnews.com/news/us-news/wisconsin-police-chief-says-he-has-no-reason-fire-officer-n1243021.

93. Wisconsin Statutes § 323.14(4)(b).

94. Karen Pilarski, "Alvin Cole Family, Tosa Officials Gather for Private Meeting," *Wauwatosa Patch*, October 20, 2020, https://patch.com/wisconsin/wauwatosa/alvin-cole-family-tosa-officials-gather-private-meeting.

95. Evan Casey, "Alvin Cole's Family 'Strongly Considering' Suing Wauwatosa after Cole's Mom Was Injured During an Arrest, Attorney Says," *Milwaukee Journal Sentinel*, October 23, 2020, https://www.jsonline.com/story/communities/west/news/wauwatosa/2020/10/23/alvin-coles-family-might-sue-wauwatosa-after-injury-during-arrest/3729506001/; Winnie Dortch, "Family of Alvin Cole meets with Wauwatosa Mayor," WDJT-TV (Milwaukee), October 21, 2020, https://www.cbs58.com/news/family-of-alvin-cole-meets-with-wauwatosa-mayor.

96. Casey and Kuhagan, "Wisconsin Police Officer"; Maria Cramer, "Wisconsin Officer Who Fatally Shot Three Men in Five Years Resigns: Joseph Mensah, a Black Officer, Most Recently Killed an Armed Black Teenager, Alvin Cole, Setting Off Protests in the Milwaukee Area," *New York Times*, November 18, 2020, https://www.nytimes.com/2020/11/18/us/joseph-mensah-wisconsin-police-resigned.html; Livia Albeck-Ripka and Orlando Mayorquin, "Tacoma Officers Cleared in Black Man's Death Will Get $500,000 Each to Resign," *New York Times*, January 16, 2024, https://www.nytimes.com/2024/01/16/us/tacoma-police-manny-ellis-death-payouts-resign.html.

97. Corinne Hess, "Kenosha County DA Won't Charge Police Officers in Jacob Blake Shooting," Wisconsin Public Radio, January 5, 2021, https://www.wpr.org/kenosha-county-da-wont-charge-police-officers-jacob-blake-shooting.

98. Casey, "Joseph Mensah"; Jacey Fortin, "Police Officer Who Resigned After Fatal Shootings Is Hired as Sheriff's Deputy," *New York Times*, January 27, 2021, https://www.nytimes.com/2021/01/27/us/wisconsin-deputy-sheriff-fatal-shootings.html.

TIME, PLACE, AND MANNER

1. *Tinius v. Choi*, 77 F.4th 691, 695 (D.C. Cir. 2023).
2. Christina Maxouris, Holly Van, and Ralph Ellis, "Cities Extend Curfews for Another Night in an Attempt to Avoid Violent Protests Over George Floyd's Death," CNN, June 2, 2020, https://www.cnn.com/2020/05/31/us/george-floyd-protests-sunday/index.html.
3. "New Lawsuit Alleges Cities Used Curfews to Crush Protest," *Los Angeles Times*, March 1, 2021, https://www.latimes.com/california/story/2021-03-01/new-lawsuit-over-summer-curfew-alleges-l-a-santa-monica-beverly-hills-conspired-to-stifle-protest.
4. Stephen Gandel, "At Least 40 Lawsuits Claim Police Brutality at George Floyd Protests Across U.S.," CBS News, June 23, 2020, https://www.cbsnews.com/news/george-floyd-protests-police-brutality-settlements-lawsuits/.
5. "Outside Lawyers for 2020 Protest Lawsuits Have Cost the City More Than $20 Million," DivestSPD, May 30, 2023, https://divestspd.substack.com/p/outside-lawyers-for-2020-protest.
6. Nicholas Bogel-Burroughs and John Eligon, "George Floyd's Family Settles Suit Against Minneapolis for $27 Million," *New York Times*, March 12, 2021, https://www.nytimes.com/2021/03/12/us/george-floyd-minneapolis-settlement.html.
7. "Minneapolis City Council Approves $700K in Settlements Over Police Actions during 2020 Protests," Minnesota Public Radio, October 21, 2022, https://www.mprnews.org/story/2022/10/21/minneapolis-city-council-approves-700k-in-settlements-over-police-actions-during-protests; "ACLU-MN Announces $600K Settlement with Mpls. for 12 Protesters Injured during George Floyd Protests," WCCO-TV (Minneapolis), November 30, 2022, https://www.cbsnews.com/minnesota/news/aclu-mn-announces-600k-settlement-with-mpls-for-12-protesters-injured-during-george-floyd-protests/.
8. Jonathan Levinson, "Jury Awards $40k to Woman Injured by Portland Police in 2020 Protests," Oregon Public Broadcasting, October 4, 2022, https://www.opb.org/article/2022/10/04/jury-awards-40k-to

-woman-injured-portland-police-2020-protests/; Conrad Wilson, "Portland Agrees to Settle 2020 Tear Gas Lawsuit Brought by Protesters for $250,000," Oregon Public Broadcasting, November 29, 2022, https://www.opb.org/article/2022/11/29/portland-police-protest-oregon-rubber-ball-devices-crowd-control/.

9. Piper McDaniel, "Recent Settlements Against Portland Police Surpass $6.7 Million," *Street Roots,* June 28, 2023, https://www.streetroots.org/news/2023/06/28/settlement-against-portland-police-millions.

10. Mike Carter, "Seattle Settles CHOP Lawsuit for $3.6 Million, with $600,000 for Deleted Texts," *Seattle Times,* February 17, 2023, https://www.seattletimes.com/seattle-news/law-justice/seattle-settles-chop-lawsuit-for-3-6m-with-600k-for-deleted-texts/; Natalie Swaby, "'This Is the Last Resort': New Lawsuits Filed Over Seattle's Handling of 2020 CHOP Protest Zone," KING-TV (Seattle), June 9, 2023, https://www.king5.com/article/news/local/new-lawsuits-filed-seattle-handling-2020-chop-zone/281-04d67365-a32e-4070-9ca1-1371ce632b51.

11. Brad Dress, "19 Austin Officers Indicted, $10M in Settlements Approved Over 2020 Protest Injuries," *The Hill,* February 17, 2023, https://thehill.com/homenews/state-watch/594844-at-least-9-austin-officers-indicted-10m-in-settlements-approved-over/.

12. Austen Erblat, "Denver City Council Approves $4.7M Settlement to Over 300 Black Lives Matter Protesters from 2020 Arrests," KCNC-TV (Denver), August 29, 2023, https://www.cbsnews.com/colorado/news/denver-city-council-approves-4-7m-settlement-to-2020-protesters-per-court-order/.

13. "$9.25 Million Settlement Announced in 2020 George Floyd Lawsuits," *PBS News Hour,* March 20, 2023, https://www.pbs.org/newshour/politics/9-25-million-settlement-announced-in-2020-george-floyd-protest-lawsuits.

14. Colin Moynihan, "New York to Pay $13 Million Over Police Actions at George Floyd Protests," *New York Times,* July 20, 2023, https://www.nytimes.com/2023/07/20/nyregion/nypd-george-floyd-protesters-settlement.html; Fola Akinnibi, "New York City to Overhaul Police Protest Response After Lawsuit," *Bloomberg News,* September 5, 2023, https://www.bloomberg.com/news/articles/2023-09-05/new-york-police-department-to-reform-tactics-in-george-floyd-protest-deal?cmpid=BBD090723_CITYLAB.

15. Keristen Holmes, "City of La Mesa Pays Woman Hit, Blinded by Bean Bag $10M," KFMB-TV (San Diego), March 16, 2023, https://www.cbs8.com/article/news/local/la-mesa-settles-with-woman-hit-by

-projectile/509-1a5ef558-fa89-491a-a91a-ff0494c2cd7a; Joseph Geha, "San Jose Poised to Settle Lawsuit Over 2020 Police Protests," *San Jose Spotlight*, September 2, 2023, https://sanjosespotlight.com/san-jose-poised-to-settle-lawsuit-over-2020-police-black-lives-matter-blm-george-floyd-protests/.

16. "Seattle Will Pay $10 Million to Protesters Who Said Police Used Excessive Force During 2020 Protests," Associated Press, January 24, 2024, https://www.usnews.com/news/best-states/washington/articles/2024-01-24/seattle-will-pay-10-million-to-protesters-who-said-police-used-excessive-force-during-2020-protests; "Court Upholds Legal Claims of Protesters Against the City of Seattle," Stritmatter Kessler Koehler Moore law firm, February 20, 2021, https://www.stritmatter.com/firm-blog/2021/2/20/court-upholds-legal-claims-of-peaceful-protesters-against-the-city-of-seattle; "Outside Lawyers," DivestSPD.

17. *Herbert v. Lando*, 441 U.S. 153, 168n16 (1979).

18. *Heffron v. International Society for Krishna Consciousness, Inc.*, 452 U.S. 640, 647 (1981).

19. Kevin Francis O'Neill, "Time, Place, and Manner Restrictions," Free Speech Center, Middle Tennessee State University, updated February 18, 2024, https://www.mtsu.edu/first-amendment/article/1023/time-place-and-manner-restrictions.

20. *Ward v. Rock Against Racism*, 491 U.S. 781, 789 (1989).

21. *Ward*, 491 U.S. at 798 n6.

22. John Futty, "Columbus Mayor Ginther Drops Curfew After Lawsuit, Reduction of Violence in Protests," *Columbus Dispatch*, June 5, 2020, https://www.dispatch.com/story/news/local/2020/06/05/columbus-mayor-ginther-drops-curfew-after-lawsuit-reduction-of-violence-in-protests/42131345/.

23. "City of Wauwatosa Announces 9pm Curfew," City of Wauwatosa, May 30, 2020, https://www.wauwatosa.net/Home/Components/News/News/2016/.

24. Hanna Fry, Matt Hamilton, and Brittany Meija, "ACLU Sues to End L.A. Curfew, Calling It a Suppression of Political Protest," *Los Angeles Times*, July 20, 2023, https://www.latimes.com/california/story/2020-06-03/l-a-s-nighttime-curfew-faces-growing-criticism-as-arrests-mount; Bridget Honaker, "Black Lives Matter Lawsuit Says LA Curfews Are Unlawful," Top Class Actions, June 8, 2020, https://topclassactions.com/civil-rights/black-lives-matter-lawsuit-says-la-curfews-are-unlawful/.

25. *Snyder v. Phelps*, 562 U.S. 443, 456 (2011), quoting *Frisby v. Schultz*, 487 U.S. 474, 479 (1988).

26. David French, "Opinion: Colleges Can't Say They Weren't Warned," *New York Times*, August 18, 2024, https://www.nytimes.com/2024/08/18/opinion/ucla-harvard-protests-rulings.html.

27. Editorial Board, "Opinion: How Smart Campuses Are Preparing for Another Wave of Gaza Protests," *Washington Post*, August 28, 2024, https://www.washingtonpost.com/opinions/2024/08/27/campus-protest-gaza-free-speech/.

28. *Tinius*, 77 F.4th at 695–697; "Extensions of Public Emergency and Public Health Emergency and Preparation for Washington, DC Reopening," District of Columbia Office of the Mayor, May 13, 2020, last updated June 27, 2023, at 7, https://perma.cc/N8ZF-V9FN.

29. *Tinius v. Choi*, 2022 WL 899238 (D.D.C. 2022); "Extensions of Public Emergency," District of Columbia Office of the Mayor, 7.

30. *Tinius*, 77 F.4th at 702.

31. Ibid. at 703.

32. "Proclamation of Emergency," City of Wauwatosa, September 30, 2020, https://www.wauwatosa.net/home/showpublisheddocument?id=3145.

33. *Tinius*, 77 F.4th at 699.

34. Complaint, ¶ 1, in *Knowlton, et al. v. City of Wauwatosa, et al.*, Case 2:20-cv-01660 (E.D. Wis.).

35. Ibid., ¶¶ 11–12.

36. "Decision and Order," in *Paige Radke v. City of Wauwatosa, et al.*, Case No. 21-C-0247 (E.D. Wis., August 24, 2022) (Adelman, J.), https://www.wied.uscourts.gov/sites/wied/files/documents/opinions/21-CV-247%20Radke%20v.%20City%20of%20Wauwatosa%20et%20al%20%2844%29.pdf; Beck Andrew Salgado, "Wauwatosa Is Confident It Will Win Protest Case after Two Recent Legal Rulings. An Opposing Lawyer Disagrees," *Milwaukee Journal Sentinel*, September 2, 2022, https://www.jsonline.com/story/communities/west/news/2022/09/02/wauwatosa-confident-win-protest-case-after-legal-rulings/7949214001/.

37. "Decision and Order," in *Radke*, at 5–6, citing *Ward*, 491 U.S. at 791.

38. Ibid. at 7–8.

39. Ibid. at 8–9.

40. "Decision and Order," in *Radke*, at 8n3.

41. Ibid. at 9–14.

42. Evan Casey, "Judge Says Attorneys Must Amend Their Complaint in Wauwatosa Curfew Lawsuit," *Milwaukee Journal Sentinel*, February 4, 2022, https://www.jsonline.com/story/communities/west/news

/wauwatosa/2022/02/03/judge-dismisses-complaint-wauwatosa-curfew-lawsuit-mensah-protests/6638429001/; "Decision and Order on Defendants' Motion to Dismiss Third Amended Complaint," in *Knowlton, et al. v. City of Wauwatosa, et al.*, Case No. 20-CV-1660 (E.D. Wis.) (Joseph, Mag. J.), February 2, 2022, https://casetext.com/case/knowlton-v-city-of-wauwatosa-6; "Decision and Order on Defendants' Motion to Dismiss Fourth Amended Complaint," in *Knowlton, et al. v. City of Wauwatosa, et al.*, Case No. 20-CV-1660 (E.D. Wis.) (Joseph, Mag. J.), August 24, 2022, https://wisconsinexaminer.com/wp-content/uploads/2022/09/082422-Order-Denying-Wauwatosas-Motion-to-Dismiss-.pdf; Jim Stingl, "A Milwaukee Judge Surprises Her 'Mom' by Presiding at Her Citizenship Ceremony in NY," *Milwaukee Journal Sentinel*, April 5, 2019, https://www.jsonline.com/story/news/columnists/jim-stingl/2019/04/05/stingl-milwaukee-judge-surprises-mom-citizenship-ceremony/3364949002/; "Decision and Order on Plaintiffs' Motion for Partial Summary Judgment, Defendants' Motion for Summary Judgment, the Parties' Motions to Strike, and Plaintiffs' Motions for Sanctions," in *Knowlton et al. v. City of Wauwatosa et al.*, Case No. 20-CV-1660 (E.D. Wis.) (Joseph, Mag. J.), March 13, 2023, https://docs.justia.com/cases/federal/district-courts/wisconsin/wiedce/2:2020cv01660/92408/332; Isiah Holmes, "Judge Dismisses More Claims in Wauwatosa Curfew Lawsuit; Others Remain," *Wisconsin Examiner*, March 16, 2023, https://wisconsinexaminer.com/2023/03/16/judge-dismisses-more-claims-in-wauwatosa-curfew-lawsuit-others-remain/.

43. *Knowlton v. City of Wauwatosa*, 119 F.4th 507, 516, 516 n.1 (7th Cir. 2024).

44. Bridget Fogarty, "Federal Judge Grants a Trial in Fatal Wauwatosa Police Shooting of 17-Year-Old Alvin Cole," *Milwaukee Journal Sentinel*, March 29, 2024, https://www.jsonline.com/story/communities/north/2024/03/29/fatal-mensah-shooting-of-alvin-cole-gets-a-trial-judge-rules/73147135007/.

45. Isiah Holmes, "Baldwin and Moore Call for Civil Rights Probe of Wauwatosa PD," *Wisconsin Examiner*, July 23, 2020, https://wisconsinexaminer.com/2021/07/23/baldwin-and-moore-call-for-civil-rights-probe-of-wauwatosa-pd/; Jim Piwowarczyk and Jessica McBride, "Why Won't the Media Fully Report Tammy Baldwin Staffer's Ties to Wauwatosa Unrest?," Wisconsin Right Now, July 30, 2021, https://www.wisconsinrightnow.com/2021/07/30/tiffany-henry-2/.

46. Masood Farivar, "US Justice Department Ramps Up Investigations of Police," Voice of America, May 20, 2021, https://www.voanews.com/a/usa_us-justice-department-ramps-investigations-police/6206017.html.

47. "Special Litigation Section Case Summaries: Law Enforcement Agencies: Louisville Metro Police Department and Louisville/Jefferson County Metro Government," US Department of Justice Civil Rights Division, accessed August 22, 2023, https://www.justice.gov/crt/special-litigation-section-case-summaries#police-summ.

48. "Special Litigation Section Case Summaries: Law Enforcement Agencies: Minneapolis Police Department," US Department of Justice Civil Rights Division, accessed August 22, 2023, https://www.justice.gov/crt/special-litigation-section-case-summaries#police-summ; Robert Legare and Melissa Quinn, "DOJ Report Finds Minneapolis Police Use Dangerous 'Excessive' Force and Discriminatory Conduct," CBS News, June 16, 2023, https://www.cbsnews.com/news/garland-concludes-civil-investigation-into-minneapolis-pd/.

49. Steve Karnowski, "Minneapolis Council to Discuss Post-Floyd Policing Lawsuit," Associated Press, March 29, 2023, https://apnews.com/article/minneapolis-police-george-floyd-policing-lawsuit-f04139cd9013147cea22ed159dc07249.

50. "Special Litigation Section Case Summaries: Law Enforcement Agencies: Seattle Police Department and Portland Police Bureau," US Department of Justice Civil Rights Division, accessed August 22, 2023, https://www.justice.gov/crt/special-litigation-section-case-summaries#police-summ.

51. Ryan J. Foley, "Journalist Acquitted in Iowa Case Seen as Attack on Press," Associated Press, March 10, 2021, https://apnews.com/article/andrea-sahouri-acquitted-cd95fea66c260ec7990a2ccda06a6ca7; "Des Moines Register Editorial: Prosecution of Iowa Reporter Violates Rights: Sahouri Arrested While Documenting Protest," *USA Today*, February 24, 2021, https://www.usatoday.com/story/opinion/2021/02/24/iowa-reporter-charged-prosecution-violates-first-amendment-free-press-rights/6802177002/.

52. *Tinius*, 77 F.4th at 696.

53. Everton Bailey Jr., "Portland Bans Police from Working with Federal Law Enforcement, Targeting Journalists and Legal Observers during Protests," *Oregonian* / Oregon Live, July 22, 2020, https://www.oregonlive.com/portland/2020/07/portland-bans-police-from-working-with-federal-law-enforcement-targeting-journalists-and-legal-observers-during-protests.html; "Index Newspapers LLC v. City of Portland," ACLU Oregon, July 22, 2020, https://www.aclu-or.org/en/cases/index-newspapers-llc-v-city-portland#.

54. "Proclamation of Emergency," City of Wauwatosa.

55. "Index Newspapers LLC," ACLU Oregon.

56. Robert Gearly, "Daily Caller Reporters Say Cops Beat Them with Nightsticks during Wauwatosa Protest," Fox News, October 9, 2020, https://www.foxnews.com/us/daily-caller-reporters-say-cops-beat-them-with-nightsticks-during-wauwatosa-protest.

57. *MacIver Institute for Public Policy v. Tony Evers*, 2020 WL 1531637 (W.D. Wis. 2020).

58. *MacIver Institute for Public Policy v. Tony Evers*, 994 F.3d 602, 614 (7th Cir. 2021); Bruce Murphy, "Conservative Group Loses Suit Against Evers," *Urban Milwaukee*, April 21, 2021, https://urbanmilwaukee.com/2021/04/21/back-in-the-news-conservative-group-loses-suit-against-evers/.

59. Molly Beck, "U.S. Supreme Court Denies Appeal Over Access to Gov. Tony Evers' Press Events," *Milwaukee Journal Sentinel*, December 13, 2021, https://www.jsonline.com/story/news/politics/2021/12/13/u-s-supreme-court-denies-appeal-over-access-wisconsin-governor-tony-evers-press-events-media-maciver/6493955001/.

60. "If the [June 1] Order had excepted expressive activity, as Plaintiffs argue the First Amendment required, it would have left D.C. officials in the same position as before the curfew: hindered by the unusual volume of people on the streets from stemming the vandalism and looting. An expressive-activity exception would have effectively enabled public circulation of people intent on looting, so long as they traveled with demonstrators, wore protest messages, shouted political slogans, or carried placards." *Tinius*, 77 F.4th at 701.

61. *MacIver Institute*, 994 F.3d at 613–615.

UNCIVIL LIBERTIES

1. Olga Khazan, "Why People Are Acting So Weird," *Atlantic*, March 10, 2022, https://www.theatlantic.com/politics/archive/2022/03/antisocial-behavior-crime-violence-increase-pandemic/627076/.

2. "More Than 80 Percent of U.S. Public Schools Report Pandemic Has Negatively Impacted Student Behavior and Socio-Emotional Development," National Center for Education Statistics, July 6, 2022, https://nces.ed.gov/whatsnew/press_releases/07_06_2022.asp.

3. Jennifer Rubin, "Opinion: Gen Z Might Be the MAGA Movement's Undoing," *Washington Post*, January 28, 2024, https://www.washingtonpost.com/opinions/2024/01/28/genz-poll-republicans/.

4. Sharon O'Malley, "Sharp Rise in Abuse Targeting Mayors Highlighted by New Study," *Route Fifty*, May 11, 2022, https://www.route-fifty.com/management/2022/05/psychological-abuse-against-mayors-23-2017/366841/.

5. Jim Piwowarczyk, "Wauwatosa Mayor's House Window Shot with BB Gun; Police Called," Wisconsin Right Now, January 18, 2021, https://www.wisconsinrightnow.com/2021/01/18/wauwatosa-mayor-house-shot/.

6. "Threats and Harassment in Local Government: Initial Benchmarking Report," CivicPulse.org / Princeton University, September 2023, https://www.civicpulse.org/_files/ugd/753449_23937267f1b64a58b4b222411f1106da.pdf. See also David French, "MAGA's Violent Threats Are Warping Life in America," *Atlantic*, February 18, 2024, https://www.nytimes.com/2024/02/18/opinion/magas-violent-threats-are-warping-life-in-america.html.

7. O'Malley, "Sharp Rise in Abuse."

8. "VIDEO: Group Chants 'We Are Watching You' Outside Arizona Secretary of State Katie Hobbs' Home," KPNX-TV News (Channel 12, Phoenix), November 18, 2020, https://www.12news.com/article/news/politics/video-group-chants-we-are-watching-you-outside-arizona-secretary-of-state-katie-hobbs-home/75-a569ae35-3b62-424e-88f8-f03ca8b89458; Peter Eisler, Jason Szep, Linda So, and Sam Hart, "Anatomy of a Death Threat: Trump Supporters Have Waged a Campaign of Intimidation Against the State and Local Officials Who Administer U.S. Elections," Reuters, December 30, 2021, https://www.reuters.com/graphics/USA-ELECTION/THREATS/mopanwmlkva/; Molly Beck, "Elections Chief Meagan Wolfe Gets Extra Security While Donald Trump Foments False Accusations," *Milwaukee Journal Sentinel*, April 15, 2024, https://www.jsonline.com/story/news/politics/elections/2024/04/15/wisconsin-elections-chief-wolfe-gets-extra-security-as-trump-attacks/73297004007/.

9. Jacob Fischler, "Growing Threat of Political Violence Looms Over 2024, Former Members of Congress Warn," *Wisconsin Examiner*, December 11, 2023, https://wisconsinexaminer.com/2023/12/11/growing-threat-of-political-violence-looms-over-2024-former-members-of-congress-warn/.

10. "Threats and Harassment in Local Government: Benchmarking Report, Q1 2024," CivicPulse.org / Princeton University, May 2024, 3, 11, 13–15, https://bridgingdivides.princeton.edu/sites/g/files/toruqf6646/files/documents/BDI_Threats%20and%20Harassment%20Benchmarking%20Report_Q1%202024.pdf; Fischler, "Growing Threat of Political

Violence"; Steven Walters, "Women Politicians Still Face Double Standard," *Urban Milwaukee*, December 11, 2023, https://urbanmilwaukee.com/2023/12/11/the-state-of-politics-women-politicians-still-face-double-standard/.

11. Hannah Natanson, "Death Threats, Online Abuse, Police Protection: School Board Members Face Dark New Reality," *Washington Post*, November 9, 2021, https://www.washingtonpost.com/local/education/death-threats-online-abuse-police-protection-school-board-members-face-dark-new-reality/2021/11/09/db007706-37fe-11ec-9bc4-86107e7b0ab1_story.html; Alec Johnson, "A Fourth Oconomowoc School Board Member Has Stepped Down, Saying He and His Family Felt Unsafe in Their Home," *Milwaukee Journal Sentinel*, November 10, 2021, https://www.jsonline.com/story/communities/lake-country/news/oconomowoc/2021/11/10/oconomowoc-school-board-member-scott-roehl-resigns-says-family-felt-unsafe/6352874001/.

12. Dave Orrick, "Jacob Frey and His Wife Are Speaking Out About Death Threats," *Minneapolis Star Tribune*, March 11, 2023, https://www.startribune.com/jacob-frey-and-wife-sarah-clarke-death-threats-minneapolis-mayor/600258091/.

13. Nicole Acevedo, "Judge Esther Salas Applauds New Law Named after Her Son, Who Was Killed by a Gunman Targeting Her," NBC News, December 20, 2022, https://www.nbcnews.com/news/latino/judge-esther-salas-law-son-killed-gunman-target-rcna62637.

14. Rob Kuznia, Majlie de Puy Kamp, Alex Leeds Matthews, Kyung Lah, Anna-Maja Rappard, and Yahya Abou-Ghazala, "A Deluge of Violent Messages: How a Surge in Threats to Public Officials Could Disrupt American Democracy," CNN, December 7, 2023, https://www.cnn.com/2023/12/07/politics/threats-us-public-officials-democracy-invs.

15. "Suspect in Killing of a Maryland Judge Who Presided Over Divorce Case Is Found Dead," Associated Press / National Public Radio, October 26, 2023, https://www.npr.org/2023/10/26/1208828822/maryland-judge-suspect-found-dead-divorce#.

16. Dan Balz, "Analysis: Assault of Paul Pelosi Was Attack on Democracy. The Risks Keep Growing," *Washington Post*, October 29, 2022, https://www.washingtonpost.com/politics/2022/10/29/pelosi-attack-toxic-politics/; "Updates: Intruder Seeking Speaker Pelosi Attacked Her Husband with a Hammer," *New York Times*, October 30, 2022, https://www.nytimes.com/live/2022/10/28/us/pelosi-san-francisco-home-attack.

17. Julie Bosman, "Killing in Wisconsin Was Motivated by Judicial Matter, Attorney General Says," *New York Times*, June 3, 2022, https://www.nytimes.com/2022/06/03/us/wisconsin-killing-judge.html; Kelli Arseneau, Bill Glauber, Patrick Marley, and Daniel Bice, "Retired Wisconsin Judge John Roemer Killed in New Lisbon; Suspected Shooter Had Other 'Targets' That Sources Say Included Gov. Evers," *Milwaukee Journal Sentinel*, June 3, 2022, https://www.jsonline.com/story/news/crime/2022/06/03/police-respond-lisbon-home-john-roemer-ex-juneau-county-judge/7505230001/.

18. Sarah Dewberry and David J. Lopez, "Man Who Assisted Campaign of Failed GOP Candidate Pleads Guilty to Shootings at Democratic Officials' Homes," CNN, January 10, 2024, https://www.cnn.com/2024/01/10/us/new-mexico-shootings-trujillo-solomon-pena; "Intruder Seeking Speaker Pelosi," *New York Times*.

19. "Statement from Mayor McLean," City of Boise, March 3, 2022, https://www.cityofboise.org/news/mayor/2022/march/statement-from-mayor-mclean; Amanda Holpuch, "Boise's Mayor, Who Championed Covid Restrictions, Says She Faces Violent Threats and Harassment," *New York Times*, March 5, 2022, https://www.nytimes.com/2022/03/06/us/boise-mayor-covid.html.

20. Jessica Wolfrom and Mark Berman, "Police Clash with Protesters Outside Pittsburgh Mayor's Home as Movement Arrives at Officials' Front Doors," *Washington Post*, August 20, 2020, https://www.washingtonpost.com/national/police-clash-with-protesters-outside-house-of-pittsburgh-mayor-the-latest-public-official-to-see-protests-at-home/2020/08/20/78375c64-e31a-11ea-8181-606e603bb1c4_story.html; Charles R. Davis, "Thousands Protested outside Los Angeles Mayor's House, as the Public Also Voiced Outrage at LAPD during an Emotional Zoom Town Hall," *Business Insider*, June 2, 2020, https://www.businessinsider.com/thousands-protest-outside-los-angeles-mayors-house-2020-6; Courtney Lamon, "Racial Justice Protesters March to Burlington Mayor's House," *Seven Days Vermont*, June 17, 2020, https://www.sevendaysvt.com/OffMessage/archives/2020/06/17/racial-justice-protesters-march-to-burlington-mayors-house; Jamie Hale and Beth Nakamura, "March to Portland Mayor Ted Wheeler's Home Declared Riot Monday as Burning Debris Thrown into Building: Key Takeaways," *Oregonian* / Oregon Live, August 31, 2020, https://www.oregonlive.com/portland/2020/09/protesters-march-to-portland-mayor-ted-wheelers-residence-monday-throw-birthday-party-demand-resignation-live-updates.html; Lance

Armstrong, “George Floyd Protest Held in Mayor’s Neighborhood,” *Valley Community Newspapers*, June 18, 2020, https://www.valcomnews.com/george-floyd-protest-held-in-mayors-neighborhood/.

21. Davis, “Thousands Protested.”

22. Lamon, “Racial Justice Protesters.”

23. Wolfrom and Berman, “Police Clash with Protesters”; Leslie Brinkley, “Oakland Mayor Libby Schaaf’s Home Vandalized as Threat of Federal Troops Looms,” KGO-TV (San Francisco), July 21, 2020, https://abc7news.com/oakland-mayor-house-vandalized-libby-schaaf-defund-police/6327466/.

24. Amanda del Castillo, “San Jose Mayor’s Home Vandalized as Hundreds Protest Downtown Against Police Brutality, Jacob Blake Shooting,” KGO-TV (San Francisco), August 29, 2020, https://abc7news.com/san-jose-protest-jacob-blake-mayor-sam-liccardo-home-vandalized-downtown-sj/6394638/.

25. Hale and Nakamura, “March to Portland Mayor’s Home”; Everton Bailey Jr., “Ted Wheeler Won Reelection as Portland Mayor by an Historically Narrow Margin; Here’s How He Held On to Lead for 4 More Years,” *Oregonian* / Oregon Live, November 8, 2020, https://www.oregonlive.com/politics/2020/11/ted-wheeler-won-reelection-as-portland-mayor-by-an-historically-narrow-margin-heres-how-he-held-on-to-lead-for-4-more-years.html.

26. Nancy Rommelmann, “Guest Essay: Kenosha, Portland, and the Lies We Must Leave Behind,” *New York Times*, November 22, 2021, https://www.nytimes.com/2021/11/22/opinion/politics/kenosha-rittenhouse-2020-protests.html.

27. Evan Casey and Eddie Morales, “‘It’s a Shame’: Businesses Vandalized in Wauwatosa After the Announcement of the Decision Not to Charge Officer Mensah,” *Milwaukee Journal Sentinel*, October 8, 2020, https://www.jsonline.com/story/communities/west/news/wauwatosa/2020/10/08/wauwatosa-police-officer-joseph-mensah-decision-protests-turn-violent/5924160002/; Jake Pearson, “More Than Two Years after George Floyd’s Murder Sparked a Movement, Police Reform Has Stalled. What Happened?,” ProPublica, October 24, 2022, https://www.propublica.org/article/why-police-reform-stalled-elizabeth-glazer; James Wigderson, “Opinion: Trump’s One Hope to Win Wisconsin,” CNN, October 9, 2020, https://www.cnn.com/2020/10/09/opinions/us-elections-2020-wisconsin-conservative-wigderson/index.html; Charles M. Blow, “Opinion: The Great Erasure,” *New York Times*, May 20, 2022, https://www.nytimes

.com/interactive/2022/05/20/opinion/blm-george-floyd-mural.html.

28. Shaun Gallagher, "Protesters Arrived at Wauwatosa Mayor's Home in Defiance of City Ordinance, Mayor Says," WTMJ-TV (Milwaukee), August 14, 2020, https://www.tmj4.com/news/local-news/protesters-arrived-at-wauwatosa-mayors-home-in-defiance-of-city-ordinance-mayor-says.

29. Ibid.

30. Wauwatosa Municipal Code § 7.52.020.

31. *City of Wauwatosa v. King*, 49 Wis.2d 398, 182 N.W.2d 530 (1971).

32. *Frisby v. Schultz*, 487 U.S. 474 (1988).

33. Jim Piwowarczyk, "Inside the Peoples Revolution: Gang Ties, Felonies, a State Rep & Congressional Staffer," Wisconsin Right Now, January 30, 2021, https://www.wisconsinrightnow.com/2021/01/30/the-peoples-revolution/; "*Frisby v. Schultz, et al., 487 U.S. 474* (1988)," First Amendment Library, accessed May 23, 2022, https://www.thefire.org/first-amendment-library/decision/frisby-et-al-v-schultz-et-al/; "*Frisby v. Schultz* (1988)," Free Speech Center, Middle Tennessee State University, updated February 18, 2024, https://www.mtsu.edu/first-amendment/article/477/frisby-v-schultz.

34. *Frisby*, 487 U.S. at 486.

35. John Cassidy, "Trump's Attacks on Local Officials Are Spreading Hatred and Inciting Violence," *New Yorker*, December 8, 2020, https://www.newyorker.com/news/our-columnists/trumps-attacks-on-local-officials-are-spreading-hatred-and-inciting-violence; Hannah Knowles, Annie Gowen, and Tom Hamburger, "'A Dark, Empty Place': Public Officials Face Personal Threats as Tensions Flare," *Washington Post*, December 13, 2020, https://www.washingtonpost.com/national/public-officials-threatened-covid-election/2020/12/13/680bd380-3be7-11eb-bc68-96af0daae728_story.html.

36. Editorial Board, "Opinion: The Abortion Rights Protest at Justice Kavanaugh's Home Crossed the Line," *Washington Post*, September 15, 2021, https://www.washingtonpost.com/opinions/2021/09/15/abortion-rights-protest-justice-kavanaughs-home-crossed-line/.

37. Philip Bump, "Kanye West, Donald Trump and the Effort to Overturn the 2020 Results in Georgia," *Washington Post*, December 10, 2021, https://www.washingtonpost.com/politics/2021/12/10/kanye-west-donald-trump-effort-overturn-2020-results-georgia/; Isaac Stanley-

Becker and Yvonne Wingett Sanchez, "Leaked Call Shows Clash Between Kari Lake Campaign and Maricopa County," *Washington Post*, November 19, 2022, https://www.washingtonpost.com/politics/2022/11/19/kari-lake-maricopa-county-arizona/; Eileen Sullivan, "Jury Orders Giuliani to Pay $148 Million to Election Workers He Defamed," *New York Times*, December 15, 2023, https://www.nytimes.com/2023/12/15/us/politics/rudy-giuliani-defamation-trial-damages.html.

38. *Dobbs v. Jackson Women's Health Organization*, 597 U.S. 215 (2022).

39. *Roe v. Wade*, 410 U.S. 113 (1973).

40. Jasmine Hilton and Ann E. Marimow, "Supreme Court Marshal Presses Md., Va. Leaders to Stop Home Protests," *Washington Post*, July 2, 2022, https://www.washingtonpost.com/dc-md-va/2022/07/02/supreme-court-justices-picketing-homes/; Kathleen Parker, "Opinion: Stay Away from My House—and My Womb," *Washington Post*, May 11, 2022, https://www.washingtonpost.com/opinions/2022/05/11/kavanaugh-abortion-roe-middle-ground/.

41. Ruth Marcus, "Opinion: Even Conservative Justices Have a Right to Privacy," *Washington Post*, July 8, 2022, https://www.washingtonpost.com/opinions/2022/07/08/kavanaugh-protests-abortion-elrich/?wpisrc=nl_opinions; Editorial Board, "Abortion Rights Protest"; Edwin Chemerinsky, "No One Has a Right to Protest in My Home," *Atlantic*, April 26, 2024, https://www.theatlantic.com/ideas/archive/2024/04/campus-protest-first-amendment-berkeley/678186/.

42. Wisconsin Statutes § 62.13(5); Corrine Hess, "Activists Push for Police Firings, but Elected Officials Don't Have Power to Do That," Wisconsin Public Radio, February 8, 2021, accessed December 24, 2022, https://www.wpr.org/activists-push-police-firings-elected-officials-dont-have-power-do.

43. "Due Process," Legal Information Institute, Cornell Law School, accessed April 10, 2021, https://www.law.cornell.edu/wex/due_process.

44. Paul Rosenzweig, "Jack Smith's Daring Gambit," *Atlantic*, December 12, 2023, https://www.theatlantic.com/ideas/archive/2023/12/due-process-donald-trump-trial-jack-smith-supreme-court/676319/.

45. U.S. Const. amends. V and XIV; Wis. Const. art. I, §§ 1 and 8. For example, see, *County of Kenosha v. C. & S. Management, Inc.*, 223 Wis. 2d 373, 588 N.W.2d 236 (1999).

46. Evan Casey, "More Legal Action Coming Against Wauwatosa Police Officer Joseph Mensah, Attorney Says," *Milwaukee Journal Sentinel*, October 15, 2020, https://www.jsonline.com/story/communities/west

/news/wauwatosa/2020/10/15/attorney-kimberley-motley-promised-more-legal-action-against-tosa-cop/3663879001/; Jim Piwowarczyk and Jessica McBride, "Khalil Coleman Pressured Juvenile to Rob Drug House with Gun: Complaint," Wisconsin Right Now, February 19, 2021, https://www.wisconsinrightnow.com/2021/02/19/khalil-coleman-pressured-juvenile-to-rob-drug-house-with-gun-complaint/.

47. Allison Dirr, "Fire and Police Commission Failed to Follow Processes in Demotion of Former Police Chief Morales, Report Finds," *Milwaukee Journal Sentinel*, February 10, 2021, https://www.jsonline.com/story/news/local/milwaukee/2021/02/10/fpc-failed-follow-processes-demotion-chief-alfonso-morales/4443600001/; Jeramey Jannene, "FPC Members, City Attorney, Blew Off Inspector General Interview Requests: Fallout and Confusion from the Morales Fiasco Gets Worse," *Urban Milwaukee*, February 15, 2021, https://urbanmilwaukee.com/2021/02/15/city-hall-fpc-members-city-attorney-blew-off-inspector-general-interview-requests/; Piwowarczyk and McBride, "Khalil Coleman Pressured Juvenile."

48. Allison Dirr, "Steven DeVougas, Subject of Ethics Investigation, Resigns from Milwaukee Fire and Police Commission," *Milwaukee Journal Sentinel*, February 15, 2021, https://www.jsonline.com/story/news/local/milwaukee/2021/02/15/steven-devougas-resigns-milwaukee-fire-and-police-commission/6757629002/.

49. Elliot Hughes, "Ousted Milwaukee Police Chief Alfonso Morales Reaches Tentative $626,000 Settlement with City," *Milwaukee Journal Sentinel*, July 13, 2021, https://www.jsonline.com/story/news/2021/07/13/ousted-milwaukee-police-chief-morales-reaches-tentative-agreement-city/7957190002/; Allison Dirr, "'Totally Avoidable': Milwaukee Committee Votes to Approve Settlement with Former Police Chief Alfonso Morales," *Milwaukee Journal Sentinel*, July 19, 2021, https://www.jsonline.com/story/news/local/milwaukee/2021/07/19/milwaukee-committee-votes-approve-settlement-former-police-chief-alfonso-morales/8014378002/; Jeramey Jannene, "Morales Payment Reaches Still Higher: City Must Also Pay Its Private Legal Team; Total Cost of Lawsuit Will Exceed $668,000," *Urban Milwaukee*, July 19, 2021, https://urbanmilwaukee.com/2021/07/19/city-hall-morales-payout-rises-still-higher/.

50. Evan Casey and Christopher Kuhagan, "Wisconsin Police Officer Who Fatally Shot Three People in the Last Five Years Is Resigning," *Milwaukee Journal Sentinel*, November 18, 2020, https://www.usatoday.com/story/news/nation/2020/11/18/wisconsin-cop-who-killed-three-people-last-five-years-resigning/6337904002/; Maria Cramer, "Wisconsin

Officer Who Fatally Shot Three Men in Five Years Resigns: Joseph Mensah, a Black Officer, Most Recently Killed an Armed Black Teenager, Alvin Cole, Setting Off Protests in the Milwaukee Area," *New York Times*, November 18, 2020, https://www.nytimes.com/2020/11/18/us/joseph-mensah-wisconsin-police-resigned.html; Jeramey Jannene, "City Will Pay $237,480 for New Settlements, Lawsuits," *Urban Milwaukee*, November 23, 2022, https://urbanmilwaukee.com/2022/11/23/city-hall-city-will-pay-237480-for-new-settlements-lawsuits/.

51. Isiah Holmes, "Policing Wauwatosa After Chief Barry Weber," *Wisconsin Examiner*, February 10, 2021, https://wisconsinexaminer.com/2021/02/10/wauwatosa-after-chief-barry-weber/.

52. *McNabb v. United States*, 318 U.S. 332, 347 (1943), cited in "Felix Frankfurter," Wikiquotes, last modified September 26, 2022, https://en.wikiquote.org/wiki/Felix_Frankfurter.

53. "Saint of the Day: Saint Thomas More," Franciscan Media, accessed March 6, 2021, https://www.franciscanmedia.org/saint-of-the-day/saint-thomas-more; "Thomas More," Wikipedia, last modified March 6, 2021, https://en.wikipedia.org/wiki/Thomas_More.

54. Robert Bolt, *A Man for All Seasons: A Play in Two Acts* (New York: Vintage Books, 1990), 65–66.

BATTLEGROUND

1. Simon Montlake, "Will the 2024 Election Results Be Accepted by All? Wisconsin Is a Key Test," *Christian Science Monitor*, August 28, 2024, https://www.csmonitor.com/USA/Politics/2024/0828/wisconsin-election-integrity-trump-vote.

2. Joseph Ax, "Coronavirus Fuels Historic Legal Battles Over Voting as 2020 Election Looms," Reuters, September 24, 2020, https://www.reuters.com/article/usa-election-litigation-idINL2N2GK0M6; Lila Hassan and Dan Glaun, "COVID-19 and the Most Litigated Election in Recent U.S. History: How the Lawsuits Break Down," *PBS Frontline*, October 28, 2020, https://www.pbs.org/wgbh/frontline/article/covid-19-most-litigated-presidential-election-in-recent-us-history/; "Wisconsin Primary Recap: Voters Forced to Choose between Their Health and Their Civic Duty: The State Was the First to Hold a Major Election with In-Person Voting Since Stay-at-Home Orders Were Widely Instituted Because of the

Coronavirus," *New York Times*, April 7, 2020, https://www.nytimes.com/2020/04/07/us/politics/wisconsin-primary-election.html; Tucker Higgins, "US Supreme Court Sides with GOP in Wisconsin: Absentee Ballots Must Be Sent by Wednesday," CNBC, April 7, 2020, https://www.cnbc.com/2020/04/06/wisconsin-supreme-court-halts-absentee-ballot-deadline-extension.html; Richard Pildes, "There's a Surprising Ending to All the 2020 Election Conflicts over Absentee Ballot Deadlines," Conversation, April 7, 2021, https://theconversation.com/theres-a-surprising-ending-to-all-the-2020-election-conflicts-over-absentee-ballot-deadlines-158010; Patrick Marley, "Wisconsin Supreme Court Flips Liberal, Creating a 'Seismic Shift,'" *Washington Post*, August 27, 2023, https://www.washingtonpost.com/politics/2023/08/27/wisconsin-supreme-court-liberal/.

3. William Cummings, Joey Garrison, and Jim Sergent, "By the Numbers: President Donald Trump's Failed Efforts to Overturn the Election," *USA Today*, January 6, 2021, https://www.usatoday.com/in-depth/news/politics/elections/2021/01/06/trumps-failed-efforts-overturn-election-numbers/4130307001/; James M. Lindsay, "The 2020 Election by the Numbers," Council on Foreign Relations, December 15, 2020, https://www.cfr.org/blog/2020-election-numbers.

4. Benjamin Swasey and Connie Hanzhang Jin, "Narrow Margins in These Key States Powered Biden to the Presidency," National Public Radio, December 2, 2020, https://www.npr.org/2020/12/02/940689086/narrow-wins-in-these-key-states-powered-biden-to-the-presidency; Ronald Brownstein, "Why Politics Has Become So Stressful: Fewer Voters and States Than Ever Before Now Decide the Fate of Our Republic," *Atlantic*, October 14, 2022, https://www.theatlantic.com/politics/archive/2022/10/politics-stress-swing-states-elections/671729/; Stephen Collinson, "Why Voters Don't Want Biden or Trump but Might Get Them Anyway in 2024," CNN, December 15, 2022, https://www.cnn.com/2022/12/15/politics/biden-trump-2024-analysis/index.html.

5. Harry Enten, "Why GOP Leaders Are Playing It Smart When It Comes to Trump," CNN, May 15, 2021, https://www.cnn.com/2021/05/15/politics/republicans-trump-cheney-analysis/index.html.

6. Sabrina Tavernise and Ellen Almer Durston, "How Chaos in Kenosha Is Already Swaying Some Voters in Wisconsin," *New York Times*, August 26, 2020, https://www.nytimes.com/2020/08/26/us/kenosha-wisconsin-trump.html.

7. "2020 Republican National Convention," Wikipedia, accessed August 29, 2023, https://en.wikipedia.org/wiki/2020_Republican_National_Convention.

8. Jacqueline Alemany, "Power Up: Trump and GOP Go All In on Law-and-Order Message as Kenosha Protests Continue," *Washington Post*, August 27, 2020, https://www.washingtonpost.com/politics/2020/08/27/power-up-trump-gop-go-all-law-and-order-message-kenosha-protests-continue/; Jonathan Martin and Alexander Burns, "With Wisconsin Unrest as Backdrop, Republicans Intensify Law-and-Order Message," *New York Times*, August 26, 2020, https://www.nytimes.com/2020/08/26/us/politics/republican-national-convention-recap.html.

9. Jonathan Chait, "Intelligencer: In 2016, Trump Promised to Make America Safe Again. He Failed," *New York Magazine*, August 27, 2020, https://nymag.com/intelligencer/2020/08/trump-convention-speech-crime-rooting-violence-republican.html.

10. Adam Edelman, "Biden Responds to Pence Speech: The Violence Is in 'Trump's America,'" Axios, August 27, 2020, https://www.axios.com/2020/08/27/biden-pence-trump-kenosha-protests.

11. Tavernise and Durston, "Chaos in Kenosha"; Natasha Korecki, "'It's Playing into Trump's Hands': Dems Fear Swing-State Damage from Kenosha Unrest: Some Wisconsin Democrats Worry That the Images of Violence and Destruction Will Turn Suburban Voters Against the Party," *Politico*, August 27, 2020, https://www.politico.com/news/2020/08/27/its-playing-into-trumps-hands-dems-fear-swing-state-backlash-after-kenosha-carnage-402953; George Packer, "This Is How Biden Loses," *Atlantic*, August 28, 2020, https://www.theatlantic.com/ideas/archive/2020/08/how-biden-loses/615835/; Jim Geraghty, "Wrapping Up the RNC," *National Review*, August 28, 2020, https://www.nationalreview.com/the-morning-jolt/wrapping-up-the-rnc/.

12. Natasha Korecki, "Dems Fear Wisconsin Governor Is Becoming a Liability for Biden: Tony Evers' Performance—Especially His Response to the Kenosha Riots—Is Diminishing What Should Be a Significant Edge for the Party," *Politico*, September 17, 2020, https://www.politico.com/news/2020/09/17/tony-evers-kenosha-wisconsin-415706.

13. Korecki, "It's Playing into Trump's Hands."

14. Packer, "This Is How Biden Loses."

15. J. R. Ross, "Trump Claims He Saved Kenosha. Wisconsin Voters Aren't Buying It," *Politico*, September 1, 2020, https://www.politico.com

/news/magazine/2020/09/01/donald-trump-kenosha-wisconsin-2020-406865.

16. Zeke Miller and Jonathan Lemire, "Trump Visits Kenosha, Calls Violence 'Domestic Terrorism,'" AP News, September 1, 2020, https://apnews.com/article/virus-outbreak-election-2020-ap-top-news-politics-shootings-4a58a15c9955bb6312c1fbe42215110d.

17. Adam Edelman, "Biden to Visit Kenosha on Thursday in First Campaign Trip to Wisconsin," NBC News, September 2, 2020, https://www.nbcnews.com/politics/2020-election/biden-visit-kenosha-thursday-first-campaign-trip-wisconsin-n1239084; Molly Beck, "12 Hours to Sleep and Clean: How a Wauwatosa Home Became the Scene of a Biden Campaign Event," *Milwaukee Journal Sentinel*, September 4, 2020, https://www.jsonline.com/story/news/politics/elections/2020/09/04/biden-wisconsin-how-wauwatosa-home-became-campaign-event/5716262002/.

18. "Wauwatosa Protests for Alvin Cole and the Suburban Vote," PBS Wisconsin, October 9, 2020, https://on-demand.wvia.org/video/wauwatosa-protests-alvin-cole-and-suburban-vote-wzn2gm/.

19. Cilizza, "Why Wisconsin."

20. Frey, "Biden's Victory"; Florida et al., "How Suburbs Swung the 2020 Election."

21. "Milwaukee County, WI: General Election, November 3, 2020; Unofficial Results—Wauwatosa," City of Wauwatosa, accessed May 16, 2021, https://www.wauwatosa.net/home/showpublisheddocument/3250/637400542155470000; Florida et al., "How Suburbs Swung the 2020 Election."

22. Dan Schafer, "Wauwatosa Is at the Core of Republicans' Ugly Partisan Gerrymander," *Milwaukee Record*, May 19, 2022, https://milwaukeerecord.com/city-life/wauwatosa-is-at-the-core-of-republicans-ugly-partisan-gerrymander/; Cilizza, "Why Wisconsin."

23. Craig Gilbert, "Is Republican Domination in Rural Wisconsin Enough to Hold Off Once-Red Suburbs Becoming Significantly More Democratic?," *Milwaukee Journal Sentinel*, December 19, 2022, https://www.jsonline.com/story/news/politics/analysis/2022/12/19/wisconsin-remains-politically-purple-but-the-way-to-win-is-changing/69734911007/.

24. Charles Sykes, "Opinion: Wisconsin Democrats Have a Kenosha Problem—and It Could Cost Them Big in the Polls in 2022," *Politico*, November 22, 2021, https://www.politico.com/news/magazine/2021/11/22/wisconsin-democrats-kenosha-problem-523196; Jesse Richardson, "Civil Unrest in Kenosha Likely Helped Donald Trump," *Political Kiwi* (blog), May 13, 2021, https://politicalkiwi.wordpress.com/2021/05/13

/civil-unrest-in-kenosha-helped-donald-trump/; Editorial Board, "Opinion: Has Tony Evers Learned His Lesson? Wisconsin's Governor Deploys 500 National Guard Troops Ahead of the Rittenhouse Verdict," *Wall Street Journal*, November 17, 2021, https://www.wsj.com/articles/has-tony-evers-learned-his-lesson-wisconsin-kenosha-national-guard-kyle-rittenhouse-trial-verdict-11637189602; Joseph O'Neill, "How Milwaukee Could Decide the Next President," *New Yorker*, February 18, 2020, https://www.newyorker.com/news/news-desk/what-wins-wisconsin-milwaukee-community-organizing.

25. Cummings et al., "By the Numbers"; Farnoush Amiri, "How the Trump Fake Electors Scheme Became a 'Corrupt Plan,' According to the Indictment," Associated Press, August 2, 2023, https://apnews.com/article/donald-trump-jan-6-investigation-fake-electors-608932d4771f6e2e3c5efb3fdcd8fcce.

26. Daniel Dale, "27 Donald Trump Election Lies Listed in His Georgia Indictment," CNN, August 16, 2023, https://www.cnn.com/2023/08/16/politics/fact-check-trump-georgia-indictment-lies; Jennifer Rubin, "Opinion: Jack Smith Broadens His Phony-Elector Case," *Washington Post*, July 17, 2023, https://www.washingtonpost.com/opinions/2023/07/17/smith-more-phony-electors-states/; Cummings et al., "By the Numbers"; Amiri, "Trump Fake Electors Scheme"; Patrick Marley, "Ballot Drop Boxes Not Allowed in Wisconsin, State Supreme Court Rules," *Washington Post*, July 8, 2022, https://www.washingtonpost.com/politics/2022/07/08/wisconsin-ballot-drop-boxes/.

27. "Post-Election Lawsuits Related to the 2020 U.S. Presidential Election," Wikipedia, accessed August 27, 2023, https://en.wikipedia.org/wiki/ Post-election_lawsuits_related_to_the_2020_U.S._presidential_election#Wisconsin; Harriet Alexander, "Trump-Appointed Judges Among 86 Who Have So Far Dismissed Election Fraud Suits," *Telegraph*, December 13, 2020, https://www.telegraph.co.uk/news/2020/12/13/trump-appointed-judges-among-86-have-far-dismissed-election/; Adam Liptak, "Supreme Court Rejects Republican Challenge to Pennsylvania Vote," *New York Times*, December 8, 2020, https://www.nytimes.com/2020/12/08/us/supreme-court-republican-challenge-pennsylvania-vote.html; Adam Winkler, "Trump's Wildest Claims Are Going Nowhere in Court. Thank Legal Ethics," *Washington Post*, November 20, 2020, https://www.washingtonpost.com/outlook/trump-lawyers-legal-ethics/2020/11/20/3c286710-2ac1-11eb-92b7-6ef17b3fe3b4_story.html; Andy Sullivan and Jan Wolfe, "Trump Bid to Overturn Election Stumbles as Judge Rejects 'Meritless' Pennsylvania Lawsuit," *Sydney Morning Herald*, November

22, 2020, https://www.smh.com.au/world/north-america/trump-and-allies-launch-new-efforts-to-overturn-biden-victory-in-key-states-20201122-p56gry.html; Amy Gardner, Kati Perry, and Adriana Usero, "How Donald Trump Tried to Undo His Loss in Georgia in 2020," *Washington Post*, August 14, 2023, https://www.washingtonpost.com/national-security/interactive/2023/trump-georgia-election-investigation/.

28. *King v. Whitmer*, 556 F. Supp. 3d 680, 689 (E.D. Mich. 2021); Quinta Jurecic, "The Courtroom Is a Very Unhappy Place for Donald Trump," *Atlantic*, October 2023, https://www.theatlantic.com/magazine/archive/2023/10/trump-indictments-trials/675110/.

29. *Texas v. Pennsylvania*, 592 U.S. ___, 141 S.Ct. 1230 (2020); Cummings et al., "By the Numbers."

30. Scott Bauer, "Wisconsin Supreme Court Tosses Trump Election Lawsuit," AP News, December 14, 2020, https://apnews.com/article/wisonsin-supreme-court-trump-lawsuit-e6b3aa222b4141c0844d541c4b041964; Vanessa Romo, "Wisconsin Supreme Court Rules Trump Election Challenge 'Unreasonable in the Extreme,'" National Public Radio, December 14, 2020, https://www.npr.org/2020/12/14/946463134/wisconsin-supreme-court-rules-trump-election-challenge-unreasonable-meritless; Will Kenneally and Zac Schultz, "Breaking: Wisconsin Supreme Court Rejects Trump's Election Challenge," PBS Wisconsin, December 14, 2020, https://pbswisconsin.org/news-item/breaking-wisconsin-supreme-court-rejects-trumps-election-challenge/.

31. Patrick Marley, "Wisconsin Trump Electors Settle Lawsuit, Agree Biden Won in 2020," *Washington Post*, December 6, 2023, https://www.washingtonpost.com/politics/2023/12/06/wisconsin-trump-fake-electors-lawsuit/; Amy Gardner and Yvonne Wingett Sanchez, "Pro-Trump Electors Indicted in Nevada, the Third State to Issue Charges," *Washington Post*, December 6, 2023, https://www.washingtonpost.com/politics/2023/12/06/nevada-fake-electors-indictment-trump/.

32. Marley, "Wisconsin Supreme Court Flips Liberal."

33. "A Timeline of the Government's Response on Jan. 6, 2021," American Oversight, accessed August 31, 2023, https://www.americanoversight.org/timeline-jan6; "U.S. Capitol Riot," History Channel, accessed August 31, 2023, https://www.history.com/this-day-in-history/january-6-capitol-riot; Adam Serwer, "Who's Afraid of Calling Donald Trump an Insurrectionist?," *Atlantic*, January 5, 2024, https://www.theatlantic.com/ideas/archive/2024/01/donald-trump-insurrection/677028/.

34. John Danforth et al., *Lost, Not Stolen: The Conservative Case That Trump Lost and Biden Won the 2020 Presidential Election*, Lost, Not Stolen,

July 2022, 4, https://lostnotstolen.org/; Peter Wehner, "The Polite Zealotry of Mike Johnson," *Atlantic,* October 31, 2023, https://www.theatlantic.com/ideas/archive/2023/10/polite-zealotry-mike-johnson/675845/; Robby Brod, "These Republicans Did a Deep Dive into 2020 Election Lawsuits, Including in Pa. Here's Why Most of Them Failed," WITF-TV (Harrisburg, PA), September 1, 2022, https://www.witf.org/2022/09/01/these-republicans-did-a-deep-dive-into-2020-election-lawsuits-including-in-pa-heres-why-most-of-them-failed/.

35. Brownstein, "Why Politics Has Become So Stressful"; Craig Gilbert, "'It's Going to Be Very Intense': Wisconsin Will Occupy a Familiar Spot in 2022—at the Epicenter of National Politics," *Milwaukee Journal Sentinel,* March 18, 2021, https://www.jsonline.com/story/news/politics/analysis/2021/03/18/wisconsin-again-epicenter-national-politics-2022/4747123001/; Ronald Brownstein, "What the Georgia Runoff Revealed: Democrats Hold a Key Advantage in the Five States That Will Decide the Next Presidential Election," *Atlantic,* December 7, 2022, https://www.theatlantic.com/politics/archive/2022/12/raphael-warnock-wins-georgia-senate-herschel-walker/672382/; Schafer, "Wauwatosa Is at the Core"; Beck Salgado, "Democratic Growth in Suburban Milwaukee Played a Key Role in Wisconsin Elections. It's Part of a Plan Years in the Making," *Milwaukee Journal Sentinel,* November 11, 2022, https://www.jsonline.com/story/communities/west/2022/11/11/democratic-growth-in-waukesha-county-played-key-role-in-2022-election/69638019007/; Craig Gilbert, "The Indispensable State: Why Wisconsin Could Again Be the Electoral 'Tipping Point' in 2024," *Milwaukee Journal Sentinel,* August 1, 2023, https://www.jsonline.com/story/news/politics/analysis/2023/08/01/wisconsin-could-be-the-electoral-college-tipping-point-in-2024/70477587007/.

36. Greg Giroux, "Warnock Win Seals Perfect 2022 for Senators Seeking Reelection," Bloomberg Law News, December 7, 2022, https://news.bloomberglaw.com/us-law-week/warnock-win-seals-perfect-2022-for-senators-seeking-re-election.

37. David Mark, "Opinion: The Supreme Court Could Make a Trump Victory Virtually Impossible," CNN, January 1, 2024, https://www.cnn.com/2023/12/31/opinions/supreme-court-trump-2024-election-states-remove-ballot-mark; Bill Glauber, "U.S. Senator Ron Johnson Accuses Gov. Tony Evers, Lt. Gov. Mandela Barners of Inciting Kenosha Rioters," *Milwaukee Journal Sentinel,* January 23, 2022, https://www.jsonline.com/story/news/2022/01/23/ron-johnson-accuses-evers-barnes-inciting

-kenosha-rioters/6629299001/; Molly Beck, "On the 2-Year Anniversary of Kenosha Unrest After the Jacob Blake Shooting, Tim Michels Criticizes Tony Evers' Response to the Riots," *Milwaukee Journal Sentinel*, August 24, 2022, https://www.jsonline.com/story/news/politics/elections/2022/08/23/tim-michels-hits-evers-kenosha-response-after-jacob-blake-shooting/7870319001/.

38. Aaron Blakey, "Why the 2022 Election Was Such a Disaster for Trump," *Washington Post*, November 6, 2022, https://www.washingtonpost.com/politics/2022/11/09/trump-candidates-underperform-2022/.

39. Kelsey Snell and Maayan Silver, "Republicans' Focus on Milwaukee Shows Wisconsin Will Be a Crucial State Again in 2024," National Public Radio, August 22, 2023, https://www.npr.org/2023/08/22/1195024667/republican-debate-milwaukee-wisconsin-politics; Michael Scherer, Clara Ence Morse, Josh Dawsey, and Marianne LeVine, "Small Segment of Voters Will Wield Outsize Power in 2024 Presidential Race," *Washington Post*, December 8, 2023, https://www.washingtonpost.com/nation/2023/12/08/electoral-college-votes-swing-states-decline/; Ronald Brownstein, "Why the Blue Wall Looms So Large," *Atlantic*, August 22, 2024, https://www.theatlantic.com/politics/archive/2024/08/blue-wall-democrats-kamala-harris/679548/.

40. Nick Robertson, "Trump and Harris Neck and Neck in Battleground States, Nationally: CBS Poll," *Hill*, August 4, 2024, https://thehill.com/homenews/campaign/4810063-donald-trump-kamala-harris-battleground-states-poll/; Diana Glebova and Ryan King, "Kamala Harris Chooses Minnesota Gov. Tim Walz as Running Mate," *New York Post*, August 6, 2024, https://nypost.com/2024/08/06/us-news/kamala-harris-chooses-minnesota-gov-tim-walz-as-running-mate/; Rachel Hale, "'I Basically Live in Wisconsin Now': JD Vance Slams Democrats on Crime in Visit to Kenosha," *Milwaukee Journal Sentinel*, August 20, 2024, https://www.jsonline.com/story/news/politics/elections/2024/08/20/jd-vance-slams-democrats-on-crime-in-visit-to-kenosha/74856760007/.

41. Montlake, "2024 Election Results."

42. Caitlin Yilek, "Trump Clinches Wisconsin, Winning Presidency, CBS News Projects. See the County-by-County Results," CBS News, November 5, 2024, https://www.cbsnews.com/live-updates/wisconsin-election-results-2024/; Robert Yoon, "Why AP Called Wisconsin and the White House for Donald Trump," Associated Press, November 6, 2024, https://apnews.com/article/trump-harris-wisconsin-president-race-call-winner-explain-d07049f884d25ceae0d1376157d07c35.

43. Dave Keating, "We cannot leave the security of Europe in the hands of voters in Wisconsin every 4 years," X (Twitter), October 25, 2024, https://x.com/davekeating/status/1849915556335407543?s=46.

MASS SHOOTING

1. Roni Caryn Rabin, "Why Some Americans Buy Guns: Sociologists Are Just Beginning to Understand Who Is Buying Guns and How Gun Ownership Makes Them Feel," *New York Times*, June 29, 2023, https://www.nytimes.com/2023/06/23/health/gun-violence-psychology.html; Emma Tucker and Peter Nickeas, "The US Saw Significant Crime Rise Across Major Cities in 2020. And It's Not Letting Up," CNN, April 3, 2021, https://www.cnn.com/2021/04/03/us/us-crime-rate-rise-2020/index.html; Ellen Francis, "Guns Killed a Record Number of U.S. Children in 2021, Study Finds," *Washington Post*, August 23, 2023, https://www.washingtonpost.com/nation/2023/08/23/gun-deaths-children-record-2021/.

2. Reis Thebault, Joe Fox, and Andrew Ba Tran, "2020 Was the Deadliest Gun Violence Year in Decades. So Far, 2021 Is Worse," *Washington Post*, June 14, 2021, https://www.washingtonpost.com/nation/2021/06/14/2021-gun-violence/.

3. Ibid.; Elliot Hughes, "As Milwaukee Closes Book on Historic Year of Violence, There's Some Optimism for 2021. But Just Some," *Milwaukee Journal Sentinel*, January 1, 2021, https://www.jsonline.com/story/news/2021/01/01/cascade-factors-led-2020-milwaukee-violence-they-change/4073573001/; Marco della Cava and Mike Stucka, "Mass Shootings Surge in Wisconsin as Nation Faces Record High," *USA Today*, March 5, 2021, https://www.jsonline.com/story/news/2021/03/05/gda-mass-shootings-rise-in-2020-wi-pmjs/43442219/; Tom Jackman, "Homicides Rose 30 Percent in 2020, Survey of 34 U.S. Cities Finds: Robbery and Burglary Fell, Likely Related to the Pandemic, Expert Says," *Washington Post*, February 3, 2021, https://www.washingtonpost.com/crime-law/2021/02/03/homicides-rose-2020/; Derek Thompson, "Why America's Great Crime Decline Is Over: Even before the Recent Mass Shootings, Violent Crime Was Surging to Its Highest Rate in 30 Years. Patrick Sharkey Illuminates What's Happening," *Atlantic*, March 24, 2021, https://www.theatlantic.com/ideas/archive/2021/03/is-americas-great-crime-decline-over/618381/; Tucker and Nickeas, "US Saw Significant Crime Rise"; John McWhorter, "Opinion: Our Racial Reckoning Could Have Come Sooner.

What Made 2020 Different?," *New York Times*, June 10, 2022, https://www.nytimes.com/2022/06/10/opinion/pandemic-police-race.html.

4. "2020 Gun Deaths, by the Numbers," Alliance for Gun Responsibility, May 9, 2022, https://gunresponsibility.org/blog/2020-gun-deaths-by-the-numbers/.

5. Brakkton Booker, "Amid Protests and Virus Fears, Firearms Background Checks Hit All-Time High," National Public Radio, July 2, 2020, https://www.npr.org/sections/live-updates-protests-for-racial-justice/2020/07/02/886545589/amid-virus-fears-and-protests-firearm-background-checks-hit-all-time-high.

6. Chauncey Alcorn, "Guns and Ammunition Sales Soar as Defund-the-Police Movement Grows," CNN, June 24, 2020, https://www.cnn.com/2020/06/24/business/gun-sales-spike/index.html; Dalvin Brown, "Americans Are Loading Up on Guns and Ammo in Wake of Race Protests," *USA Today*, June 3, 2020, https://www.usatoday.com/story/money/2020/06/03/americans-buying-guns-and-ammo-wake-race-protests/3124011001/.

7. Ray Sanchez, Brynn Gingras, and Laura Dolan, "Gun Violence Surges in Major American Cities in the Midst of a Pandemic and a Policing Crisis," CNN, July 1, 2020, https://www.cnn.com/2020/07/01/us/homicides-shootings-spike-us-cities/index.html; Neil MacFarquhar, "Murders Spiked in 2020 in Cities across the United States," *New York Times*, September 27, 2021, https://www.nytimes.com/2021/09/27/us/fbi-murders-2020-cities.html.

8. Neil MacFarquhar, "With Homicides Rising, Cities Brace for a Violent Summer," *New York Times*, June 1, 2021, https://www.nytimes.com/2021/06/01/us/shootings-in-us.html; Della Cava and Stucka, "Mass Shootings Surge in Wisconsin"; Jackman, "Homicides Rose 30 Percent"; Hughes, "As Milwaukee Closes Book"; Thompson, "America's Great Crime Decline"; Vanessa Swales, "Acting Mayor Johnson Announces Public Safety Plan to Tackle Gun Violence, Car Thefts and Reckless Driving in Milwaukee," *Milwaukee Journal Sentinel*, January 12, 2022, https://www.jsonline.com/story/news/local/milwaukee/2022/01/12/cavalier-johnson-unveils-plan-to-tackle-milwaukee-citys-public-safety-crisis/9187218002/.

9. Sanchez, Gingras, and Dolan, "Gun Violence Surges"; Tucker and Nickeas, "US Saw Significant Crime Rise"; MacFarquhar, "Murders Spiked in 2020"; Henry Olsen, "Opinion: What's to Blame for the Murder Spike? Certainly Anti-police Fervor Didn't Help," *Washington Post*, September 28, 2021, https://www.washingtonpost.com/opinions/2021/09/28

/whats-blame-murder-spike-certainly-anti-police-fervor-didnt-help/; David Lauter, "Killings in the U.S. Are Dropping at a Historic Rate. Will Anyone Notice?," *Los Angeles Times*, October 20, 2023, https://www.latimes.com/politics/newsletter/2023-10-20/killings-in-the-u-s-are-dropping-at-an-historic-rate-will-anyone-notice-essential-politics.

10. Thebault et al., "2020 Deadliest Gun Violence Year."

11. Holly Bailey and Tim Craig, "Officials Worry the Rise in Violent Crime Portends a Violent Summer: 'It's Trauma on Top of Trauma,'" *Washington Post*, May 31, 2021, https://www.washingtonpost.com/nation/2021/05/30/summer-crime-spike/.

12. Jeff Asher, "The Murder Rate Is Suddenly Falling," *Atlantic*, June 5, 2023, https://www.theatlantic.com/ideas/archive/2023/06/us-murder-rate-decline-crime-statistics/674290/; Mark Berman, "Homicides Fell in Many Big U.S. Cities in 2023," *Washington Post*, January 25, 2024, https://www.washingtonpost.com/nation/2024/01/25/homicides-fell-many-big-us-cities-2023-report-says/.

13. Berman, "Homicides Fell."

14. Evan Casey, "Milwaukee Sees Decline in Homicides in 2023, but Numbers Still Not Back to Pre-pandemic Levels," Wisconsin Public Radio, January 3, 2024, https://www.wpr.org/justice/milwaukee-decline-homicides-2023-still-up-from-pre-pandemic-levels.

15. "Homicide, Other Crimes Decline in U.S. Cities But Remain Above Pre-pandemic Levels," Council on Criminal Justice, July 20, 2023, accessed September 5, 2023, https://counciloncj.org/homicide-other-violent-crimes-decline-in-u-s-cities-but-remain-above-pre-pandemic-levels/; Alexander Nazaryan, "Violent Crime Is Dropping Nationwide, Report Shows," Yahoo News, May 22, 2023, https://news.yahoo.com/violent-crime-is-dropping-nationwide-report-shows-200015787.html.

16. Asher, "Murder Rate Suddenly Falling"; Peter Hermann, "Homicides Are Falling in Many Big Cities. In D.C., They're Rising," *Washington Post*, August 19, 2023, https://www.washingtonpost.com/dc-md-va/2023/08/19/dc-homicides-rising-major-cities/.

17. Paul LeBlanc and Annette Choi, "United States Tops 400 Mass Shootings in 2023," CNN, July 24, 2023, https://www.cnn.com/2023/07/24/politics/us-400-mass-shootings/index.html; Sareen Habeshian, "Mass Shootings Increased While Gun Violence Deaths Dropped in 2023," Axios, January 9, 2024, https://www.axios.com/2024/01/09/mass-shooting-gun-violence-us-2023.

18. Chip Brownlee, "Gun Violence by the Numbers in 2024," *The Trace*, December 31, 2024, https://www.thetrace.org/2024/12/data-gun-violence-shooting-stats-america/.

19. Elaina Athans, "Man Killed Wife, 3 Children, Family Dog before Killing Self in Craven County, Police Say," WTVD-TV (Durham), January 25, 2020, accessed September 5, 2023, https://abc11.com/murder-suicide-5-dead-michael-ireland-ray/5881935/; "Milwaukee Police Identify Victims, Suspect in Shooting at Molson Coors Milwaukee Campus," Wisconsin Public Radio, February 27, 2020, https://www.wpr.org/milwaukee-police-identify-victims-suspect-shooting-molson-coors-milwaukee-campus; Jane Morice, "18 Shot, One Killed Following Fight Between Multiple Motorcycle Clubs on Cleveland's East Side," Advance Ohio (Cleveland), March 9, 2020, https://www.cleveland.com/crime/2020/03/18-shot-1-killed-following-fight-between-multiple-motorcycle-clubs-on-clevelands-east-side.html; Sophie Carson, Ashley Luthern, and Gina Barton, "'Nobody Understands This Situation': Five Dead in a Shooting at a Home on Milwaukee's North Side," *Milwaukee Journal Sentinel*, April 27, 2020, https://www.jsonline.com/story/news/crime/2020/04/27/milwaukee-police-called-shooting-multiple-victims-home/3033403001/; "'People Were Running Everywhere': 4 Killed, 10 Hurt in North Charlotte Shooting," WCNC-TV (Charlotte), June 22, 2020, https://www.wcnc.com/article/news/crime/deadly-shooting-north-charlotte-beatties-ford-road/275-781db2ad-0768-402f-8ebc-09f252617 2a7; "Man Killed, 4 Wounded in Lawndale Shooting," *Chicago Sun-Times*, July 18, 2020, https://chicago.suntimes.com/crime/2020/7/18/21329379/twan-thigpen-lawndale-shooting-5-shot-man-killed-homicide-gun-violence-keeler; "Shooting at Illinois Bowling Alley Leaves 3 Dead, 3 Injured," Associated Press, December 26, 2020, https://apnews.com/article/ap-top-news-rockford-shootings-chicago-illinois-8fd8b49a766a96aab43528539ffca3f9.

20. Evan Casey and Jordyn Noennig, "A 15-Year-Old Boy Has Been Arrested in Connection with the Mayfair Mall Shooting," *Milwaukee Journal Sentinel*, November 22, 2020, https://www.jsonline.com/story/communities/west/news/wauwatosa/2020/11/22/mayfair-mall-shooting-15-year-old-arrested/6384531002/; Bruce Vielmetti, "Commissioner Orders 15-Year-Old Mayfair Shooting Suspect Held in Detention," *Milwaukee Journal Sentinel*, November 24, 2020, https://www.jsonline.com/story/news/crime/2020/11/24/commissioner-orders-15-year-old-mayfair-mall-suspect-held-detention/6407450002/; Elliott Hughes and Evan Casey, "Longstanding Feud Between Two Groups Preceded Mayfair Mall

Shooting, Police Report Says," *Milwaukee Journal Sentinel*, April 9, 2021, https://www.jsonline.com/story/news/2021/04/09/report-says-long-feud-between-2-groups-preceded-mayfair-mall-shooting/7166344002/; Mark Stevens, "Police Release New Records in Mayfair Mall Shooting Investigation," WDJT-TV (Milwaukee), April 8, 2021, https://www.cbs58.com/news/police-release-new-records-in-mayfair-mall-shooting-investigation.

21. "Wauwatosa Community 'Terrified and Terrorized' After Mayfair Mall Shooting; Police Looking for Shooter," WDJT-TV (Milwaukee), November 21, 2020, https://www.cbs58.com/news/wauwatosa-police-continue-to-search-for-mayfair-mall-shooter.

22. "Teen Charged in Mall Shooting to Contest Move to Adult Court: Attorneys for the 15-Year-Old Boy Charged in a Shooting at a Wisconsin Mall That Left Eight People Wounded Plan to Contest Prosecutors' Attempts to Move His Case to Adult Court," *U.S. News and World Report*, December 3, 2020, https://www.usnews.com/news/best-states/wisconsin/articles/2020-12-03/teen-charged-in-mall-shooting-to-contest-move-to-adult-court; Casey and Noennig, "15-Year-Old Boy Arrested."

23. Casey and Noennig, "15-Year-Old Boy Arrested"; "Know Your Rights: Protesters' Rights," American Civil Liberties Union, accessed December 26, 2021, https://www.aclu.org/know-your-rights/protesters-rights/; David French, "Free Speech for Me but Not for Thee," *Atlantic*, April 11, 2022, https://www.theatlantic.com/ideas/archive/2022/04/republican-dont-say-gay-bill-florida/629516/.

24. Bruce Vielmetti, "The Teenager Charged in the Mayfair Mall Shooting Will Remain in Juvenile Court," *Milwaukee Journal Sentinel*, February 25, 2021, https://www.jsonline.com/story/news/crime/2021/02/25/teen-charged-mayfair-mall-shooting-remain-juvenile-court/6762142002/; Hughes and Casey, "Longstanding Feud"; Bruce Vielmetti, "Supreme Court Orders Teen Charged in Mayfair Mall Shooting to Be Tried as an Adult," *Milwaukee Journal Sentinel*, June 29, 2022, https://www.jsonline.com/story/news/2022/06/29/supreme-court-teen-mayfair-mall-shooting-tried-adult/7749317001/; Bruce Vielmetti, "Teen Accused in 2020 Mayfair Mall Shooting Now Charged as an Adult," *Milwaukee Journal Sentinel*, July 12, 2022, https://www.jsonline.com/story/news/2022/07/12/mayfair-mall-shooting-suspect-now-charged-adult-2020-incident/10034749002/; "Man Gets 15 Years for Mayfair Mall Shooting That Wounded 8," *Milwaukee Journal Sentinel*, April 4, 2023, https://www.jsonline.com/story/news/crime/2023/04/04/xavier-sevilla-gets-15-years-for-mayfair-mall-shooting/70080217007/; Tajma Hall, "Mayfair

Mall Shooter Sentenced to 15 Years in Prison," WDJT-TV (Milwaukee), April 4, 2023, https://www.cbs58.com/news/mayfair-mall-shooter-sentenced-to-15-years-in-prison.

25. The facts of this incident are taken primarily from an investigative report by the West Allis (Wisconsin) Police Department and a statement from the Milwaukee County District Attorney's Office.

26. Evan Casey and Sophie Carson, "Wauwatosa Police Officer Shoots, Injures Woman in Village Area Following 'Altercation' and Reported Attack of Another Woman," *Milwaukee Journal Sentinel*, December 11, 2020, https://www.jsonline.com/story/news/local/2020/12/10/wauwatosa-police-respond-report-shots-fired/3891971001/; "Wauwatosa Protesters Demand Reform after Latest Police Shooting," WISN-TV (Milwaukee), December 13, 2020, https://www.wisn.com/article/wauwatosa-protesters-demand-reform-after-latest-police-shooting/34937219#; Isiah Holmes, "Wauwatosa Police Shooting Rekindles Tensions in Suburb," *Wisconsin Examiner*, December 11, 2020, https://wisconsinexaminer.com/brief/wauwatosa-police-shooting-rekindles-tensions-in-suburb; Evan Casey, "Milwaukee County District Attorney's Office Will Not Pursue Charges against a Wauwatosa Officer Who Shot a Woman in 2020," *Milwaukee Journal Sentinel*, December 9, 2021, https://www.jsonline.com/story/communities/west/news/wauwatosa/2021/12/09/milwaukee-da-not-charge-wauwatosa-police-officer-2020-shooting-district-attorney/6446726001/.

27. Peter Charalambous, "'Vicious Cycle': Inside the Police Recruiting Crunch with Resignations on the Rise," ABC News, April 6, 2023, https://abcnews.go.com/US/police-departments-face-vicious-cycle-challenges-retaining-recruiting/story?id=98363458#:~:text=AsurveyreleasedonApril2022comparedto2019; Ryan Young and Devon M. Sayers, "Why Police Forces Are Struggling to Recruit and Keep Police Officers," CNN, February 3, 2022, https://www.cnn.com/2022/02/02/us/police-departments-struggle-recruit-retain-officers/index.html; Frank Vaisvilas, "Oneida Police Department Teams with UWM Professor to Address Suicide Prevention for Officers," *Milwaukee Journal Sentinel*, April 10, 2024, https://www.jsonline.com/story/news/local/wisconsin/2024/04/10/oneida-police-team-with-uwm-professor-on-suicide-prevention-program/73180395007/.

28. Christopher Kuhagen, "A Heartbreaking St. Patrick's Day: Gov. Tony Evers, Sen. Tammy Baldwin and Others React to the Killings at Roundy's in Oconomowoc," *Milwaukee Journal Sentinel*, March 17, 2021, https://www.jsonline.com/story/communities/lake-country/news/oconomowoc/2021/03/17/oconomowoc-shooting-governor-tony-evers

-tammy-baldwin-barbara-dittrich-react-roundys/4735985001/; Elliot Hughes and Evan Frank, "New Documents in Roundy's Shooting Give Insight into Shooter's Actions," *Milwaukee Journal Sentinel*, May 13, 2021, https://www.jsonline.com/story/news/local/wisconsin/2021/05/13/new-roundys-oconomowoc-shooting-documents-no-motive-give-insight-cornelius/5081529001/.

29. Quinn Clark, "Wauwatosa Is Investing $1.5 Million in City Funds in Its Police Department. Here's a Breakdown of the Spending," *Milwaukee Journal Sentinel*, April 26, 2023, https://www.jsonline.com/story/communities/west/2023/04/26/wauwatosa-police-department-to-receive-additional-1-5m-in-city-funds/70151162007/; Jesse Paul, Jordan Steffen, and John Ingold, "Planned Parenthood Shooting: 3 Killed, including 1 Police Officer, in Colorado Springs," *Denver Post*, November 27, 2015, https://web.archive.org/web/20151127230543/http://www.denverpost.com/news/ci_29172660/colorado-springs-firefighters-respond-active-shooter-at-planned; Deanna Bettineschi, "Orlando Police Use Armored Vehicle to Get inside Building," WJAX-TV (Jacksonville), June 13, 2016, https://www.actionnewsjax.com/news/local/orlando-police-use-armored-vehicle-to-get-inside-nightclub/340918441/.

30. Ariel Edwards-Levy, "CNN Poll: Most Americans Want Stricter Gun Control, but They're Divided on Whether Guns Make Public Places Safer," CNN, May 26, 2023, https://www.cnn.com/2023/05/26/politics/cnn-poll-gun-laws/index.html; Ivana Saric, "Fox News Poll Shows Americans Overwhelmingly Want Restrictions on Guns," Axios, April 29, 2023, https://www.axios.com/2023/04/28/fox-news-poll-voters-want-gun-control; "Guns," Gallup Inc., 2022, https://news.gallup.com/poll/1645/guns.aspx.

31. "A List of Mass Killings in the United States This Year," Associated Press, March 31, 2024, https://apnews.com/article/mass-killings-list-united-states-2024-796844f3291e1c9031013a14268a8e78; Gun Violence Archive, accessed May 26, 2024, https://www.gunviolencearchive.org/.

POLICE BLUES

1. Sam Levin, "What Does 'Defund the Police' Mean? The Rallying Cry Sweeping the US—Explained," *Guardian*, June 6, 2020, https://www.theguardian.com/us-news/2020/jun/05/defunding-the-police-us-what-does-it-mean; Ernesto Londoño, "How 'Defund the Police' Failed," *New York Times*, June 16, 2023, https://www.nytimes.com/2023/06/16/us

/defund-police-minneapolis.html; Melina Abdullah, "Statement Regarding the Ongoing Trial of Jussie Smollett," Black Lives Matter, December 7, 2021, https://blacklivesmatter.com/statement-regarding-the-ongoing-trial-of-jussie-smollett/; Jessie Opoien, "State Rep. Ryan Clancy Stands by Comments about Police Derided as 'Inane' and 'Clueless,'" *Milwaukee Journal Sentinel,* August 17, 2023, https://www.jsonline.com/story/news/politics/2023/08/17/ryan-clancy-stands-by-comments-about-police-derided-as-clueless/70596858007/; Fola Akinnibi, Sarah Holder, and Christopher Cannon, "Cities Say They Want to Defund Police. Their Budgets Say Otherwise," *Bloomberg CityLab,* January 12, 2021, https://www.bloomberg.com/graphics/2021-city-budget-police-funding/.

2. Erin Durkin, "De Blasio Confirms He'll Cut $1B from NYPD Budget," *Politico,* June 29, 2020, https://www.politico.com/states/new-york/city-hall/story/2020/06/29/de-blasio-confirms-hell-cut-1b-from-nypd-budget-1295930; Jeffery C. Mays, "Who Opposes Defunding the N.Y.P.D.? These Black Lawmakers," *New York Times,* August 10, 2020, https://www.nytimes.com/2020/08/10/nyregion/defund-police-nyc-council.html; David Freedlander, "Bill de Blasio Did What New Yorkers Wanted, Yet as the Mayor Prepares to Leave Office, He Remains Stubbornly Unpopular," *New York* magazine, December 16, 2021, https://nymag.com/intelligencer/2021/12/bill-de-blasio-remains-unpopular.html.

3. Liz Navratil, "Momentum Slows in Minneapolis City Council's Plan to Remake Police," *Minneapolis Star-Tribune,* September 6, 2020, https://www.startribune.com/momentum-slows-in-minneapolis-city-council-s-plan-to-remake-police/572329932/; Astead Herndon, "How a Pledge to Dismantle the Minneapolis Police Collapsed," *New York Times,* September 26, 2020, https://www.nytimes.com/2020/09/26/us/politics/minneapolis-defund-police.html; Sarah Holder and Fola Akinnibi, "Minneapolis One Year Later," *Bloomberg CityLab,* May 24, 2021, https://www.bloomberg.com/news/features/2021-05-24/how-george-floyd-s-death-changed-minneapolis; Londoño, "How 'Defund the Police' Failed."

4. Navratil, "Momentum Slows"; Eric Roper, "Polls: Cuts to Minneapolis Police Ranks Lack Majority Support," *Minneapolis Star-Tribune,* August 15, 2020, https://www.startribune.com/poll-cuts-to-minneapolis-police-ranks-lack-majority-support/572119932/; Herndon, "Pledge to Dismantle Minneapolis Police"; Holder and Akinnibi, "Minneapolis One Year Later"; Londoño, "How 'Defund the Police' Failed."

5. Jeramey Jannene, "Groups Call for Defunding the Police to Solve Milwaukee Pension Crisis: Move Would Strip $78 Million from MPD Budget, Leave Others Intact," *Urban Milwaukee,* October 1, 2021, https://

urbanmilwaukee.com/2021/10/01/groups-calls-for-defunding-the-police-to-solve-milwaukee-pension-crisis/.

6. Scott Wilson, "Anarchists and an Increase in Violent Crime Hijack Portland's Social Justice Movement," *Washington Post*, May 31, 2021, https://www.washingtonpost.com/national/anarchists-and-an-increase-in-crime-hijack-portlands-social-justice-movement/2021/05/28/d49ee1b6-bf1a-11eb-a55f-4871b8ac676f_story.html; Shane Dixon Kavanaugh, "Amid Calls to 'Defund the Police,' Most Portland Residents Want Police Presence Maintained or Increased, Poll Finds," *Oregonian* / Oregon Live, May 18, 2021, https://www.oregonlive.com/news/2021/05/amid-calls-to-defund-the-police-most-portland-residents-want-police-presence-maintained-or-increased-poll-finds.html.

7. Nicole Celestine, "Abraham Maslow, His Theory and Contribution to Psychology," Positive Psychology, September 29, 2017, https://positivepsychology.com/abraham-maslow/#needs-abraham-maslow.

8. Deja Thomas and Juliana Menasce Horowitz, "Support for Black Lives Matter Has Decreased Since June [2020] but Remains Strong Among Black Americans," Pew Research Center, https://www.pewresearch.org/short-reads/2020/09/16/support-for-black-lives-matter-has-decreased-since-june-but-remains-strong-among-black-americans/; Emma Tucker and Peter Nickeas, "The US Saw Significant Crime Rise Across Major Cities in 2020. And It's Not Letting Up," CNN, April 3, 2021, https://www.cnn.com/2021/04/03/us/us-crime-rate-rise-2020/index.html; Patrick Marley, "Police Union Poll Finds Broad Support for Body Cameras and Tougher Penalties for Property Destruction," *Milwaukee Journal Sentinel*, May 11, 2021, https://www.jsonline.com/story/news/politics/2021/05/11/wisconsin-police-union-poll-finds-public-support-body-cameras/5029472001/.

9. "United States Racial Unrest (2020–Present)," Wikipedia, last modified May 21, 2024, https://en.wikipedia.org/wiki/2020-2023_United_States_racial_unrest; Herndon, "Pledge to Dismantle Minneapolis Police"; Jonathan Martin, Alexander Burns, and Thomas Kaplan, "Biden Walks a Cautious Line as He Opposes Defunding the Police," *New York Times*, June 8, 2020, https://www.nytimes.com/2020/06/08/us/politics/biden-defund-the-police.html; Fadel Allassan, "Bernie Sanders Pushes Back on Idea of Abolishing Police Departments," Axios, June 9, 2020, https://www.axios.com/2020/06/09/bernie-sanders-defund-police; Thomas and Horowitz, "Support for Black Lives Matter"; Katie Glueck, Adam Nagourney, and Maggie Haberman, "Trump Steps Up His Assault

on Biden with Scattershot Attacks, Many False," *New York Times*, September 29, 2020, https://www.nytimes.com/2020/07/17/us/trump-biden-2020-election.html.

10. Mays, "Who Opposes Defunding the N.Y.P.D.?"

11. Herndon, "Pledge to Dismantle Minneapolis Police."

12. Wilson, "Anarchists and an Increase."

13. Emily Bazelon, "Speaking Truth to Both the Right and the Left," *New York Times*, June 14, 2021, https://www.nytimes.com/2021/06/14/books/review/george-packer-last-best-hope-jonathan-rauch-the-constitution-of-knowledge.html.

14. Akinnibi et al., "Cities Say."

15. Everton Bailey Jr., "Ted Wheeler Won Reelection as Portland Mayor by An Historically Narrow Margin; Here's How He Held On to Lead for 4 More Years," *Oregonian* / Oregon Live, November 9, 2020, https://www.oregonlive.com/politics/2020/11/ted-wheeler-won-reelection-as-portland-mayor-by-an-historically-narrow-margin-heres-how-he-held-on-to-lead-for-4-more-years.html.

16. Griff Witte, Holly Bailey, and Joanna Slater, "In Mayoral Elections Nationwide, Voters Opt for Pragmatism Over Ideology," *Washington Post*, November 3, 2021, https://www.washingtonpost.com/national/in-mayoral-elections-nationwide-voters-opt-for-pragmatism-over-ideology/2021/11/03/a854bc30-3ce1-11ec-a67c-d7c2182dac83_story.html.

17. "Buffalo Mayor Who Lost Primary Reelected with Write-In Votes," Associated Press (Spectrum News 1), November 19, 2021, https://spectrumlocalnews.com/nys/buffalo/news/2021/11/19/india-walton-concedes-buffalo-mayoral-race.

18. Akinnibi et al., "Cities Say"; "Mayoral Election in Seattle, Washington (2021)," *Ballotpedia*, accessed November 30, 2023, https://ballotpedia.org/Mayoral_election_in_Seattle,_Washington_(2021).

19. Akinnibi et al., "Cities Say"; Holder and Akinnibi, "Minneapolis One Year Later."

20. Londoño, "How 'Defund the Police' Failed"; "Minneapolis-St. Paul Election Results," *New York Times*, November 2, 2021, https://www.nytimes.com/interactive/2021/11/02/us/elections/results-minneapolis-st-paul-minnesota.html; Witte et al., "In Mayoral Elections Nationwide."

21. "Minneapolis-St. Paul Election Results," *New York Times*.

22. Katie Glueck, "Eric Adams Is Elected Mayor of New York City," *New York Times*, November 2, 2021, https://www.nytimes.com/2021/11/02/nyregion/eric-adams-mayor.html; Juan Williams, "Eric Adams Is

Making White Liberals Squirm," *Atlantic*, August 24, 2021, https://www.theatlantic.com/ideas/archive/2021/08/eric-adams-police-new-york/619869/.

23. James Downie, "Opinion: Democrats Don't Win by Punching Left," *Washington Post*, July 4, 2021, https://www.washingtonpost.com/opinions/2021/07/04/democrats-dont-win-by-punching-left/.

24. Witte et al., "In Mayoral Elections Nationwide"; Jonathan Weisman and Michael C. Bender, "Chicago's Choice Points to a Democratic Divide the G.O.P. Hopes to Exploit," *New York Times*, March 1, 2023, https://www.nytimes.com/2023/03/01/us/politics/chicago-mayor-republicans-democrats-trump.html; Alexi McCammond, "Opinion: Being 'Tough on Crime' Isn't an Appeal to White Voters," *Washington Post*, April 8, 2024, https://www.washingtonpost.com/opinions/2024/04/08/democrats-crime-hochul-2024-biden/.

25. "Analysis of Police Department, Wauwatosa, Wisconsin: Recruitment Strategies, Alternative Responses and Efficiency in Delivering Services, Policy Review, Training Assessment, Promotional Process, Strategic Planning," Center for Public Safety Management, July 2021, https://www.wauwatosa.net/home/showpublisheddocument/4251/637726909146070000; "CPSM Progress," City of Wauwatosa, accessed December 10, 2022, https://www.wauwatosa.net/government/departments/police/cpsm-progress; Evan Casey, "Wauwatosa Lacks Diversity and Affordable Housing, Report Says. Here's How the City Plans to Address That," *Milwaukee Journal Sentinel*, March 10, 2021, https://www.jsonline.com/story/communities/west/news/wauwatosa/2021/03/10/how-wauwatosa-plans-address-lack-diversity-affordable-housing/4636244001/; Evan Casey, "Wauwatosa Will Likely Elect a Person of Color for the First Time in the 125-Year History of the Common Council This Spring," *Milwaukee Journal Sentinel*, January 20, 2022, https://www.jsonline.com/story/communities/west/news/wauwatosa/2022/01/20/margaret-arney-running-unopposed-wauwatosa-spring-election/6513383001/.

26. "Making Wauwatosa More Inclusive," City of Wauwatosa, accessed December 11, 2022, https://www.wauwatosa.net/government/open-government/making-wauwatosa-more-inclusive.

27. Evan Casey, "Wauwatosa Police Chief Barry Weber Is Retiring This Spring after 48 Years in Law Enforcement," *Milwaukee Journal Sentinel*, February 1, 2021, https://www.jsonline.com/story/communities/west/news/wauwatosa/2021/02/01/wauwatosa-police-chief-barry-weber-retiring-spring/4345288001/.

28. Wisconsin Statutes § 62.13(5)(j); Claire Silverman, "Removal of Officers; Governing Body Procedures and the Recall Procedure," *Municipality* (League of Wisconsin Municipalities newsletter), August 2018, https://www.lwm-info.org/DocumentCenter/View/2171/August-Removal-of-Officers.

29. "Wauwatosa Police Chief Barry Weber Submits Retirement Notice," City of Wauwatosa, February 1, 2021, https://www.wauwatosa.net/Home/Components/News/News/2393/17.

30. Gregory Krieg, "There's No Playbook for the Battle between Mayors and Police Right Now," CNN, June 20, 2020, https://www.cnn.com/2020/06/20/politics/mayors-police/index.html; Noam Scheiber, Farah Stockman, and J. David Goodman, "How Police Unions Became Such Powerful Opponents to Reform Efforts: Half a Decade after a Spate of Officer-Involved Deaths Inspired Widespread Protest, Many Police Unions Are Digging In to Defend Members," *New York Times*, June 6, 2020, https://www.nytimes.com/2020/06/06/us/police-unions-minneapolis-kroll.html.

31. Daniel DiSalvo, "The Trouble with Police Unions," *National Affairs*, Fall 2020, https://www.nationalaffairs.com/publications/detail/the-trouble-with-police-unions; Scheiber et al., "Police Unions"; Eve L. Ewing, "Blue Bloods: America's Brotherhood of Police Officers: To Understand the Citadel of Law Enforcement, We Must Reckon with Its Unions—Which Resemble Fraternities More Than Labor Unions," *Vanity Fair*, August 25, 2020, https://www.vanityfair.com/culture/2020/08/americas-brotherhood-of-police-officers; Adam Serwer, "The Authoritarian Instincts of Police Unions," *Atlantic*, July/August 2021, https://www.theatlantic.com/magazine/archive/2021/07/bust-the-police-unions/619006/.

32. Kirk Johnson and Sergio Olmos, "After a Year of Protests, Portland Is Ready to Move On. But Where?," *New York Times*, June 9, 2021, https://www.nytimes.com/2021/06/09/us/portland-protests.html.

33. Evan Casey, "The Wauwatosa Police Officer Who Has Shot and Killed Three People in the Last Five Years Has Been Suspended, Commission Rules," *Milwaukee Journal Sentinel*, July 15, 2020, https://www.jsonline.com/story/communities/west/news/wauwatosa/2020/07/15/officer-joseph-mensah-suspended-wauwatosa-police-and-fire-commission/5446849002/.

34. Isiah Holmes, "Tosa Officer's Suspension Is Just One Chapter in an Ongoing Saga: Officials Raise 'Improper' Public Influence in the Case

of Police Shootings," *Wisconsin Examiner*, July 17, 2020, https://wisconsinexaminer.com/2020/07/17/tosa-officers-suspension-is-just-one-chapter-in-an-ongoing-saga/.

35. Evan Casey, "Wauwatosa's Mayor Says the Police Union Is 'a Problem' and 'Has Not Been a Good Partner' with the City," *Milwaukee Journal Sentinel*, May 25, 2021, https://www.jsonline.com/story/communities/west/news/wauwatosa/2021/05/25/wauwatosa-police-union-and-mayor-odds-again/5172570001/.

36. Adam Serwer, "The Capitol Rioters Attacked Police. Why Isn't the FOP Outraged?—Police Unions Aren't Usually Bashful About Defending Officers, but They've Been Conspicuously Subdued in Discussing the January 6 Attacks," *Atlantic*, August 5, 2021, https://www.theatlantic.com/ideas/archive/2021/08/blue-wall-silence/619612/.

37. Evan Casey, "Officer Joseph Mensah Was Physically Assaulted by Protesters and a Gunshot Was Fired into His Home, Wauwatosa Police Say," *Milwaukee Journal Sentinel*, August 9, 2020, https://www.jsonline.com/story/communities/west/news/wauwatosa/2020/08/09/wauwatosa-police-officer-joseph-mensah-physically-assaulted/3330610001/.

38. See Isiah Holmes, "Wauwatosa PD's High Value Target Internal Investigation: Tosa PD Incident Reports Contradict the Findings of Internal Investigation into Why Mayor McBride Was Placed on a Higher Value Target List," *Wisconsin Examiner*, May 12, 2021, https://wisconsinexaminer.com/2021/05/12/wauwatosa-pds-high-value-target-internal-investigation/.

39. John Rappaport and Ben Grunwald, "Opinion: It Will Take More Than the George Floyd Justice in Policing Act to Fix Our Broken System," *Washington Post*, February 5, 2021, https://www.washingtonpost.com/opinions/it-will-take-more-than-the-george-floyd-justice-in-policing-act-to-fix-our-broken-system/2021/02/04/e59f8b2c-66fb-11eb-886d-5264d4ceb46d_story.html.

40. Evan Casey and Eddie Morales, "Milwaukee County District Attorney Will Not Charge Police Officer Joseph Mensah in Shooting Death of Alvin Cole," *Milwaukee Journal Sentinel*, October 7, 2020, https://www.jsonline.com/story/communities/west/news/wauwatosa/2020/10/07/wauwatosa-police-officer-joseph-mensah-da-decision-coming/3446512001/; Associated Press, "Protests Break Out, Windows Broken in Wauwatosa after Wisconsin Police Officer Involved in Several Shootings Is Cleared in Mall Death," *Chicago Tribune*, October 8, 2020, https://www.chicagotribune.com/midwest/ct-milwaukee-police-joseph-mensah-20201007-f42mhenqxrbqfnl2sxyt3yvhby-story.html.

41. "Report of Independent Investigator Steven M. Biskupic to the Wauwatosa Police and Fire Commission Regarding the Conduct of Wauwatosa Police Officer Joseph Mensah," WLUK Fox 11, October 7, 2020, 1, http://fox11digital.com/news/PDFs/Report%20of%20Independent%20Investigator_Part1.pdf; Ashley Luthern, "Outside Investigator: Tosa Officer Should Be Fired, Citing 'Extraordinary' Risk of a Fourth Fatal Shooting," *Milwaukee Journal Sentinel*, October 7, 2020, https://www.jsonline.com/story/news/crime/2020/10/07/wauwatosa-police-officer-joseph-mensah-should-fired-shootings-report-says/5909137002/; Associated Press, "Protests Break Out"; Rappaport and Grunwald, "Opinion."

42. Evan Casey, "Wauwatosa Detectives Made a PowerPoint That Said the Mayor 'Sanctioned Violence' Against Former Officer Joseph Mensah," *Milwaukee Journal Sentinel*, January 14, 2021, https://www.jsonline.com/story/communities/west/news/wauwatosa/2021/01/14/wauwatosa-police-said-mayor-dennis-mcribe-sanctioned-violence-against-mensah/4145935001/.

43. Ibid.; Holmes, "Wauwatosa PD's Internal Investigation."

44. Isiah Holmes, "Wauwatosa Mayor Dennis McBride Named as 'Target' by Police," *Wisconsin Examiner*, January 13, 2021, https://wisconsinexaminer.com/2021/01/13/wauwatosa-mayor-dennis-mcbride-named-as-target-by-police/; Casey, "Wauwatosa Detectives Made a PowerPoint"; Derrick Rose, "Wauwatosa Mayor: Police Considered Me 'Higher Value Target,'" WISN-TV (Milwaukee), January 13, 2021, https://www.wisn.com/article/wauwatosa-mayor-police-considered-me-higher-value-target/35203049.

45. Bruce Murphy, "8 Ways Police Mishandled Protests: From Los Angeles to New York, Milwaukee and Wauwatosa, Police Made Similar Mistakes," *Urban Milwaukee*, March 25, 2021, https://urbanmilwaukee.com/2021/03/24/murphys-law-8-ways-police-mishandled-protests/.

46. Holmes, "Wauwatosa PD's Internal Investigation."

47. "WTMJ Conversations: Dennis McBride," WTMJ-AM (Milwaukee), May 16, 2021, https://wtmj.com/wtmj-conversations/2021/05/16/wtmj-conversations-dennis-mcbride/.

48. Isiah Holmes, "Detective Who Labeled Wauwatosa Tosa [*sic*] Mayor a 'Higher Value Target' Is Now Sergeant," *Wisconsin Examiner*, September 24, 2021, https://wisconsinexaminer.com/brief/detective-who-labeled-wauwatosa-tosa-mayor-a-higher-value-target-is-now-sergeant/; Holmes, "Wauwatosa PD's Internal Investigation."

49. Tony Kushner, *Lincoln: The Screenplay* (New York: Theatre Communications Group, 2012), 76–78.

50. Corrine Hess, "Activists Push for Police Firings, but Elected Officials Don't Have Power to Do That," Wisconsin Public Radio, February 8, 2021, https://www.wpr.org/activists-push-police-firings-elected-officials-dont-have-power-do; Jeramey Jannene, "Should Mayor Appoint Police and Fire Chiefs? Council Members Think System Is Broken; Many Support Change in State Legislation," *Urban Milwaukee*, December 7, 2020, https://urbanmilwaukee.com/2020/12/07/city-hall-should-mayor-appoint-police-and-fire-chiefs/; Editorial Board, "Opinion: Court-Packing Isn't the Right Fix for Our Courts. Ending Life Tenure Is," *Washington Post*, April 10, 2021, https://www.washingtonpost.com/opinions/court-packing-isnt-the-right-fix-for-our-courts-ending-life-tenure-is/2021/04/09/.

51. Ruy Teixeira and Dan Adams, "Step Away from the Noise of Social Media and Cable News and There's a Lot of Common Ground in Wisconsin," *Milwaukee Journal Sentinel*, October 10, 2022, https://www.jsonline.com/story/opinion/2022/10/10/despite-noise-social-media-theres-common-ground-wisconsin/8191449001/.

52. Neil MacFarquhar, "Why Police Have Been Quitting in Droves in the Last Year," *New York Times*, June 24, 2021, https://www.nytimes.com/2021/06/24/us/police-resignations-protests-asheville.html; Thomas Friedman, "Opinion: Want to Get Trump Reelected? Dismantle the Police," *New York Times*, June 22, 2021, https://www.nytimes.com/2021/06/22/opinion/gop-democrats-defund-police-voting.html; Mitch Smith, "As Applications Fall, Police Departments Lure Recruits with Bonuses and Attention: Many Police Chiefs Say Staffing Levels Have Not Rebounded from a Wave of Resignations That Started with the Pandemic and the 2020 Unrest," *New York Times*, December 25, 2022, https://www.nytimes.com/2022/12/25/us/police-officer-recruits.html; Robert Klemko, "Police Agencies Are Desperate to Hire. But They Say Few Want the Job," *Washington Post*, May 27, 2023, https://www.washingtonpost.com/national-security/2023/05/27/police-vacancies-hiring-recruiting-reform/.

53. Michele Fiore, "Area Police Departments Offer Sign-On Incentives as They Struggle to Attract New Officers," WDJT-TV (Milwaukee), February 4, 2022, https://cbs58.com/news/police-departments-offer-sign-on-incentives-as-they-face-difficulty-attracting-new-officers; "Career Pages: Police Officer," City of Wauwatosa, accessed December 27, 2022, https://www.governmentjobs.com/careers/wauwatosawi/jobs/3381087/police-officer.

54. Jake Pearson, "More Than Two Years after George Floyd's Murder Sparked a Movement, Police Reform Has Stalled. What Happened?,"

ProPublica, October 24, 2022, https://www.propublica.org/article/why-police-reform-stalled-elizabeth-glazer.

55. "WTMJ Conversations: Dennis McBride," WTMJ-AM (Milwaukee).

56. Wilson, "Anarchists and an Increase"; Casey, "Wauwatosa's Mayor."

ECHOES AND AFTERSHOCKS

1. "William Faulkner: Quotes," Goodreads.com, accessed April 22, 2024, https://www.goodreads.com/quotes/12124-the-past-is-never-dead-it-s-not-even-past.

2. Jon Collins, "How Minneapolis Has Changed Three Years after the Murder of George Floyd," Minnesota Public Radio, May 25, 2023, https://www.mprnews.org/story/2023/05/24/how-minneapolis-has-changed-three-years-after-the-murder-of-george-floyd; "How George Floyd Died, and What Happened Next," *New York Times*, July 29, 2022, https://www.nytimes.com/article/george-floyd.html.

3. Christina Morales, "What We Know About the Shooting of Jacob Blake," *New York Times*, November 16, 2021, https://www.nytimes.com/article/jacob-blake-shooting-kenosha.html; Becky Sullivan, "Kyle Rittenhouse Is Acquitted of All Charges in the Trial Over Killing 2 in Kenosha," National Public Radio, November 19, 2021, https://www.npr.org/2021/11/19/1057288807/kyle-rittenhouse-acquitted-all-charges-verdict.

4. J. David Goodman, "Texas Governor Pardons Man in Fatal Shooting of Protester in 2020," *New York Times*, May 16, 2024, https://www.nytimes.com/2024/05/16/us/texas-abbott-pardon-daniel-perry.html.

5. David Nakamura, "Former Louisville Officer Faces Third Trial in Breonna Taylor Slaying," *Washington Post*, March 11, 2024, https://www.washingtonpost.com/national-security/2024/03/11/former-louisville-officer-faces-third-trial-breonna-taylor-slaying/; "Ex-Louisville Officer Convicted of Using Excessive Force on Breonna Taylor During Deadly Raid," PBS News, November 2, 2024, https://www.pbs.org/newshour/nation/ex-louisville-officer-convicted-of-using-excessive-force-on-breonna-taylor-during-deadly-raid.

6. Jamiles Lartey, "How Policing Has—and Hasn't—Changed Since George Floyd," Marshall Project, August 6, 2022, https://www.themarshallproject.org/2022/08/06/how-policing-has-and-hasn-t-changed-since-george-floyd; Neil Gross, "The Myths Holding Back Police

Reform," *TIME*, September 26, 2023, https://time.com/6316258/myths-police-reform/; Robert Klemko, Emily Davies, and Tom Jackman, "Killings by Police Brought Reforms. Fear of Crime Is Unraveling Them," *Washington Post*, March 10, 2024, https://www.washingtonpost.com/national-security/2024/03/10/police-reform-rollback-tyre-nichols-floyd-breonna/; Robert Samuels and Toluse Olorunnipa, "Four Years Later, Has the Racial-Justice Movement Lost the Fight?," *Washington Post*, May 25, 2024, https://www.washingtonpost.com/nation/2024/05/25/george-floyd-anniversary-retrenchment/.

7. Julie Bosman, "Four Years On, Covid Has Reshaped Life for Many Americans," *New York Times*, March 13, 2024, https://www.nytimes.com/2024/03/13/us/covid-national-emergency-anniversary.html.

8. "Milwaukee Health Systems Deferring Some Elective Procedures Amid COVID-19 Surge," WTMJ-TV (Milwaukee), December 31, 2021, https://www.tmj4.com/news/coronavirus/amid-covid-19-surge-froedtert-delaying-some-deferrable-surgical-procedures-requiring-beds; Ahmed Aboulenein, "Overwhelmed by Omicron Surge, U.S. Hospitals Delay Surgeries," Reuters, January 7, 2022, https://www.reuters.com/world/us/overwhelmed-by-omicron-surge-us-hospitals-delay-surgeries-2022-01-07/; Emily Anthes and Benjamin Mueller, "U.S. Life Expectancy Creeps Up as Covid Deaths Fall," *New York Times*, November 29, 2023, https://www.nytimes.com/2023/11/29/health/us-life-expectancy-covid-deaths.html.

9. Emily Harris, "Life Expectancy in US Climbed after Declines Related to COVID-19," *JAMA Network*, December 13, 2023, https://jamanetwork.com/journals/jama/article-abstract/2813157; Azeen Ghorayshi, "An 'Unsettling' Drop in Life Expectancy for Men," *New York Times*, November 13, 2023, https://www.nytimes.com/2023/11/13/health/men-life-expectancy-drops.html.

10. Frances Stead Sellers, "Four Years On, Long Covid Still Confounds Us. Here's What We Know Now," *Washington Post*, December 31, 2023, https://www.washingtonpost.com/health/2023/12/31/long-covid-symptoms-treatment-research/; Nicole D. Ford, Abrahm Agedew, Alexandra F. Dalton, Jordan Singleton, Cria G. Perrine, and Sharon Saydah, "Notes from the Field: Long COVID Prevalence among Adults—United States, 2022," US Centers for Disease Control and Prevention, February 15, 2024, https://www.cdc.gov/mmwr/volumes/73/wr/mm7306a4.htm; Madeline Miller, "Opinion: Long Covid Has Derailed My Life. Make No Mistake: It Could Yours, Too," *Washington Post*, August 9, 2023, https://

www.washingtonpost.com/opinions/2023/08/09/madeline-miller-long-covid-post-pandemic/; Sarah Mervosh and Francesca Paris, "Why School Absences Have 'Exploded' Almost Everywhere," *New York Times*, March 29, 2024, https://www.nytimes.com/interactive/2024/03/29/us/chronic-absences.html; Donna St. George, "Behavioral Issues, Absenteeism at Schools Increase, Federal Data Shows," *Washington Post*, July 6, 2022, https://www.washingtonpost.com/education/2022/07/05/absenteeism-behavioral-issues-pandemic-data/.

11. "Stress in America 2023: A Nation Recovering from Collective Trauma," American Psychological Association, accessed April 24, 2024, https://www.apa.org/news/press/releases/stress/2023/collective-trauma-recovery.

12. Ana Marie Cox, "We Are Not Just Polarized. We Are Traumatized," *New Republic*, September 14, 2023, https://newrepublic.com/article/175311/america-polarized-traumatized-trump-violence; Roxane Cohen Silver, E. Alison Holman, and Dana Rose Garfin, "Coping with Cascading Collective Traumas in the United States," *Nature Human Behavior* 5 (2020): 4–6, https://www.nature.com/articles/s41562-020-00981-x; Stephanie Zacharek, "2020 Tested Us beyond Measure. Where Do We Go from Here?," *TIME*, December 8, 2020, https://time.com/5917394/2020-in-review/; Reis Thebault and Hannah Natanson, "College Protests. A Trump Trial. Raging Wars. Is Everything 'on Fire'?," *Washington Post*, May 5, 2024, https://www.washingtonpost.com/nation/2024/05/04/university-protest-trump-trial-israel-gaza-ukraine-news/.

13. Sarah Mervosh, Claire Cain Miller, and Francesca Paris, "What the Data Says About Pandemic School Closures, Four Years Later," *New York Times*, March 18, 2024, https://www.nytimes.com/2024/03/18/upshot/pandemic-school-closures-data.html; Tom Nichols, "When Experts Fail," *Atlantic*, March 22, 2024, https://www.theatlantic.com/ideas/archive/2024/03/experts-failure-covid-19-pandemic/677816/.

14. *Youth Risk Behavior Survey Data Summary and Trends Report: 2011–2021*, US Centers for Disease Control and Prevention National Center for HIV, Viral Hepatitis, STD, and TB Prevention Division of Adolescent and School Health, accessed October 13, 2023, https://www.cdc.gov/healthyyouth/data/yrbs/pdf/YRBS_Data-Summary-Trends_Report2023_508.pdf.

15. "More Than 80 Percent of U.S. Public Schools Report Pandemic Has Negatively Impacted Student Behavior and Socio-emotional

Development," National Center for Education Statistics, July 6, 2022, https://nces.ed.gov/whatsnew/press_releases/07_06_2022.asp; Mervosh and Paris, "Why School Absences Have 'Exploded'"; St. George, "Behavioral Issues"; William Bornhoft, "Half of Milwaukee Students Were 'Chronically Absent' in 2023: Report," *Milwaukee Patch*, April 1, 2024, https://patch.com/wisconsin/wauwatosa/s/ivnhv/half-of-milwaukee-students-were-chronically-absent-in-2023-report.

16. Mervosh and Paris, "Why School Absences Have 'Exploded'"; St. George, "Behavioral Issues."

17. Mervosh et al., "What the Data Says"; Mervosh and Paris, "Why School Absences Have 'Exploded'"; St. George, "Behavioral Issues."

18. Mervosh and Paris, "Why School Absences Have 'Exploded.'"

19. Matthew Stone, "Why America Has a Youth Mental Health Crisis, and How Schools Can Help," Education Week, October 16, 2023, https://www.edweek.org/leadership/why-america-has-a-youth-mental-health-crisis-and-how-schools-can-help/2023/10; Donna St. George and Valerie Strauss, "The Crisis of Student Mental Health Is Much Vaster Than We Realize," *Washington Post*, December 5, 2022, https://www.washingtonpost.com/education/2022/12/05/crisis-student-mental-health-is-much-vaster-than-we-realize/.

20. "Social Work," City of Wauwatosa, accessed April 26, 2024, https://www.wauwatosa.net/government/departments/social-work; Olivia Randi, "American Rescue Plan Act Presents Opportunities for States to Support School Mental Health Systems," National Academy for State Health Policy, August 2, 2021, https://nashp.org/american-rescue-plan-act-presents-opportunities-for-states-to-support-school-mental-health-systems/.

21. Emma Goldberg, "What We Do and Don't Know About the Effects of Remote Work," *New York Times*, October 10, 2023, https://www.nytimes.com/2023/10/10/business/remote-work-effects.html.

22. Edward L. Glaeser and Carlo Ratti, "26 Empire State Buildings Could Fit into New York's Empty Office Space. That's a Sign," *New York Times*, May 10, 2023, https://www.nytimes.com/interactive/2023/05/10/opinion/nyc-office-vacancy-playground-city.html.

23. Nicholas Bloom, "The Five-Day Office Week Is Dead," *New York Times*, October 18, 2023, https://www.nytimes.com/2023/10/16/opinion/office-work-home-remote.html.

24. Ian Smith, "Many Federal Agency Offices Remain Largely Vacant Post COVID," FedSmith, December 12, 2023, https://www.fedsmith

.com/2023/12/12/many-federal-agency-offices-remain-largely-vacant-post-covid/.

25. Yelena Mandenberg, "NYC Has So Much Empty Office Space It Could Fill Up 30 Empire State Buildings," *Mirror*, January 16, 2024, https://www.mirror.co.uk/news/us-news/nyc-much-empty-office-space-31890001.

26. Heather Long, "Opinion: Finally, Someone Wants to Buy Your Old Office," *Washington Post*, August 15, 2024, https://www.washingtonpost.com/opinions/2024/08/15/downtown-office-sales-makeover-price/; Nazzmul Ahasan, "A Record Number of Office Buildings Will Be Converted into Apartments in 2024," *TIME*, January 22, 2024, https://time.com/6565216/offices-apartments-conversion-2024-remote-hybrid-work/.

27. Jordan Wolman, "Big-City Dems Face Return-to-Office Reckoning—with Their Own Workers," *Politico*, August 25, 2023, https://www.politico.com/news/2023/08/25/blue-city-officials-face-reckoning-with-own-staff-on-return-to-office-00112820; Toluse Olorunnipa and Lisa Rein, "White House Urges Federal Workers to Return to Office This Fall," *Washington Post*, August 4, 2023, https://www.washingtonpost.com/politics/2023/08/04/white-house-urges-federal-workers-return-office-this-fall/; Goldberg, "Effects of Remote Work"; Ian Smith, "Another Bill Introduced to Slash Telework for Federal Employees," FedSmith, May 8, 2024, https://www.fedsmith.com/2024/05/08/another-bill-introduced-to-slash-telework-for-federal-employees/.

28. Natalie Sherman, "Zoom Orders Workers Back to the Office," BBC, August 7, 2023, https://www.bbc.com/news/business-66432173.

29. Danielle Abril, "Return to the Office? These Workers Quit Instead," *Washington Post*, September 21, 2023, https://www.washingtonpost.com/technology/2023/09/21/return-office-mandates-employees-quit/.

30. Ben Wigert, Jim Harter, and Sangeeta Agrawal, "The Future of the Office Has Arrived: It's Hybrid," Gallup Inc., October 9, 2023, https://www.gallup.com/workplace/511994/future-office-arrived-hybrid.aspx.

31. Taylor Telford, "Ordered Back to the Office, Top Tech Talent Left Instead, Study Finds," *Washington Post*, May 12, 2024, https://www.washingtonpost.com/business/2024/05/12/rto-microsoft-apple-spacex/.

32. Glaeser and Ratti, "26 Empire State Buildings."

33. Michael Sasso, "Record Wave of Americans Fled Big Cities for Small Ones in 2023," *Bloomberg CityLab*, May 7, 2024, https://www.bloomberg.com/news/articles/2024-05-07/record-wave-of-americans-fled-big-cities-for-small-ones-in-2023.

34. Tracy Alloway and Laura Nahmias, "'Urban Family Exodus' Continues with Number of Young Kids in NYC Down 18%," *Bloomberg CityLab*, July 10, 2024, https://www.bloomberg.com/news/articles/2024-07-10/-urban-family-exodus-continues-with-number-of-young-kids-in-nyc-down-18; Connor O'Brien, "Young Families Have Continued Leaving Big Cities Post-pandemic," Economic Innovation Group, July 10, 2024, https://eig.org/families-exodus/.

35. Richard Florida, "The Pandemic Didn't Upend US Geography," Bloomberg News, April 14, 2023, https://www.bloomberg.com/news/features/2023-04-14/three-years-into-the-pandemic-the-urban-exodus-was-overblown; Justine McDaniel, "U.S. Cities See More Improvement After Pandemic Population Loss, Census Shows," *Washington Post*, May 16, 2024, https://www.washingtonpost.com/nation/2024/05/16/census-population-cities-pandemic/.

36. Claire Reid, "The Milwaukee Area Is One of the Most Competitive Rental Markets in the Nation, Forbes Says," *Milwaukee Journal Sentinel*, April 24, 2024, https://www.jsonline.com/story/money/business/2024/04/24/why-milwaukee-has-one-of-the-countrys-most-competitive-rental-markets/73424211007/; Joe Schulz, "'I'm Essentially Breaking Even Every Month': Wisconsin Renters Struggle with Rising Prices," Wisconsin Public Radio, March 15, 2024, https://www.wpr.org/economy/im-essentially-breaking-even-every-month-wisconsin-renters-struggle-with-rising-prices; Evan Casey, "Brookfield Has the Highest Average Rent in Wisconsin, Report Says. Here's Why," *Milwaukee Journal Sentinel*, January 24, 2020, https://www.jsonline.com/story/communities/west/news/brookfield/2020/01/24/brookfield-has-highest-average-rent-rate-wisconsin-rentcafe/4540586002/.

37. Ben [Smith], "Mayor Says Solution to Lack of Affordable Housing Is More Housing," *Wauwastoa* [*sic*], January 26, 2023, https://wauwastoa.substack.com/p/mayor-solution-to-lack-of-affordable.

38. Goldberg, "Effects of Remote Work."

39. Sydney Ember, "They Never Could Work from Home. These Are Their Stories," *New York Times*, September 22, 2021, https://www.nytimes.com/2021/09/22/business/never-remote-workers-covid.html.

40. Sigrid Nunez, *The Vulnerables* (New York: Riverhead Books, 2023), 98; Dwight Garner, "In the Early Days of Lockdown, a Writer Considers a Perplexing Age," *New York Times*, October 30, 2023, https://www.nytimes.com/2023/10/30/books/review/sigrid-nunez-the-vulnerables.html.

41. Amanda Mull, "After the Pandemic, the Office Dress Code Should Never Come Back," *Atlantic,* May 2020, https://www.theatlantic.com/magazine/archive/2020/05/kill-the-office-dress-code/609070/; Estelle Tang, "The Pandemic Destroyed My Personal Style, and I'm Not Alone," *BuzzFeed News,* May 19, 2021, https://www.buzzfeednews.com/article/estelletang/pandemic-era-style; Jeffrey M. Jones, "U.S. Church Attendance Still Lower Than Pre-pandemic," Gallup, June 28, 2023, https://news.gallup.com/poll/507692/church-attendance-lower-pre-pandemic.aspx; Thomas Floyd, "Fewer People Are Going to Movies, Theater and Museums, NEA Study Shows," *Washington Post,* October 18, 2023, https://www.washingtonpost.com/entertainment/2023/10/18/nea-study-arts-audience-decline/; Linda Poon, "Americans Are Walking 36% Less since Covid," *CityLab* (Bloomberg News), November 3, 2023, https://www.bloomberg.com/news/articles/2023-11-03/as-us-cycling-boomed-walking-trips-crashed-during-covid; Kim Severson, "Hungry (but Not for Human Contact), Americans Head for the Drive-Through," *New York Times,* November 7, 2023, https://www.nytimes.com/2023/11/07/dining/drive-through.html; Vanessa Friedman, "Will the Tie Ever Make a Comeback?," *New York Times,* November 13, 2023, accessed November 26, 2023, https://www.nytimes.com/2023/11/13/style/tie-necktie-fashion.html; Abha Bhattarai, "Covid Changed How We Spend: More YOLO Splurging but Less Saving," *Washington Post,* March 29, 2024, https://www.washingtonpost.com/business/2024/03/29/consumer-spending-savings-yolo-us/; Caitlin Gilbert and Luis Melgar, "Americans Are Sleeping More Than Ever. See How You Compare," *Washington Post,* April 30, 2024, https://www.washingtonpost.com/wellness/interactive/2024/sleep-data-survey-americans/.

42. Erin Blakemore, "'Zoom Fatigue' May Take Toll on the Brain and the Heart, Researchers Say," *Washington Post,* November 25, 2023, https://www.washingtonpost.com/health/2023/11/25/zoom-fatigue-brain-heart-effects/.

43. Glaeser and Ratti, "26 Empire State Buildings."

44. Ian Smith, "Trump Issues Memorandum Ending Remote Work for Federal Employees," FedSmith, January 20, 2025, https://www.fedsmith.com/2025/01/20/trump-signs-executive-order-ending-remote-work-for-federal-employees/; Terina Allen, "Trump Signs Order Ending Remote Work; Mandates Federal Workers Return to Office," *Forbes,* January 28, 2025, https://www.forbes.com/sites/terinaallen/2025/01/20/trump-signs-order-ending-remote-work-mandates-federal-workers-return-to-office/.

45. Kathryn Westcott, "Is King Canute Misunderstood?," *BBC News*, May 26, 2011, https://www.bbc.com/news/magazine-13524677.

46. Matthew Shaer, "Why Are American Drivers So Deadly?," *New York Times*, January 10, 2024, https://www.nytimes.com/2024/01/10/magazine/dangerous-driving.html; Kim Lombard, "Reckless Driving: A Silent Epidemic," Froedtert and Medical College of Wisconsin, July 7, 2021, https://www.froedtert.com/stories/reckless-driving-wisconsin-silent-epidemic.

47. Shaer, "American Drivers"; "Stress in America 2023," American Psychological Association.

48. Drew Dawson, "What to Know About Reckless Driving, Car Thefts and the Kia Boyz, including an Upcoming Trial," *Milwaukee Journal Sentinel*, March 9, 2023, https://www.jsonline.com/story/news/crime/2023/03/09/a-man-seen-in-a-kia-boyz-car-theft-video-goes-to-trial-in-milwaukee/69989487007/; Allison Dirr, "What to Know About Milwaukee's Possible Lawsuit against Kia and Hyundai and Other Efforts to Stop Car Thefts and Reckless Driving," *Milwaukee Journal Sentinel*, March 21, 2023, https://www.jsonline.com/story/news/local/milwaukee/2023/03/21/milwaukee-leaders-explore-lawsuit-following-kia-hyundai-thefts/69937113007/; David Lauter, "Killings in the U.S. Are Dropping at a Historic Rate. Will Anyone Notice?," *Los Angeles Times*, October 20, 2023, https://www.latimes.com/politics/newsletter/2023-10-20/killings-in-the-u-s-are-dropping-at-an-historic-rate-will-anyone-notice-essential-politics; Claire Reid, "Milwaukee Is among the Cities with the Worst Drivers in America, Forbes Study Says," *Milwaukee Journal Sentinel*, February 22, 2024, https://www.jsonline.com/story/news/local/milwaukee/2024/02/22/milwaukee-has-some-of-the-worst-drivers-in-the-u-s-forbes-study-says/72687014007/.

49. Vanessa Swales, "Acting Mayor Johnson Announces Public Safety Plan to Tackle Gun Violence, Car Thefts and Reckless Driving in Milwaukee," *Milwaukee Journal Sentinel*, January 12, 2022, https://www.jsonline.com/story/news/local/milwaukee/2022/01/12/cavalier-johnson-unveils-plan-to-tackle-milwaukee-citys-public-safety-crisis/9187218002/; Reid, "Milwaukee among the Cities."

50. Evan Casey, "A Woman Died in Wauwatosa After She Tried to Stop an Auto Theft and Was Struck by an SUV, Police Say," *Milwaukee Journal Sentinel*, October 14, 2021, https://www.jsonline.com/story/communities/west/news/wauwatosa/2021/10/14/wauwatosa-hit-and-run-claims-life-47-year-old-woman/6013677001/; Michele Fiore,

"13-Year-Old Charged as Adult in Deadly Wauwatosa Hit-and-Run," WDJT-TV (Milwaukee), October 20, 2021, https://www.cbs58.com/news/13-year-old-charged-as-adult-in-deadly-wauwatosa-hit-and-run; Evan Casey, "Wauwatosa Is Looking to Address Reckless Driving. Here Are Some Ways the City Could Buck the Trend," *Milwaukee Journal Sentinel*, May 12, 2022, https://www.jsonline.com/story/communities/west/news/wauwatosa/2022/05/12/wauwatosa-leaders-looking-address-reckless-driving/9707010002/; Taylor Lumpkin, "Wauwatosa Residents Voice Driving Concerns to DOT at Safe Streets Roadshow," WTMJ-TV (Milwaukee), July 13, 2023, https://www.tmj4.com/news/project-drive-safer/wauwatosa-residents-voice-driving-concerns-to-dot-at-safe-streets-roadshow.

51. Shaer, "American Drivers"; "Road Diets (Roadway Reconfiguration)," Federal Highway Administration, accessed April 24, 2024, https://highways.dot.gov/safety/proven-safety-countermeasures/road-diets-roadway-reconfiguration; "Proven Safety Countermeasures," Federal Highway Administration, accessed April 24, 2024, https://highways.dot.gov/safety/proven-safety-countermeasures; Stephanie Desmon, "Narrower Traffic Lanes Could Help Reduce Crashes," Bloomberg School of Public Health, Johns Hopkins University, November 21, 2023, https://publichealth.jhu.edu/2023/narrower-lanes-safer-streets; "Stress in America 2023," American Psychological Association.

52. Angie Schmitt, "What Can Cities Do About the Most Dangerous Drivers?," Bloomberg News, April 4, 2023, https://www.bloomberg.com/news/articles/2023-04-04/how-cities-can-get-the-very-worst-drivers-off-the-streets; "How to Give Streets Back to People: Implementation Considerations for New York City's Next Leader," NYC 25x25, accessed April 27, 2024, https://nyc25x25.org/implementation.html.

53. "How Much Does a Road Diet Cost?," Federal Highway Administration, accessed April 24, 2024, https://safety.fhwa.dot.gov/road_diets/resources/fhwasa16100/.

54. "NYC 25x25: A Challenge to New York City's Leaders to Give Streets Back to People," NYC 25x25, accessed April 27, 2024, https://nyc25x25.org/25x25report.html.

55. Daniel Arkin, "Columbia Unrest Echoes Chaotic Campus Protest Movement of 1968," NBC News, April 30, 2024, https://www.nbcnews.com/news/us-news/columbia-unrest-echoes-chaotic-campus-protest-movement-1968-rcna149967; Richard Fausset, "From Free Speech to Free Palestine: Six Decades of Student Protest," *New York Times*, May 4, 2024,

https://www.nytimes.com/2024/05/04/us/college-protests-free-speech.html; "*The Strawberry Statement*," Wikipedia, accessed April 30, 2024, https://en.wikipedia.org/wiki/The_Strawberry_Statement.

56. Jeremy W. Peters, "It's Not Just Gaza: Student Protesters See Links to a Global Struggle," *New York Times*, May 1, 2024, https://www.nytimes.com/2024/05/01/us/pro-palestinian-college-protests.html.

57. Katherine Rosman, "Universities Face an Urgent Question: What Makes a Protest Antisemitic?," *New York Times*, April 29, 2024, https://www.nytimes.com/2024/04/29/nyregion/college-protests-columbia-campus.html; Celina Tebor, Zoe Sottile, and Matt Egan, "Columbia University Faces Full-Blown Crisis as Rabbi Calls for Jewish Students to 'Return Home,'" CNN, April 22, 2024, https://www.cnn.com/2024/04/21/us/columbia-university-jewish-students-protests/index.html; Michael Powell, "We Want *All* of It," *Atlantic*, May 3, 2024, https://www.theatlantic.com/ideas/archive/2024/05/columbia-protesters-israel-palestinian/678251/; Max Boot, "Opinion: I've Read Student Protesters' Manifestos. This Is Ugly Stuff. Clueless, Too," *Washington Post*, May 6, 2024, https://www.washingtonpost.com/opinions/2024/05/06/student-protests-mistakes-gaza-help-trump/.

58. Arkin, "Columbia Unrest"; Shimon Prokupecz, Mark Morales, and Celina Tebor, "Here's What We Know About the Arrests at Campus Protests in New York City on Tuesday Night," CNN, May 2, 2024, https://www.cnn.com/business/live-news/university-protests-pro-palestinian-israel-05-02-24/index.html.

59. Chandelis Duster, Ramishah Maruf, Rachel Ramirez, and Holly Yan, "Biden Weighs In on Protests Disrupting Colleges Across the US," CNN, May 2, 2024, https://www.cnn.com/business/live-news/university-protests-pro-palestinian-israel-05-02-24/index.html; Will Creeley, "Those Who Preach Free Speech Need to Practice It," *Atlantic*, April 30, 2024, https://www.theatlantic.com/ideas/archive/2024/04/colleges-protests-free-speech/678238/.

60. Yair Rosenberg, "The New AOC: The Progressive Congresswoman Is No Longer Speaking Solely to the Left Wing, but to the Party as a Whole," *Atlantic*, August 20, 2024, https://www.theatlantic.com/politics/archive/2024/08/aoc-speech-dnc-2024/679528/.

61. John McWhorter, "Opinion: The Columbia Protests Made the Same Mistake the Civil Rights Movement Did," *New York Times*, May 3, 2024, https://www.nytimes.com/2024/05/03/opinion/columbia-protests-civil-rights.html; Aaron Blake, "Pro-Palestinian College Protests

Have Not Won Hearts and Minds," *Washington Post*, May 22, 2024, https://www.washingtonpost.com/politics/2024/05/22/gaza-israel-college-protests/.

62. Luke McGee, "What Is the Good Friday Agreement? How a Historic Deal Ended the Troubles in Northern Ireland," CNN, April 10, 2023, https://www.cnn.com/2023/04/07/uk/good-friday-agreement-explained-intl-cmd-gbr/index.html; Thomas Friedman, "Opinion: Why the Campus Protests Are So Troubling," *New York Times*, May 8, 2024, https://www.nytimes.com/2024/05/08/opinion/campus-protests-gaza.html. According to an article in the *Milwaukee Journal Sentinel*, "Robert Cohen, a New York University professor who studies the history of student activism, said today's demonstrations are much smaller than in the 1960s and 1970s. That's in part because pro-Israeli and pro-Palestinian camps tend to only talk about their own side's suffering, he said, which has prevented the movement from gaining the broader support that defined the antiwar efforts of the Vietnam era." (Kelly Meyerhofer, "After 12-Day Encampment, UW-Madison Protesters Reached Deal. Why? And What's Next?," *Milwaukee Journal Sentinel*, May 13, 2024, https://www.jsonline.com/story/news/education/2024/05/13/inside-university-of-wisconsins-deal-with-encampment-protesters/73632345007/.)

63. Zack Beauchamp, "Why America's Israel-Palestine Debate Is Broken—and How to Fix It," Vox, May 2, 2024, https://www.vox.com/politics/2024/5/2/24147192/israel-palestine-student-protest-columbia-ucla-radicalism.

64. *Cole v. City of Wauwatosa*, 23-CV-1321, and *Rivera v. City of Wauwatosa*, 23-CV-1330 (E.D. Wis., April 17, 2024) (Joseph, M.J.), https://casetext.com/case/cole-v-city-of-wauwatosa.

65. Bridget Fogarty, "Wauwatosa's October 2020 Citywide Curfew Order Violated State Statute, Wisconsin Judge Rules," *Milwaukee Journal Sentinel*, July 9, 2024, https://www.jsonline.com/story/communities/north/2024/07/09/wauwatosas-october-2020-curfew-violated-state-law-judge-rules/74309914007/.

66. "Decision and Order," in *Paige Radke v. City of Wauwatosa, et al.*, Case No. 21-C-0247 (E.D. Wis., August 24, 2022) (Adelman, J.), https://www.wied.uscourts.gov/sites/wied/files/documents/opinions/21-CV-247%20Radke%20v.%20City%20of%20Wauwatosa%20et%20al%20%2844%29.pdf, at 5n2.

67. "Decision and Order on Defendants' Motion to Dismiss Fourth Amended Complaint," in *Knowlton v. City of Wauwatosa*, Case No.

20-CV-1660 (E.D. Wis.) (Joseph, Mag. J.), August 24, 2022, at 26, citing *Pasiewicz v. Lake County Forest Preservation District*, 270 F.3d 520, 526 (7th Cir. 2001).

68. Evan Casey and Christopher Kuhagen, "Wisconsin Police Officer Who Fatally Shot Three People in the Last Five Years Is Resigning," *Milwaukee Journal Sentinel*, November 18, 2020, https://www.usatoday.com/story/news/nation/2020/11/18/wisconsin-cop-who-killed-three-people-last-five-years-resigning/6337904002/; Todd Richmond, "Protests Break Out, Windows Broken in Wauwatosa after Wisconsin Police Officer Involved in Several Shootings Is Cleared in Mall Death," *Chicago Tribune*, October 8, 2020, https://www.chicagotribune.com/midwest/ct-milwaukee-police-joseph-mensah-20201007-f42mhenqxrbqfnl2sxyt3yvhby-story.html; "Cleanup Underway after Damage, Looting in Wauwatosa Unrest," WDJT-TV (Milwaukee), October 8, 2020, https://www.cbs58.com/news/damage-looting-in-wauwatosa-after-das-decision-not-to-charge-officer; Cassidy Williams, "Businesses Damaged, Looted Hours after Peaceful Protests in Wauwatosa," Fox 32 (Chicago), October 8, 2020, https://www.fox32chicago.com/news/businesses-damaged-looted-hours-after-peaceful-protests-in-wauwatosa; Ryan Jenkins, "Residents Host 'Let's Heal Wauwatosa' Cleanup after Night of Unrest," WTMJ-TV (Milwaukee), October 8, 2020, https://www.tmj4.com/news/local-news/wauwatosa-locals-host-lets-heal-wauwatosa-cleanup-after-night-of-unrest.

69. "In Wake of Wisconsin's Racial Justice Protests, Curfew Tickets Raise Equity and Speech Questions," Wisconsin Watch, April 26, 2021, https://pbswisconsin.org/news-item/in-wake-of-wisconsins-racial-justice-protests-curfew-tickets-raise-equity-and-speech-questions/; "Stifling Free Speech: Blacks Targeted with Curfew Tickets in Wake of Wisconsin's Racial Justice Protests," *Milwaukee Independent*, June 4, 2021, http://www.milwaukeeindependent.com/syndicated/stifling-free-speech-blacks-targeted-curfew-tickets-wake-wisconsins-racial-justice-protests/; "Minutes of Wauwatosa Common Council Meeting," City of Wauwatosa, October 13, 2020, http://wauwatosacitywi.iqm2.com/Citizens/FileOpen.aspx?Type=15&ID=2809&Inline=True; Evan Casey, "Was Wauwatosa's Curfew and Emergency Proclamation Necessary? Here's What City Officials Think," *Milwaukee Journal Sentinel*, October 21, 2020, https://www.jsonline.com/story/communities/west/news/wauwatosa/2020/10/21/wauwatosa-officials-discuss-whether-citys-curfew-necessary/3713386001/.

70. Fogarty, "Wauwatosa's October 2020 Citywide Curfew"; Bridget Fogarty, "Fate of Wauwatosa Citations Remains Unclear Despite Judge Ruling October 2020 Curfew Was Illegal," *Milwaukee Journal Sentinel*, July

22, 2024, https://www.jsonline.com/story/communities/west/2024/07/22/fate-of-wauwatosa-citations-unclear-despite-judge-ruling-curfew-illegal/74476383007/.

71. Fogarty, "Wauwatosa's October 2020 Citywide Curfew"; Bridget Fogarty, "Milwaukee County judge says he erred, now sides with City of Wauwatosa on curfew ruling," *Milwaukee Journal Sentinel*, December 6, 2024, https://www.jsonline.com/story/communities/north/2024/12/06/judge-reverses-ruling-now-sides-with-wauwatosa-in-curfew-case/76807945007/.

72. *Ex parte Merryman*, 17 F. Cas. 144 (C.C.D. Md.).

73. Scott Bomboy, "Lincoln and Taney's Great Writ Showdown," National Constitution Center, May 28, 2023, https://constitutioncenter.org/blog/lincoln-and-taneys-great-writ-showdown; James A. Dueholm, "Lincoln's Suspension of the Writ of Habeas Corpus: An Historical and Constitutional Analysis," *Journal of the Abraham Lincoln Association* 29, no. 2 (Summer 2008), https://quod.lib.umich.edu/j/jala/2629860.0029.205/--lincoln-s-suspension-of-the-writ-of-habeas-corpus?rgn=main;view=fulltext; "*Ex parte Merryman*," Wikipedia, October 19, 2024, https://en.wikipedia.org/wiki/Ex_parte_Merryman.

74. Evan Casey, "The Wauwatosa Council Has Passed an Equity and Inclusion Statement to Guide the City. Here's What It Says," *Milwaukee Journal Sentinel*, January 27, 2022, accessed February 1, 2022, https://www.jsonline.com/story/communities/west/news/wauwatosa/2022/01/27/wauwatosa-common-council-passes-equity-statement-wisconsin/9204961002/; "City of Wauwatosa, Wisconsin: Strategic Plan, 2023–2027," City of Wauwatosa website, accessed December 10, 2022, https://www.wauwatosa.net/home/showpublisheddocument/4758/637998985496170000.

75. Evan Casey, "Melissa Dolan Wins Race to Be the Next Wauwatosa District 8 Alderperson," *Milwaukee Journal Sentinel*, April 6, 2022, https://www.jsonline.com/story/communities/west/news/wauwatosa/2022/04/06/wauwatosa-district-8-alderman-election-results-april-5-2022-melissa-dolan-john-larry/7215060001/; Evan Casey, "Wauwatosa Elects the First Person of Color in the 125-year History of the Wauwatosa Common Council," *Milwaukee Journal Sentinel*, April 7, 2022, https://www.jsonline.com/story/communities/west/news/wauwatosa/2022/04/07/margaret-arney-wauwatosas-first-alderperson-color/9484449002/; Evan Casey, "Wauwatosa Will Likely Elect a Person of Color for the First Time in the 125-Year History of the Common Council This Spring," *Milwaukee Journal Sentinel*, January 20, 2022, https://www.jsonline.com

/story/communities/west/news/wauwatosa/2022/01/20/margaret-arney-running-unopposed-wauwatosa-spring-election/6513383001/.

76. Alec Johnson, "Wauwatosa School Board Appoints Jessica Willis to Vacant Board Seat Left by Steve Doman's Abrupt Resignation," *Milwaukee Journal Sentinel*, June 28, 2022, https://www.jsonline.com/story/communities/west/news/wauwatosa/2022/06/28/jessica-willis-appointed-wauwatosa-school-board/7756106001/.

77. Sofia Andrade and Janay Kingsberry, "Bad Behavior at 'Barbenheimer' Reflects a Worrying Trend," *Washington Post*, August 5, 2023, https://www.washingtonpost.com/lifestyle/2023/08/05/barbenheimer-bad-movie-behavior/; "Stress in America 2023," American Psychological Association; Olga Khazan, "Why People Are Acting So Weird," *Atlantic*, March 10, 2022, https://www.theatlantic.com/politics/archive/2022/03/antisocial-behavior-crime-violence-increase-pandemic/627076/; Helaine Olen, "Opinion: Air-Rage Incidents Are Rising—for Lots of Reasons," *Washington Post*, July 15, 2021, https://www.washingtonpost.com/opinions/2021/07/15/airline-rage-incidents-flying/.

78. Cox, "We Are Not Just Polarized"; George Makari and Richard A. Friedman, "It's Not the Economy. It's the Pandemic," *Atlantic*, March 21, 2024, https://www.theatlantic.com/health/archive/2024/03/covid-grief-trauma-memory-biden-trump/677828/?gift=obxF8VkM-AIIkF4coxW-MwEDqTEH090AOLQrw9TawcI; Lisa Lerer, Jennifer Medina, and Reid J. Epstein, "How a Pandemic Malaise Is Shaping American Politics," *New York Times*, March 24, 2024, https://www.nytimes.com/2024/03/24/us/politics/pandemic-politics-malaise.html.

78. Sam Wang, "The Hardened Divide in American Politics," *American Prospect*, October 7, 2016, https://prospect.org/power/hardened-divide-american-politics/.

80. Michael Dimock and John Gramlich, "How America Changed during Donald Trump's Presidency," Pew Research Center, January 29, 2021, https://www.pewresearch.org/politics/2021/01/29/how-america-changed-during-donald-trumps-presidency/; Adam Gabbatt, "Same World, Different Planet: Trump's Arrest Lays Bare US Polarization," *Guardian*, April 8, 2023, https://www.theguardian.com/us-news/2023/apr/08/us-political-polarization-trump-arrest.

81. Brett Samuels, "Trump Signals He's Out for Revenge in Second Term," *Hill*, November 16, 2023, https://thehill.com/homenews/campaign/4311194-trump-signals-revenge-in-second-term/.

82. Peter Wehner, "Vengeance Is Trump's," *Atlantic*, March 13, 2023, https://www.theatlantic.com/ideas/archive/2023/03/donald-trump

-cpac-republican-primary-retribution/673373/; Maggie Haberman and Shane Goldmacher, "Trump, Vowing 'Retribution,' Foretells a Second Term of Spite," *New York Times*, March 7, 2023, https://www.nytimes.com/2023/03/07/us/politics/trump-2024-president.html.

83. Marianne Sotomayor, "GOP House Hard-Liners Won't Compromise. They're Losing Key Fights Because of It," *Washington Post*, April 29, 2024, https://www.washingtonpost.com/politics/2024/04/29/house-republicans-mike-johnson-motion-to-vacate/; Lisa Desjardins, "How Dysfunction Has Defined the House," *PBS NewsHour*, March 21, 2024, https://www.pbs.org/newshour/show/how-dysfunction-has-defined-the-house.

84. Frank Benest, Rusty Kennedy, and Erica L. Manuel, "Managing Angry Mobs Disrupting Governing Board Meetings," Institute for Local Government, March 2022, https://www.ca-ilg.org/sites/main/files/ilg_managing_angry_mobs_ver4.pdf; Karin Brulliard, "Free Speech or Out of Order? As Meetings Grow Wild, Officials Try to Tame Public Comment," *Washington Post*, January 17, 2023, https://www.washingtonpost.com/nation/2023/01/17/public-comment-new-rules-free-speech/; Beck Andrew Salgado, "Wauwatosa Schools Change Their Sex Education Curriculum Amid Protests, Will Start Teachings as Early as Kindergarten This Year," *Milwaukee Journal Sentinel*, August 23, 2022, https://www.jsonline.com/story/communities/west/news/wauwatosa/2022/08/23/wauwatosa-school-board-approves-new-sex-education-curriculum/7873012001/.

85. "Threats and Harassment in Local Government: Benchmarking Report, Q1 2024," CivicPulse.org / Princeton University, May 2024, 3, 11, 13–15, https://bridgingdivides.princeton.edu/sites/g/files/toruqf6646/files/documents/BDI_Threats%20and%20Harassment%20Benchmarking%20Report_Q1%202024.pdf.

86. Ibid.; Maresa Strano, "Where Have All the Local Candidates Gone?," New America, November 6, 2023, https://www.newamerica.org/political-reform/blog/where-have-all-the-local-candidates-gone/; Sharon O'Malley, "Sharp Rise in Abuse Targeting Mayors Highlighted by New Study," *Route Fifty*, May 11, 2022, https://www.route-fifty.com/management/2022/05/psychological-abuse-against-mayors-23-2017/366841/.

87. "Analysis of Uncontested Elections, 2024," *Ballotpedia*, April 2024, https://ballotpedia.org/Analysis_of_uncontested_elections,_2024?_wcsid=23001E272D784B8B3E7911DD397C42142EA78F8ECA70B4BE.

88. Sophia Voight, "Political Divides, Declining Population Are Causing Fewer People to Run in Rural Local Elections," *Appleton Post-Crescent*, March 28, 2024, https://www.jsonline.com/story/news/politics/elections/2024/03/28/rural-wisconsin-communities-struggle-to-attract-candidates-for-elections/73032197007/.

89. David Ignatius, "Opinion: How Rep. Mike Gallagher, a Rising GOP Star, Was Driven Out of Politics," *Washington Post*, August 27, 2024, https://www.washingtonpost.com/opinions/2024/08/27/gallagher-republican-trump-populism-rebirth/.

90. Steve Forrester, "Writer's Notebook: Politics Is a Contact Sport, but Death Threats Are a New Thing," *Astorian*, October 26, 2023, https://www.dailyastorian.com/opinion/columns/writers-notebook-politics-is-a-contact-sport-but-death-threats-are-a-new-thing/article_0f053414-72be-11ee-8130-d3c07cdd782b.html.

91. Philippe Naughton, "It Really Was the Economy, Stupid," *Daily Beast*, November 6, 2024, https://www.thedailybeast.com/donald-trumps-victory-really-was-about-the-economy-stupid/.

92. Derek Thompson, "How Donald Trump Won Everywhere: This Was the Second COVID Election," *Atlantic*, November 6, 2024, https://www.theatlantic.com/politics/archive/2024/11/donald-trump-covid-election/680559/.

93. Jess Bidgood, "The Second Pandemic Election: Covid Cost Trump the Presidency in 2020, and It May Have Cleared the Path for His Return," *New York Times*, November 6, 2024, https://www.nytimes.com/2024/11/06/us/politics/trump-election-covid-2020.html.

94. "Yogi Berra Quotes," GoodReads, accessed November 9, 2024, https://www.goodreads.com/quotes/261863-it-s-tough-to-make-predictions-especially-about-the-future.

THE SECOND-HARDEST JOB IN GOVERNMENT

1. Lisa Kashinsky, "'It Was Exhaustion, It Was Sadness, It Was Fatigue': America's Mayors Call It Quits," *Politico*, June 16, 2021, https://www.politico.com/news/2021/06/16/americas-mayors-covid-year-494753; Perry Bacon Jr., "Opinion: The Second-Hardest Job in Politics," *Washington Post*, December 16, 2021, https://www.washingtonpost.com/opinions/2021/12/16/second-hardest-job-politics/.

2. Robert A. Caro, *The Power Broker: Robert Moses and the Fall of New York* (New York: Vintage Books, 1975), 60; Jason Stein, "With Budget

Leaning More Heavily on the Property Tax, Wisconsin Towns Face New Challenges," *Milwaukee Journal Sentinel*, July 27, 2022, https://www.jsonline.com/story/news/solutions/2022/07/27/wisconsin-towns-face-challenges-budget-lean-property-tax/10147304002/; Stephanie Murray, Jason Stein, and Rob Henken, "Dollars and Sense: Is It Time for a New Municipal Financing Framework in Wisconsin?," Wisconsin Policy Forum, February 2019, 12, 14–15, https://wispolicyforum.org/wp-content/uploads/2019/02/DollarsAndSense_Full.pdf.

3. Richard Faussett, "Keisha Lance Bottoms Won't Seek Second Term as Atlanta Mayor," *New York Times*, May 7, 2021, https://www.nytimes.com/2021/05/06/us/keisha-lance-bottoms-atlanta-mayor.html; Zak Cheney-Rice, "Why Did Keisha Lance Bottoms Quit? The Mayor of Atlanta Was a Rising Star in Democratic Politics. Then the Crime Wave Hit," *Intelligencer*, January 3, 2022, https://nymag.com/intelligencer/2022/01/keisha-lance-bottoms-atlanta-mayor-quits.html.

4. Ellen Barry, "Drained by a Year of Covid, Many Mayors Head for the Exit: Local Officials Nationwide Are Announcing Plans to Step Back from Elected Office. Many Offer the Same Explanation: Covid Burnout," *New York Times*, April 11, 2021, https://www.nytimes.com/2021/04/11/us/covid-burnout-mayors.html.

5. Linda Poon, "What U.S. Mayors Are Really Worried About: A Survey of 126 Mayors Reveals That City Leaders Are More Concerned About the Long-Term Mental Health Consequences of the Pandemic Than Other Headline-Grabbing Issues," *Bloomberg CityLab*, November 30, 2021, https://www.bloomberg.com/news/articles/2021-11-30/the-pandemic-fallout-that-u-s-mayors-are-worried-about.

6. Maureen Groppe, "Facing Death Threats and No Pay, Georgia Mayor among Leaders Who Are the Front-Line Commanders of the Coronavirus Pandemic," *USA Today*, May 26, 2020, https://www.savannahnow.com/story/news/2020/05/26/facing-death-threats-georgia-mayor-among-leaders-who-are-front-line-commanders-coronavirus-pandemic/1150314007/.

7. Matt Wotton and Graham Johnston, "What Politicians Can Learn from Athletes Opening Up About Their Mental Health," Politics.co.uk, October 18, 2021, https://www.politics.co.uk/comment/2021/10/18/what-politicians-can-learn-from-athletes-opening-up-about-their-mental-health/.

8. Barry, "Drained by a Year of Covid"; Faussett, "Keisha Lance Bottoms"; Wilborn P. Nobles III, J. D. Capelouto, and Ben Brasch, "Atlanta Mayor Calls End of Her Reelection Bid a 'Very Difficult Decision,'"

Atlanta Journal-Constitution, May 7, 2021, https://www.ajc.com/news/atlanta-news/mayor-bottoms-not-running-for-reelection-was-very-difficult-decision/PSMN2ZMV3RGZPLNFS2XMB56EIY/; Kashinsky, "It Was Exhaustion."

9. Barry, "Drained by a Year of Covid"; Astead W. Herndon and Jennifer Medina, "'Everybody Will Second-Guess': Liberal Mayors Navigate Protesters and Police," *New York Times*, June 1, 2020, https://www.nytimes.com/2020/06/01/us/politics/floyd-protests-chicago-la-mayors.html.

10. Griff Witte, Holly Bailey, and Joanna Slater, "In Mayoral Elections Nationwide, Voters Opt for Pragmatism over Ideology," *Washington Post*, November 3, 2021, https://www.washingtonpost.com/national/in-mayoral-elections-nationwide-voters-opt-for-pragmatism-over-ideology/2021/11/03/a854bc30-3ce1-11ec-a67c-d7c2182dac83_story.html; "Minneapolis-St. Paul Election Results," *New York Times*, November 2, 2021, https://www.nytimes.com/interactive/2021/11/02/us/elections/results-minneapolis-st-paul-minnesota.html.

11. Andrew Zhang, "Sheila Jackson Lee Loses Houston Mayor's Race to Tough-on-Crime State Senator," *Politico*, December 9, 2023, https://www.politico.com/news/2023/12/09/john-whitmire-sheila-jackson-lee-houston-mayor-00130873.

12. A. J. Bayatpour, "Housing, Relationships Shape Race for Tosa Mayor," WDJT-TV (CBS 58, Milwaukee), March 29, 2024, https://www.cbs58.com/news/housing-relationships-shape-race-for-tosa-mayor.

13. Compare Becca Rothfeld, "Nelly Bowles Thinks You Should Outgrow Progressivism," *Washington Post*, May 2, 2024, https://www.washingtonpost.com/books/2024/05/02/morning-after-revolution-nellie-bowles-review/.

14. Helen Lewis, "The Left Can't Afford to Go Mad," *Atlantic*, December 8, 2023, https://www.theatlantic.com/magazine/archive/2024/01/trump-biden-democratic-left-opposition/676141/. See also the following argument:

> In the first half of the 20th century, the United States actually had a powerful leftist force in the form of the Socialist Party of America. Its members won municipal races in places such as Berkeley, California, and Schenectady, New York. The party's proud centerpiece was Milwaukee, which had three socialist mayors for a total of 38 years from 1910 to 1960. Those further to the left often made fun of them as "sewer socialists" who cared more about the city's excellent public-sanitation system than about the socialist revolution. . . . But Milwaukee's sewer socialists could boast something that purists simply can't: They made a difference in the lives of millions of working people. Those are

the politics—result-oriented and pragmatic—that convince people to give the socialist left and its ideas a chance. If American socialists truly want to emerge as a serious political force in the world's most powerful country, they need to stop cosplaying radicalism and learn how to defend democracy, build broad coalitions, and run successful governments. (Arash Azizi, "Too Much Purity Is Bad for the Left," *Atlantic*, March 21, 2024, https://www.theatlantic.com/international/archive/2024/03/american-left-socialist-lessons-from-abroad/677804/)

15. To blunt the Socialist Party's popularity in Milwaukee, Republicans and Democrats in the Wisconsin Legislature passed a bill in 1912 to make local offices nonpartisan. They were only temporarily successful. Socialists dominated Milwaukee's mayoral and Common Council elections and elections to the Milwaukee County Board of Supervisors for years thereafter. Milwaukee's last Socialist mayor left office in 1960. "Nonpartisan Elections," *Encyclopedia of Milwaukee* (University of Wisconsin–Milwaukee), 2016, https://emke.uwm.edu/entry/non-partisan-elections/.

16. Jeremy Jannene, "Mayors Offer Plea to Republicans for Federal Support," *Urban Milwaukee*, July 15, 2024, https://urbanmilwaukee.com/2024/07/15/mayors-make-their-plea-to-republicans-for-federal-support/. I had been using that expression for years before I learned that Mayor LaGuardia, who governed New York City from 1934 to 1946, had used a similar expression, variously recorded as "There is no Republican or Democratic way of taking out the garbage" or "There is no Republican or Democratic way of cleaning the streets." (Aaron M. Renn, "The Pandemic and the Strengths of Our Networked Governance," Governing.com, April 7, 2020, https://www.governing.com/now/the-pandemic-and-the-strengths-of-our-networked-governance.html; BrainyQuote.com, accessed December 28, 2024, https://www.brainyquote.com/quotes/fiorello_laguardia_227727.)

17. Bridget Fogarty, "Wauwatosa Mayor Dennis McBride Wins a Second Term, Other Tosa Incumbents Win," *Milwaukee Journal Sentinel*, April 2, 2024, https://www.jsonline.com/story/communities/north/2024/04/02/here-are-the-results-for-wauwatosa-mayor-and-districts-8-and-3-alders/73143961007/.

18. Isabel Wilkerson, *The Warmth of Other Suns: The Epic Story of America's Great Migration* (New York: Random House, 2010), 535.

19. Adam Carlson, "Retiring Republican Congressman Slams GOP Leaders for 'Lying to America,'" ABC News, November 1, 2023, https://abcnews.go.com/Politics/republicans-ken-buck-kay-granger-retire-congress-buck/story?id=104547157; Joanna Slater, "Connecticut Jury

Orders Alex Jones to Pay Nearly $1 Billion to Sandy Hook Families," *Texas Tribune*, October 12, 2022, https://www.texastribune.org/2022/10/12/alex-jones-sandy-hook-shooting/; Wesley R. Moy and Kacper Gradon, "COVID-19 Effects and Russian Disinformation," *Homeland Security Affairs* 16 8 (December 2020): 8, www.hsaj.org/articles/16533.

20. Em Steck and Andrew Kaczynski, "Marjorie Taylor Greene Indicated Support for Executing Prominent Democrats in 2018 and 2019 before Running for Congress," CNN, January 26, 2021, https://www.cnn.com/2021/01/26/politics/marjorie-taylor-greene-democrats-violence/index.html; Brian Klaas, "Trump Floats the Idea of Executing Joint Chiefs Chairman Milley," *Atlantic*, September 25, 2023, https://www.theatlantic.com/ideas/archive/2023/09/trump-milley-execution-incitement-violence/675435/.

21. George Thomas, "The GOP Is Abandoning the American Idea," *Bulwark*, July 3, 2020, https://www.thebulwark.com/p/the-gop-is-abandoning-the-american-idea; Greg Jaffe and Patrick Marley, "The Pandemic Is Over in This Michigan County. The Mistrust Never Ended," *Washington Post*, October 22, 2023, https://www.washingtonpost.com/politics/2023/10/22/ottawa-county-michigan-covid-mistrust/; Maeve Reston, Hannah Knowles, and Meryl Kornfield, "Led by Trump, GOP Candidates Take Polarizing Stances on Race and History," *Washington Post*, December 30, 2023, https://www.washingtonpost.com/elections/2023/12/30/trump-desantis-haley-race-slavery/.

22. Liz Crampton, "GOP Sees 'Huge Red Wave' Potential by Targeting Critical Race Theory," *Politico*, January 5, 2022, https://www.politico.com/news/2022/01/05/gop-red-wave-critical-race-theory-526523; Reston, Knowles, and Kornfield, "Led by Trump"; Michael Goldberg, "Republican Lawmakers Are Backing Dozens of Bills Targeting Diversity Efforts on Campus and Elsewhere," Associated Press, February 10, 2024, https://apnews.com/article/dei-state-legislation-diversity-4d80ec7e9d372e74b129efc402ac0b76; Jessie Opolen, "Republican Legislators Launch Audit of DEI Activities in Wisconsin State Agencies," *Milwaukee Journal Sentinel*, May 7, 2024, https://www.jsonline.com/story/news/politics/2024/05/07/wisconsin-republicans-launch-audit-of-dei-activities-in-state-agencies/73588362007/.

23. *Students for Fair Admissions, Inc. v. President and Fellows of Harvard College, et al.*, 600 U.S. 181 (2023).

24. Daniel Arkin, "Virginia School Board Votes to Restore Names of Confederate Leaders to Schools," NBC News, May 9, 2024, https://www

.nbcnews.com/news/us-news/virginia-school-board-vote-restoring-names-confederate-leaders-schools-rcna151458.

25. "Trump Orders End of Government DEI Programs, LGBT Protections," France24, January 22, 2025, https://www.france24.com/en/americas/20250122-trump-orders-end-of-government-dei-programs-lgbt-protections.

26. Sally Satel, "The Experts Somehow Overlooked Authoritarians on the Left: Many Psychologists Wrongly Assumed That Coercive Attitudes Exist Only Among Conservatives," *Atlantic,* September 25, 2021, https://www.theatlantic.com/ideas/archive/2021/09/psychological-dimensions-left-wing-authoritarianism/620185/; Robert Kagan, "Opinion: We Have a Radical Democracy. Will Trump Voters Destroy It?," *Washington Post,* April 24, 2024, https://www.washingtonpost.com/opinions/2024/04/24/trump-tyranny-christian-nationalist-democracy/.

27. Bryan McKenzie, "Americans Say to Meet Political Agendas, Rights May Be Left Behind," *UVA Today,* October 20, 2023, https://news.virginia.edu/content/americans-say-meet-political-agendas-rights-may-be-left-behind; Theodore R. Johnson, "Opinion: Illiberalism Is a Threat to Democracy—on the Right and Left," *Washington Post,* May 4, 2023, https://www.washingtonpost.com/opinions/2023/05/04/democracy-challenged-right-left/.

28. Lydia Saad, "The U.S. Remained Center-Right, Ideologically, in 2019," Gallup Inc., January 8, 2020, https://news.gallup.com/poll/275792/remained-center-right-ideologically-2019.aspx; Gary Fields and Amelia Thomson Deveaux, "Yes We're Divided. But New AP-NORC Poll Shows Americans Still Agree on Most Core American Values," Associated Press, April 3, 2024, https://apnews.com/article/ap-poll-democracy-rights-freedoms-election-b1047da72551e13554a39594 87e5181a; "Who Are the Moderates?," Citizen Data, February 26, 2023, https://citizendata.com/report/who-are-the-moderates/; Megan McArdle, "Opinion: Democratic Politicians Aren't Looking for Student Protesters' Support," *Washington Post,* May 2, 2024, https://www.washingtonpost.com/opinions/2024/05/02/student-protesters-politics-democrats-tactics/.

29. "Party Affiliation," Gallup Inc., April 1–22, 2024, https://news.gallup.com/poll/15370/party-affiliation.aspx.

30. Meilan Solly, "The True History Behind 'The Plot Against America,'" *Smithsonian Magazine,* March 16, 2020, https://www.smithsonianmag.com/history/true-history-behind-plot-against-america-180974365/.

31. Fareed Zakaria, "Opinion: Biden Is Showing the World That U.S. Government Can Work Again," *Washington Post*, March 4, 2021, https://www.washingtonpost.com/opinions/biden-is-showing-the-world-that-us-government-can-work-again/2021/03/04/2cf54be2-7d27-11eb-85cd-9b7fa90c8873_story.html.

32. Jeffrey Owen Jones, "The Man Who Wrote the Pledge of Allegiance," *Smithsonian Magazine*, November 2003, https://www.smithsonianmag.com/history/the-man-who-wrote-the-pledge-of-allegiance-93907224/.

33. Lee Ann Potter, "A Republic, If You Can Keep It," US Library of Congress, September 8, 2016, https://blogs.loc.gov/teachers/2016/09/a-republic-if-you-can-keep-it/.

34. Jennifer Rubin, "Opinion: Why Centrism Might Be Our Salvation," *Washington Post*, July 23, 2024, https://www.washingtonpost.com/opinions/2024/07/23/american-democracy-reform-cenrist-solutions/.

DENNIS R. MCBRIDE is the mayor of Wauwatosa, Wisconsin. He holds a journalism degree from the University of Wisconsin–Milwaukee, a master of public administration degree from Princeton University, and a law degree from New York University.

For Indiana University Press

Sabrina Black, *Editorial Assistant*
Tony Brewer, *Artist and Book Designer*
Gary Dunham, *Acquisitions Editor and Director*
Anna Francis, *Assistant Acquisitions Editor*
Anna Garnai, *Production Coordinator*
Katie Huggins, *Production Manager*
Alyssa Nicole Lucas, *Marketing and Publicity Manager*
David Miller, *Lead Project Manager/Editor*
Dan Pyle, *Online Publishing Manager*
Jennifer L. Wilder, *Senior Artist and Book Designer*